TABLE OF CONTENTS

COMPACT GREEK-ENGLISH LEXICON OF THE NEW TESTAMENT

revised and edited by

Mark A. House

Based on *A Pocket Lexicon to the Greek New Testament*

by Alexander Souter

HENDRICKSON PUBLISHERS

Compact Greek-English Lexicon of the New Testament

Published by Hendrickson Publishers
an imprint of Hendrickson Publishing Group
P. O. Box 3473
Peabody, Massachusetts 01961-3473
www.hendricksonpublishinggroup.com

ISBN 978-1-61970-717-7

This work is based on an earlier work by Alexander Souter, entitled *A Pocket Lexicon to the Greek New Testament* (Oxford: Clarendon, 1916).

Printed in the United States of America

Library of Congress Cataloging-in-Publication Data

Compact Greek-English lexicon of the New Testament / revised and edited by Mark A. House.
p. cm.
Based on: A pocket lexicon to the Greek New Testament / by Alexander Souter. Oxford : Clarendon Press, 1916.
ISBN 978-1-59856-325-2 (alk. paper)
1. Greek language, Biblical--Dictionaries--English. I. House, Mark A. II. Souter, Alexander, 1873-1949. Pocket lexicon to the Greek New Testament.
PA881.C66 2008
487'.4--dc22

2008028603

PREFACE

The *Compact Greek-English Lexicon of the New Testament* is a revision and expansion of Alexander Souter's popular *A Pocket Lexicon to the Greek New Testament* (Oxford: Clarendon, 1916). Souter's *Pocket Lexicon* is the third installment of what he termed a "tiny trilogy" of tools for students of the Greek New Testament that also includes a popular edition of the Greek New Testament (1910)[1] and a widely used guide to the text and canon of the New Testament (1913).[2] With its succinct yet lucid definitions of the entire New Testament vocabulary and its helpful Scripture references, Souter's *Pocket Lexicon* became one of the most widely used compact Greek dictionaries of his own and the succeeding generation. Souter's interest in creating such a compact resource was not only that theological students and clergy would have a convenient, accessible tool for the study of the Greek New Testament, but also that such a resource would be available at a reasonable price.

The publication of *A Pocket Lexicon* came closely on the heels of a period in which the knowledge of Hellenistic Greek had blossomed. The discovery in Egypt of hoards of ancient, nonliterary Greek papyri written in the κοινὴ διάλεκτος ("common dialect"), or *lingua franca,* spoken and written throughout nearly the entire first-century Greco-Roman world, brought with it a wealth of fresh insights into the meanings of New Testament words and phrases. Souter desired to offer students and pastors as much of this new knowledge as possible in a compact, unobtrusive format. In doing so, he laid out briefly, yet fully, the range of meanings of each of the Greek words of the New Testament, without encumbering the volume with extensive morphological detail.

In creating his work, Souter expressed profound indebtedness to J. H. Moulton and G. Milligan,[3] whose work he described as encompassing with unequalled philological discipline "all the important lexical knowl-

---

1 *Novum Testamentum Graece, Texui a Retractatoribus Anglis adhibito brevem Adnotationem Criticam subiecit* (Oxford: Clarendon Press, 1910, repr. 1947).

2 *The Text and Canon of the New Testament* (New York: Scribner's Sons, 1913, repr. 1923).

3 J.H. Moulton and G. Milligan, *The Vocabulary of the Greek Testament: Illustrated from the Papyri and Other Non-Literary Sources* (Peabody, Mass. : Hendrickson Publishers, 1997).

edge accruing from the recent finds." Yet in compiling his *Pocket Lexicon,* he avoided slavish dependence on the work of his colleagues and predecessors. Rather, by doing original concordance work and consulting the best commentaries of his time, he sought to reflect meanings that best fit the New Testament contexts in which the words occur.

In this revised and expanded edition, Souter's classic work has been enhanced by the addition of several helpful features:

- English definitions, still set apart in italicized type, have been moved to the beginning of each entry and are followed with grammatical, etymological, and other extraneous information.
- Parts of complex word definitions have been more consistently numbered to simplify analysis.
- Definitions have been revised, where needed, to keep pace with current English usage.
- Several new Greek word entries that reflect New Testament textual discoveries made since Souter's day have been added.
- Analyzed forms of over one thousand irregular verbs and other unusual words have been added to aid the reader in identifying difficult forms.
- Definite articles and genitive word endings have been included for each noun to indicate gender and pattern of declension.
- Adjective endings have been provided to offer help in the identification of regular and irregular forms.
- Prepositions and adverbs have been more explicitly and consistently identified.
- Biblical references have been converted from Roman to Arabic numerals and set forth in a format more familiar to contemporary readers.
- Latin equivalents to Greek words, with the exception of cognate forms, have been eliminated.
- An abbreviations list has been added, and abbreviations have been updated and applied more consistently throughout the lexicon.

ABBREVIATIONS

Biblical Books

Gen	Genesis	Nah	Nahum
Exod	Exodus	Hab	Habakkuk
Lev	Leviticus	Zeph	Zephaniah
Num	Numbers	Hag	Haggai
Deut	Deuteronomy	Zech	Zechariah
Josh	Joshua	Mal	Malachi
Judg	Judges	Matt	Matthew
1–2 Sam	1–2 Samuel	Rom	Romans
1–2 Kgs	1–2 Kings	1–2 Cor	1–2 Corinthians
1–2 Chr	1–2 Chronicles	Gal	Galatians
Neh	Nehemiah	Eph	Ephesians
Ps	Psalms	Phil	Philippians
Prov	Proverbs	Col	Colossians
Isa	Isaiah	1–2 Thess	1–2 Thessalonians
Jer	Jeremiah	1–2 Tim	1–2 Timothy
Ezek	Ezekiel	Phlm	Philemon
Dan	Daniel	Heb	Hebrews
Hos	Hosea	Jas	James
Obad	Obadiah	1–2 Pet	1–2 Peter
Mic	Micah	Rev	Revelation

General

absol.	absolute(ly)	cf.	compare
abstr.	abstract	cog.	cognate
acc.	accusative	comp.	comparative
act.	active	concr.	concrete
A.D.	anno domini (Common Era)	cond.	conditional
adj(s).	adjective(s)	conj.	conjunction
adv(s).	adverb(s), adverbial	constr.	construction
aor.	aorist	dat.	dative
Aram.	Aramaic	def.	definite
B.C.	before Christ (before the Common Era)	demons.	demonstrative
		e.g.	for example
c.	century	Eng.	English

esp.	especially
etc.	et cetera
fem.	feminine
fut.	future
gen.	genitive
Gk.	Greek
Heb.	Hebrew
i.e.	that is
imper.	imperative, imperatival
impers.	impersonal(ly)
impf.	imperfect
indef.	indefinite
indic.	indicative
indir.	indirect
infin.	infinitive
interj.	interjection
interrog.	interrogative
intrans.	intransitive
Lat.	Latin
lit.	literal(ly)
LXX	Septuagint
masc.	masculine
met.	metaphorical(ly)
mid.	middle
mod.	modern
MSS	manuscripts
neut.	neuter
nom.	nominative
NT	New Testament
obj.	object(ive)
opp.	opposite (of)
opt.	optative
orig.	original(ly)
OT	Old Testament
par(s).	parallel(s)
part(s).	participle(s)
pas.	passive
perf.	perfect
pers.	person(al)
plup.	pluperfect
plur.	plural
pred.	predicate
prep(s).	preposition(s)
pres.	present (tense)
pron.	pronoun
q.v.	which see
refl.	reflexive
rel.	relative
repr.	reprinted
sing.	singular
subj.	subject
subjun.	subjunctive
subst.	substantive
superl.	superlative
Syr.	Syriac
temp.	temporal
trans.	transitive
var.	textual variant
voc.	vocative
w.	with

A

A the first letter of the Greek alphabet, see ἄλφα.

᾿Ααρών, ὁ *Aaron*, son of Amram and Jochebed, younger brother of Moses [Heb.].

᾿Αβαδδών, ὁ *Destroyer* (i.e., *Destroying Angel*) or *"place of destruction"* (personified) [Heb.].

ἀβαρής, ές *not burdensome, bringing no weight or oppression upon.*

ἀββά (ἀββᾶ), ὁ *Father!* (voc., from Aram.).

᾿Αβειληνή, ῆς, ἡ *the Abilenian territory* (understand χώρα), *the territory of Abila* (in Syria), a small principality in the mountains northwest of Damascus.

῞Αβελ, ὁ *Abel*, second son of Adam and Eve, brother of Cain [Heb.].

᾿Αβιά, ὁ *Abjah*, founder of the eighth class of priests (1 Chr 24:10) [Heb.].

᾿Αβιάθαρ (᾿Αβιαθάρ), ὁ *Abiathar*, a priest in King David's time [Heb.].

᾿Αβιληνή, ῆς, ἡ see ᾿Αβειληνή.

᾿Αβιούδ, ὁ *Abiud*, son of Zorobabel and father of Eliakim [Heb.].

᾿Αβραάμ, ὁ *Abraham*, progenitor of the Hebrew race; hence the phrase θυγατέρα ᾿Αβραάμ (Luke 13:16) means simply *a woman of Hebrew race* [Heb.].

ἄβυσσος, ου, ἡ *the abyss, the unfathomable depth*, an especially Jewish conception, the home of the dead and of evil spirits.

῞Αγαβος (῞Αγαβος), ου, ὁ *Agabus*, a Christian prophet (Acts 11:28; 21:10).

ἀγαγεῖν aor. act. infin. → ἄγω.

ἀγαθοεργέω (ἀγαθουργέω) *I work that which is good, I perform good deeds.*

ἀγαθοποιέω *I do that which is good* (opp. κακοποιέω).

ἀγαθοποιΐα (ἀγαθοποιΐα), ας, ἡ *the doing of that which is good.*

ἀγαθοποιός, οῦ, ὁ *a doer of that which is good*, opp. of κακοποιός (adj. as noun, ἀγαθοποιῶν gen. plur. masc., 1 Pet 2:14).

ἀγαθός, ή, όν (1) *good* (intrinsically), *good* (in nature), *good* (whether it be seen to be so or not), the widest and most colorless of all words with this meaning (opp. πονηρός, κακός); (2) subs. τὰ ἀγαθά, *the goods*, Luke 12:18.

ἀγαθουργέω see ἀγαθοεργέω.

ἀγαθωσύνη, ης, ἡ *goodness* (intrinsic, especially as a personal quality), with stress on the kindly (rather than the righteous) side of goodness.

ἀγαλλίασις, εως, ἡ *wild joy, ecstatic delight, exultation, exhilaration.*

ἀγαλλιάω *I exult, I am full of joy.*

ἄγαμος, ου, ὁ or **ἡ** *unmarried, not married*, of a person not in a state of wedlock, whether he or she has formerly been married or not.

ἀγανακτέω *I am angry, I am incensed.*

ἀγανάκτησις, εως, ἡ *feeling of anger, vexation.*

ἀγαπάω *I love* (never of love between the sexes, but nearly always of the love of God or Christ to us, and of our love to Him and to our fellow creatures, as inspired by His love for us).

ἀγάπη, ης, ἡ (1) *love* (this was the sense of the word *charity* in the time of the Authorized Version), as that of God or Christ to us, and our love to Him and to our fellow creatures thus inspired (a word exclusively biblical, curtailed from ἀγάπησις (from ἀγαπάω); (2) in LXX generally of sexual love; first in higher sense not before about 100 B.C.); (3) ἀγάπη τοῦ θεοῦ, τοῦ χριστοῦ are sometimes ambiguous, when it is doubtful whether

God's/Christ's love for us, or our love for God/Christ, is intended; in most cases the former is probably the primary thought; (4) ἀγάπαι plur. concr., of the *love feasts* of the Christians, evening meals partaken of by Christians in the early Church, either accompanied or followed by the Eucharist (Jude 12). Such common meals were sacred, and intended to be expressive of the union of Christians in their Head.

ἀγαπητός, ή, όν *loved, beloved,* with two special applications, (1) ὁ ἀγαπητός, *the Beloved,* a title of the Messiah (Christ), as beloved beyond all others by the God who sent Him; (2) of Christians, as beloved by God, Christ, and one another.

Ἄγαρ (Ἁγάρ), ἡ *Hagar,* the servant of Sarah, wife of Abraham, and interpreted by Rabbinic lore, countenanced by Paul, as a type of Mount Sinai, where the Mosaic Law was given (Gal 4:24–25) [Heb.].

ἀγγαρεύω *I impress* (into my service), *I send* (on an errand); from a Persian word, meaning *to impress for the postal service.*

ἀγγεῖον, ου, τό *a vessel, flask, can.*

ἀγγελία, ας, ἡ *a message.*

ἀγγέλλω *I report, I announce* (as a messenger).

ἄγγελος, ου, ὁ (1) *a messenger,* generally; (2) *a* (supernatural) *messenger from God, an angel,* conveying news or requests from God to men; (3) almost *an intermediary,* Gal 3:19.

ἄγγος, ους, τό *a vessel.*

ἄγε *come now! Ho now!* (an interj., properly imper. of ἄγω).

ἀγέλη, ης, ἡ *a herd.*

ἀγενεαλόγητος, ον *not provided with a genealogy, whose descent cannot be traced.*

ἀγενής, ές *ignoble,* lit., *without* γένος *(family).*

ἁγιάζω *I make* ἅγιος *(set apart, holy);* apparently exclusively biblical.

ἁγιασμός, οῦ, ὁ *the process of making* or *becoming* ἅγιος *(set apart, holy).*

ἅγιος, α, ον *set apart* by (or for) the God, *holy, sacred,* e.g., (of Jerusalem) ἁγία πόλις (Matt 4:5); τὸ ἅγιον πνεῦμα, practically synonymous with τὸ πνεῦμα τοῦ θεοῦ; ὁ ἅγιος τοῦ θεοῦ (Mark 1:24) of the Messiah; οἱ ἅγιοι, of the Christians as the new people of God, taking the place of the Hebrews; τὸ ἅγιον, τὰ ἅγια, *the temple;* τὰ ἅγια τῶν ἁγίων, *the inmost part of the temple, the inner shrine.*

ἁγιότης, ητος, ἡ *holiness* (see ἅγιος), as an abstr. quality.

ἁγιωσύνη, ης, ἡ *a holy* or *sanctified state,* the resulting state of the ἅγιος.

ἀγκάλη, ης, ἡ *an arm,* especially as bent to receive a burden.

ἄγκιστρον, ου, τό *a fishhook.*

ἄγκυρα, ας, ἡ *an anchor.*

ἄγναφος, ον *unshrunken* (of cloth), *unmilled, not yet dressed* (by the fuller).

ἁγνεία, ας, ἡ *purity, chastity.*

ἁγνίζω *I make pure,* either (1) ceremonially (e.g., Acts 21:24), or (2) actually (e.g., 1 Pet 1:22).

ἁγνισμός, οῦ, ὁ *purification* (ceremonial).

ἀγνοέω *I do not know, I am ignorant of* (a person, thing, or fact), sometimes with the idea of willful ignorance.

ἀγνόημα, ατος, τό *an offence committed through ignorance, an error due to* (willful or culpable) *ignorance.*

ἄγνοια, ας, ἡ *ignorance, inadver-*

tence; sometimes with the idea of *willful blindness* (Eph 4:18).

ἁγνός, ή, όν (1) *pure* (either ethically, or ritually, ceremonially); (2) *chaste* (orig., *in a condition prepared for worship*).

ἁγνότης, ητος, ἡ *purity, chastity.*

ἁγνῶς adv., *purely, with pure motives, honestly.*

ἀγνωσία, ας, ἡ disgraceful *ignorance.*

ἄγνωστος, ον *unknown, unknowable.*

ἀγορά, ᾶς, ἡ *marketplace, market.*

ἀγοράζω *I buy.*

ἀγοραῖος, ου, ὁ (1) *a lounger in the marketplace,* perhaps with the idea of *agitator* (Acts 17:5); (2) ἀγοραῖοι (understand ἡμέραι), *market days;* (3) (understand σύνοδοι) *judicial inquests.*

ἄγρα, ας, ἡ *catching, a catch.*

ἀγράμματος, ον *unlettered, illiterate, uneducated,* perhaps with the narrower idea, *unacquainted with Rabbinic teaching.*

ἀγραυλέω *I spend the night in the open, bivouac.*

ἀγρεύω *I catch, capture.*

ἀγριέλαιος, ου, ἡ *a wild olive.*

ἄγριος, α, ον *wild.*

Ἀγρίππας, α, ὁ *Agrippa,* i.e., Herod Agrippa II (M. Iulius Agrippa, A.D. 28–c. 93), son of Agrippa I (the Herod of Acts 12), king of Chalcis (A.D. 50), and afterwards of the old tetrarchies of Philip and Lysanias also.

ἀγρός, οῦ, ὁ (1) *a field* (a word rare in papyrus documents, and now obsolete), especially as bearing a crop; (2) *the country,* Mark 15:21; 16:12: plur. ἀγροί, *lands, property in land, a country estate.*

ἀγρυπνέω (1) *I am not asleep, I am awake;* (2) especially *I am watchful, careful.*

ἀγρυπνία, ας, ἡ *the state of being awake* (at night).

ἄγω (1) *I lead, I lead away, I bring* (a person, or animal); thus *I bring* before a court of justice; (2) especially in first pers. plur. subjun. ἄγωμεν, intrans., *let us depart* (e.g., Mark 1:38); (3) *I hold, keep, celebrate;* ἀγοραῖοι ἄγονται (Acts 19:38), *judicial inquests are held.*

ἀγωγή, ῆς, ἡ (1) *leading;* (2) hence, *mode of life, conduct.*

ἀγών, ῶνος, ὁ (1) *an* (athletic) *contest;* (2) hence, *a struggle* (in the soul).

ἀγωνία, ας, ἡ (1) *great fear, terror,* of death; (2) *anxiety* (properly the feeling of the athlete before a contest).

ἀγωνίζομαι *I am struggling* (as in an athletic contest or warfare); sometimes w. the obj. ἀγῶνα expressed.

Ἀδάμ, ὁ *Adam,* the first man, the first parent of the human race; ὁ ἔσχατος Ἀδάμ, its latest ideal representative, who inaugurates the new age, Jesus the Messiah (1 Cor 15:45) [Heb.].

ἀδάπανος, ον *without expense, for which nothing has to be paid.*

Ἀδδεί (Ἀδδί), ὁ *Addei,* son of Cosam, and father of Melchei, one of the ancestors of Jesus (Luke 3:28) [Heb.].

ἀδελφή, ῆς, ἡ (1) *a sister;* (2) *a woman (fellow) member of a church, a Christian woman* (Rom 16:1; 1 Cor 7:15, etc.).

ἀδελφός, οῦ, ὁ (1) *a brother* (so probably even in Rom 16:23; 2 Cor 12:18); (2) *a member of the same religious community,* especially *a fellow Christian* (particularly in the plur., a use characteristic of Jewish literature but not confined to it).

ἀδελφότης, ητος, ἡ *brotherhood*

(in the collective sense), *the members of the Christian Church, Christendom.*

ἄδηλος, ον *unseen, inconspicuous, indistinct* (also of sound).

ἀδηλότης, ητος, ἡ *the quality of being unseen (of disappearing), indefiniteness, uncertainty.*

ἀδήλως adv., (1) *out of sight, obscurely, inconspicuously;* (2) in 1 Cor 9:26 perhaps = *uncertainly, without certain aim.*

ἀδημονέω (1) *I feel fear, I lack courage;* (2) *I am distressed* (orig., *I am bewildered,* from δήμων, *knowing, prudent*).

ᾅδης, ου, ὁ *Hades, the unseen world,* into which the spirits of all persons pass at death (in LXX = Heb. *šĕʾôl,* Sheol).

ἀδιάκριτος, ον *without divisions of mind, undivided, wholehearted.*

ἀδιάλειπτος, ον *unceasing, unremitting.*

ἀδιαλείπτως adv., *unceasingly, without remission.*

ἀδικέω *I act unjustly towards, I injure, I harm* (animate or inanimate).

ἀδίκημα, ατος, τό (1) *a legal wrong, a crime* (with which one is charged), *a misdeed;* (2) *a crime against God, a sin* (Rev 18:5).

ἀδικία, ας, ἡ *injustice, unrighteousness, hurt;* sometimes in a Hebraistic gen., equivalent to the adj. ἄδικος (e.g., Luke 16:8; 18:6).

ἄδικος, ον *unjust, unrighteous* (opp. δίκαιος).

ἀδίκως adv., *unjustly.*

Ἀδμείν (Ἀδμίν), ὁ *Admein,* son of Arnei, father of Naasson, one of the ancestors of Jesus [Heb.].

ἀδόκιμος, ον *failing to pass the test, unapproved, counterfeit.*

ἄδολος, ον *unadulterated, pure.*

Ἀδραμυντηνός (Ἀδραμυττηνός), ή, όν *belonging to Adramyttium,* a port in Mysia, northwest Asia Minor.

Ἀδρίας (Ἀδρίας), ου, ὁ *the Hadria,* a name given by sailors not merely to the Adriatic Sea, to which it properly belonged, but also to the open Mediterranean to the southeast of Italy, to the sea that lay between Malta, Italy, Greece, and Crete.

ἁδρότης, ητος, ἡ *lavishness, lavish generosity.*

ἀδυνατέω of things, *to be impossible.*

ἀδύνατος, ον (1) of persons, *incapable* (Acts 14:8; Rom 15:1); (2) of things, *impossible;* τὸ ἀδύνατον, either *the inability,* or *that which is impossible* (Rom 8:3).

ἀδυσβάστακτος, ον *not too difficult to bear* (cf. δυσβάστακτος).

ᾄδω (ᾄδω) *I sing.*

ἀεί adv., *always* (rare in colloquial Gk.).

ἀετός, οῦ, ὁ *an eagle.*

ἄζυμος, ον (1) *unleavened,* especially in the neut. plur., τὰ ἄζυμα, *the unleavened bread,* a festival of the Hebrews, held from 15 to 21 Nisan, in commemoration of their deliverance from Egypt; (2) in a moral sense, 1 Cor 5:7–8.

Ἀζώρ, ὁ *Azor,* son of Eliakim and father of Zadok, an ancestor of Jesus [Heb.].

Ἄζωτος, ου, ἡ *Azotus, Ashdod,* a coast town of Palestine belonging to the ancient Philistia, and part of Herod's kingdom.

ἀήρ, έρος, ὁ *air,* the lower air we breathe.

ἀθανασία, ας, ἡ *immortality, imperishability, freedom from death.*

ἀθέμιτος, ον (1) *illegal, unlawful;* (2) thus *abominable.*

ἄθεος, ον *without god, without (the only true) god, godless.*

ἄθεσμος, ον *lawless, ignoring the* (divine) *ordinances.*
ἀθετέω (1) *I annul, make of no eject, set aside, ignore, slight;* (2) *I break faith with,* Mark 6:26.
ἀθέτησις, εως, ἡ *annulment.*
᾿Αθῆναι, ῶν, ἡ *Athens,* the intellectual capital of Greece.
᾿Αθηναῖος, α, ον *Athenian, belonging to Athens.*
ἀθλέω *I engage, compete, in an* (athletic) *contest.*
ἄθλησις, εως, ἡ *a struggling* (as in an athletic contest).
ἀθροίζω *I gather together, collect.*
ἀθυμέω *I lose heart, am despondent.*
ἀθῷος, ον *guiltless, innocent* (sometimes, *unpunished*).
αἴγειος, α, ον *of a goat.*
αἰγιαλός, οῦ, ὁ (1) *sea coast,* (sandy) *beach;* (2) *shore* (of sea or lake), *land.*
Αἰγύπτιος, α, ον *Egyptian.*
Αἴγυπτος, ου, ἡ *Egypt.*
ἀΐδιος, ον *lasting for ever.*
αἰδώς, οῦς, ἡ *shame, modesty.*
Αἰθίοψ, οπος, ὁ *Ethiopian, Abyssinian* (apparently absent from papyri).
αἷμα, ατος, τό *blood* (especially as shed); σὰρξ καὶ αἷμα (αἷμα καὶ σὰρξ), a Hebraistic expression for *a human being, human beings, human nature.*
αἱματεκχυσία, ας, ἡ *a shedding* or *pouring forth of blood* (in sacrifice).
αἱμορροέω *I suffer from a continual flow (oozing) of blood.*
Αἰνέας, ου, ὁ *Aeneas,* a citizen of Lydda.
αἴνεσις, εως, ἡ *praise, commendation.*
αἰνέω *I praise.*
αἴνιγμα, ατος, τό *a riddle.*
αἶνος, ου, ὁ *praise.*
Αἰνών, ἡ *Aenon.* Eusebius and Jerome place this site eight (Roman) miles south of Scythopolis near the Jordan.
αἵρεσις, εως, ἡ (1) *a self-chosen opinion;* (2) a religious or philosophical *sect* (orig., *choosing, choice*).
αἱρετίζω *I choose.*
αἱρετικός, ή, όν *disposed to form sects, sectarian, factious.*
αἱρέω mid. *I choose.*
αἴρω (1) *I raise, lift up;* (2) *I take away, remove.*
αἰσθάνομαι *I perceive.*
αἴσθησις, εως, ἡ *perception.*
αἰσθητήριον, ου, τό *perceptive faculty.*
αἰσχροκερδής, ές *fond of base gain.*
αἰσχροκερδῶς adv., *in a spirit of eagerness for base gain.*
αἰσχρολογία, ας, ἡ *filthy, obscene speech.*
αἰσχρός, ά, όν *base, disgraceful.*
αἰσχρότης, ητος, ἡ *baseness.*
αἰσχύνη, ης, ἡ (1) *shame;* (2) *shamefacedness.*
αἰσχύνομαι *I am ashamed.*
αἰτέω *I ask, request, beg, petition;* mid. voice αἰτέομαι, *I ask for myself* (perhaps w. entreaty).
αἴτημα, ατος, τό *a request.*
αἰτία, ας, ἡ (1) *a cause, reason; excuse;* (2) *a charge, accusation;* (3) *guilt;* (4) *relationship, matter, circumstances, case,* Matt 19:10.
αἴτιον, ου, τό (1) *cause* shading into *crime;* (2) *guilt, criminality* (neut. of adj. αἴτιος).
αἴτιος, ου, ὁ (1) *the cause of the originator of;* (2) *responsible for* (adj.).
αἰτίωμα, ατος, τό *a charge, accusation.*
αἰφνίδιος, ον *sudden.*
αἰχμαλωσία, ας, ἡ (1) *captivity;* (2) Hebraistically = *captives,* Eph 4:8.

αἰχμαλωτεύω *I take captive* (in war).

αἰχμαλωτίζω *I take captive* (in war), *I subdue, I ensnare.*

αἰχμάλωτος, ου, ὁ *a captive* (in war), hence generally.

αἰών, ῶνος, ὁ *an age, a cycle* (of time), especially of the present age as contrasted with the future age, and of one of a series of ages stretching to infinity; ἀπ' αἰῶνος, from *the beginning of the present age, from the beginning of time,* Luke 1:70, etc.; εἰς αἰῶνα *for eternity;* αἰῶνες αἰώνων, a Hebraistic expression, more emphatic than the simple αἰῶνες, Gal 1:5, etc. (From a root meaning *life,* especially *long life, old age.*)

αἰώνιος, ον (1) *age-long,* and, therefore, practically *eternal, unending;* (2) partaking of the character of that which lasts for an age, as contrasted with that which is brief and fleeting.

ἀκαθαρσία, ας, ἡ *uncleanness, impurity.*

ἀκάθαρτος, ον *unclean, impure;* in reference to demons, spirits, Matt 10:1, etc.

ἀκαιρέομαι *I am without a suitable opportunity* (to effect something).

ἀκαίρως adv., *unseasonably, out of due season, inopportunely.*

ἄκακος, ον (1) *innocent, guileless;* (2) *simple,* Rom 16:18.

ἄκανθα, ης, ἡ *a thorn bush.*

ἀκάνθινος, η, ον *made of thorns.*

ἄκαρπος, ον *fruitless, profitless.*

ἀκατάγνωστος, ον *uncondemned, unimpeachable.*

ἀκατακάλυπτος, ον *not veiled, unveiled.*

ἀκατάκριτος, ον *uncondemned* (probably an attempt to translate the Lat. *re incognita* or *causâ indictâ,* "[our, one's] case not having been tried").

ἀκατάλυτος, ον *indissoluble, that cannot be broken up.*

ἀκατάπαστος, ον a colloquial spelling of ἀκατάπαυστος.

ἀκατάπαυστος, ον *not ceasing from, not abandoning (giving up),* w. gen.

ἀκαταστασία, ας, ἡ *disturbance, upheaval, revolution,* almost *anarchy,* first in the political, and thence in the moral sphere.

ἀκατάστατος, ον *unsettled, unstable* (though these are hardly strong enough equivalents), almost *anarchic;* (in LXX *staggering, reeling*).

Ἀκελδαμάχ see Ἁχελδαμάχ.

ἀκέραιος, ον *simple, unsophisticated* (lit. *unmixed*).

ἀκήκοα perf. act. → ἀκούω.

ἀκλινής, ές *unbent, unyielding, resolute.*

ἀκμάζω (1) *I reach maturity, become ripe;* (2) *I am in full vigor.*

ἀκμήν adv., *thus* (properly adv. acc. of ἀκμή [full time, maturity], and meaning *just now*), Matt 15:16 where par. in Mark 7:18 has οὕτως).

ἀκοή, ῆς, ἡ (1) *hearing, faculty of hearing, ear;* in ἀκοῇ ἀκούειν (Matt 13:14, etc.), a Hebraistic(?) expression, the ἀκοῇ is emphatic; (2) *report, rumor.*

ἀκολουθέω *I accompany, attend* (takes the place of the old ἕπομαι).

ἀκούω *I hear, listen;* in the pas., *is heard, is reported;* ἀκοῇ ἀκούειν, see ἀκοή.

ἀκρασία (= ἀκράτεια), ας, ἡ *incontinence, intemperance* (in wide sense).

ἀκρατής, ές (*impotent*), hence, *lacking self control, inclined to excess.*

ἄκρατος, ον *unmixed, undiluted* (from κεράννυμι).

ἀκρίβεια, ας, ἡ *accuracy, exactness, attention to detail, scrupulousness.*

ἀκριβής, ές *careful, accurate, exact, strict, scrupulous, precise.*

ἀκριβόω *I examine carefully, inquire strictly.*

ἀκριβῶς adv., *carefully, exactly, strictly.*

ἀκρίς, ίδος, ἡ *a locust.*

ἀκροατήριον, ου, τό (1) *auditorium, recitation hall;* (2) *court room* (for hearing cases).

ἀκροατής, οῦ, ὁ *a hearer of, a listener to.*

ἀκροβυστία, ας, ἡ *foreskin, prepuce* (a technical word of Jewish use, perhaps adapted from ἀκροποσθία); *uncircumcision,* a slang term used by Jews to refer to Gentiles, (Eph 2:11).

ἀκρογωνιαῖος, α, ον adj., *in the corner* (of a building), *corner*(stone) [= Attic γωνιαῖος].

ἀκροθίνιον, ου, τό *spoil, treasure* (taken in war); lit. *top of a heap.*

ἄκρον, ου, τό *edge, tip* (neut. of adj. ἄκρος).

᾿Ακύλας acc. **-αν, ὁ** the Gk. way of writing the Lat. *Aquila,* a male proper name; the husband of Priscilla (Prisca), and a Jew, of a family belonging to (Sinope in) Pontus.

ἀκυρόω *I annul, make of no eject, cancel.*

ἀκωλύτως adv., *without let or hindrance* (characteristic of legal documents).

ἄκων adj., *unwilling,* generally used where Eng. would express by an adv., *unwillingly.*

ἀλάβαστρος (or -ον), ου, τό *an alabaster phial* or *bottle.*

ἀλαζονεία, ας, ἡ (1) *arrogant display, ostentation;* (2) plur. = *occasions of ostentation.*

ἀλαζών, όνος, ὁ *boastful,* giving one's self airs in a loud and flaunting way.

ἀλαλάζω (1) *I cry aloud,* generally of persons (in Mark 5:38 from sorrow); (2) κύμβαλον ἀλαλάζον, a *clanging* or *clashing* cymbal (1 Cor 13:1); onomatopoeic, cf. Heb.

ἀλάλητος, ον *unutterable, that baffles words.*

ἄλαλος, ον *dumb.*

ἅλας, ατος, τό *salt.*

ἁλεεύς (ἁλιεύς), έως, ὁ *a fisherman* (a modification of the earlier ἁλιεύς).

ἀλείφω *I anoint.*

ἀλεκτοροφωνία, ας, ἡ *cockcrow,* as a period of time, between midnight and 3 a.m.

ἀλέκτωρ, ορος, ὁ *a cock.*

᾿Αλεξανδρεύς, έως, ὁ *an Alexandrian,* a native (or resident) of Alexandria in Egypt.

᾿Αλεξανδρινός (᾿Αλεξανδρῖνος), ἡ, όν *belonging to Alexandria* in Egypt.

᾿Αλέξανδρος, ου, ὁ *Alexander,* a proper name of Gk. origin, borne by four, possibly five, persons in the NT, (1) an early Christian, son of Simon of Cyrene, who carried the Cross, Mark 15:21; (2) a leading non-Christian Jew in Jerusalem, Acts 4:6; (3) an Ephesian Jew, Acts 19:33; (4) a renegade Christian at Rome (1 Tim 1:20), probably to be identified with Alexander the coppersmith (2 Tim 4:14).

ἄλευρον, ου, τό *meal.*

ἀλήθεια, ας, ἡ *truth,* but not merely truth as spoken; truth of idea, reality, sincerity, truth in the moral sphere, straightforwardness; ἐπ' ἀληθείας, *really, truly.*

ἀληθεύω (1) *I say (speak) truth,* Gal 4:16; (2) *I do truth, I maintain truth (the truth);* see ἀλήθεια for the sense of "truth."

ἀληθής, ές *true* in fact; hence more widely (see ἀλήθεια).
ἀληθινός, ή, όν *true* (lit., *made of truth*), *real, genuine* (less common than ἀληθής).
ἀλήθω *I grind.*
ἀληθῶς adv., *truly, verily.*
ἁλιεύς, έως, ὁ see ἁλεεύς.
ἁλιεύω *I fish.*
ἁλίζω *I salt, salten, sprinkle with salt* (of sacrifices or of those who offer sacrifice), *keep fresh and sound,* and so acceptable to God.
ἀλίσγημα, ατος, τό *pollution,* perhaps *a polluted thing* (especially of food); from ἀλισγέω, read in Freer manuscript at Mark 9:49.
ἁλισθήσομαι fut. pas. → ἁλίζω.
ἀλλά (1) *but;* (2) *except* (used very like πλήν), Mark 4:22; Matt 20:23; ἀλλ' ἤ, *except,* 2 Cor 1:13; in Mark 6:9 ἀλλά is probably a misrendering of an Aram. word meaning *and not.*
ἀλλαγήσομαι fut. pas. → ἀλλάσσω.
ἀλλάσσω trans., *I change, alter.*
ἀλλαχόθεν adv., *from another quarter,* practically *by another way.*
ἀλλαχοῦ adv., *elsewhere* (= ἄλλοσε, ἀλλαχόσε, *to another place*).
ἀλληγορέω *I allegorize, I interpret as an allegory.*
ἀλληλουιά (ἀλληλουϊά) *Hallelujah, Praise the Lord* [Heb.].
ἀλλήλων, ους *one another* (a reciprocal word).
ἀλλογενής, οῦς, ὁ *a man of another race, a foreigner.*
ἅλλομαι *I leap, leap up.*
ἄλλος, η, ο (1) *other, another* (of more than two), *different;* (2) see under ἕτερος; ὁ ἄλλος, *the other* (of two only), Matt 5:39, etc.; ἄλλοι . . . ἄλλο τι . . . *some . . . one thing, some . . . another thing.*
ἀλλοτρι(ο)επίσκοπος, ου, ὁ *one who pries into other men's affairs* by means of soothsayers, astrologers, etc. (a word of uncertain application).
ἀλλότριος, α, ον *belonging to another person, belonging to others.*
ἀλλόφυλος, ον *a foreigner.*
ἄλλως *otherwise;* τὰ ἄλλως ἔχοντα, *things that are otherwise.*
ἀλοάω *I thresh* (corn).
ἄλογος, ον (1) *without (devoid of) human reason;* (2) *unreasonable, senseless.*
ἀλόη, ης, ἡ *aloes,* the powdered fragrant aloe wood.
ἅλς, ἁλός, ὁ *salt.*
ἁλυκός, ή, όν *salty, saline.*
ἄλυπος, ή, όν *free from pain (grief, trouble),* comp. in Phil. 2:28.
ἅλυσις, εως, ἡ *a* (light) *chain.*
ἀλυσιτελής, ές *profitless, unprofitable.*
ἄλφα, τό *alpha,* the first letter of the Greek alphabet, cf. A.
Ἀλφαῖος, ου, ὁ *Alphaeus,* apparently two persons, (1) father of Levi (Mark 2:14); and (2) father of James (Mark 3:18, etc.). (Some say = Aram. Chalphai, and identify with Clopas, John 19:25.)
ἅλων, ωνος, ἡ *a threshing floor* (= ἅλως).
ἀλώπηξ, εκος, ἡ *a fox.*
ἅλωσις, εως, ἡ *capture, capturing.*
ἅμα (1) adv., *at the same time, therewith;* (2) prep. w. dat., *along with, together with.*
ἀμαθής, ές *unlearned* (very rare in Hellenistic period).
ἀμαράντινος, η, ον *unfading, fadeless.*
ἀμάραντος, ον *unfading.*
ἁμαρτάνω orig., *I miss the mark;* hence, (1) *I make a mistake;* (2) *I sin, I commit a sin* (against God); sometimes (Luke 17:4; Acts 25:8, etc.) the idea of sinning against a fellow creature is present.
ἁμάρτημα, ατος, τό *a fault, a sin.*

ἁμαρτία, ας, ἡ (error, *a wrong state of mind* or *soul*), *a sin.*

ἀμάρτυρος, ον *unwitnessed, untestified to.*

ἁμαρτωλός, όν (1) *sinning, sinful;* (2) frequent as a translation of a contemptuous Aram. word, w. reference to particular classes despised by strict Jews, *a sinner.*

ἄμαχος, ον *not quarrelsome, peaceable* (orig. a military word).

ἀμάω *I mow, reap.*

ἀμέθυστος, ου, ἡ *amethyst* (a kind of rock crystal; the best specimens are the color of unmixed wine, whence perhaps the name).

ἀμελέω *I neglect.*

ἄμεμπτος, ον *blameless.*

ἀμέμπτως adv., *blamelessly.*

ἀμέριμνος, ον *free from anxiety* (though "anxiety" is rather too strong a word).

ἀμετάθετος, ον *unchanged, unchangeable.*

ἀμετακίνητος, ον *immovable.*

ἀμεταμέλητος, ον *not to be repented of, about which no change of mind can take place, not affected by change of mind.*

ἀμετανόητος, ον *unrepentant.*

ἄμετρος, ον *unmeasurable, immeasurable;* εἰς τὰ ἄμετρα, *to a limitless degree.*

ἀμήν *verily, truly;* at the end of sentences may be paraphrased by *So let it be!* [Heb.]

ἀμήτωρ, ορος *whose mother's name is not recorded* (or *known*); lit., *motherless.*

ἀμίαντος, ον *undefiled, untainted.*

Ἀμιναδάβ, ὁ *Aminadab,* son of Aram and father of Naasson, one of the ancestors of Jesus [Heb.].

ἄμμος, ου, ἡ *sand.*

ἀμνός, οῦ, ὁ *a lamb* (as a type of innocence, and w. sacrificial connotation).

ἀμοιβή, ῆς, ἡ (1) a *change, an exchange;* (2) hence, plur. *reciprocal good deeds (services), a fitting requital.*

ἄμπελος, ου, ἡ *a vine.*

ἀμπελουργός, οῦ, ὁ *a vinedresser.*

ἀμπελών, ῶνος, ὁ *a vineyard* (-ών indicates "plantation of," cf. ἐλαιών).

Ἀμπλιᾶτος, ου, ὁ *Ampliatus,* a male member of the church at Rome, probably of the imperial household (pet form Ἀμπλίας).

ἀμύνομαι *I attack in defense, I defend* (by force); (very rare in the colloquial language).

ἀμφιάζω *I clothe, I put clothing (covering) on (over);* from ἀμφί, as ἀντιάζω is from ἀντί.

ἀμφιβάλλω *I cast* (a fishing net), *I fish.*

ἀμφίβληστρον, ου, τό *a* (casting) *net.*

ἀμφιέζω see ἀμφιάζω.

ἀμφιέννυμι *I clothe* (a survival of literary language).

Ἀμφίπολις, εως, ἡ *Amphipolis,* a leading city of Macedonia.

ἄμφοδον, ου, τό *a street,* or rather *a quarter* or *block* of a city.

ἀμφότεροι, αι, α *both* (of two); in Acts 19:16; 23:8, perhaps = *all* (of more than two); so in common speech and in Byzantine Gk.

ἀμώμητος, ον *unblemished* (a literary word; the Gk. properly means *not to be blamed,* but under the influence of Heb. the other sense has come into prominence).

ἄμωμον, ου, τό *spice,* an odorous unguent derived from an Eastern plant with fruit like grapes, Rev 18:13.

ἄμωμος, ον (1) *blameless,* the original sense, which may be that in Eph 1:4; 5:27, etc.; (2) *without blemish, unblemished,* a sense almost invariable in the LXX, of sacrificial animals, and possibly the only sense intended in NT (cf. ἀμώμητος).

᾿Αμώς, ᾿Αμών, ὁ *Amos,* son of Manasseh and father of Josiah, an ancestor of Jesus [Heb. = ’amon, OT].

ἄν (1) an untranslatable word *(under the circumstances, in that case, anyhow),* the general effect of which is to make a statement contingent, which would otherwise be definite; it is thus regularly used w. the subjun. mood; cf. ἕως ἄν, *until such time as,* ὃς ἄν, ὅστις ἄν, *whosoever,* ὅσοι ἄν, *as many as . . . may,* ὅπως ἄν, ὡς ἄν (1 Cor 11:34, etc., not in 1 Cor 12:2), *that so;* so, w. the indic. past, in the apodosis of a cond. sentence, e.g., Matt 11:21 ἂν . . . μετένοησαν, "*would* have repented," where μετένοησαν alone would have meant "repented"; cf. also Mark 7:11 (reading ὃ ἂν . . . ὠφελήθης); and w. the opt. (rare in NT), e.g., τί ἂν θέλοι, "how he *would* like" (Luke 1:62), where τί θέλοι would be "how he *might* like"; (2) *if* (= Attic ἤν, ἐάν), e.g., John 12:32 (var.), 13:20.

ἀνά prep. w. acc., (1) *up;* hence, *up along;* (2) ἀνὰ μέσον, *in the middle;* (3) most commonly w. a distributive force, e.g., ἀνὰ δηνάριον (Matt 20:9), "a denarius *each,*" ἀνὰ δύο χιτῶνας (Luke 9:3), "two tunics *each,*" ἀνὰ πεντήκοντα (Luke 9:14), "in fifties," "in *groups of* fifty," ἀνὰ δύο (Luke 10:1), "two by two" (where perhaps ἀνὰ δύο δύο, a mixed distributive, ought to be read).

ἀναβαθμός, οῦ, ὁ (1) *a step;* (2) plur. *a flight of steps,* the well known "stairs" leading up from the temple to the tower of Antonia at Jerusalem.

ἀναβαίνω *I go up, mount, ascend.*

ἀναβάλλομαι *I postpone,* especially *I postpone the trial of,* w. acc. of the person affected.

ἀναβέβηκα perf. act. → ἀναβαίνω.

ἀναβιβάζω *I cause to come up, bring up,* regularly from sea to land.

ἀναβλέπω (1) *I look up,* e.g., Matt 14:19; (2) *I recover my sight,* e.g., Matt 11:5.

ἀνάβλεψις, εως, ἡ *recovery of sight.*

ἀναβοάω *I shout upwards, cry out, raise my voice,* Matt 27:46, var.

ἀναβολή, ῆς, ἡ *postponement, delay, putting off.*

ἀνάγαιον, ου, τό *an upper room;* another form is ἀνώγεον.

ἀναγγέλλω *I announce, report.*

ἀναγγελῶ fut. act. → ἀναγγέλλω.

ἀναγεννάω *I beget again, I beget into a new life.*

ἀναγινώσκω *I read aloud* (in the scriptures, i.e., the OT).

ἀναγκάζω *I compel, I constrain.*

ἀναγκαῖος, α, ον (1) *necessary, essential;* (2) *intimate,* Acts 10:24.

ἀναγκαστῶς adv., *by way of compulsion, by force.*

ἀνάγκη, ης, ἡ *necessity, constraint, compulsion;* ἔχω ἀνάγκη, *I am obliged.*

ἀναγνωρίζω *I make known to again, I make to be recognized* (var. in Acts 7:13).

ἀναγνωσθῆναι aor. pas. infin. → ἀναγινώσκω.

ἀνάγνωσις, εως, ἡ public *reading* (of the law and prophets in synagogue or church).

ἀνάγω (1) *I lead up;* (2) mid., and pas. *I put to sea, set sail.*

ἀναδείκνυμι (1) *I show forth* or *clearly;* (2) hence, *I proclaim* (a person's appointment to an office), *I appoint.*

ἀνάδειξις, εως, ἡ (1) *the proclamation of an appointment* (to an office); (2) perhaps rather *admission to membership* of a society.

ἀναδέχομαι (1) *I welcome, receive kindly;* (2) in Heb 11:17 perhaps *I undertake, I assume the responsibility of.*

ἀναδίδωμι *I send up, deliver, hand over.*

ἀναδούς aor. act. part. → ἀναδίδωμι.

ἀναζάω *I come to life again, I revive* (var. in Luke 15:24).

ἀναζητέω *I seek out, search for* (implying the difficulty of the task).

ἀναζώννυμι *I gird up, brace up* (with a view to active exertion). A metaphor from the girding of the flowing tunic, to prevent its hampering one in active work.

ἀναζωπυρέω *I stir up the fire, fan the flame of.*

ἀναθάλλω *I cause to bloom again.*

ἀνάθεμα, ατος, τό *a curse, a cursed thing* (properly, a devoting to the vengeance of the infernal goddesses). Distinguish from ἀνάθημα, q.v.

ἀναθεματίζω *I curse, I invoke curses.*

ἀναθεωρέω *I look up at, I gaze up at.*

ἀνάθημα, ατος, τό an *offering dedicated* (hung up in a temple) by a worshipper to a god, in return for a favor received, Luke 21:5.

ἀναίδεια, ας, ἡ *shamelessness, shameless persistence* (e.g., in greed).

ἀναίρεσις, εως, ἡ *taking away* (of life), *killing, slaying, murder.*

ἀναιρέω (1) *I take up,* e.g., Acts 7:21; more often (2) *I take away the life of, murder* (2 Thess 2:8, var.).

ἀναίτιος, ον *guiltless.*

ἀνακαθίζω *I sit up* (in classical Gk. *I cause to sit up*); var. in Luke 7:15.

ἀνακαινίζω *I make fresh again, I make fresh as at the first.*

ἀνακαινόω *I renew, I make new again* (cf. ἀνακαινίζω); not cited before Paul.

ἀνακαίνωσις, εως, ἡ *renewing* (not cited earlier).

ἀνακαλύπτω *I unveil.*

ἀνακάμπτω *I return.*

ἀνάκειμαι *I recline* (especially at a dinner table).

ἀνακεφαλαιόομαι (1) *I sum up, summarize, recapitulate;* (2) in Eph 1:10 *gather up in one* (a literary word, from κεφάλαιον, *chapter, section*).

ἀνακλίνω (1) *I make to recline* (especially at a dinner table); (2) mid. and pas. *I recline at a table.*

ἀνακράζω *I shout* (aloud); colloquial.

ἀνακρίνω *I examine, inquire into* (judicially; see ἀνάκρισις); of the preliminary examination, preceding the trial proper; hence with derived applications.

ἀνάκρισις, εως, ἡ *judicial examination, preliminary inquiry.*

ἀνακυλίω *I roll back.*

ἀνακύπτω (1) *I raise myself, become erect* (Luke 13:11); (2) *I look up* (Luke 21:28).

ἀναλαμβάνω (1) *I take up, raise;* (2) *I pick up,* 2 Tim 4:11, or *take on board,* Acts 20:13, 14; (3) *I carry off, lead away,* Acts 23:31.

ἀνάλημψις, εως, ἡ *a taking up, lifting up* (of the Ascension); lit. *Assumption.*

ἀναλίσκω (ἀναλόω) *I destroy, annihilate* (var. in 2 Thess 2:8).

ἀναλογία, ας, ἡ *proportion, measure.*

ἀναλογίζομαι *I reckon up, count over* (from λόγος = *account*).

ἀναλοῖ aor. opt. → ἀναλίσκω.

ἄναλος, ον *saltless, tasteless, flat.*

ἀναλόω see ἀναλίσκω.

ἀνάλυσις, εως, ἡ *departing, departure* (from this life, probably a metaphor from the yoking and unyoking of transport animals).

ἀναλύω (1) *I depart,* Phil 1:23; (2) perhaps, *I return,* Luke 12:36 (see ἀνάλυσις).

ἀναλώσω fut. act. → ἀναλίσκω.

ἀναμάρτητος, ον *sinless.*

ἀναμένω *I await* (one whose coming is expected).

ἀναμιμνῄσκω (1) act. *I remind;* (2) mid. or pas. *I am reminded, remind myself, remember, recall.*

ἀνάμνησις, εως, ἡ *a recalling, remembrance, memory.*

ἀναμνήσω fut. act. → ἀναμιμνῄσκω.

ἀνανεόομαι *I am renewed* (regularly a legal word).

ἀνανήφω *I become sober again, I recover sound sense.*

Ἀνανίας (Ἁνανίας), ου, ὁ *Ananias,* (1) husband of Sapphira, a member of the early church at Jerusalem, Acts v; (2) a member of the church at Damascus, Acts 9:10, etc.; (3) the high priest at Jerusalem, Acts 23:2; 24:1.

ἀναντίρ(ρ)ητος, ον *that cannot be gainsaid, undeniable.*

ἀναντιρ(ρ)ήτως adv., *without saying anything against* (the request), *unquestioningly.*

ἀνάξιος, ον *unworthy.*

ἀναξίως adv., *unworthily, in an unworthy manner.*

ἀναπαήσομαι fut. pas. → ἀναπαύω.

ἀνάπαυσις, εως, ἡ *a resting, rest,* especially *a respite* or *temporary rest* as a preparation for future toil.

ἀναπαύω (1) act. *I make to rest, I give rest to;* (2) mid. and pas. *I rest, take my ease* (see ἀνάπαυσις).

ἀναπείθω *I urge by* (evil) *persuasion, I tempt.*

ἀνάπειρος see ἀνάπηρος.

ἀναπέμπω (1) *I send up* (to a higher tribunal), Luke 23:7; Acts 25:21, etc.; (2) *I send back,* Phlm 12, etc.

ἀναπηδάω *I leap up.*

ἀνάπηρος, όν *maimed.*

ἀναπίπτω (1) *I lie down, recline* (at a dinner table); (2) *I fall back upon* (the breast of another person reclining at dinner).

ἀναπληρόω (1) *I fill up, make up, complete the measure of,* Phil 2:30; (2) *I fulfill, I carry out the commands* (*provisions,* etc.) *of,* Matt 13:14; Gal 6:2, etc.

ἀναπολόγητος, ον *without* (ground of) *defense, indefensible, inexcusable.*

ἀναπτύσσω *I unroll* (reading uncertain).

ἀνάπτω *I kindle.*

ἀναρίθμητος, ον *uncountable, innumerable, that cannot be numbered.*

ἀνασείω *I shake up, stir up, excite.*

ἀνασκευάζω (1) *I pack up;* (2) hence, *I carry away,* or *dismantle;* (3) hence, *I upset, destroy, overthrow, subvert* (lit. and met.).

ἀνασπάω *I drag up, pull up.*

ἀνάστα aor. act. imper. → ἀνίστημι.

ἀναστάς aor. act. part. → ἀνίστημι.

ἀνάστασις, εως, ἡ *a rising again, resurrection.*

ἀναστατόω *I turn upside dawn, upset, unsettle* (perhaps a political metaphor).

ἀνασταυρόω *I crucify again* (so the sense seems to require, but elsewhere simply = σταυρόω, *I crucify*).

ἀναστενάζω *I groan.*

ἀνάστηθι aor. act. imper. → ἀνίστημι.

ἀναστῆναι aor. act. infin. → ἀνίστημι.

ἀναστήσας aor. act. part. → ἀνίστημι.

ἀναστήσω fut. act. → ἀνίστημι.

ἀναστρέφω (1) *I overturn, turn upside down,* John 2:15 (var.); (2) *I return,* Acts 5:22; 15:16 (in a Hebraistic idiom, where the verb means little more than the adv. *again*); (3) mid. and pas. *I conduct (behave) myself, live* (w. reference to the manner of life, especially in a moral and religious aspect), Matt 17:22 (var.), etc., often w. ἐν and a noun indicating condition or circumstances.

ἀναστροφή, ῆς, ἡ *dealing with* other men, *going up and down* among men, *life, manner of life* (not in papyri, common in inscriptions).

ἀνατάσσομαι *I arrange, draw up,* but perhaps, as Blass thought, *I set down from memory, I restore from memory,* Luke 1:1.

ἀνατέλλω (1) *I make to rise,* Matt 5:45; (2) *I rise, shine* (generally of the sun, and hence met.).

ἀνατέταλκα perf. act. → ἀνατέλλω.

ἀνατίθεμαι *I lay* (a case) *before, I impart, I communicate, I relate* (with a view to consulting).

ἀνατολή, ῆς, ἡ (1) *rising* of the sun; (2) hence, the quarter whence the sun rises, *the east* (sing. and plur.).

ἀνατρέπω *I overturn* (lit. or met.); var. in John 2:15.

ἀνατρέφω *I rear, bring up* (var. in Luke 4:16).

ἀναφαίνω (1) a nautical term, *I sight* (a place); (2) mid. *I appear* (as it were, out of the unseen).

ἀναφέρω (1) *I carry up, lead up;* (2) *I offer up* (on a high altar) as a sacrifice, *I offer up* to God on high.

ἀναφωνέω *I call out, shout.*

ἀναχθῆναι aor. pas. infin. → ἀνάγω.

ἀνάχυσις, εως, ἡ *outpouring, excess* (probably literary).

ἀναχωρέω (1) *I return,* Matt 2:12; (2) *I retire, depart* (underlying idea perhaps of taking refuge from danger or of going into retirement).

ἀνάψυξις, εως, ἡ *refreshing, refreshment.*

ἀναψύχω *I refresh, revive, comfort.*

ἀνδραποδιστής, οῦ, ὁ *an enslaver,* one who forcibly enslaves, *a kidnapper.*

'Ανδρέας, ου, ὁ *Andrew,* brother of Simon Peter, and one of the disciples of Jesus, belonging to Bethsaida (John 1:44) [a Gk. name].

ἀνδρίζομαι *I act in manly fashion, I play the man, I display manly qualities.*

'Ανδρόνικος, ου, ὁ *Andronicus,* a member of the Roman church, probably husband of Junia, and a kinsman or fellow tribesman of Paul.

ἀνδροφόνος, ου, ὁ *a murderer.*

ἀνεβαλόμην aor. mid. → ἀναβάλλω.

ἀνέβην aor. act. → ἀναβαίνω.

ἀνέγκλητος, ον *irreproachable* (especially in private life), *blameless.*

ἀνέγνων aor. act. → ἀναγινώσκω.

ἀνέδειξα aor. act. → ἀναδείκνυμι.

ἀνεζώσαμαι aor. mid. → ἀναζώννυμαι.

ἀνέθαλον aor. act. → ἀναθάλλω.

ἀνεθέμην aor. mid. → ἀνατίθεμαι.

ἀνέθην aor. pas. → ἀνίημι.

ἀνεῖλα aor. act. → ἀναιρέω.

ἀνεῖλον aor. act. → ἀναιρέω.

ἀνείς aor. act. part. → ἀνίημι.

ἀνεκδιήγητος, ον *indescribable, that cannot be thoroughly related.*

ἀνεκλάλητος, ον *incapable of expression in speech.*

ἀνέκλειπτος (ἀνέγλειπτος), ον *unfailing.*

ἀνεκρίθην aor. pas. → ἀνακρίνω.

ἀνεκτός, όν *endurable, tolerable.*

ἀνέλαβον aor. act. → ἀναλαμβάνω.

ἀνελεήμων, ον *unpitying, unmerciful.*
ἀνελεῖ fut. act. 3 sing. → ἀναιρέω.
ἀνελεῖν aor. act. infin. → ἀναιρέω.
ἀνέλεος, ον *unmerciful.*
ἀνελήμφθην aor. pas. → ἀναλαμβάνω.
ἀνέλοι aor. opt. → ἀναιρέω.
ἀνέλω aor. act. subj. → ἀναιρέω.
ἀνελῶ fut. act. → ἀναιρέω.
ἀνεμίζομαι *I am blown with the wind* (referring to the gentler motions of the air).
ἀνεμνήσθην aor. pas. → ἀναμιμνήσκω.
ἄνεμος, ου, ὁ (1) *wind* (lit., and in Eph 4:14 met.); (2) in the sense *quarter of the heaven, cardinal point,* as both Greeks and Romans habitually defined the quarters of the heaven by the winds which came from those quarters, Matt 24:31 (Mark 13:27).
ἀνένδεκτος, ον *impossible.*
ἀνενέγκαι aor. act. infin. → ἀναφέρω.
ἀνενεγκεῖν aor. act. infin. → ἀναφέρω.
ἀνεξεραύνητος, ον *that cannot be searched into, inscrutable.*
ἀνεξίκακος, ον *enduring evil, patient of evil.*
ἀνεξιχνίαστος, ον *that cannot be tracked out, unexplorable, unsearchable* (perhaps from Job [LXX]).
ἀνεπαίσχυντος, ον *not ashamed* (of his work).
ἀνέπεσον aor. act. → ἀναπίπτω.
ἀνεπίλημπτος, ον *giving no cause for accusation.*
ἀνέρχομαι *I go up* (to the capital).
ἄνεσις, εως, ἡ (1) *relief, remission, indulgence, freedom,* Acts 24:23; (2) *rest* (opp. θλῖψις, lit., *loosening, relaxing*).
ἀνέστην aor. act. → ἀνίστημι.
ἀνέστησα aor. act. → ἀνίστημι.
ἀνεστράφην aor. pas. → ἀναστρέφω.
ἀνεσχόμην aor. mid. → ἀνέχομαι.
ἀνετάζω *I examine* (a person on trial, a witness) *judicially* (frequently by the aid of torture).
ἀνέτειλα aor. act. → ἀνατέλλω.
ἄνευ prep. w. gen., *without, without the cooperation* (or *knowledge*) *of* (Matt 10:29).
ἀνεύθετος, ον *unfitted, unsuitable.*
ἀνευρίσκω *I find by seeking out.*
ἀνεῦρον aor. act. → ἀνευρίσκω.
ἀνέφανα aor. act. → ἀναφαίνομαι.
ἀνέχομαι *I endure,* Matt 6:24 (= Luke 16:13); 2 Thess 1:4 (var.).
ἀνεψιός, οῦ, ὁ *cousin* (male), whether on the father's or on the mother's side.
ἀνέῳγα perf. act. → ἀνοίγω.
ἀνέῳγμαι perf. mid./pas. → ἀνοίγω.
ἀνέῳξα aor. act. → ἀνοίγω.
ἀνεῴχθην aor. pas. → ἀνοίγω.
ἀνήγαγον aor. act. → ἀνάγω.
ἀνήγγειλα aor. act. → ἀναγγέλλω.
ἀνηγγέλην aor. pas. → ἀναγγέλλω.
ἄνηθον, ου, τό *dill (anethum graveolens).*
ἀνήκω *is due, becoming, suitable, proper;* in third pers., especially of impf. (cf. Eng. *ought = owed*).
ἀνῆλθον aor. act. → ἀνέρχομαι.
ἀνηλώθην aor. pas. → ἀναλίσκω.
ἀνήλωσα aor. act. → ἀναλίσκω.
ἀνήμερος, ον (1) *ungentle;* (2) *untamed.*
ἀνήνεγκον aor. act. → ἀναφέρω.
ἀνήρ, ἀνδρός, ὁ (1) *a male human being, a man* (contrast ἄνθρωπος); (2) often in addresses, at the beginning of speeches, *Gentlemen;* (3) *a husband.*
ἀνηρέθην aor. pas. → ἀναιρέω.
ἀνήφθην aor. pas. → ἀνάπτω.
ἀνήχθην aor. pas. → ἀνάγω.

ἀνθέξομαι fut. mid. → ἀντέχομαι.
ἀνθέστηκα perf. act. → ἀνθίστημι.
ἀνθίστημι *I take a stand against, oppose, resist;* only in intrans. tenses of act., and in all tenses of the mid. or pas.
ἀνθομολογέομαι *I confess (*so e.g., the Lat. and Sahidic versions), (1) *acknowledge, formally admit;* (2) *I give thanks* (so e.g., the Peshitta Syriac and the Bohairic versions, and moderns generally). (The senses *I agree, I answer to [come up to], I come to an understanding with,* appear in papyri.)
ἄνθος, ους, τό *bloom,* possibly a reference to the bright flowers, such as poppies (among the grass).
ἀνθρακιά, ᾶς, ἡ *a coal fire.*
ἄνθραξ, ακος, ὁ a *coal.*
ἀνθρωπάρεσκος, ον *a men-pleaser, one who renders service to human beings* (as opposed to God).
ἀνθρώπινος, η, ον (1) *belonging to human beings* (especially as contrasted with God), *human* (as contrasted with divine); (2) perhaps *moderate,* Rom 6:19; 1 Cor 10:13.
ἀνθρωποκτόνος, ου, ὁ *a murderer* (borrowed from poetry).
ἄνθρωπος, ου, ὁ *a human being;* υἱὸς ἀνθρώπου, notable because of the sing. (rather than the plur. ἀνθρώπων), a Hebraistic expression of a somewhat frequent type (see under υἱός), indicating *a human being with all the characteristics of a human being* (ὁ υἱὸς τοῦ ἀνθρώπου, a Messianic title especially favored by our Lord for this very reason).
ἀνθύπατος, ου, ὁ *a proconsul,* a title applied to the governor of a senatorial province under the Empire, such as Cyprus (Acts 13:7, 8, 12), Achaia (Acts 18:12), and Asia (Acts 19:38, where the plur. is general and does not mean that there were more than one at a time). The word means orig. *one with the rank and insignia of a consul* (i.e., the chief Roman magistrate), but was later applied to those who had not yet held the office of consul as well as to those who had.
ἀνίημι *I let go, loosen, release, give up.*
ἄνιπτος, ον *unwashed.*
ἀνίστημι (1) *I raise up, set up;* only the fut. ἀναστήσω and the 1 aor. ἀνέστησα are used in this trans. sense in the NT; (2) much more frequent are the mid. voice and the 2 aor. of the act. in the intrans. sense, *I rise,* especially ἐκ νεκρῶν, *from among (the) dead bodies, dead persons, the dead.*
Ἄννα (Ἅννα), ας, ἡ *Anna,* a prophetess, who visited the infant Jesus. (The aspirated form Ἅννα, favored by WH, is contradicted by the evidence of the versions.)
Ἄννας (Ἅννας), α, ὁ *Annas,* high priest at Jerusalem.
ἀνόητος, ον *senseless* (in Gal 3:1 pathos is behind the use of the word, according to Ramsay, *Historical Commentary,* pp. 308 ff., and it describes a state of culture unworthy of the Romanized Galatians).
ἄνοια, ας, ἡ *senselessness.*
ἀνοίγω *I open.*
ἀνοικοδομέω (1) *I rebuild, build up* (what has fallen or been razed to the ground); (2) sometimes merely *I build.*
ἄνοιξις, εως, ἡ *opening* (abstr.).
ἀνομία, ας, ἡ (1) *lawlessness;* (2) especially *disobedience to the divine law, sin.*
ἄνομος, ον (1) *lawless, disobedient to the law* of God, *sinful;* (2) *illegal;* ἄνομος θεοῦ = ἄνευ νόμου θεοῦ (1 Cor 9:21).
ἀνόμως adv., *without law.*

ἀνορθόω *I make upright (straight) again, I rear again, restore.*
ἀνόσιος, ον *regarding nothing as holy.*
ἀνοχή, ῆς, ἡ (1) *forbearance;* (2) *suspense* or *delay* (of punishment).
ἀνταγωνίζομαι *I struggle against.*
ἀντάλλαγμα, ατος, τό *an exchange, purchasing price.*
ἀνταναπληρόω *I fill up in place of someone else.*
ἀνταπεδόθην aor. pas. → ἀνταποδίδωμι.
ἀνταποδίδωμι *I give in return.*
ἀνταπόδομα, ατος, τό *a gift in return* (for another), *a return, a recompense.*
ἀνταπόδοσις, εως, ἡ orig. abstr., *giving in return,* but in Col 3:24 practically = ἀνταπόδομα.
ἀνταποδοῦναι aor. act. infin. → ἀνταποδίδωμι.
ἀνταποδώσω fut. act. → ἀνταποδίδωμι.
ἀνταποκρίνομαι *I give a hostile answer.*
ἀντεῖπον *I said in reply* (with idea of hostility, contradiction); 2 aor. act. of **ἀντιλέγω.**
ἀντελαβόμην aor. mid. → ἀντιλαμβάνομαι.
ἀντέστην aor. act. → ἀνθίστημι.
ἀντέχομαι *I hold fast (firmly) to.*
ἀντί prep. w. gen. (1) *instead of, in return for, in exchange for, as a substitute for;* λύτρον ἀντὶ πολλῶν Mark 10:45 (= Matt 20:28), *a ransom to buy the many, for the many;* cf. Heb 12:16 and ἀντίλυτρον; (2) ἀντὶ ἐμοῦ, *on my behalf,* Matt 17:27; (3) ἀνθ' ὧν (lit., *in return for which things*) has become a conj., *wherefore, because;* (orig. local, *in front of, opposite*).
ἀντιβάλλω (1) *I throw at in opposition* (or quasi-opposition), *I exchange* (words) *with;* (2) perhaps, *I compare.*
ἀντιδιατίθεμαι *I am adversely affected against, I oppose.*
ἀντίδικος, ου, ὁ *an opponent* (in a lawsuit); probably so even in 1 Pet 5:8.
ἀντίθεσις, εως, ἡ *a proposition, tenet, opinion* advanced by one party *against* another.
ἀντικαθίστημι *I stoutly resisted* (2 aor.).
ἀντικαλέω *I invite in return.*
ἀντικατέστην aor. act. → ἀντικαθίστημι.
ἀντίκειμαι *I resist, oppose* (used as a pas. for ἀντιτίθημι, just as κεῖμαι is a pas. for τίθημι).
ἄντικρυς prep. w. gen., *right opposite, off* (nautical sense).
ἀντιλαμβάνομαι (1) *I lay hold of* (in order to help), *I aid (succor);* (2) *I take in hand* (lit. and met.), *I undertake;* (3) *I partake of, enjoy,* 1 Tim 6:2.
ἀντιλέγω *I speak* or *say in opposition, I contradict (oppose, resist);* σημεῖον ἀντιλεγόμενον, *a disputed sign, a sign that is debated about.*
ἀντίλημψις, εως, ἡ *a lending a hand to, a helping* (cf. ἀντιλαμβάνομαι, both being often used in petitions).
ἀντιλογία, ας, ἡ *contradiction, dispute.*
ἀντιλοιδορέω *I abuse in return, I give abuse for abuse.*
ἀντίλυτρον, ου, τό a stronger form of λύτρον, *a ransom.*
ἀντιμετρέω *I measure in return, I give equivalent measure,* Luke 6:38 (var.).
ἀντιμισθία, ας, ἡ *a reward, recompense* (a more emphatic expression than the simple μισθός).
Ἀντιόχεια, ας, ἡ *Antioch* (derived from Antiochus, a king of the

Seleucid dynasty), (1) *Antioch* on the river Orontes, capital of the Province Syria; (2) "Pisidian" *Antioch,* not in Pisidia, but near Pisidia, in the Roman Province Galatia, where was a Roman colony founded by Augustus, Acts 13:14; 14:19, 21; 2 Tim 3:11.

'Αντιοχεύς, έως, ὁ *an Antiochian, an inhabitant of* (Syrian) *Antioch.*

ἀντιπαρέρχομαι *I pass opposite,* on the *opposite* side of the road.

ἀντιπαρῆλθον aor. act. → ἀντιπαρέρχομαι.

'Αντίπας ('Αντιπᾶς, 'Αντείπας, 'Αντίφας), α, ὁ *Antipas,* a Christian martyr of Pergamum (a pet form of 'Αντίπατρος).

'Αντιπατρίς, ίδος, ἡ *Antipatris,* a town, where was a Roman colony, on the road between Caesarea and Jerusalem.

ἀντίπερα (ἀντιπέρα) prep. w. gen., *opposite.*

ἀντιπίπτω (1) *I fall foul of;* (2) *I resist, oppose.*

ἀντιστρατεύομαι *I campaign against, war against.*

ἀντιτάσσομαι *I range myself against, resist* (the attack of).

ἀντίτυπος, ον (1) *typical of, representing by type* (or *pattern*), *corresponding to;* (2) neut., as noun, *an image* (from τύπος, *impress, impression left by a die*).

ἀντίχριστος, ου, ὁ *antichrist,* either *one who puts himself in the place of* or *the enemy (opponent) of the Messiah,* a figure first appearing in the NT, identified with various historical persons; the plur., of many such, in 1 John 2:18.

ἀντλέω (1) *I draw* (generally water from a deep well in the ground); (2) perhaps, *I draw out,* John 2:9.

ἄντλημα, ατος, τό *a pail* attached to a rope, by which it is let down into a well.

ἀντοφθαλμέω (1) *I face* (lit. "I present my eye to"); (2) *I resist.*

ἄνυδρος, ον *waterless.*

ἀνυπόκριτος, ον *unfeigned, genuine* (literary).

ἀνυπότακτος, ον *disorderly, unruly.*

ἄνω adv., *up, above;* ἕως ἄνω, *up to the top, up to the brim,* John 2:7; τὰ ἄνω, *things above, heaven, the heavenly region;* see ἀνώτερον.

ἀνῶ aor. act. subj. → ἀνίημι.

ἄνωθεν adv. (1) from *above,* sometimes strengthened by ἀπό, *from heaven* (locally and spiritually); (2) *from the beginning, from their origin (source), from of old,* Luke 1:3; Acts 26:5; Gal 4:9; Jas 1:17; (3) *again* (the meaning taken out of Jesus' words by Nicodemus, John 3:4, where δεύτερον is his paraphrase of ἄνωθεν [3:3]).

ἀνωτερικός, ή, όν *upper, higher-lying* (the high central plateau of Asia Minor in contrast to the road through the valley).

ἀνώτερον adv. (1) *higher, to a more honorable place* (at the dinner table), Luke 14:10; (2) *previously, in an earlier passage* (of the book), *above,* (comp. of ἄνω, q.v.).

ἀνωφελής, ές *useless, unprofitable* (perhaps also with the further idea, *harmful,* as in Plato).

ἀξίνη, ης, ἡ *axe.*

ἄξιος, α, ον (1) *worthy;* (2) *worthy of, deserving.*

ἀξιόω *I account* or *treat as worthy.*

ἀξίως adv., *worthily, in a manner worthy of.*

ἀόρατος, ον *unseen, invisible.*

'Αουλία *see* 'Ιουλία.

ἀπαγγέλλω *I report* (from one place to another), *I bring a report, I announce.*

ἀπάγχομαι *I choke, strangle, hang myself.*

ἀπάγω (1) *I lead away,* (e.g., *I lead away* to execution, Acts 12:19);

(2) hence, in the moral sphere, 1 Cor 12:2; (3) also, of a road *leading* to a place.

ἀπαίδευτος, ον *untrained, uneducated, showing a want of training or education.*

ἀπαίρω *I take away, remove.*

ἀπαιτέω *I ask back,* or *I ask what is my due.*

ἀπαλγέω *I am past feeling, cease to care* (suggesting sometimes despair, sometimes recklessness), *I become callous;* (lit. *I cease to feel [my] pain*).

ἀπαλλάσσω (1) *I free* (a person) *from* (anything); (2) oftener in the mid. voice, *I am released from, I am rid of* (a person or thing).

ἀπαλλοτριόομαι (1) lit. *I am being alienated from;* (2) the perf. part. pas. is practically a noun, *aliens.*

ἁπαλός, ή, όν *tender.*

ἀπαντάω *I meet.*

ἀπάντησις, εως, ἡ the act of *meeting;* εἰς ἀπάντησιν, *to meet* (a phrase seemingly almost technical for the reception of a newly arrived official).

ἅπαξ adv., (1) *once;* (2) *once for all.*

ἀπαράβατος, ον *inviolate, inviolable.*

ἀπαρασκεύαστος, ον *unprepared.*

ἀπαρνέομαι *I deny, disown, repudiate* (either another person or myself).

ἀπάρτι (1) *henceforth;* (2) *even now* (properly ἀπ' ἄρτι, lit., *from now*).

ἀπαρτισμός, οῦ, ὁ (1) *setting up, erection;* (2) hence, *completion.*

ἀπαρχή, ῆς, ἡ (1) *firstfruits, the earliest crop* of the year; (2) hence also met., e.g., of the earliest converts in a district. There is evidence in favor of rendering in some passages merely by *sacrifice, gift.*

ἅπας, ασα, αν *all, whole* (cf. πᾶς). It is rather a literary word and is used by preference after consonants.

ἀπασπάζομαι *I greet at parting, I give parting greetings to.*

ἀπατάω *I deceive, cheat* (becoming obsolete in most countries).

ἀπάτη, ης, ἡ *deceit, deception,* (or more probably, according to a Hellenistic sense), *pleasure* in Mark 4:19 (= Matt 13:22, cf. Luke 8:14); 2 Pet 2:13.

ἀπάτωρ, ορος *without* (recorded) *father, of unknown father.*

ἀπαύγασμα, ατος, τό *a light flashing forth* (from), *radiation, gleam.*

ἀπαχθῆναι aor. pas. infin. → ἀπάγω.

ἀπέβαλον aor. act. → ἀποβάλλω.

ἀπέβην aor. act. → ἀποβαίνω.

ἀπέδειξα aor. act. → ἀποδείκνυμι.

ἀπεδόμην aor. mid. → ἀποδίδωμι.

ἀπέθανον aor. act. → ἀποθνῄσκω.

ἀπεθέμην aor. mid. → ἀποτίθημι.

ἀπείθεια, ας, ἡ *disobedience, rebellion, contumacy;* for υἱοὶ τῆς ἀπειθείας, see υἱός.

ἀπειθέω *I disobey, I rebel, I am disloyal.*

ἀπειθής, ές *disobedient.*

ἀπειλέω *I threaten* (apparently going out of popular speech).

ἀπειλή, ῆς, ἡ *threatening, a threat.*

ἄπειμι (1) *I am absent;* (2) *I shall go away, I go away* (only Acts 17:10).

ἀπειπάμην aor. mid. → ἀπολέγομαι.

ἀπεῖπον in mid., ἀπειπάμην, *I have renounced.*

ἀπείραστος, ον (1) *untried, inexperienced* (c. gen. = *in*); (2) or *untempted* (c. gen. = *to*).

ἄπειρος, ον *inexperienced* (in), *without experience* (of), *unacquainted* (with); from πεῖρα.

ἀπεκαλύφθην aor. pas. → ἀποκαλύπτω.

ἀπεκατεστάθην aor. pas. → ἀποκαθίστημι.

ἀπεκατέστην aor. act. → ἀποκαθίστημι.
ἀπεκδέχομαι *I expect eagerly, I wait for eagerly* (rare).
ἀπεκδύομαι *I put off* (as a garment) *from myself, I throw off* (probably coined by Paul).
ἀπέκδυσις, εως, ἡ *a putting off* (as of a garment), *a casting off* (probably coined by Paul).
ἀπεκρίθην aor. pas. → ἀποκρίνομαι.
ἀπεκτάνθην aor. pas. → ἀποκτείνω.
ἀπέκτεινα aor. act. → ἀποκτείνω.
ἀπέλαβον aor. act. → ἀπολαμβάνω.
ἀπελαύνω *I drive away.*
ἀπελεγμός, οῦ, ὁ (1) *refutation, rejection;* (2) hence, *disrepute.*
ἀπελεύθερος, ου, ὁ *a freedman,* one who has been a slave but has been manumitted by his master.
ἀπελεύσομαι fut. mid. → ἀπέρχομαι.
ἀπελήλυθα perf. act. → ἀπέρχομαι.
ἀπέλιπον aor. act. → ἀπολείπω.
Ἀπελλῆς, οῦ, ὁ *Apelles,* a Christian (man) in Rome.
ἀπελπίζω (ἀφελπίζω) *I despair;* in Luke 6:35, if μηδέν be the correct reading, μηδὲν ἀφελπίζοντες must be translated, *despairing not at all,* if μηδένα ἀφ., *despairing of no one.*
ἀπέναντι prep. w. gen., (1) *over against, opposite;* (2) *in view of, in presence of.*
ἀπενεγκεῖν aor. act. infin. → ἀποφέρω.
ἀπενεχθῆναι aor. pas. infin. → ἀποφέρω.
ἀπέπεσα aor. act. → ἀποπίπτω.
ἀπέπλευσα aor. act. → ἀποπλέω.
ἀπεπνίγην aor. pas. → ἀποπνίγω.
ἀπέραντος, ον *unaccomplished, unending, endless.*
ἀπερισπάστως adv., *without distraction, without being distracted.*
ἀπερίτμητος, ον (1) *uncircumcised;* (2) hence practically, *unclean;* (3) met, used of rankness, want of restraint.
ἀπέρχομαι *I go away from* (a place).
ἀπεστάλην aor. pas. → ἀποστέλλω.
ἀπέσταλκα perf. act. → ἀποστέλλω.
ἀπέστειλα aor. act. → ἀποστέλλω.
ἀπέστην aor. act. → ἀφίστημι.
ἀπέστησα aor. act. → ἀφίστημι.
ἀπεστράφην aor. pas. → ἀποστρέφω.
ἀπέχω (1) trans., *I have received* (payment), a formula of receipts; so prob. also in Mark 14:41, ὁ Ἰούδας being understood as subj. (there is hardly any other example in Gk. of the meaning *it is sufficient*); (2) intrans., *I am away (from, distant from),* of places and objects; (3) mid., *I keep myself away* (from), *I refrain* (from), *I abstain* (from).
ἀπήγαγον aor. act. → ἀπάγω.
ἀπήγγειλα aor. act. → ἐπαγγέλλομαι.
ἀπηγγέλην aor. pas. → ἐπαγγέλλομαι.
ἀπηγξάμην aor. mid. → ἀπάγχομαι.
ἀπῄεσαν imperf. 3 plur. → ἄπειμι.
ἀπήλασα aor. act. → ἀπελαύνω.
ἀπῆλθον aor. act. → ἀπέρχομαι.
ἀπηλλάχθαι perf. mid./pas. infin. → ἀπαλλάσσω.
ἀπήνεγκα aor. act. → ἀποφέρω.
ἀπήρθην aor. pas. → ἀπαίρω.
ἀπιστέω (1) *I am unfaithful;* (2) *I disbelieve.*
ἀπιστία, ας, ἡ *unbelief.*
ἄπιστος, ον (1) *unbelieving, incredulous;* (2) *unchristian;* sometimes substantivally, *unbeliever.*
ἁπλότης, ητος, ἡ *singleness of mind, sincerity.*

ἁπλοῦς, ῆ, οῦν (1) *single;* (2) of the eye, *directed towards one object.*

ἁπλῶς adv., (1) *singly, simply;* (2) in Jas 1:5 either *graciously* or *unreservedly, without reserve.*

ἀπό prep. w. gen., w. nouns or advs., *from,* (as distinguished from ἐκ) = *from the outside of, away from;* (1) ἀπ' ἀγορᾶς, *fresh from market,* Mark 7:4; ἀπ' ἀγροῦ, *fresh from the country,* Mark 15:21; Rev 1:4, constr. is peculiar; (2) οἱ ἀπὸ τῆς Ἰταλίας, *those who are in(?) Italy,* Heb 13:24; (3) φοβεῖσθαι ἀπό, see φοβέομαι; (4) *by* (expressing agent), e.g., Luke 8:43; (5) = gen. of material, Matt 3:4; 27:21.

ἀποβαίνω (1) *I disembark;* (2) ἀποβαίνειν εἰς, *to result in, to end in* (lit. *I go away*).

ἀποβάλλω (1) *I cast away, I cast off;* (2) *I lose,* Heb 10:35.

ἀποβήσομαι fut. mid. → ἀποβαίνω.

ἀποβλέπω *I look away from* one thing to another, *I turn my attention* to.

ἀπόβλητος, ον *worthy to be cast away, worthless.*

ἀποβολή, ῆς, ἡ *a casting away, a loss.*

ἀπογίνομαι w. the dat., *I die away from* (opp. γίνομαι; therefore, *I go out of being, I cease to be*).

ἀπογραφή, ῆς, ἡ *an enrollment, a census taking,* in which particulars not only of the persons but also of their property were generally given on the census papers. The system began 10–9 B.C., and such an enrollment took place every fourteen years.

ἀπογράφομαι *I enroll myself* (for the census); hence Heb 12:23, in another connection.

ἀποδέδειγμαι perf. mid./pas. → ἀποδείκνυμι.

ἀποδείκνυμι (1) *I show off, display, exhibit,* 1 Cor 4:9; (2) *I make good, demonstrate,* Acts 25:7; (3) *I make out* (to be so and so), *proclaim* (to be), 2 Thess 2:4; (4) *I designate, nominate, appoint,* Acts 2:22.

ἀπόδειξις, εως, ἡ *(1) display, exhibition* (abstr.); (2) the ordinary sense is *proof.*

ἀποδεκατεύω *I take off (deduct) a tenth part* (of my property to give away), *I pay tithe.*

ἀποδεκατόω (1) as ἀποδεκατεύω; (2) w. acc. pers. *I take a tenth part from.*

ἀπόδεκτος, ον *worthy to be received (welcomed), acceptable, welcome.*

ἀποδέχομαι (1) *I receive, welcome, entertain* (with hospitality); (2) hence, met. Acts 2:41; 24:3.

ἀποδημέω *I am away from my parish, I am away from home, I am absent* (ἀπό *from,* δῆμος *parish*).

ἀπόδημος, ον *away from home* (see ἀποδημέω).

ἀποδίδωμι (1) *I give back, return, restore;* (2) *I give, render,* as due; (3) mid., *I sell,* Acts 5:8, etc.

ἀποδιορίζω *(I make a [logical] distinction), I make an* (invidious) *distinction.*

ἀποδοθῆναι aor. pas. infin. → ἀποδίδωμι.

ἀποδοκιμάζω *I reject after testing (examination), I disqualify.*

ἀποδοχή, ῆς, ἡ *acceptance, appreciation, approbation* (properly *reception, welcome,* of guests).

ἀποθανοῦμαι fut. mid. → ἀποθνήσκω.

ἀποθέμενος aor. mid. part. → ἀποτίθημι.

ἀποθέσθαι aor. mid. infin. → ἀποτίθημι.

ἀπόθεσις, εως, ἡ *a putting off, a laying down.*

ἀποθήκη, ης, ἡ *a storehouse, storeroom* for foodstuffs, *a barn.*

ἀποθησαυρίζω *I store up, treasure up.*

ἀποθλίβω *I jostle;* (lit. *I rub*).

ἀποθνήσκω *I am dying* (= obsolete θνήσκω), Luke 8:42; 2 Cor 6:9; Heb 11:21; aor. ἀποθανεῖν, *to die;* the pres. is frequentative in 1 Cor 15:22; Heb 7:8; 10:28; Rev 14:13 (different individuals), iterative in 1 Cor 15:31 (same person), equivalent to the fut., John 21:23; 1 Cor 15:32.

ἀποίσω fut. act. → ἀποφέρω.

ἀποκαθίστημι (ἀποκαθιστάνω) (1) *I set up again, I restore to its original position* or *condition;* (2) hence, *I restore, give back.*

ἀποκαλύπτω *I unveil, reveal* (correlative to μυστήριον, *secret*).

ἀποκάλυψις, εως, ἡ *an unveiling, uncovering, revealing.*

ἀποκαραδοκία, ας, ἡ *eager expectation* (perhaps coined by Paul).

ἀποκαταλλάσσω *I reconcile.*

ἀποκατάστασις, εως, ἡ *reestablishment, restoration.*

ἀποκαταστήσω fut. act. → ἀποκαθίστημι.

ἀποκατηλλάγην aor. pas. → ἀποκαταλλάσσω.

ἀπόκειμαι *I have been put away, I am stored.*

ἀποκεφαλίζω *I behead.*

ἀποκλείω *I shut.*

ἀποκόπτω (1) *I cut off, I cut loose;* (2) *I emasculate, castrate* (Gal 5:12, where mid. = pas., probably).

ἀπόκριμα, ατος, τό *an answer* (of God to the apostle's appeal, preserved in his heart).

ἀποκρίνομαι (1) *I answer* (either a spoken or an unspoken question), ἀπεκρίθην, etc. (absent from papyri after second c. B.C.), are borrowed by NT from LXX; (2) ἀπεκρινάμην, *I uttered solemnly,* Luke 3:16; John 5:17, 19; Acts 3:12; (3) *I replied* in a court of law, Matt 27:12; Mark 14:61; Luke 23:9 (cf. John 5:11 var.).

ἀπόκρισις, εως, ἡ *answering, answer* (rare in NT times).

ἀποκρύπτω *I hide away, conceal.*

ἀπόκρυφος, ον *hidden away, secret.*

ἀποκτείνω (ἀποκτέννω, ἀποκτεννύω) *I kill* (absent from papyri of NT times).

ἀποκτενῶ fut. act. → ἀποκτείνω.

ἀποκυέω *I bring forth, give birth to* (a child), a medical or physical word, marking the close of pregnancy.

ἀποκυλίω trans., *I roll away from*

ἀπολαμβάνω (1) *I get back, I receive back;* (2) *I get (receive) as due (deserved);* (3) mid., *I draw aside, separate,* Mark 7:33.

ἀπόλαυσις, εως, ἡ *the faculty* or *experience of enjoyment.*

ἀπολείπω *I leave behind;* in Heb 4:6 ἀπολείπεται is impers., *it remains.*

ἀπολέσαι aor. act. infin. → ἀπόλλυμι.

ἀπολέσω fut. act. → ἀπόλλυμι.

ἀπολήμψομαι fut. mid. → ἀπολαμβάνω.

ἀπόλλυμι (1) *I destroy;* (2) *I lose;* (3) mid., *I am perishing* (the resultant death being viewed as certain).

Ἀπολλύων, ονος, ὁ *The Destroying One,* a Gk. translation of the Heb. ʾ*Abaddôn* (properly pres. part. of ἀπολλύω, cf. ἀπόλλυμι).

Ἀπολλωνία, ας, ἡ *Apollonia,* a city of Macedonia.

Ἀπολλῶς (Ἀπολλῶς), ῶ, ὁ *Apollos,* a Jew of Alexandria (a pet, familiar form of Ἀπολλώνιος).

ἀπολογέομαι *I give a defense, I defend myself* (especially in a law court); it can take an obj. of what is said in defense.

ἀπολογία, ας, ἡ *a defense* (particularly in a law court).

ἀπολοῦμαι fut. mid. → ἀπόλλυμι.
ἀπολούω (1) *I wash off;* (2) mid. *I wash away* (my sins, in baptism).
ἀπολύτρωσις, εως, ἡ *ransoming, deliverance, liberation* (from captivity), *ransoming away, emancipation, manumission* (of a slave by his master); the idea of payment, though orig. present, seems wholly to have disappeared in NT.
ἀπολύω (1) *I let loose, set free, release, permit to depart;* (2) mid., *I withdraw myself, depart,* Acts 28:25.
ἀπολωλώς perf. act. part. → ἀπόλλυμι.
ἀπομάσσομαι *I wipe off myself* (on to another).
ἀπονέμω *I apportion, render (as due).*
ἀπονίπτω (ἀπονίζω) *I wash* dirt *off.*
ἀποπίπτω *I fall away* (from), *I fall off.*
ἀποπλανάω *I cause to wander astray;* 1 Tim 6:10 (aor. pas.), *I have wandered away.*
ἀποπλέω *I sail away.*
ἀποπληρόω *I fulfill* (Gal 6:2, var.).
ἀποπνίγω (1) *I choke, drown;* (2) *I stop the growth of.*
ἀπορέω (lit. *I lose the way*), esp. in mid., *I am in difficulties, I am at my wits' end.*
ἀπορία, ας, ἡ *state of difficulty, distress.*
ἀπορίπτω *I throw away* from, *I throw overboard.*
ἀπορφανίζω *I separate from* some one.
ἀποσκίασμα, ατος, τό either *a shadow cast* by an object, or *a faint image* or *copy* of an object.
ἀποσπάω (1) lit. *I wrench away from, I drag away;* (2) but perhaps sometimes in the well attested weakened sense, *I withdraw.*
ἀποστάς aor. act. part. → ἀφίστημι.
ἀποστασία, ας, ἡ *a revolting, revolt,* especially religious *apostasy.*
ἀποστάσιον, ου, τό *divorce.*
ἀποστεγάζω *I unroof, take the roof off.*
ἀποστέλλω (1) *I send away, commission;* (2) *I put forth,* Mark 4:29.
ἀποστελῶ fut. act. → ἀποστέλλω.
ἀποστερέω *I deprive* one *of* something, *I rob;* absol. in Mark 10:19; 1 Cor 7:5, var.
ἀποστῆναι aor. act. infin. → ἀφίστημι.
ἀποστήσομαι fut. mid. → ἀφίστημι.
ἀποστολή, ῆς, ἡ *commission, duty of* ἀπόστολος *(apostle), apostleship.*
ἀπόστολος, ου, ὁ *a messenger, an envoy, a delegate,* one commissioned by another to represent him in some way, especially a man sent out by Jesus Christ Himself to preach the Gospel, *an apostle.*
ἀποστοματίζω *I draw out* by questioning (literary, from ἀπὸ στόματος).
ἀποστρέφω (1) *I turn away (from);* (2) mid., *I turn myself away from;* (3) met., *I pervert,* Luke 23:14; (trans., seems mostly literary).
ἀποστυγέω *I shrink from* (with horror).
ἀποσυνάγωγος, ον *away from the synagogue, expelled the synagogue, excommunicated.*
ἀποτάσσομαι (1) *I give parting instructions;* (2) *I say farewell (good bye), I take leave.*
ἀποτελέω (1) *I complete, accomplish,* Luke 13:32; (2) *I form fully,* Jas 1:15.
ἀποτίθεμαι (1) *I put off (away), cast off (away) from myself;* (2) hence, *I put, store (in).*
ἀποτινάσσω *I shake off.*
ἀποτίνω *I repay, pay what is due* (by way of punishment or fine).
ἀποτίσω fut. act. → ἀποτίνω.

ἀποτολμάω *I break out boldly* (literary).
ἀποτομία, ας, ἡ *peremptoriness, inexorableness, harshness, severity* (lit. *sheerness,* of a rock).
ἀποτόμως adv., *sharply, severely.*
ἀποτρέπομαι *I turn myself away from.*
ἀπουσία, ας, ἡ *absence.*
ἀποφέρω *I carry, bear away* (sometimes with violence, as Mark 15:1).
ἀποφεύγω *I flee from.*
ἀποφθέγγομαι *I utter forth, speak out.*
ἀποφορτίζομαι *I discharge my cargo.*
ἀπόχρησις, εως, ἡ *using up.*
ἀποχωρέω *I go away, depart.*
ἀποχωρίζομαι *I separate myself from.*
ἀποψύχω *I faint* or *I die.*
Ἄππιος *Appius* (censor 312 B.C.), after whom the township *Appi Forum* (Ἀππίου Φόρον) on the Appian Way, 43 Roman miles from Rome, was named.
ἀπρόσιτος, ον *unapproachable.*
ἀπρόσκοπος, ον (*free from hurt or harm*), hence, *not offending, not causing offence, blameless.*
ἀπροσωπολήμπτως adv., *without any preference* (*undue favor, partiality*) *for a person* (literary and Jewish).
ἄπταιστος, ον *not stumbling* (literary and rare).
ἅπτω (1) act. *I light, kindle;* (2) mid. w. gen. *I lay hold of, I cling to* (eagerly).
Ἀπφία (Ἀφφία), ας, ἡ *Apphia,* a Christian lady of Colossae, either wife or sister of Philemon.
ἀπωθέομαι *I push (thrust) away from myself.*
ἀπώλεια, ας, ἡ *destruction, ruin, loss.*
ἀπώλεσα aor. act. → ἀπόλλυμι.
ἀπωλόμην aor. mid. → ἀπόλλυμι.
ἀπών pres. part. → ἄπειμι.
ἀπωσάμην aor. mid. → ἀπωθέομαι.
Ἅρ (Ἄρ) *Ar, Har,* only in the combined expression Ἅρ **Μαγεδών**, Heb. *har măgiddôn,* "the hill of Megiddo." In the neighborhood of Megiddo the sovereignty of Palestine was often decided by battle. Hence name transferred to the place of the decisive battle on the Day of Judgment.
ἄρα an inferential particle, *then, therefore;* found also in combination w. other particles, such as γε and οὖν, etc.; εἰ ἄρα, *if perchance,* Mark 11:13, etc.
ἆρα a particle asking a question, to which a neg. answer is expected.
ἀρά, ᾶς, ἡ *cursing, a curse.*
Ἀραβία, ας *Arabia,* the district south of Palestine.
ἆραι aor. act. infin. → αἴρω.
Ἀράμ, ὁ *Aram,* son of Esrom and father of Aminadab.
ἄραφος, ον *without seam* [Heb.].
Ἄραψ, βος, ὁ *an Arabian.*
ἀργέω *I am idle (unemployed, without occupation);* generally, outside NT, of necessity, and not blame worthily.
ἀργός, ἡ, όν (1) *idle, lazy;* (2) *thoughtless,* Matt 12:36.
ἀργύρεος (ἀργυροῦς), ᾶ, οῦν *made of silver, silver.*
ἀργύριον, ου, τό *a piece of silver money* (except 1 Cor 3:12, where *silver*).
ἀργυροκόπος, ου, ὁ *a silversmith* (lit., *silver cutter*).
ἄργυρος, ου, ὁ *silver* as a metal (except Matt 10:9, where *silver used as money*); rare in papyri.
ἀρεῖ fut. act. 3 sing. → αἴρω.
Ἄρειος Πάγος, ὁ *the Aeropagus,* a hill in Athens (lit. *Hill of Ares,* the Athenian war god, corresponding to Mars). As on this hill the

Council of the Areopagus (ἡ ἐξ 'Αρείου Πάγου βουλή), the supreme court of Athens, had met in early times, the expression ὁ Ἄρειος Πάγος came to be used (as in Acts 17:19, 22) for the *Council of the Aeropagus,* wherever it met.

'Αρεοπαγίτης, ου, ὁ *member of the Council of the Areopagus, an Areopagite.*

ἀρέσαι aor. act. infin. → ἀρέσκω.

ἀρέσκεια (ἀρεσκεία), ας, ἡ *pleasing, willing service.*

ἀρέσκω (1) *I please,* with the idea of willing service rendered to others; (2) hence almost, *I serve.*

ἀρεστός, ή, όν *pleasing, satisfactory, acceptable.*

'Αρέτας ('Αρέτας, for **'Αρέθας), α, ὁ** Arabic *Ḥāriṯā, Aretas,* Aretas IV, King of the Nabataeans.

ἀρετή, ῆς, ἡ (1) *excellence,* particularly *moral excellence;* (2) *manifestation of power,* 2 Pet 1:3 (a word of wide significance in non-Christian ethics).

'Αρηί see 'Αρνεί.

ἀρήν, ἀρνός, ὁ *a lamb;* acc. plur. ἄρνας (Luke 10:3); the nom. (= Ϝαρήν) is found only in early times, and its place is taken by ἀρνίον.

ἀρθήσομαι fut. pas. → αἴρω.

ἀριθμέω *I number, count.*

ἀριθμός, οῦ, ὁ *a number, total.*

'Αριμαθαία ('Αριμαθαία), ας, ἡ *Arimathaea,* a place in Palestine, identical with Ramathaim, the birthplace of Samuel. Orig. part of Samaria, it with its surrounding district was united to Judaea under the Maccabees.

'Αρίσταρχος, ου, ὁ *Aristarchus,* a Christian, belonging to Thessalonica in Macedonia.

ἀριστάω *I breakfast.*

ἀριστερός, ά, όν *on the left hand;* ἡ ἀριστερά (understand χείρ), Matt 6:3; ἐξ ἀριστερῶν, *on the left hand.*

'Αριστόβουλος, ου, ὁ *Aristobulus,* a Christian in Rome.

ἄριστον, ου, τό *breakfast.*

ἀρκετός, ή, όν *sufficient* (rare).

ἀρκέω (1) act. *I am sufficient, I suffice;* impers. John 14:8; (2) mid. w. dat. *I am content, satisfied (with).*

ἄρκος, ου, ὁ *a bear* (a later form of ἄρκτος).

ἅρμα, ατος, τό *a chariot.*

'Αρμαγεδών ('Αρμαγεδών) see Ἅρ.

ἁρμόζομαι *I fit, join* (the mid. indicating deep personal interest).

ἁρμός, οῦ, ὁ a *joint* of the body.

'Αρνεί ('Αρνί), ὁ *Arnei,* son of Esrom, and father of Admein [Heb.].

ἀρνέομαι (1) *I deny* (a statement); (2) *I repudiate* (a person, or belief).

ἀρνίον, ου, τό *a lamb* (orig., *a little lamb,* but diminutive force was lost), see ἀρήν.

ἄρνας see ἀρήν.

ἀροτριάω *I plough.*

ἄροτρον, ου, τό *a plough.*

ἁρπαγείς aor. pas. part. → ἁρπάζω.

ἁρπαγή, ῆς, ἡ *robbery, robbing.*

ἁρπαγμός, οῦ, ὁ either (1) *snatching, robbery, the action of plundering, rapacity, self-aggrandizement,* or (2) *a thing to be snatched, plunder, prey, booty, a prize, spoil.*

ἁρπάζω *I seize, snatch, obtain by robbery.*

ἅρπαξ, αγος (1) *snatching, robbing, greedy;* (2) subst. *swindler, extortioner,* 1 Cor 5:10.

ἀρραβών (ἀραβών), ῶνος, ὁ *an earnest, earnest money,* a large part of the payment, given in advance as a security that the whole will be paid afterwards (a word of Semitic origin).

ἄρραφος see ἄραφος.

ἄρρην see ἄρσην.
ἄρρητος, ον *not to be uttered* (because too sacred), secret.
ἄρρωστος, ον (1) *infirm;* (2) *sick, ill.*
ἀρσενοκοίτης, ου, ὁ *a pederast.*
ἄρσην (ἄρρην), εν, gen. **ενος** *male.*
Ἀρτεμᾶς, ᾶ, ὁ *Artemas,* a Christian in Rome (a pet form of Ἀρτεμίδωρος).
Ἄρτεμις, ιδος, ἡ *Artemis,* a goddess, worshipped principally at Ephesus, typifying fertility (she had no relation with the other Artemis, the maiden huntress, to whom corresponded the Lat. Diana).
ἀρτέμων, ωνος, ὁ *a foresail,* set on the bow.
ἄρτι adv., *now, just now* (of present time).
ἀρτιγέννητος, ον *newly begotten, newly born.*
ἄρτιος, α, ον *perfect.*
ἄρτος, ου, ὁ *bread, a loaf.*
ἀρτύω *I season.*
Ἀρφαξάδ, ὁ *Arphaxad,* son of Shem, and father of Cainam [Heb.].
ἀρχάγγελος, ου, ὁ *a ruler of angels, a superior angel, an archangel.*
ἀρχαῖος, α, ον (1) *original, primitive;* (2) *ancient,* Matt 5:21, etc.
Ἀρχέλαος, ου, ὁ *Archelaus,* Herod Archelaus, son and successor of Herod I, reigned over Judaea from 4 B.C. to A.D. 6 and died before A.D. 18.
ἀρχή, ῆς, ἡ (1) *rule* (kingly or magisterial); (2) plur., in a quasi-personal sense, almost *rulers, magistrates,* Titus 3:1; (3) *beginning.* In the very difficult John 8:25 τὴν ἀρχήν would naturally mean *originally,* but the passage is not yet explained.
ἀρχηγός, οῦ, ὁ *originator, author, founder.*
ἀρχιερατικός, όν *high priestly, to which the chief priest belongs.*
ἀρχιερεύς, έως, ὁ *high priest, chief priest.*
ἀρχιποίμην, ενος, ὁ *chief shepherd.*
Ἄρχιππος, ου, ὁ *Archippus,* a Christian of Colossae.
ἀρχισυνάγωγος, ου, ὁ *a leader of the synagogue,* a leading man (or woman) connected with the synagogue; sometimes there was only one, and the name was in some cases merely honorary.
ἀρχιτέκτων, ονος, ὁ *master builder.*
ἀρχιτελώνης, ου, ὁ *head of a custom house, chief tax gatherer.*
ἀρχιτρίκλινος, ου, ὁ *master of ceremonies* at a dinner, *master of the feast.*
ἄρχω (1) act. w. gen. *I rule;* (2) mid. *I begin;* sometimes in this sense the word is otiose, being merely an imitation of OT language or a lit. translation of Heb. or Aram., e.g., repeatedly in the Synoptic Gospels, and particularly in Mark, Luke 3:8, etc.
ἄρχων, οντος, ὁ (1) *a ruler, governor, leader, leading man;* (2) with the Jews, *an official member (a member of the executive)* of the γερουσία.
ἄρωμα, ατος, τό *spice.*
ἀσάλευτος, ον *unshaken, immovable.*
Ἀσάφ, Ἀσά, ὁ *Asaph, Asa,* son of Abijah and father of Jehoshaphat, king of Judah about 900 B.C. for 41 years [Heb.].
ἄσβεστος, ον *inextinguishable, unquenchable.*
ἀσέβεια, ας, ἡ *impiety, irreverence.*
ἀσεβέω (1) intrans., *I am impious, irreverent;* (2) trans., *I do impiously.*
ἀσεβής, ές *impious, irreverent, irreligious.*
ἀσέλγεια, ας, ἡ *wantonness, lewdness,(outrageous conduct; conduct shocking to public decency; a wanton violence).*

ἄσημος, ον *undistinguished, obscure* (lit., *unmarked, unstamped*).

Ἀσήρ, ὁ *Asher,* one of the sons of Jacob, and founder of one of the Twelve Tribes [Heb.].

ἀσθένεια, ας, ἡ *want of strength, weakness, illness.*

ἀσθενέω (1) (physically) *I am weak;* (2) (then morally) *I am sick.*

ἀσθένημα, ατος, τό *weakness.*

ἀσθενής, ές lit. *not strong;* (1) *weak* (physically or morally); (2) *ill.*

Ἀσία, ας, ἡ *the Roman province Asia,* roughly the western third of Asia Minor.

Ἀσιανός, οῦ, ὁ *belonging to the Roman province Asia.*

Ἀσιάρχης, ου, ὁ *Asiarch,* an official connected with the worship of Rome and the Emperor in the Roman province Asia.

ἀσιτία, ας, ἡ either *lack of corn, lack of food* (the lit. meaning), or *abstinence from food, loss of appetite, seasickness* (the extended meaning).

ἄσιτος, ον either *without corn, without food,* or *seasick.*

ἀσκέω *I train, practice, exercise.*

ἀσκός, οῦ, ὁ *a wineskin.*

ἀσμένως adv., *joyfully, with delight.*

ἄσοφος, ον *unskilled, unwise, foolish.*

ἀσπάζομαι (1) *I greet, salute;* (2) *I pay my respects to,* Acts 25:13 (a term regularly used at the end of a letter).

ἀσπασμός, οῦ, ὁ *a greeting, salutation* (very rare in papyri).

ἄσπιλος, ον *unstained, undefiled.*

ἀσπίς, ίδος, ἡ *an asp (hooded snake, cobra da capello).*

ἄσπονδος, ον *untrue to one's promise.*

ἀσσάριον, ου, τό *a penny* (one sixteenth of a denarius and one tenth of a drachma).

ἆσσον adv., *nearer* (comp. of ἄγχι).

Ἆσσος, ου, ἡ *Assos,* a port of Mysia, in the Roman province Asia.

ἀστατέω *I am unsettled, have no place of abode, lead a vagabond life.*

ἀστεῖος, α, ον *elegant, pretty, fair, fine* (lit. *belonging to the city;* then *witty, clever*).

ἀστήρ, έρος, ὁ *a star.*

ἀστήρικτος, ον *unsteady, unstable* (rather literary, lit. *unpropped*).

ἄστοργος, ον *unloving, devoid of affection.*

ἀστοχέω *I miss the mark, miss my aim, make a false aim.*

ἀστραπή, ῆς, ἡ *a flash of lightning.*

ἀστράπτω *I flash,* (with, then like, lightning).

ἄστρον, ου, τό *a star.*

Ἀσύγκριτος, ου, ὁ *see* Ἀσύνκριτος.

ἀσύμφωνος, ον *inharmonious, disagreeing.*

ἀσύνετος, ον *unintelligent, without wisdom, unwise, undiscerning* (implying probably moral defect, like ἀμαθής sometimes in classical Gk.).

ἀσύνθετος, ον *not covenanting, untrue to an agreement, treacherous.*

Ἀσύνκριτος *Asyncritus,* a Christian in Rome.

ἀσφάλεια, ας, ἡ (1) *safety;* (2) *security, reliability,* Luke 1:4.

ἀσφαλής, ές *safe, reliable, trustworthy* (lit., *unfailing*).

ἀσφαλίζω *I make safe (secure, fast).*

ἀσφαλῶς adv., *securely.*

ἀσχημονέω (1) *I am unseemly, I behave unbecomingly* (or even *dishonorably*); (2) perhaps, *I consider* (something) *unseemly.*

ἀσχημοσύνη, ης, ἡ *unseemly behavior, indecency,* or concr., *an indecent (lewd) act.*

ἀσχήμων, ον *unseemly, indecent.*

ἀσωτία, ας, ἡ *wantonness, profligacy.*

ἀσώτως adv., *prodigally;* ζῶν ἀσώτως, *with prodigal living.*

ἀτακτέω *I am disorderly, I neglect my duty, I am careless* (or *idle*) *in*

habits (lit. *I march out of order;* then *I riot, I rebel*).
ἄτακτος, ον *disorderly, slack* (in performance of duty), (lit. *out of order*).
ἀτάκτως adv., *in a disorderly manner* (see ἄτακτος, ἀτακτέω).
ἄτεκνος, ον *childless.*
ἀτενίζω *I direct my gaze, I look steadily.*
ἄτερ prep., *apart from, without* (orig. poetic).
ἀτιμάζω (1) *I disgrace, treat disgracefully, dishonor, insult;* (2) *I despise.*
ἀτιμία, ας, ἡ *disgrace, dishonor.*
ἄτιμος, ον *unhonored, without honor, unesteemed.*
ἀτμίς, ίδος, ἡ (1) *breath;* (2) *steam, vapor.*
ἄτομος, ον an indivisible part of time, *a second* (lit., *that cannot be cut*).
ἄτοπος, ον (1) *improper, unrighteous, perverse, froward;* (2) almost = *evil,* Acts 28:6; (lit., *out of place, unusual, unbecoming*).
᾿Αττάλεια, ας, ἡ *Attalia,* the port of Perga in Pamphylia.
αὐγάζω *I flash, gleam, appear white, bright* (as in LXX), but perhaps, *I see, I see clearly* (as in classical poetry).
αὐγή, ῆς, ἡ *light (of day).*
Αὔγουστος (Αὐγοῦστος), ου, ὁ *Augustus,* a title conferred on the first Roman Emperor, C. Iulius Octauianus, denoting sanctity (almost divinity); grecized as Σεβαστός (q.v.).
αὐθάδης, ες *self-satisfied;* hence, *arrogant.*
αὐθαίρετος, ον *of one's own accord.*
αὐθεντέω *I domineer over* (a colloquial word, from αὐθέντης, "master," "autocrat," = αὐτός + root *sen,* "accomplish," in ἀνύω).
αὐλέω *I play the flute.*
αὐλή, ῆς, ἡ (1) *courtyard, forecourt;* (2) but it may be understood as *palace, house,* e.g., Matt 26:3.
αὐλητής, οῦ, ὁ *a flute player.*
αὐλίζομαι *I bivouac, I pass the night.*
αὐλός, οῦ, ὁ *a flute.*
αὐξάνω (αὔξω) (1) trans., *I cause to increase;* (2) intrans., *I increase, grow;* w. cog. acc. Col 2:19.
αὔξησις, εως, ἡ *increasing, increase, growth.*
αὐξήσω fut. act. → αὐξάνω.
αὔξω see αὐξάνω.
αὔριον adv., *tomorrow.*
αὐστηρός, ά, όν (1) *grim, severe;* (2) *strict, exacting.*
αὐτάρκεια, ας, ἡ *self-sufficiency, independence.*
αὐτάρκης, ες *self-sufficient, independent, contented* (a literary use).
αὐτοκατάκριτος, ον *self-condemned* (perhaps a new coinage).
αὐτόματος, η, ον *of its own accord.*
αὐτόπτης, ου, ὁ *eyewitness.*
αὐτός, ή, ό (1) *he,* etc.; (2) *self;* e.g., αὐτός ὁ, etc., *the very,* but often weakened to mean simply *that;* αὐτός = αὐτόματος, *of his own accord,* John 16:27; (3) ὁ αὐτὸς, etc., *the same.* Parts of αὐτός are sometimes added pleonastically to the rel. pron. (colloquial; where the usage is not due to inferior culture, it is due to translation Gk.), cf. Mark 7:25; (4) αὐτοῦ, adv., *there;* (5) ἐπὶ τὸ αὐτό, κατὰ τὸ αὐτό, *together.*
αὑτοῦ = ἑαυτοῦ, of altogether uncertain existence in NT.
αὐτοῦ adv. see αὐτός.
αὐτόφωρος, ον ἐπ' αὐτοφώρῳ, *in the act* (αὐτός and φώρ, *a thief*).
αὐτόχειρ, ος *with one's own hand* (probably exclusively literary).
αὐχέω *I speak with proud confidence of, I boast of* (mostly in poetry).
αὐχμηρός, α, όν *dingy, dusky, obscure, dark, funereal* (poetic, lit.

dry and parched; then *squalid and rough*).
ἀφαιρέω *I take away.*
ἀφανής, ές *invisible.*
ἀφανίζω (1) *I cause to disappear, hide, remove;* (2) *I disfigure* (probably by leaving unwashed for a long period), Matt 6:16.
ἀφανισμός, οῦ, ὁ *disappearing, disappearance.*
ἄφαντος, ον *disappearing, invisible, hidden* (orig. poetic).
ἀφεδρών, ῶνος, ὁ *a drain, latrine.*
ἀφέθην aor. pas. → ἀφίημι.
ἀφεθήσομαι fut. pas. → ἀφίημι.
ἀφειδία, ας, ἡ *severe treatment* (lit. *unsparingness*).
ἀφεῖλον aor. act. → ἀφαιρέω.
ἀφείς aor. act. part. → ἀφίημι.
ἀφεῖς pres. act. 2 sing. → ἀφίημι.
ἀφελεῖν aor. act. infin. → ἀφαιρέω.
ἀφελότης, ητος, ἡ *simplicity.*
ἀφελῶ fut. act. → ἀφαιρέω.
ἄφες aor. act. imper. → ἀφίημι.
ἄφεσις, εως, ἡ (1) a *sending away, a letting go, release;* (2) hence, *remission, forgiveness* (cf. in inscriptions, *remission* from debt or punishment; from ἀφίημι).
ἄφετε aor. act. imper. 2 plur. → ἀφίημι.
ἀφέωμαι perf. mid./pas. → ἀφίημι.
ἀφή, ῆς, ἡ *a band, fastening* (hence, possibly, *a ligament*).
ἀφῆκα aor. act. → ἀφίημι.
ἀφήσω fut. act. → ἀφίημι.
ἀφθαρσία, ας, ἡ (1) *indestructibility, incorruptibility;* (2) hence, *immortality.*
ἄφθαρτος, ον (1) *indestructible, imperishable, incorruptible;* (2) hence, *immortal.*
ἀφθορία, ας, ἡ *(moral) incorruptness, incorruption, purity, freedom from taint.*
ἀφίημι (1) *I send away;* (2) *I let go* or *away, release, permit to depart;* (3) *I remit, forgive;* (4) *I permit,* followed by the subjun. w. (or without) ἵνα, or w. acc. obj. and infin.; ἄφες ἐκβάλω (Matt 7:4 = Luke 6:42), *let me (allow me to) cast out;* so also Matt 27:49 = Mark 15:36; John 12:7.
ἀφικνέομαι *I arrive, reach* (in ordinary use very rare at this time).
ἀφικόμην aor. mid. → ἀφικνέομαι.
ἀφιλάγαθος, ον *not loving that which is good.*
ἀφιλάργυρος, ον *not loving money, not avaricious.*
ἄφιξις, εως, ἡ *departure.* (This is the sense required by Acts 20:29, but as the word comes from ἀφικνέομαι, it ought to mean *arrival.*)
ἀφίστημι (1) 1 aor. trans., *I made to stand away, I drew away,* Acts 5:37; *I repelled;* (2) other tenses of act., and mid. *I take up a position away from, I withdraw from, I leave.*
ἄφνω adv., *suddenly.*
ἀφόβως adv., *fearlessly* (literary).
ἀφομοιόω *I make like to.*
ἀφοράω *I look away from (something else) to;* ἀφίδω, Phil 2:23, aspirated from ἀπίδω by analogy w. ἀφοράω; (cf. ἀποβλέπω).
ἀφορίζω *I rail off, I separate, I place apart.*
ἀφορίσω fut. act. → ἀφορίζω.
ἀφοριῶ fut. act. → ἀφορίζω.
ἀφορμή, ῆς, ἡ (1) *a starting, a start;* (2) *cause, occasion, opportunity.*
ἀφρίζω *I foam* (at the mouth).
ἀφρός, οῦ, ὁ *foam* (at the mouth).
ἀφροσύνη, ης, ἡ *want of sense, foolishness.*
ἄφρων, ον *senseless, foolish, inconsiderate.*
ἀφυπνόω *I fall asleep* (very rare).
ἀφυστερέω *I withdraw, take away.*
ἀφῶ aor. act. subj. → ἀφίημι.
ἄφωνος, ον *soundless, voiceless, speechless, dumb.*
Ἄχαζ (Ἀχάζ, Ἄχας), ὁ *Achaz,*

son of Joatham and father of Hezekiah [Heb.].

Ἀχαΐα, ας, ἡ *the Roman Province Achaia,* governed by a proconsul, and practically conterminous w. mod. Greece before 1912.

Ἀχαϊκός, οῦ, ὁ *Achaicus,* a Corinthian Christian.

ἀχάριστος, ον *ungrateful.*

Ἀχείμ (Ἀχίμ), ὁ *Acheim,* son of Zadok and father of Eliud [Heb.].

ἀχειροποίητος, ον *not made by hand, not handmade* (unknown outside NT).

Ἀχελδαμάχ *Acheldamach,* the place where Judas Iscariot committed suicide [Aram.].

ἀχθήσομαι fut. pas. → ἄγω.

ἀχλύς, ύος, ἡ *mist.*

ἀχρεῖος, ον *unprofitable, useless, unworthy.*

ἀχρεόομαι (earlier **ἀχρειόομαι**) *I am good for nothing* (lit. *I become sour, I turn,* of milk).

ἄχρηστος, ον *unprofitable, useless* (a play upon words, w. ὀνήσιμος).

ἄχρι, ἄχρις prep. w. gen., *as far as, up to,* conj. *until;* ἄχρι τοῦ νῦν = *until now;* ἄχρι οὗ (with or without ἄν) w. the subjun., *until.*

ἄχυρον, ου, τό *chaff.*

ἄψας aor. act. part. → ἅπτω.

ἀψευδής, ές *not guilty of falsehood, truthful.*

ἄψινθος (Ἄψινθος), ου, ὁ *wormwood;* ὁ Ἄψινθος, a star.

ἄψυχος, ον *lifeless.*

B

Βάαλ, ὁ (Bahal, properly *Lord,* and so not a proper name), *Baal,* a god worshipped by the Hebrews (in Rom 11:4 fem., because Jews in reading substituted αἰσχύνη), being the highest god of all the West Semitic peoples.

Βαβυλών, ῶνος, ἡ (1) *Babylon,* the ancient city on the Euphrates, to which the people of Jerusalem, etc., were transported; (2) hence allegorically of Rome, from the point of view of the Christian people, Rev (6 times), 1 Pet 5:13 (probably).

βαθμός, οῦ, ὁ (1) *a step* (of a stairway); (2) hence, *a stage* in a career, *a position.*

βάθος, ους, τό (1) *depth;* (2) *a depth, a deep* (also met.).

βαθύνω *I deepen.*

βαθύς, εῖα, ύ *deep* (lit., and met.); ὄρθρου βαθέως, *in the depths of the early morning, while still very early.*

βαΐον (βάϊον), ου, τό *a palm branch.*

Βαλαάμ, ὁ *Balaam* (Balaham), son of Beor of Pethor on the Euphrates, a soothsayer in the OT [Heb.].

Βαλάκ, ὁ *Balac, Balak,* son of Zippor, King of Moab [Heb.].

βαλλάντιον, ου, τό *a purse.*

βάλλω (1) *I cast, throw;* (2) intrans., *I rush,* Acts 27:14; (3) often, in the weaker sense, *I place, put, drop;* βεβλημένος, *lying in bed,* Matt 8:14.

βαπτίζω lit. *I dip, submerge,* but specifically of ceremonial dipping (whether immersion or pouring), *I baptize;* when the prep. εἰς w. a noun in the acc. follows, it appears to indicate that through this ceremony the baptized person becomes the property of the person indicated after εἰς; met. Mark 10:38.

βάπτισμα, ατος, τό *a dipping, a baptism;* w. gen. μετανοίας, belonging to a change of mental attitude, sign of a change of mental attitude.

βαπτισμός, οῦ, ὁ *dipping, washing* (of a ceremonial character).

βαπτιστής, οῦ, ὁ *the baptizer, the baptist,* epithet used only of John, the son of Zechariah and Elizabeth, forerunner of Jesus.

βάπτω (1) *I dip;* (2) *I dye;* Rev 19:13, cf. δίβαφα, twice-dyed garments.

Βαραββᾶς, ᾶ, ὁ *Barabbas* (really *Jesus Barabbas,* according to certain MSS of Matt 27:17), a highway robber.

Βαράκ, ὁ *Barak,* one of the judges of Israel [Heb.].

Βαραχίας, ου, ὁ *Barachias, Baruch* [Heb.]. His identity is uncertain, perhaps father of the Zacharias killed by the Zealots in the last Jewish War (Josephus, *B.J.* 4.5.4). See Ζαχαρίας.

βάρβαρος, ον *a foreigner,* one who speaks neither Gk. nor Lat.; as adj., *foreign.*

βαρέω *I weight, load, burden,* lit. and met.

βαρέως adv., *heavily, with difficulty.*

Βαρθολομαῖος, ου, ὁ *Bartholomew,* one of the twelve disciples of Jesus (son of Tholmai [= Ptolomaeus], Aram.).

Βαριησοῦς, οῦ, ὁ *Bar-Jesus* (i.e., son of Jesus), the name of the magician and false prophet at Paphos in Cyprus. He is also called *Elymas* [Aram.].

Βαριωνᾶ (Βαριωνᾶς), ᾶ, ὁ *Barjonas,* son of Jonas, the surname of Simon Peter [Aram.].

Βαρνάβας (Βαρναβᾶς), α, ὁ *Barnabas* (son of Nebo), a Cypriote Jew, uncle of John Mark; his other name was Joseph [Aram.].

βάρος, ους, τό (1) *a weight, a burden,* lit. or met.; (2) in 1 Thess 2:7 there may be a play on the derived sense, *authority, dignity.*

Βαρσαββᾶς, ᾶ, ὁ *Barsabbas,* son of Sabbas, a surname of Joseph (Acts 1:23) and Judas (Acts 15:22) [Aram.].

Βαρτίμαιος (Βαρτιμαῖος), ου, ὁ *Bartimaeus,* son of(?) Timaeus [Aram.].

βαρύς, εῖα, ύ *heavy, weighty, burdensome,* lit. and met.

βαρύτιμος, ον *heavy in price, very expensive.*

βασανίζω *I torture.*

βασανισμός, οῦ, ὁ *torture.*

βασανιστής, οῦ, ὁ *a torturer.*

βάσανος, ου, ἡ *torture.*

βασιλεία, ας, ἡ (1) *kingship, sovereignty, authority, rule,* especially of God, both in the world, and in the hearts of men; (2) hence, *kingdom,* in the concr. sense; ἡ βασιλεία τῶν οὐρανῶν perhaps always signifies the *coming* kingdom, but ἡ βασιλεία τοῦ θεοῦ is wider.

βασίλειος, ον (1) in Luke 7:25 either masc. *courtiers,* or neut. *palaces;* (2) the LXX intended βασίλειον as subst., *a body of kings,* in the passage quoted by 1 Pet 2:9, but Peter clearly takes βασίλειον as adj., *royal.*

βασιλεύς, έως, ὁ *a king,* but in some passages, as 1 Pet 2:17, clearly to be translated *emperor;* ὁ βασιλεὺς τῶν βασιλέων (βασιλευόντων), *the King of Kings,* an oriental type of phrase, used for the Persian king as overlord of other kings, and in scripture of God.

βασιλεύω (1) *I rule, reign;* (2) *I reign over,* w. gen.

βασιλικός, ή, όν (1) *connected with a king, royal, regal* in Jas 2:8 βασιλικὸς νόμος, a supreme law is referred to, the more important parts of the law; (2) substantivally, (a) *an officer in the service of the king* (Herod Antipas), John 4:46, 49, (b) ἡ βασιλική (understand χώρα), *the king's country,* Acts 12:20.

βασίλισσα, ης, ἡ *a queen.*

βάσις, εως, ἡ *a foot* (properly, that on which something may rest).
βασκαίνω *I give the evil eye to, fascinate, bewitch, overpower.*
βαστάζω (1) *I carry, bear;* (2) *I carry (take) away,* Matt 3:11; John 20:15; (3) *I pilfer,* John 12:6.
βάτος, ου ὁ or ἡ *a thorn bush;* ἐπὶ τοῦ (Luke τῆς) βάτου, *in the passage about the thorn bush,* Mark 12:26; Luke 20:37.
βάτος, ου, ὁ *a batus,* a liquid measure among the Jews, containing between eight and nine gallons [Heb.].
βάτραχος, ου, ὁ *a frog.*
βατταλογέω *I chatter, am long-winded, utter empty words.*
βδέλυγμα, ατος, τό *an abominable thing, an accursed thing.*
βδελυκτός, ἡ, όν *abominable, detestable.*
βδελύσσομαι *I abominate, detest.*
βέβαιος, α, ον *firm, steadfast, enduring.*
βεβαιόω *I confirm, ratify.*
βεβαίωσις, εως, ἡ *confirmation, ratification, establishment.*
βέβαμμαι perf. mid./pas. → βάπτω.
βέβηλος, ον (1) *profane, secular;* (2) *unspiritual, godless, worldly,* Heb 12:16.
βεβηλόω *I profane.*
βέβληκα perf. act. → βάλλω.
βεβρωκώς perf. act. part. → βιβρώσκω.
Βεεζεβούλ (Βεελζεβούλ), ὁ *Beezebul, Beelzebul,* a name of uncertain derivation, the chief of evil spirits among the Jews. The form Beelzebub = god of Flies at Ekron (2 Kgs 1:2, 3); the better attested form perhaps = the Phoenician sun god as lord of the heavenly dwelling.
Βελίαρ (Βελιάρ), ὁ *Beliar* (spelled sometimes Belial, Beliab), a demon, among the Jews, and in fact a name for Satan (orig. a Heb. word = *uselessness, corruption*).
βελόνη, ης, ἡ *a needle.*
βέλος, ους, τό *a missile, dart.*
βέλτιον adv., *best,* an adv., comp. in form, superl. in meaning, (very rare in this period).
Βενιαμείν (Βενιαμίν), ὁ *Benjamin,* youngest son of Jacob, founder of one of the twelve tribes of Israel [Heb.].
Βερνίκη, ης, ἡ *Bernice,* (born A.D. 29) daughter of Agrippa I and Kypros, and sister of M. Iulius Agrippa II, in whose company she appears, Acts 25, 26.
Βέροια, ας, ἡ *Beroea,* a town of the province Macedonia.
Βεροιαῖος, α, ον *belonging to Beroea, Beroean.*
Βεώρ, ὁ *Beor,* father of Balaam [Heb.]. (The var. Βόσορ has no authority in LXX, and is probably due to textual corruption here).
Βηθαβαρά, ἡ *Bethabara,* one reading in John 1:28. If the place existed, it was on east side of Jordan, see Βηθανία.
Βηθανία, ας, ἡ (1) *Bethany,* the home of Lazarus, Martha, and Mary, near Jerusalem; (2) *Bethany,* beyond Jordan, the reading with the strongest attestation in John 1:28, see Βηθαβαρά.
Βηθεσδά, ἡ see Βηθζαθά.
Βηθζαθά, ἡ *Bethzatha* (= House of Olives), name of a pool in Jerusalem. (But there is great doubt as to the real form).
Βηθλέεμ (Βηθλεέμ), ἡ *Bethlehem,* a town of Judaea.
Βηθσαϊδά, ἡ *Bethsaida,* a city of Galilee.
Βηθφαγή, ἡ *Bethphage,* a village in the neighborhood of Jerusalem, on the Mount of Olives.
βῆμα, ατος, τό (1) βῆμα ποδός,

the space covered by a step of the foot; (2) *tribunal;* (from root of ἔβην, *I went*).
Βηρεύς, έως, ὁ *Bereus* (Acts 16:15 var.)
βήρυλλος, ου, ὁ *a beryl,* a precious stone of various colors, the best known being sea green.
βία, ας, ἡ *force.*
βιάζομαι (1) mid. *I use force, I force my way, I come forward violently,* cf. Matt 11:12 (where perhaps pas.); (2) pas. *I am forcibly treated.*
βίαιος, α, ον *strong, violent.*
βιαστής, οῦ, ὁ *a forceful, violent man.*
βιβλαρίδιον, ου, τό *a little papyrus roll.*
βιβλίον, ου, τό (1) *a papyrus roll;* (2) ἀποστασίου, document of divorce, handed by the husband to the wife whom he divorces; (3) ζωῆς, of life, preserved in heaven and containing the names of those who share in (eternal) life; (orig. a diminutive).
βίβλος, ου, ἡ *a papyrus roll,* with a sacred connotation; ζωῆς, see βιλίον, which had almost ousted it.
βιβρώσκω *I eat.*
Βιθυνία, ας, ἡ *Bithynia,* a Roman province, northwest of Asia Minor and southwest of the Black Sea.
βίος, ου, ὁ (1) *life;* (2) *manner of life;* (3) *livelihood.*
βιόω *I live.*
βίωσις, εως, ἡ *manner of life.*
βιωτικός, ή, όν *belonging to ordinary life,* with somewhat contemptuous attitude.
βλαβερός, ά, όν *injurious.*
βλάπτω *I injure.*
βλαστάνω (βλαστάω) (1) intrans., *I sprout;* (2) trans., *I cause to sprout, make to grow up,* Jas 5:18.
Βλάστος, ου, ὁ *Blastus,* chamberlain of King Herod Agrippa I.
βλασφημέω *I speak evil against, I use abusive* or *scurrilous language about* (God or men).
βλασφημία, ας, ἡ *abusive* or *scurrilous language.*
βλάσφημος, ον *abusive, scurrilous.*
βλέμμα, ατος, τό *look,* the faculty of looking.
βλέπω (1) *I look, see* (primarily physical); βλέποντες βλέψετε, Hebraistic; βλέπειν ἀπό, *to look away from, to beware of;* βλέπειν μή, *to take care lest;* βλτέπειν πῶς, *to take care how;* (2) almost *I find,* Rom 7:23 (cf. 21).
βληθήσομαι fut. pas. → βάλλω.
βλητέος, α, ον *one must put* (verbal adj. from βάλλω, understand ἐστίν).
Βοανηργές *Boanerges,* a name of doubtful origin and meaning.
βοάω *I shout, call aloud.*
Βοές, Βόες see Βοός.
βοή, ῆς, ἡ *a shout.*
βοήθεια, ας, ἡ (1) abstr., *assistance;* (2) concr. (a technical term of nautical language), *a help.*
βοηθέω *I come to the rescue of, come to help, help.*
βοηθός, οῦ, ὁ *helper.*
βόθυνος, ου, ὁ *a hole in the earth, ditch.*
βολή, ῆς, ἡ *a casting, throw;* in acc. as measure of distance.
βολίζω *I cast the line* (for sounding), *I sound.*
Βοός (Βοές, Βόες), ὁ *Boos* or *Boes (Boaz),* son of Salmon (Sala) and Rahab, husband of Ruth, father of Iobed [Heb.].
βόρβορος, ου, ὁ *a miry dungeon, hole.*
βορρᾶς, ᾶ, ὁ *the north wind,* hence, *the north.*
βόσκω *I feed.*
Βοσόρ, ὁ *Bosor,* father of Balaam; but see Βεώρ.
βοτάνη, ης, ἡ *fodder, food.*

βότρυς, υος, ὁ *cluster (bunch) of grapes.*
βουλεύομαι *I deliberate, take counsel.*
βουλευτής, οῦ, ὁ *a member of a* βουλή, *(city council),* in NT of the συνέδριον, Sanhedrin at Jerusalem.
βουλή, ῆς, ἡ *counsel, deliberate wisdom.*
βούλημα, ατος, τό *will, desire.*
βούλομαι *I will.*
βουνός, οῦ, ὁ *a hillock, hill.*
βοῦς, βοός, ὁ *an ox, cow, head of cattle.*
Βραβεῖον, ου, τό *a prize.*
βραβεύω (1) *I decide* (in a conflict between contending forces); (2) hence, *I rule, I administer.*
βραδύνω *I am slow, I delay;* followed by gen., 2 Pet 3:9.
βραδυπλοέω *I sail slowly.*
βραδύς, εῖα, ύ *slow.*
βραδύτης (βραδυτής), ητος, ἡ *tardiness, dilatoriness.*
βραχίων, ονος, ὁ *arm.*
βραχύς, εῖα, ύ *little;* mostly in various adv. phrases, indicating degree or time.
βρέφος, ους, τό *infant, baby, child in arms;* ἀπὸ βρέφους, *from babyhood.*
βρέχω (1) *I wet;* (2) *I rain,* having orig. the rain god (Ζεύς, Jupiter) as subj. (cf. Matt 5:45); (3) hence, of a shower from the sky other than rain, Luke 17:29.
βροντή, ῆς, ἡ *thunder.*
βροχή, ῆς, ἡ *a wetting, rain.*
βρόχος, ου, ὁ *a noose.*
βρυγμός, οῦ, ὁ *gnashing, crunching.*
βρύχω *I gnash, crunch.*
βρύω *I cause to gush forth, send forth.*
βρῶμα, ατος, τό *food.*
βρώσιμος, ον *eatable, suitable for food.*
βρῶσις, εως, ἡ (1) (abstr.) *eating;* (2) *food, a meal,* Heb 12:16; (3) *rust.*
βυθίζω *I cause to sink.*
βυθός, οῦ, ὁ *the deep sea.*
βυρσεύς, έως, ὁ *a tanner.*
βύσσινος, η, ον *of fine linen, of lawn.*
βύσσος, ου, ἡ *fine linen* (Semitic origin, some authorities consider *cotton* to be meant; others *silk*).
βωμός, οῦ, ὁ *an altar.*

Γ

Γαββαθά *Gabbatha,* i.e., *Gab Baitha,* "the ridge (back) of the House," i.e., the Aram. name for what the Greeks called Λιθόστρωτον, a sort of paved square, on which the procurator had his judgment seat.
Γαβριήλ, ὁ *Gabriel,* a messenger of God [Heb.].
γάγγραινα, ης, ἡ *a cancerous sore, a cancer.*
Γάδ, ὁ *Gad,* one of the twelve tribes of Israel [Heb.].
Γαδαρηνός, ή, όν *Gadarene, belonging to Gadara* (an important Hellenized town, one of the Decapolis, and southeast of the Sea of Galilee), see Γερασηνός, Γεργεσηνός.
Γάζα, ης, ἡ *Gaza,* an old town in the south of Palestine, on the sea coast.
γάζα, ης, ἡ *treasure* (a Persian loanword).
γαζοφυλάκιον, ου, τό *treasury.*
Γάϊος, ου, ὁ *Gaius,* (1) a Corinthian, Rom 16:23; 1 Cor 1:14; (2) a Macedonian(?), Acts 19:29; (3) a citizen of Derbe, Acts 20:4; (4) an Ephesian(?), 3 John 1, It may be that (2) and (3) or even (2), (3), and (4) are identical.
γάλα, γάλακτος, τό *milk.*
Γαλάτης, ου, ὁ *a Galatian* (meaning any inhabitant of the Roman *province* Galatia).
Γαλατία, ας, ἡ *Galatia,* a large

Roman province in central Asia Minor, comprising the districts of Paphlagonia, Pontus Galaticus, Galatia (in the narrower sense, which some still think is intended in the NT), Phrygia Galatica, Lycaonia Galatica, Pisidia and Isaurica. In 2 Tim 4:10 the reference may be to *Gaul,* even if we read Γαλατίαν.

Γαλατικός, ή, όν *Galatic,* belonging to the province Galatia; τὴν φρυγίαν καὶ Γαλατικὴν χώραν, Acts 16:6, "the region which is both Phrygian (racially) and Galatic (by administration)."

γαλήνη, ης, ἡ *a calm.*

Γαλιλαία, ας, ἡ *Galilee,* a district towards the southern end of the Roman province Syria.

Γαλιλαῖος, α, ον *a Galilaean,* an inhabitant of Galilee.

Γαλλία, ας, ἡ *Gaul,* a var. reading in 2 Tim 4:10, indicating one of the four provinces called by this name, which together comprised for the most part the territory of mod. France.

Γαλλίων, ωνος, ὁ *Gallio,* Lucius Iunius Gallio, who received this name by adoption into another family, but was born brother of the philosopher Seneca and orig. named L. Annaeus Nouatus; proconsul of the Roman province Achaia from spring A.D. 52 to spring 53.

Γαμαλιήλ, ὁ *Gamaliel,* a noted Pharisee, teacher of Saul [Heb.].

γαμέω *I marry,* used of either sex.

γαμίζω *I give in marriage;* this sense probably even in 1 Cor 7:38, where the older view took it as equal to γαμέω.

γαμίσκομαι *I am given in marriage* (only as var.).

γάμος, ου, ὁ (1) *a marriage, wedding, wedding ceremony;* (2) γάμοι (plur.), *a wedding feast.*

γάρ conj., *for.*

γαστήρ, τρός, ἡ *belly;* often ἐν γαστρὶ ἔχειν, of a woman, *to be pregnant* (lit., *to have* [a child] *in the belly*).

Γαύδη see Καῦδα.

γέ *at least, indeed, really,* an enclitic, emphasizing particle generally too subtle to be represented in Eng.

Γεδεών, ὁ *Gideon,* one of the Judges of Israel [Heb.].

γεγένημαι perf. mid./pas. → γίνομαι.

γέγονα perf. act. → γίνομαι.

γεγόνει plup. act. 3 sing. → γίνομαι.

γέγραπται perf. mid./pas. 3 sing. → γράφω.

γέγραφα perf. act. → γράφω.

γέεννα, ης, ἡ *gehenna,* and orig. *gē ben hinnôm,* name of a valley or cavity near Jerusalem, Jer 7:31; 2 Kgs 23:10, a place underneath the earth, a place of punishment (retributive or purificatory) for evil [Aram.].

Γεθσημανί (Γεθσημανεί) *Gethsemani,* a small place between the brook Kidron and the Mount of Olives near Jerusalem.

γείτων, ονος, ὁ or ἡ *a neighbor.*

γελάω *I laugh.*

γέλως, ωτος, ὁ *laughter.*

γεμίζω *I fill, load.*

γέμω *I am full of.*

γενεά, ᾶς, ἡ *a generation;* in combination w. another γενεά, or w. αἰών, practically indicates infinity of time.

γενεαλογέομαι *I am put into a genealogy.*

γενεαλογία, ας, ἡ *genealogy.*

γενέσθαι aor. mid. infin. → γίνομαι.

γενέσια, ων, τά *birthday or anniversary feast.*

γένεσις, εως, ἡ *birth, creation, beginning.*
γενετή, ῆς, ἡ *birth.*
γενηθήτω aor. pas. imper. 3 sing. → γίνομαι.
γένημα, ατος, τό of vegetable, never of animal, products (contrast γέννημα), *fruit, crop, produce of the earth* (from γίνομαι).
γενήσομαι fut. mid. → γίνομαι.
γεννάω *I beget* (of the male), more rarely (e.g., Luke 1:13), (of the female) *I bring forth.*
γέννημα, ατος, τό of animal, never of vegetable, products (contrast γένημα), *offspring, child* (from γεννάω).
Γεννησαρέτ, ἡ *Gennesaret,* a fertile district by the lake of Tiberias, which was in consequence sometimes called the Lake of Gennesaret.
γέννησις, εως, ἡ *birth.*
γεννητός, ή, όν *begotten,* used as subst.
γένοιτο aor. mid. opt. 3 sing. → γίνομαι.
γένος, ους, τό (1) *race;* (2) *kind.*
Γερασηνός, ή, όν *Gerasene, of Gerasa,* a town on the east of the Lake of Tiberias. Wherever this people is mentioned, the variants Γαδαρηνός and Γεργεσηνός occur.
Γεργεσηνός, ή, όν *Gergesene, of Gergesa* (mod. Kursi), a place on a hill on the Lake of Tiberias. It is best perhaps to regard Γερασηνός as a by form of this word, Γαδαρηνός being a conscious alteration.
γερουσία, ας, ἡ *the assembly* or *body of elders,* probably as synonymous w. or explicative of συνέδριον and πρεσβύτεροι. (The term γερουσία was often used in such a collective sense in the cities of Asia Minor.)
γέρων, οντος, ὁ *an old man.*
γεύομαι (1) *I taste;* (2) *I experience.*
γεωργέω *I work the soil, I cultivate the soil.*
γεώργιον, ου, τό *a cultivated field.*
γεωργός, οῦ, ὁ *a worker of the soil, husbandman, farmer, farm laborer.*
γῆ, γῆς, ἡ *the earth, soil, land.*
γήμας aor. act. part. → γαμέω.
γῆρας, ως or **ους** (dat. **γήρᾳ** or **γήρει), τό** *old age.*
γηράσκω *I become old, grow old.*
γίνομαι (1) *I come into being, am born,* John 8:58; Gal 4:4, etc.; (2) *I become, come about, happen.* (In aor. ἐγένετο used by Luke, to give Hebraistic coloring, in various constructions: ἐγένετο ἦλθεν, ἐγένετο καὶ ἦλθεν, ἐγένετο ἐλθεῖν [the latest of the three and non-Hebraistic].)
γινώσκω (1) *I am taking in knowledge, come to know, learn;* (2) aor. *I ascertained, realized,* but not in John 17:25; 2 Tim 2:19.
γλεῦκος, ους, τό *sweet wine,* made perhaps from a small specially sweet grape.
γλυκύς, εῖα, ύ *sweet.*
γλῶσσα, ης, ἡ (1) *tongue,* especially as an organ of speech; (2) *tongue, language;* (3) also, usually in the plur., for the unintelligible sounds uttered in spiritual ecstasy.
γλωσσόκομον, ου, τό *bag, purse;* some prefer to take as *box, chest* (a vernacular word).
γναφεύς, έως, ὁ *fuller.*
γνήσιος, α, ον (lit. *born*), hence, *real, true, genuine;* τὸ γνήσιον, *the true, genuine element.*
γνησίως adv., (1) *truly, genuinely;* (2) *honorably.*
γνοῖ aor. act. subj. 3 sing. → γινώσκω.
γνούς aor. act. part. → γινώσκω.
γνόφος, ου, ὁ *darkness.*
γνῶ aor. act. subj. 3 sing. → γινώσκω.

γνῶθι aor. act. imper. 2s → γινώσκω.

γνώμη, ης, ἡ *opinion, counsel.*

γνῶναι aor. act. infin. → γινώσκω.

γνωρίζω *I make known.*

γνωσθήσομαι fut. pas. → γινώσκω.

γνῶσις, εως, ἡ *knowledge.*

γνώσομαι fut. mid. → γινώσκω.

γνώστης, ου, ὁ *a knower, expert.*

γνωστός, ή, όν (1) *known;* (2) subst. *an acquaintance.*

γνώτω aor. act. imper. → γινώσκω.

γογγύζω *I whisper, murmur, grumble* (generally of smoldering discontent).

γογγυσμός, οῦ, ὁ *murmuring, grumbling.*

γογγυστής, οῦ, ὁ *murmurer, grumbler.*

γόης, ητος, ὁ (1) *a conjuror, juggler, sorcerer;* (2) *a tricky (crafty) deceiver, impostor.*

Γολγοθᾶ (Γολγοθά), ἡ *Golgotha,* a knoll outside the wall of Jerusalem.

Γόμορρα, ας or **ων, ἡ** or **τά** *Gomorrha,* one of the destroyed cities on the Dead Sea.

γόμος, ου, ὁ *a cargo, freight.*

γονεύς, έως, ὁ *a parent.*

γόνυ, γόνατος, τό *a knee.*

γονυπετέω *I fall on my knees before* (in supplication), *supplicate, entreat.*

γράμμα, ατος, τό *a letter of the alphabet;* collectively, *written* (revelation), Rom 2:27: γράμματα, *writings,* (1) *a written document,* Luke 16:6, 7; *a letter an epistle,* Acts 28:21; (2) *writings, literature,* John 5:47; 7:15; Acts 26:24; 2 Tim 3:15.

γραμματεύς, έως, ὁ (1) in Jerusalem, *a scribe,* one learned in the Jewish Law, a religious teacher; (2) at Ephesus, *the town clerk, the secretary of the city,* Acts 19:35.

γραπτός, ή, όν *written.*

γραφή, ῆς, ἡ (1) *a writing;* (2) *a passage of scripture;* plur. αἱ γραφαί, *the scriptures* (of the OT, and in 2 Pet 3:16 also of the New).

γράφω (1) *I write;* (2) γέγραπται, *it is written, it stands written* (in the scriptures of the OT; so in ordinary life, a formula introducing an unalterable agreement); (3) = προγράφω, Rom 15:4.

γραώδης, ες *belonging to old women, such as old women tell.*

γρηγορέω (1) *I am awake* (in the night), *watch;* (2) *I am watchful, on the alert.*

γυμνάζω (1) *I train by physical exercise;* (2) hence, *train* in widest sense; w. gen. of sphere, 2 Pet 2:14.

γυμνασία, ας, ἡ (physical) *exercise,* in a wide sense.

γυμνιτεύω *I am habitually* γυμνός, i.e., *I wear the undergarment* (χιτών) *only,* it being the regular practice to wear two garments.

γυμνός, ή, όν (1) rarely *stark naked,* generally *wearing only the undergarment* (χιτών), see γυμνιτεύω; (2) γυμνὸς κόκκος *a simple seed, a seed* per se.

γυμνότης, ητος, ἡ *nakedness,* cf. γυμνός, γυμνιτεύω.

γυναικάριον, ου, τό *a poor weak woman* (physically or morally).

γυναικεῖος, α, ον *belonging to woman, of woman.*

γυνή, αικός, ἡ (1) *a* (married) *woman, a wife;* so even in Matt 5:28 (2) voc., γύναι, *my lady,* Luke 22:57; John 2:4.

Γώγ, ὁ *Gog,* a name borrowed from Ezekiel (38:2 ff., where = prince over Mesech and Thubal), to indicate a race or races to be led astray by Satan at the end of the thousand years.

γωνία, ας, ἡ *a corner.*

Δ

δαιμονίζομαι *I am under the power of an evil spirit* or *demon.*

δαιμόνιον, ου, τό *an evil spirit, demon.*

δαιμονιώδης, ες *demon-like, such as demons have.*

δαίμων, ονος, ὁ *an evil spirit, a demon,* much less common than the diminutive δαιμόνιον.

δάκνω (1) *I bite;* (2) hence, *I backbite,* or *harm seriously.*

δάκρυον (δάκρυ), ου, τό *a tear.*

δακρύω *I shed tears, weep.*

δακτύλιος, ου, ὁ *a finger ring.*

δάκτυλος, ου, ὁ *a finger;* the picturesque δακτύλῳ of Luke 11:20 is represented by πνεύματι in Matt 12:28.

Δαλμανουθά, ἡ *Dalmanutha;* nothing is known of name or place, and text is probably corrupt.

Δαλματία, ας, ἡ *Dalmatia,* a province of the Roman Empire, east of the Adriatic, a later name for part of what was earlier called *Illyricum* (Rom 15:19).

δαμάζω *I tame, subdue,* involving obedience and restraint.

δάμαλις, εως, ἡ *a heifer.*

Δάμαρις, ιδος, ἡ *Damaris,* an Athenian woman.

Δαμασκηνός, ή, όν *a Damascene, an inhabitant of Damascus.*

Δαμασκός, οῦ, ἡ *Damascus,* an ancient city of Syria.

δαν(ε)ίζω (1) *I lend;* (2) mid. δανείζομαι, *I borrow.*

δάν(ε)ιον, ου, τό *a loan.*

δαν(ε)ιστής, οῦ, ὁ *a lender, creditor.*

Δανιήλ, ὁ *Daniel,* loosely called a "prophet" [Heb.].

δαπανάω *I spend.*

δαπάνη, ης, ἡ *cost, expense.*

δαρήσομαι fut. pas. → δέρω.

Δαυίδ (Δαυείδ), ὁ *David,* King of Israel, to whose name the OT collection of Psalms was attached [Heb.].

δέ a weak adversative particle, generally placed second in its clause, (1) *but, on the other hand;* (2) *and.* See μέν.

δέδεκται perf. mid. 3 sing. → δέχομαι.

δεδεκώς perf. act. part. → **δέω.**

δέδεμαι perf. mid./pas. → **δέω.**

δέδομαι perf. mid./pas. → **δίδωμι.**

δέδωκα perf. act. → **δίδωμι.**

δεδώκειν plup. act. → **δίδωμι.**

δέησις, εως, ἡ *a requesting, a begging, request.*

δεθῆναι aor. pas. infin. → **δέω.**

δεῖ (1) *it is necessary, inevitable;* (2) less frequently, *it is a duty,* **τὰ μὴ** δέοντα, *what is improper, wrong;* δέον (ἐστίν) = **δεῖ,** Acts 19:36; 1 Pet 1:6.

δεῖγμα, ατος, τό *an example, type.*

δειγματίζω *I hold up as an example.*

δείκνυμι (δεικνύω) *I point out, show.*

δειλία, ας, ἡ *cowardice.*

δειλιάω *I shrink, am fearful.*

δειλός, ή, όν *cowardly, timid.*

δεῖνα, ὁ, ἡ or τό ὁ δεῖνα, *so and so, a certain one,* where the name of the person is known but not used.

δεινός ή, όν *terrible.*

δεινῶς adv., *terribly.*

δείξω fut. act. → δείκνυμι.

δειπνέω *I dine.*

δεῖπνον, ου, τό *a dinner, an afternoon* or *evening meal.*

δείρας aor. act. part. → **δέρω.**

δεισιδαιμονία, ας, ἡ *superstition, religion.*

δεισιδαίμων, ον gen. **ονος** *respectful of what is divine, religious* perhaps, rather than *superstitious* (the usual meaning). Comp. δεισιδαιμονέστερος used as superl., *very devout* (Acts 17:22).

δειχθείς aor. pas. part. → **δείκνυμι.**

δέκα *ten.*

δεκαπέντε (δεκάπεντε) *fifteen.*

Δεκάπολις, εως, ἡ *Decapolis,*

meaning a group or district of ten cities (of the Greek type) in Palestine, mostly southeast of the Lake of Tiberias. The names and number vary in ancient authorities.

δεκατέσσαρες *fourteen.*

δεκάτη, ης, ἡ *a tenth part, a tithe.*

δέκατος, η, ον *tenth.*

δεκατόω *I tithe, I collect tithe from.*

δεκτός, ή, όν *acceptable.*

δελεάζω *I allure* (by a bait).

δένδρον, ου, τό *a tree.*

δεξιολάβος, ου, ὁ a word of uncertain meaning, indicating some class of *soldier.*

δεξιός, ά, όν *on the right hand, right hand, right.*

δέομαι *I request, beg.*

δέον pres. act. part. → δεῖ.

δέος, ους, τό *fear.*

Δερβαῖος, α, ον *Derbean, belonging to Derbe.*

Δέρβη, ης, ἡ *Derbe,* a town in Lycaonia and in the southern part of the Roman province Galatia.

δέρμα, ατος, τό *a hide, skin.*

δερμάτινος, η, ον *made of hide or leather.*

δέρω *I flay, flog, beat.*

δεσμεύω *I bind.*

δέσμη, ης, ἡ *a bond.*

δέσμιος, α, ον (1) *bound, captive, in chains;* (2) sometimes substantivally *prisoner, captive.*

δεσμός, οῦ, ὁ *a bond, chain;* in Acts 23:29; 26:31, the reference is to the form of "capital" punishment involving loss of freedom and work in chains in the quarries; plur. sometimes δεσμά.

δεσμοφύλαξ, ακος, ὁ *a prison governor, jailer.*

δεσμωτήριον, ου, τό *a prison, jail.*

δεσμώτης, ου, ὁ *a prisoner, captive.*

δεσπότης, ου, ὁ *a master.* particularly a master and owner of slaves, *lord.*

δεῦρο adv. (1) exclamatory, *come;* (2) temp., *now, the present,* Rom 1:13 (orig. *hither*).

δεῦτε adv., *come hither, come, hither,* an exclamatory word (plur. of δεῦρο).

δευτεραῖος, α, ον *on the second day, on the next day* (adj. where Eng. requires adv.).

δευτερόπρωτος, ον a word of doubtful meaning; a doubtful var. in Luke 6:1.

δεύτερος, α, ον (1) *second;* (2) (τὸ) δεύτερον is used adverbially, *in the second place, for the second time.*

δέχομαι *I receive, welcome.*

δέω *I bind.*

δή (1) in a clause expressing demand, *so, then,* 1 Cor 6:20; (2) *indeed,* Luke 2:15, etc.; (3) *truly,* Matt 13:23.

δηλαυγῶς *with perfect clearness* (from δῆλος and αὐγή), but see τηλαυγῶς.

δῆλος, η, ον *clear, manifest.*

δηλόω *I show, make clear, reveal.*

Δημᾶς, ᾶ, ὁ *Demas,* a helper of Paul in Rome (a pet form, probably of Δημήτριος).

δημηγορέω *I make a public speech, I address a multitude.*

Δημήτριος, ου, ὁ *Demetrius;* a silversmith of Ephesus.

δημιουργός, οῦ, ὁ *a constructor, builder.*

δῆμος, ου, ὁ properly *the people,* especially the citizens of a Greek city in popular assembly (ἐκκλησία), but in NT = *multitude, rabble.*

δημόσιος, α, ον (1) *public;* (2) dat. as adv., δημοσίᾳ, *publicly.*

δηνάριον, ου, ὁ *a denarius,* a small Roman silver coin, weighing in Nero's time 53 grams. Its value and purchasing power varied from time to time.

δήποτε (δή ποτε) adv., *even at that time, at any time,* var. in John 5:4.

δήπου (δή που) adv., *of course, surely,* qualifying and yet strengthening the assertion.

Δία acc. → Ζεύς.

διά (1) w. gen. *through; throughout* (διὰ παντός, *always*); *by the instrumentality of;* denoting mediate and not original authorship, e.g., Matt 1:22; John 1:3; 1 Cor 8:6; (2) w. acc. *on account of, by reason of, for the sake of, because of; through,* Luke 17:11(?).

διαβαίνω *I cross.*

διαβάλλω (1) *I slander;* (2) merely *I complain of* (without idea of malice), Luke 16:1.

διαβάς aor. act. part. → διαβαίνω.

διαβεβαιόομαι *I assert emphatically.*

διαβλέπω *I see thoroughly.*

διάβολος, η, ον (1) *slanderous* (1 Tim 3:11; 2 Tim 3:3; Titus 2:3); (2) adj. used oftener as noun, almost always ὁ Διάβολος, *the Slanderer* (par excellence), *the Devil.*

διαγγέλλω *I announce throughout* the world, *I spread the news of.*

διαγίνομαι *I pass* (of time).

διαγινώσκω *I learn thoroughly, I determine* (Acts 24:22).

διάγνωσις, εως, ἡ *decision resulting from an investigation.*

διαγογγύζω *I murmur greatly, I continue murmuring.*

διαγρηγορέω *I awake out of sleep, I am thoroughly awake.*

διάγω *I spend time, pass time, live* (either trans. or intrans.).

διαδέχομαι *I receive in my turn.*

διάδημα, ατος, τό *a chaplet, crown.*

διαδίδωμι *I offer here and there, distribute.*

διάδος imper. 2 sing. → διαδίδωμι.

διάδοχος, ου, ὁ *a successor.*

διαζώννυμι *I gird myself,* by pulling up the tunic and allowing a fold to fall over the belt (ζώνη).

διαθήκη, ης, ἡ (1) = συνθήκη, *a covenant* between two parties; (2) *a will, testament* (the ordinary, everyday sense, found a countless number of times in papyri), Gal 3:15, 17; Heb 9:16.

διαθήσομαι fut. pas. → διατίθημι.

διαίρεσις, εως, ἡ *division, distribution.*

διαιρέω *I divide, distribute.*

διακαθαίρω *I clean thoroughly.*

διακαθαρίζω *I clean thoroughly.*

διακαθαριῶ fut. act. → διακαθαρίζω.

διακατελέγχομαι *I effectively (utterly) refute (confute).*

διακονέω (1) *I wait at table* (particularly of a slave who pours out wine to the guests); (2) *I serve* (generally).

διακονία, ας, ἡ (1) *waiting at table;* (2) in a wider sense, *service, ministration.*

διάκονος, ου, ὁ or ἡ (1) *a waiter, servant;* (2) then of any one who performs any service, *an administrator,* etc.

διακόσιοι, αι, α *two hundred.*

διακούω *I hear throughout,* of a judicial hearing.

διακρίνω (1) *I separate, distinguish, discern* one thing *from* another; (2) mid., *I doubt, hesitate, waver.*

διάκρισις, εως, ἡ (1) *distinguishing;* (2) hence, *deciding, passing sentence on* (Rom 14:1).

διακωλύω *I obstinately prevent.*

διαλαλέω *I interchange talk,* of conversation passing from mouth to mouth.

διαλέγομαι (1) *I converse,* Mark 9:34; (2) elsewhere, *I address, preach, lecture.*

διαλείπω *I cease, give over, give up.*

διάλεκτος, ου, ἡ *language, speech.*

διαλιμπάνω *I cease, stop, quit,* a by-form of διαλείπω.

διαλλάγηθι aor. pas. imper. 2 sing. → διαλλάσσομαι.

διαλλάσσομαι *I become reconciled to, I reconcile myself with.*
διαλογίζομαι *I reason (with), debate (with), consider.*
διαλογισμός, οῦ, ὁ *a calculation, reasoning, thought, movement of thought, deliberation, plotting.*
διαλύω *I break up, disperse.*
διαμαρτύρομαι *I give solemn evidence, I testify (declare) solemnly.*
διαμάχομαι *I strive greatly.*
διαμένω *I remain throughout.*
διαμερίζω (1) *I divide up into parts, break up;* (2) *I distribute.*
διαμερισμός, οῦ, ὁ (1) *breaking up;* (2) *discord, hostility.*
διανέμω (1) *I divide into portions, distribute;* (2) *I spread abroad.*
διανεύω *I nod continually.*
διανόημα, ατος, τό *a reasoning, thought, cogitation.*
διάνοια, ας, ἡ *understanding, intellect, mind* (*process of reasoning* in Plato).
διανοίγω *I open up.*
διανυκτερεύω *I spend the whole night.*
διανύω *I finish, complete.*
διαπαντός = διὰ παντός; see διά.
διαπαρατριβή, ῆς, ἡ *perpetual wrangling.*
διαπεράω *I cross over.*
διαπλέω *I sail over (across).*
διαπονέομαι *I am greatly troubled.*
διαπορεύομαι *I journey through (past).*
διαπορέω *I am in trouble, doubt, difficulty.*
διαπραγματεύομαι *I gain by business (trading).*
διαπρίω *I cut to the quick* (with indignation and envy), lit. *I saw through.*
διαρπάζω *I plunder, rob thoroughly.*
δια(ρ)ρήγνυμι (δια[ρ]ρήσσω) *I tear asunder.*
διασαφέω *I make clear, explain.*
διασείω *I blackmail, extort from.*
διασκορπίζω *I scatter.*
διασπάω *I tear apart, burst.*
διασπείρω *I scatter (like seed).*
διασπορά, ᾶς, ἡ (1) lit. *scattering abroad of seed* by the sower; (2) hence, *dispersion,* used especially of the Jews who had migrated and were scattered over the ancient world. In Jas 1:1 and 1 Pet 1:1 the reference may be to the New Israel, the Christians.
διαστάς aor. act. part. → διΐστημι.
διαστέλλομαι *I give a commission (instructions), I order.*
διάστημα, ατος, τό *an interval.*
διαστήσας aor. act. part. → διΐστημι.
διαστολή, ῆς, ἡ *distinction, separation.*
διαστρέφω *I pervert.*
διασώζω (διασῴζω) (1) *I save (rescue) through* (some danger); (2) διασώζω πρός (Acts 23:34), *I bring safely to,* so διεσώθησαν εἰς (1 Pet 3:20), *escaped into.*
διαταγείς aor. act. part. → διατάσσω.
διαταγή, ῆς, ἡ *ordaining, ordinance, disposition.*
διάταγμα, ατος, τό *a commandment.*
διαταράσσω *I disturb greatly.*
διατάσσω *I command.*
διαταχθείς aor. pas. part. → διατάσσω.
διατελέω *I continue,* (act. and) mid.
διατέταγμαι perf. mid./pas. → διατάσσω.
διατηρέω *I keep safe, hold fast.*
διατί = διὰ τί.
διατίθεμαι (1) *I appoint, make* (of a covenant); (2) *I make* (a will), Heb 9:16, 17, regular in papyri.
διατρίβω *I tarry, continue, stay* in a place.
διατροφή, ῆς, ἡ *nourishment, food.*
διαυγάζω *I dawn* (of the light coming *through* the shadows).

διαυγής, ές *through which light passes, transparent.*
διαφέρω (1) trans., *I carry through, hither and thither;* (2) intrans., *I am different, I differ,* sometimes w. gen.; (3) hence w. gen., *I surpass, I excel.*
διαφεύγω *I flee through, I escape.*
διαφημίζω *I spread about* (by *word* of mouth).
διαφθείρω (1) *I destroy, waste;* (2) hence met., *I corrupt.*
διαφθορά, ᾶς, ἡ (1) *destruction, dissolution;* (2) *corruption.*
διάφορος, ον (1) *differing, different;* (2) hence, *excellent.*
διαφύγω aor. act. subj. → διαφεύγω.
διαφυλάσσω *I guard securely, I preserve,* or *guard through* (a danger), *save.*
διαχειρίζομαι *I lay my hands upon,* and so, *I slay, kill.*
διαχλευάζω *I mock (scorn) greatly,* with words and gesture.
διαχωρίζομαι *I separate myself from, I part from.*
διδακτικός, ή, όν *able to teach, apt to teach.*
διδακτός, ή, όν *taught.*
διδασκαλία, ας, ἡ *teaching.*
διδάσκαλος, ου, ὁ *teacher.*
διδάσκω *I teach.*
διδαχή, ῆς, ἡ *teaching.*
δίδραχμον, ου, τό (1) *a double-drachma, two drachmae,* a Greek silver coin. In the time of Christ 1 drachma roughly = 1 denarius = ¼ shekel; (2) δίδραχμον, the yearly temple tax thus = ½ shekel.
Δίδυμος, ου, ὁ *the Twin.*
δίδωμι (1) *I offer, give;* used elliptically in Rev 2:23; (2) Hebraistic (= τίθημι), *I put, place,* Rev 3:8.
διέβην aor. act. → διαβαίνω.
διεβλήθην aor. pas. → διαβάλλω.
διεγείρω (1) *I wake out of sleep;* (2) *I arouse,* in general.
διεγερθείς aor. pas. part. → διεγείρω.
διέδωκα aor. act. → διαδίδωμι.
διέζωσα aor. act. → διαζώννυμι.
διεζωσμένος perf. mid./pas. part. → διαζώννυμι.
διεθέμην aor. act. → διατίθημι.
διεῖλον aor. act. → διαιρέω.
διεκρίθην aor. pas. → διακρίνομαι.
διελεύσομαι fut. mid. → διέρχομαι.
διελέχθην aor. pas. → διαλέγομαι.
διελήλυθα perf. act. → διέρχομαι.
διεληλυθώς perf. act. part. → διέρχομαι.
διελθεῖν aor. act. infin. → διέρχομαι.
διέλιπον aor. act. → διαλείπω.
διενέγκω aor. act. subj. → διαφέρω.
διενθυμέομαι *I weigh in my mind, ponder.*
διέξοδος, ου, ἡ (1) *a going out in various directions, a parting;* (2) hence, *the issue* of a street, where it leads out of the city into the country.
διερμηνευτής, οῦ, ὁ *an interpreter.*
διερμηνεύω *I translate, interpret, explain.*
διέρρηξα aor. act. → διαρρήγνυμι.
διέρχομαι (1) *I go (come, journey) all the way through;* (2) in Acts seems frequently to imply, *I itinerate, evangelize as I go.*
διερωτάω *I inquire for.*
διεσπάρην aor. pas. → διασπείρω.
διεστειλάμην aor. mid. → διαστέλλομαι.
διέστην aor. act. → διΐστημι.
διέστραμμαι perf. mid./pas. → διαστρέφω.
διεσώθην aor. pas. → διασῴζω.
διεταράχθην aor. pas. → διαταράσσομαι.
διετής, ές *two years old.*
διετία, ας, ἡ *a period of two years,*

two years. (According to ancient practice this means any period between one and two years.)
διεφθάρην aor. pas. → διαφθείρω.
διέφθαρμαι perf. mid./pas. → διαφθείρω.
διήγειρα aor. act. → διεγείρω.
διηγέομαι *I relate, narrate.*
διήγησις, εως, ἡ *a narrative.*
διῆλθον aor. act. → διέρχομαι.
διηνεκής, ές (1) *continuous;* (2) εἰς τὸ διηνεκές, *perpetually.*
διηνοίχθην aor. pas. → διανοίγω.
διθάλασσος, ον *between two seas, which has sea on both sides.*
διϊκνέομαι (διικνέομαι) *I pass through (to), come through (to).*
διΐστημι (διίστημι) (1) διαστήσαντες (Acts 27:28) trans. w. τὸ πλοῖον understood, *having moved (the ship) some distance;* (2) διαστῆναι, intrans., *to be distant from, to be separated from;* (3) *to pass away.*
διϊσχυρίζομαι (διισχυρίζομαι) *I assert emphatically.*
δικαιοκρισία, ας, ἡ *just judging, just judgment.*
δίκαιος, α, ον (1) *just;* (2) especially, *just* in the eyes of God, *righteous;* (3) οἱ δίκαιοι in Matt *the elect* (a Jewish idea); (4) κρίνω τὸ δίκαιον, *I give just judgment,* Luke 12:57.
δικαιοσύνη, ης, ἡ (1) *justice, justness;* (2) *righteousness* (cf. δίκαιος); (3) δικαιοσύνη θεοῦ strictly, *righteousness of which God is the source* or *author,* but practically, *a divine righteousness* and equivalent to βασιλεία τοῦ θεοῦ (usually if not always in Jewish atmosphere).
δικαιόω (1) *I make* δίκαιος *(righteous), I defend the cause of, plead for the righteousness (innocence) of, I acquit, justify;* (2) hence, *I regard as* δίκαιος *(righteous).*
δικαίωμα, ατος, τό (1) *(an argument, a piece justificative),* hence, *a thing pronounced (by God) to be* δίκαιος *(just, the right);* (2) or *the restoration* of a criminal, a fresh chance given him; (3) *a righteous deed* (e.g., Rom 5:18).
δικαίως adv., *justly, righteously.*
δικαίωσις, εως, ἡ *justifying, justification, a process of absolution.*
δικαστής, οῦ, ὁ *a judge.*
δίκη, ης, ἡ (1) (orig. *custom, usage*); hence, *right, justice,* Acts 28:4, where rather *Justice* (the goddess); (2) *process of law, judicial hearing;* (3) *execution of sentence, punishment, penalty,* 2 Thess 1:9; Jude 7.
δίκτυον, ου, τό *a net.*
δίλογος, ον *double-tongued.*
διό *wherefore* (= δι' ὅ, *on account of which thing*).
διοδεύω *I travel through.*
Διονύσιος, ου, ὁ *Dionysius,* an Athenian.
διόπερ *therefore, for this very reason* (= δι' ὅπερ, an emphatic διό).
διοπετής, ές *fallen from the sky.*
διόρθωμα, ατος, τό *a correction, reform.*
διόρθωσις, εως, ἡ *amendment, improvement* (orig. *right ordering;* then *bettering*).
διορύσσω *I dig through, break through.*
διορυχθῆναι aor. pas. infin. → διορύσσω.
Διόσκουροι, ων, οἱ *the Dioscuri,* Castor and Pollux, sons of Zeus and Leda, and patrons of sailors (= Διὸς κοῦροι, *boys of Zeus*).
διότι (1) = διὰ ὅ τι, *wherefore;* (2) = ὅτι Rom 8:21 (var.).
Διοτρέφης, ους, ὁ *Diotrephes.*
διπλοῦς, ῆ, οῦν *double* (contracted from διπλόος).
διπλόω *I double.*
δίς adv., *twice.*
δισμυριάς, άδος, ἡ = δὶς μυριάς, *a double myriad, 20,000.*

διστάζω *I doubt.*
δίστομος, ον *two-edged* (lit. *two-mouthed;* hence of a sword, as a drinker of blood).
δισχίλιοι, αι, α *two-thousand.*
διυλίζω (διϋλίζω) *I strain, put through a sieve.*
διχάζω *I make to differ from, I make to be hostile.*
διχοστασία, ας, ἡ *division* (between persons).
διχοτομέω *I cut in two.*
διψάω *I thirst.*
δίψος, ους, τό *thirst.*
δίψυχος, ον *double-minded, wavering* (lit. *of two souls, of two selves*).
διωγμός, οῦ, ὁ *persecution.*
διώκτης, ου, ὁ *a persecutor.*
διώκω (1) *I pursue;* (2) hence, *I persecute.*
δόγμα, ατος, τό *a decree.*
δογματίζομαι *I subject myself to regulations,* or *I am decree-ridden.*
δοθείς aor. pas. part. → δίδωμι.
δοθήσομαι fut. pas. → δίδωμι.
δοῖ aor. act. subj. 3 sing. → δίδωμι.
δοκέω (1) *I seem, am thought;* (2) δοκεῖ impers. w. dat., *it seems good, it is resolved by.*
δοκιμάζω (1) *I put to the test, I prove, examine;* (2) in Rom 2:18; Phil 1:10 either *I distinguish by testing,* or, more probably, *I approve after testing;* (3) *I think fit,* Rom 1:28.
δοκιμασία, ας, ἡ *testing, proving.*
δοκιμή, ῆς, ἡ (1) *approved status;* (2) hence, *character.*
δοκίμιον, ου, τό *what is genuine, the approved part, the pure part* (neut. of δοκίμιος *genuine,* as opposed to *alloyed, counterfeit*).
δόκιμος, ον *approved.*
δοκός, οῦ, ἡ *a beam.*
δόλιος, α, ον *treacherous, deceitful.*
δολιόω *I act deceitfully, treacherously.*
δόλος, ου, ὁ *deceit, guile, treachery.*
δολόω *I adulterate* (cf. ἄδολος).
δόμα, ατος, τό *a gift.*
δόξα, ης, ἡ (1) *glory,* an especially divine quality, the unspoken manifestation of God; (2) in Jas 2:1 it is in apposition to Ἰησοῦ Χριστοῦ, and is personified (cf. 1 Cor 2:8; Acts 7:2, and the Shekinah of Targums and post-canonical Jewish writings).
δοξάζω (1) *I glorify, bestow glory on;* (2) τὸν θεόν, *I acknowledge the glory of God.*
Δορκάς, άδος, ἡ the Gk. name of Tabitha, *Dorcas* (lit. *gazelle*).
δός aor. act. imper. → δίδωμι.
δόσις, εως, ἡ *giving* (from God).
δότης, ου, ὁ *giver.*
Δουβέριος, α, ον *Douberius,* a Macedonian city; Acts 20:4 (var.).
δουλαγωγέω *I enslave.*
δουλεία, ας, ἡ *slavery.*
δουλεύω *I serve as a slave, I am a slave.*
δούλη, ης, ἡ *a female slave.*
δοῦλος, ου, ὁ *a (male) slave.*
δουλόω *I enslave.*
δοῦναι aor. act. infin. → δίδωμι.
δούς aor. act. part. → δίδωμι.
δοχή, ῆς, ἡ *a reception, party.*
δράκων, οντος, ὁ *a serpent.*
δραμών aor. act. part. → τρέχω.
δράσσομαι *I take hold of, grasp.*
δραχμή, ῆς, ἡ *a drachma,* a Gk. silver coin.
δρέπανον, ου, τό *a sickle.*
δρόμος, ου, ὁ *a run, a course* (in running).
Δρούσιλλα, ης, ἡ *Drusilla* (born A.D. 39), daughter of Herod Agrippa I and his cousin Kypros, wife, first of Azizos, King of Emesa, and then of Antonius Felix, procurator of Judaea.
δύναμαι (1) *I am powerful, I have (the) power;* (2) *I am able, I can.*
δύναμις, εως, ἡ (1) *physical power, force, might;* (2) in plur., *powerful*

deeds, deeds showing (physical) *power, marvelous works.*
δυναμόω *I empower, fill with power.*
δυνάστης, ου, ὁ (1) *a ruler, potentate;* (2) Acts 8:27 in appos., seems = *courtier, member of the court* (lit. *a man who rules by force*).
δυνατέω *I am powerful, I have power, I am able.*
δυνατός, ή, όν (1) of persons, *powerful, able;* (2) of things, *possible.*
δύνω intrans., *I sink*
δύο (1) *two;* (2) δυὸ δυό and ἀνὰ (κατὰ) δύο, *two by two;* ἀνὰ δύο δύο in some MSS of Luke 10:3 is a mistaken fusion of the two phrases.
δυσβάστακτος, ον *difficult to carry.*
δυσεντέριον, ου, τό *dysentery.*
δυσερμήνευτος, ον *difficult to interpret.*
δύσις, εως, ἡ *west.*
δύσκολος, ον *difficult.*
δυσκόλως adv., *with difficulty.*
δυσμή, ῆς, ἡ (1) *a setting* (of the sun); (2) hence, *the West;* always plur.
δυσνόητος, ον *hard to understand.*
δυσφημέω *I am badly spoken of, I have a bad reputation.*
δυσφημία, ας, ἡ *evil repute.*
δῷ aor. act. subj. 3 sing. → δίδωμι.
δώδεκα (1) *twelve;* (2) οἱ δώδεκα, the usual way in which *the Twelve* disciples of Jesus are referred to.
δωδέκατος, η, ον *twelfth.*
δωδεκάφυλον, ου, τό *the Twelve Tribes* (of Israel).
δώῃ aor. act. subj. 3 sing. → δίδωμι.
δῴη aor. opt. 3 sing. → δίδωμι.
δῶμα, ατος, τό *the roof* (of a house), *the top of the house.*
δωρεά, ᾶς, ἡ *a (free) gift, a gift (without repayment).*
δωρεάν (= acc. of δωρεά used as adv.), *as a free gift, without payment, freely, gratis.*
δωρέομαι *I give, grant, donate.*
δώρημα, ατος, τό *a gift;* in Jas 1:17 *(of God).*
δῶρον, ου, τό *a gift.*
δωροφορία, ας, ἡ *bringing of a gift or offering* (Rom 15:31, var.).
δώσω fut. act. → δίδωμι.

E

ἔα an interj., *ho!* It is supposed to imply surprise, fear and indignation.
ἐάν (1) introducing a clause, *if,* w. subjun., but 1 Thess 3:8; 1 John 5:15 have the indic.; (2) within a clause, modifying, generalizing, ὅς, ὅστις, ὅσος, ὁσάκις, ὅπου, οὗ (a usage beginning about 133 B.C., exactly as ἄν does in Attic Gk.), thus ὅς = *who,* ὅς ἐάν, *whosoever,* etc.
ἐάνπερ *if indeed.*
ἑαυτοῦ, ῆς, οῦ *self, selves;* not used in nom., used for all three persons, according to context, *ourselves; yourself, yourselves; himself, herself, itself, themselves.*
ἐάω *I allow, permit, leave.*
ἔβαλον aor. act. → βάλλω.
ἑβδομήκοντα *seventy.*
ἑβδομηκοντάκις *seventy times.*
ἕβδομος, η, ον *seventh.*
ἐβεβλήμην plup. mid./pas. → βάλλω.
Ἔβερ, ὁ *Eber,* father of Phalek and son of Sala [Heb.].
ἐβλάστησα aor. act. → βλαστάω.
ἐβλήθην aor. pas. → βάλλω.
ἐβουλήθην aor. pas. → βούλομαι.
Ἑβραϊκός, ή, όν *Hebrew.*
Ἑβραῖος, ου, ὁ *a Hebrew,* particularly one who speaks Hebrew (Aramaic), cf. Acts 6:1; Ἑβραῖος ἐξ Ἑβραίων, *a Hebrew descended from Hebrews* (Phil 3:5).
Ἑβραΐς, ΐδος, ἡ *Hebrew,* or rather *Aramaic.*
Ἑβραϊστί adv., *in the Hebrew,* or rather, *in the Aramaic dialect.*
ἐγάμησα aor. act. → γαμέω.

ἐγγίζω *I come near, approach.*
ἐγγράφω *I write (in), inscribe.*
ἔγγυος, ου, ὁ *a surety, security.*
ἐγγύς adv., *near;* comp. ἐγγύτερον, superl. ἔγγιστα.
ἐγεγόνει plup. act. 3 sing. → γίνομαι.
ἐγείρω (1) *I wake, arouse;* intrans. in imper., ἔγειρε, ἐγείρεσθε, *wake up!;* (2) *I raise up;* pas. sometimes = *I rise,* e.g., Mark 16:6.
ἐγενήθην aor. pas. → γίνομαι.
ἐγενόμην aor. mid. → γίνομαι.
ἔγερσις, εως, ἡ *a waking up.*
ἐγήγερμαι perf. mid./pas. → ἐγείρω.
ἔγημα aor. act. → γαμέω.
ἐγκάθετος, ου, ὁ *a snare setter, spy.*
ἐγκαίνια, ίων, τά *festival of dedication* of the Temple, to celebrate the rededication of the Temple by Judas Maccabeus in 164 B.C., held at Jerusalem about the middle of December.
ἐγκαινίζω (*I restore or carry out anew,* then) *I dedicate.*
ἐγκακέω (ἐκκακέω) *I lose heart* (*from* κακός in the sense of *cowardly;* very rare outside the Bible).
ἐγκαλέω *I bring a charge against.*
ἐγκαταλείπω *I leave in the lurch, I abandon* (one who is in straits), *I desert.*
ἐγκατοικέω *I am settled among, dwell among.*
ἐγκαυχάομαι *I boast in (because of)* something.
ἐγκεντρίζω *I graft.*
ἔγκλημα, ατος, τό *an accusation, charge.*
ἐγκομβόομαι *I clothe myself* (orig., *I tie round in a knot*).
ἐγκοπή (ἐκκοπή), ῆς, ἡ *a block, check, obstacle, hindrance.*
ἐγκόπτω *I block, check, hinder* (by *introducing an obstacle sharply in the way of a moving object*).
ἐγκράτεια, ας, ἡ *self-mastery, self-restraint, self-control, continence.*
ἐγκρατεύομαι *I exercise self-control, I am continent.*
ἐγκρατής, ές *self-controlled.*
ἐγκρίνω *I judge (reckon) to belong to, I class with.*
ἐγκρύπτω *I hide (within).*
ἔγκυος, ον *pregnant.*
ἔγνωκα perf. act. → γινώσκω.
ἐγνώκειν plup. act. → γινώσκω.
ἔγνων aor. act. → γινώσκω.
ἐγνώσθην aor. pas. → γινώσκω.
ἐγράφην aor. pas. → γράφω.
ἐγχρίω *I besmear, anoint.*
ἐγώ First pers. pron., *I, me;* plur. ἡμεῖς; τί ἐμοὶ (ἡμῖν) καὶ σοί; *What have I (we) to do with thee?,* but in John 2:4 ἐμοὶ καὶ σοί may be simply equal to ἡμῖν; τὸ (τὰ) κατ' ἐμέ, *so far as I am concerned;* in letters ἡμεῖς often alternates w. ἐγώ without real difference of meaning.
ἐδαφίζω *I dash to the ground.*
ἔδαφος, ους, τό *ground.*
ἐδεδώκειν plup. act. → δίδωμι.
ἐδεήθην aor. pas. → δέομαι.
ἔδειξα aor. act. → δείκνυμι.
ἔδειρα aor. act. → δέρω.
ἐδιδάχθην aor. pas. → διδάσκω.
ἐδόθην aor. pas. → δίδωμι.
ἔδοξα aor. act. → δοκέω.
ἑδραῖος, α, ον *firm, steadfast* (lit. *seated*).
ἑδραίωμα, ατος, τό *a foundation.*
ἔδραμον aor. act. → τρέχω.
ἔδυν aor. act. → δύνω.
ἔδωκα aor. act. → δίδωμι.
Ἑζεκίας, ου, ὁ *Hezekiah,* son of Achas (Ahaz), father of Manasseh, and king of Judah (727–686? B.C.) [Heb.].
ἔζην imperf. → ζάω.
ἐθελοθρησκία (-εία), ας, ἡ *service (worship) of the will, worship of self,* practically, *worship of the angels* (cf. ἐθελοδουλεία).

ἐθέλω see θέλω.
ἔθηκα aor. act. → τίθημι.
ἐθίζω (1) *I accustom;* (2) τὸ εἰθισμένον, *the custom.*
ἐθνάρχης, ου, ὁ *ethnarch, tribal lord,* a subordinate ruler.
ἐθνικός, ή, όν *a Gentile,* a non-Jew (in biblical Hebrew = *nation,* but in rabbinic Heb. = *non-Jew*).
ἐθνικῶς adv., *in the manner of Gentiles.*
ἔθνος, ους, τό (1) *a race, people* (orig., a rustic or village people as opposed to those dwelling in organized cities or πόλεις; usually outside the privileged Jewish people, but also sometimes in the singular for it; sometimes = the inhabitants of a Roman province); (2) τὰ ἔθνη, *the nations* outside Judaism, *the Gentiles.*
ἔθος, ους, τό *a custom.*
ἔθου aor. mid. 2 sing. → τίθημι.
ἔθρεψα aor. act. → τρέφω.
ἔθω see εἴωθα.
εἰ (1) *if;* (2) *verily, indeed, assuredly* (Semitic, sometimes negative, *assuredly not,* Mk 8:12; Heb 3:11), (a) in strong statements, approaching oaths in character, and as the first word in an interrog. clause, probably a mere graphic equivalent, first appearing second c. B.C., of ἦ, (b) merely a particle asking a question. εἰ μή; (3) *but only,* e.g., Luke 4:26–27; John 15:4; Acts 27:22; Rev 21:27; (4) *and not,* in Mark 6:8, probably due to a misreading of an Aram. word; (5) εἰ δὲ μή, εἰ δὲ μήγε (Aramaism?), *otherwise;* (6) εἴπερ (= εἴ περ) a more emphatic εἰ, *if indeed.*
εἷα imperf. act. 3 sing. → ἐάω.
εἴασα aor. act. → ἐάω.
εἰδέα, ας, ἡ see ἰδέα.
εἶδα (εἶδον) *I saw,* 1 and 2 aor. respectively, cf. ὁράω; ἰδὼν εἶδον, a Hebraistic repetition.
εἰδέναι perf. act. infin. → οἶδα.
εἰδήσω fut. act. → οἶδα.
εἶδος, ους, τό (1) *visible form, shape, appearance, outward show;* (2) in 1 Thess 5:22 = *kind, species, class.*
εἰδυῖα perf. act. part. fem → οἶδα.
εἰδῶ plup. act. subj. → οἶδα.
εἰδώς perf. act. part. → οἶδα.
εἰδωλεῖον, ου, τό *a temple for (containing) an image* (of a god).
εἰδωλόθυτος, ου, τό (meat) *sacrificed to an image* (of a god).
εἰδωλολατρία (-εία), ας, ἡ *service (worship) of an image* (of a god).
εἰδωλολάτρης, ου, ὁ *a server (worshipper) of an image* (of a god).
εἴδωλον, ου, τό *an image of a god.*
εἴθισμαι perf. mid./pas. → ἐθίζω.
εἰκῇ (εἰκῆ) adv.; (1) *without a cause;* (2) *purposelessly, in vain, for nothing,* used both with reference to antecedent causes and purposes for the future,
εἴκοσι *twenty.*
εἴκω *I yield.*
εἰκών, όνος, ἡ *image, likeness, bust.*
εἱλάμην aor. mid. → αἱρέομαι.
εἴλημμαι perf. mid./pas. → λαμβάνω.
εἴληφα perf. act. → λαμβάνω.
εἰλικρίνεια, ας, ἡ *purity.*
εἰλικρινής, ές (orig. *unmixed*), *pure, uncontaminated.*
εἰλίσσω see ἑλίσσω.
εἵλκυσα aor. act. → ἕλκω.
εἵλκωμαι perf. mid./pas. → ἑλκόομαι.
εἰμί *I am, exist.* Note periphrasis w. parts., the special frequency of which in the impf. is due to the Aramaic basis of the language. ὁ ἦν ungrammatically, in Rev, where an aor. part. would be expected.
εἶναι pres. infin. → εἰμί.
εἵνεκεν see ἕνεκα.
εἶξα aor. act. → εἴκω.
εἶπα see εἶπον.
εἰπεῖν aor. act. infin. → λέγω.

εἴπερ see εἰ (6).
εἶπον (εἶπα) (aor. of λέγω) *I spoke, said;* ὡς ἔπος εἰπεῖν, *one might almost say (almost, about).*
εἰργασάμην aor. mid. → ἐργάζομαι.
εἴργασμαι perf. mid./pas. → ἐργάζομαι.
εἴρηκα perf. act. → λέγω.
εἰρήκειν plup. act. → λέγω.
εἴρημαι perf. mid./pas. → λέγω.
εἰρηνεύω *I am peaceful, I keep the peace, I am at peace.*
εἰρήνη, ης, ἡ (1) *peace, undisturbed condition;* (2) invocation of peace a common Jewish farewell (Mark 5:34, etc.), in the Hebraistic sense of *the health (welfare)* of an individual.
εἰρηνικός, ή, όν *making for peace, productive of peace.*
εἰρηνοποιέω *I make peace.*
εἰρηνοποιός, ου, ὁ *peacemaking, peacemaker.*
εἰς prep. w. acc. (1) *into, until, for;* (2) εἰς τό w. infin. (a) generally final, (b) but also expressing tendency, result, e.g., Rom 12:3; 2 Cor 8:6; Gal 3:17, (c) content of command or entreaty, e.g., 1 Thess 2:12, or (d) simply = explanatory infin., 1 Thess 4:9; (3) encroaches on ἐν and = *in,* e.g., John 1:18; Acts 7:12; 2 Cor 11:10; 1 John 5:8; (4) εἰς ἑκατόν, *etc., a hundredfold.*
εἷς, μία, ἕν, gen. **ἑνός, μιᾶς, ἑνός** *one;* καθ' εἷς, *each single one, one by one;* sometimes no different from τις (Mark 14:10), and sometimes too = πρῶτος, *first.*
εἰσάγω *I lead in, bring in.*
εἰσακούω *I hear.*
εἰσδέχομαι *I welcome in.*
εἰσδραμών aor. act. part. → εἰστρέχω.
εἴσειμι *I go in, enter* (orig., *I shall go in*).
εἰσελεύσομαι fut. mid. → εἰσέρχομαι.
εἰσελήλυθα perf. act. → εἰσέρχομαι.
εἰσενεγκεῖν aor. act. infin. → εἰσφέρω.
εἰσέρχομαι *I go in.*
εἰσήγαγον aor. act. → εἰσάγω.
εἰσῄει imperf. 3 sing. → εἴσειμι.
εἰσῆλθον aor. act. → εἰσέρχομαι.
εἰσήνεγκον aor. act. → εἰσφέρω.
εἰσίασιν pres. 3 plur. → εἴσειμι.
εἰσιέναι pres. infin. → εἴσειμι.
εἰσκαλέομαι *I call in* (to my house).
εἴσοδος, ου, ἡ (1) abstr., *(act of) entering, entrance, entry;* (2) concr., *the entrance* itself, Heb 10:19 (cf. 20); 2 Pet 1:11.
εἰσπηδάω *I leap into, rush into.*
εἰσπορεύομαι *I journey in(to), I go in(to).*
εἱστήκειν plup. act. → ἵστημι.
εἰστρέχω *I run in(to).*
εἰσφέρω *I carry (bring) in.*
εἶτα adv., *then, thereafter, next* (marking a fresh stage).
εἴτε lit. *and if;* εἴτε . . . εἴτε, *whether . . . or.*
εἶτεν = εἶτα.
εἴτις = εἴ τις.
εἶχον imperf. act. → ἔχω.
εἴωθα (1) *I am accustomed* (perf. of obsolete pres. ἔθω); (2) τὸ εἰωθός (verbal adj. as subst.), *custom, what was customary.*
ἐκ, ἐξ prep. w. gen., *from out, out from among, from,* suggesting from the interior outwards; ἐξ Ἑβραίων, *descended from Hebrews,* Phil 3:5; w. gen. of price, Matt 20:2; Acts 1:18; in partitive phrase, as subj. of sentence, John 16:17; cf. the periphrasis οἱ ἐξ ἐριθείας, Rom 2:8.
ἕκαστος, η, ον *each* (of more than two); εἷς ἕκαστος, *each individual;*

plur. ἕκαστοι, etc., *each class, group.*

ἑκάστοτε adv., *on each occasion.*

ἑκατόν *a hundred;* εἰς ἑκατόν, see εἰς.

ἑκατονταετής, ές *a hundred years old.*

ἑκατονταπλασίων, ον *a hundredfold.*

ἑκατοντάρχης (ἑκατοντάρχος), ου, ὁ *a centurion* of the Roman army (see κεντουρίων).

ἐκβαίνω *I go out.*

ἐκβάλλω (1) *I throw (cast, put) out;* (2) *I banish,* Gal 4:30; 3 John 10; (3) *I bring forth, I produce,* Matt 12:35.

ἐκβαλῶ fut. act. → ἐκβάλλω.

ἔκβασις, εως, ἡ (1) *a way out, escape,* 1 Cor 10:13; (2) *result,* Heb 13:7.

ἐκβεβλήκειν plup. act. → ἐκβάλλω.

ἐκβολή, ῆς, ἡ *a throwing out, a jettisoning* of cargo, to lighten a ship.

ἔκγονος, ου, τό *descended,* hence subst., *a descendant.*

ἐκδαπανάω *I spend (give out) completely.*

ἐκδέχομαι *I wait for, expect.*

ἔκδηλος, ον *perfectly evident, manifest.*

ἐκδημέω *I am away from the* δῆμος, *from my parish, from home.*

ἐκδίδωμι (1) *I give out, let;* (2) mid., *I let out for my own advantage,* Mark 12:1.

ἐκδιηγέομαι *I give a complete narrative of.*

ἐκδικέω *I give justice over, defend, avenge, vindicate.*

ἐκδίκησις, εως, ἡ (1) *defense, avenging, vindication, vengeance;* (2) *full (complete) punishment,* 2 Thess 1:8; 1 Pet 2:14.

ἔκδικος, ου, ὁ *avenging, an avenger.* (The word occurs frequently in the sense of a special *advocate* or *champion* of a city.)

ἐκδιώκω *I drive out.*

ἔκδοτος, ον *given up, delivered up.*

ἐκδοχή, ῆς, ἡ *waiting, expectation.*

ἐκδύω *I put off, take off, strip off* w. acc. of person or garment or both.

ἐκδώσομαι fut. mid. → ἐκδίδομαι.

ἐκεῖ adv. (1) *there, yonder;* (2) *thither, there.*

ἐκεῖθεν adv., *thence, from that place.*

ἐκείνης adv., *there* (Luke 19:4, var.)

ἐκεῖνος, η, ο *that, yonder* (of what is distant, or great); in 1 John usually = Christ.

ἐκεῖσε adv. (1) *thither,* Acts 21:3; (2) *there,* Acts 22:5.

ἐκέκραξα aor. act. → κράζω.

ἐκέρασα aor. act. → κεράννυμι.

ἐκέρδησα aor. act. → κερδαίνω.

ἐκζητέω *I seek out.*

ἐκζήτησις, εως, ἡ *a seeking out, searching questioning.*

ἐκθαμβέομαι *I am greatly astonished.*

ἔκθαμβος, ον *full of astonishment.*

ἐκθαυμάζω *I wonder greatly.*

ἔκθετος, ον *exposed* (to the elements).

ἐκκαθαίρω (1) *I clean (cleanse) out,* 1 Cor 5:7; (2) *I clean thoroughly,* 2 Tim 2:21.

ἐκκαίομαι *I burn (with lust).*

ἐκκεντέω *I pierce through* (or *deeply*).

ἐκκέχυμαι perf. mid./pas. → ἐκχέω.

ἐκκλάω *I break off.*

ἐκκλείω *I shut out, exclude.*

ἐκκλησία, ας, ἡ *an assembly, meeting of assembly* (lit., *a calling out*), Acts 19:39; (1) *a community, congregation, church, society* (first used in LXX for *the congregation* of Israel), the assembly of Christians in *one* city or community; in Matt 16:18; 18:17 the body of Palestinian adherents of the Messiah is intended; (2) much more rarely, in a developed sense, especially w.

ὅλη, *the Church* (the whole body of Christians in the world).
ἐκκλίνω *I fall away from, I turn away* (from); (lit. *I bend away from*).
ἐκκολυμβάω *I swim out* (of the water).
ἐκκομίζω *I carry out* (of the city gate for burial).
ἐκκοπή see ἐγκοπή.
ἐκκόπτω *I cut out (off, away).*
ἐκκρέμαμαι (ἐκκρεμάννυμι) w. gen. *I hang upon* (met.).
ἐκλαλέω *I speak out, tell out.*
ἐκλάμπω *I shine forth (out).*
ἐκλανθάνομαι *I quite forget.*
ἔκλαυσα aor. act. → κλαίω.
ἐκλέγομαι *I pick out for myself, I choose.*
ἐκλείπω intrans., (1) *I fail utterly;* (2) *I am in a state of eclipse* (of the sun) Luke 23:45.
ἐκλεκτός, ή, όν *chosen out, selected,* sometimes as subst., of those chosen out by God for the rendering of special service to Him (of the Hebrew race, particular Hebrews, the Messiah, and the Christians); an adj. in 2 John 1, 13.
ἐκλέλησμαι perf. mid./pas. → ἐκλανθάνομαι.
ἐκλήθην aor. pas. → καλέω.
ἐκλογή, ῆς, ἡ *choosing out, selecting, choice* (by God); in Acts 9:15 a Hebraistic gen., equivalent to ἐκλεκτόν.
ἐκλύομαι *I am unstrung, become weak, fail.*
ἐκμάσσω *I wipe (off) thoroughly.*
ἐκμυκτηρίζω *I mock greatly.*
ἐκνεύω *I retire, withdraw* (lit. *I bend the head aside,* to avoid a blow).
ἐκνήφω *I am thoroughly sober* (in mind).
ἐκορέσθην aor. pas. → κορέννυμι.
ἑκούσιος, α, ον *willing;* κατὰ ἑκούσιον, *with right good will.*
ἑκουσίως adv., *willingly, with the will.*
ἔκπαλαι adv., *from of old, long since.*
ἐκπειράζω *I put to a thorough test.*
ἐκπέμπω *I send out.*
ἐκπέπτωκα perf. act. → ἐκπίπτω.
ἐκπερισσῶς adv., *most exceedingly, with exceeding emphasis.*
ἐκπετάννυμι *I spread (stretch) out.*
ἐκπηδάω *I leap (rush) out.*
ἐκπίπτω (1) *I fall out, I fall off, I fall away;* (2) hence, in nautical language, *I fall off* from the straight course; (3) of flowers, *I fade away, wither away.*
ἐκπλέω *I sail out* (of harbor), *I sail away.*
ἐκπληρόω *I fill completely, I fulfill in every particular (to the utmost), I make good.*
ἐκπλήρωσις, εως, ἡ *completion, fulfillment.*
ἐκπλήσσομαι *I am thunderstruck, astounded.*
ἐκπνέω *I breathe my last, I expire* (lit. *I breathe out*).
ἐκπορεύομαι (1) *I journey out;* (2) *I come forth.*
ἐκπορνεύω *I am guilty of fornication* (the force of ἐκ is uncertain).
ἐκπτύω *I spit upon, disdain.*
ἔκραξα aor. act. → κράζω.
ἐκρέμασα aor. act. → κρεμάννυμι.
ἐκρεμάσθην aor. pas. → κρεμάννυμι.
ἐκριζόω *I root out, root up.*
ἐκρίθην aor. pas. → κρίνω.
ἐκρύβην aor. pas. → κρύπτω.
ἔκστασις, εως, ἡ *bewilderment* (properly, *distraction* or *disturbance* of mind caused by a shock).
ἐκστρέφω *I pervert.*
ἐκσῴζω *I save completely,* var. in Acts 27:39.
ἐκταράσσω *I disturb (trouble) greatly (exceedingly).*
ἐκτεθείς aor. act. part. → ἐκτίθημι.
ἐκτείνω *I stretch out (forth).*
ἐκτελέω *I complete, bring to completion, carry out, perform.*

ἐκτένεια, ας, ἡ *earnestness, strenuousness.*
ἐκτενής, ές (1) *intent, constant, strenuous;* (2) comp. adv., ἐκτενέστερον, *more earnestly, very fervently.*
ἐκτενῶ fut. act. → ἐκτείνω.
ἐκτενῶς adv., *earnestly, strenuously.*
ἐκτίθημι (1) *I abandon* or *expose* a child; (2) mid. *I set forth, expound, explain.*
ἐκτινάσσω *I shake off;* mid. *I shake off from myself.*
ἐκτός (1) adv., (a) *without, outside,* (b) *except,* (c) τὸ ἐκτός, substantivally, *the outside;* (2) prep. w. gen., *outside, apart from.*
ἕκτος, η, ον *sixth.*
ἐκτραπήσομαι fut. pas. → ἐκτρέπομαι.
ἐκτρέπω mid. and pas. *I turn aside* (from the right road), *I wander,* and w. an obj. *I remove from myself,* 1 Tim 6:20 (lit. *I turn out from*).
ἐκτρέφω *I nourish, nurture.*
ἔκτρομος, ον *trembling greatly.*
ἔκτρωμα, ατος, τό *an untimely birth* (strictly *a lifeless abortion*).
ἐκφέρω (1) *I bring out, carry out,* sometimes out of the city for burial; (2) *I bring forth, bear,* Heb 6:8.
ἐκφεύγω *I flee out, away, I escape;* w. an acc. *I escape* something.
ἐκφοβέω *I terrify exceedingly.*
ἔκφοβος, ον *exceedingly afraid.*
ἐκφύω *I put forth, cause to sprout.*
ἐκχέω (ἐκχύννω) (1) *I pour out* (liquid or solid), *I shed;* (2) pas. *I am swept on, rush* or *I surrender,* Jude 11.
ἐκχεῶ fut. act. → ἐκχέω.
ἐκχυθήσομαι fut. pas. → ἐκχέω.
ἐκχωρέω *I go out.*
ἐκψύχω *I breathe my last, I die.*
ἑκών, οῦσα, όν *willing, willingly.*
ἔλαβον aor. act. → λαμβάνω.
ἔλαθον aor. act. → λανθάνω.
ἐλαία, ας, ἡ *an olive tree;* see ἐλαίων.
ἔλαιον, ου, τό *olive oil;* ἔλαιον ἀγαλλιάσεως, *oil of enjoyment,* the oil with which the heads of guests at banquets are anointed, Heb 1:9.
ἐλαιών (Ἐλαιών), ῶνος, ὁ *olive orchard, Olive grove, Olive yard,* probably the right text in Luke 19:29; 21:37, as well as Acts 1:12.
Ἐλαμ(ε)ίτης, ου, ὁ *an Elamite,* one of a people living to the north of the Persian Gulf in the southern part of Persia.
ἐλάσσων (ἐλάττων), ον (1) *less, smaller;* (2) *poorer, inferior,* John 2:10; (3) adv., ἔλαττον, *less.*
ἐλαττονέω *I have less, I lack.*
ἐλαττόω *I make less (inferior).*
ἐλαύνω (1) trans., *I drive (on), propel;* (2) intrans., *I row,* Mark 6:48; John 6:19.
ἐλαφρία, ας, ἡ *levity, fickleness.*
ἐλαφρός, ά, όν *light.*
ἐλάχιστος, η, ον (1) *least, smallest* (Matt; 1 Cor 15:9), but perhaps oftener in the weaker sense, *very little, very small* (Luke; 1 Cor 4:3; 6:2; James); ὁ ἐλαχιστότερος, *the smallest, the least important;* εἰς ἐλάχιστόν ἐστιν, *it matters very little;* (2) adv., ἐλάχιστον, *a very little.*
ἔλαχον aor. act. → λαγχάνω.
Ἐλεάζαρ, ὁ *Eleazar,* son of Eliud, and father of Matthan [Heb.].
ἐλεάω see ἐλεέω.
ἐλεγμός, οῦ, ὁ *reproof.*
ἔλεγξις, εως, ἡ *rebuke, reproof.*
ἔλεγχος, ου, ὁ (1) *a proof;* (2) possibly *a persuasion.*
ἐλέγχω (1) *I reprove, rebuke;* (2) *I expose, show to be guilty,* John 3:20; 1 Cor 14:24; Eph 5:11, 13; Jas 2:9.
ἐλεεινός, ή, όν *merciful, pitiful.*
ἐλεέω (ἐλεάω) *I pity.*
ἐλεημοσύνη, ης, ἡ (1) abstr. *alms-*

giving, charity; (2) concr. *alms, charity.*
ἐλεήμων, ον gen. **ονος** *pitiful, merciful.*
Ἐλεισάβετ see Ἐλισάβετ.
ἔλεος, ους, τό *pity, mercy.*
ἐλευθερία, ας, ἡ *freedom, liberty,* especially *a state of freedom* from slavery.
ἐλεύθερος, α, ον *free* (opp. *enslaved,* cf. 1 Cor 12:13).
ἐλευθερόω *I free, set free, liberate.*
ἐλεύκανα aor. act. → λευκαίνω.
ἔλευσις, εως, ἡ *coming, arrival.*
ἐλεύσομαι fut. mid. → ἔρχομαι.
ἐλεφάντινος, η, ον *made of ivory.*
ἐλήλακα perf. act. → ἐλαύνω.
ἐλήλυθα perf. act. → ἔρχομαι.
ἐλθεῖν aor. act. infin. → ἔρχομαι.
Ἐλιακ(ε)ίμ, ὁ *Eliakim,* son of Abiud and father of Azor (Matt 1:13), son of Melea and father of Jonam (Luke 3:30) [Heb.].
ἔλιγμα, ατος, τό *a roll.*
Ἐλιέζερ, ὁ *Eliezer,* son of Joreim and father of Joshua [Heb.].
Ἐλιούδ, ὁ *Eliud,* son of Acheim, and father of Eleazar [Heb.].
Ἐλισάβετ, ἡ *Elisabeth,* mother of John the Baptizer [Heb.].
Ἐλισαῖος (Ἑλισαῖος), ου, ὁ *Helisaeus,* grecized form of *Elisha.*
ἑλίσσω *I roll, roll up.*
ἑλκόομαι *I am covered with sores.*
ἕλκος, ους, τό *a (festering) sore.*
ἑλκύσω fut. act. → ἕλκω.
ἑλκύω, ἕλκω *I drag, draw, pull.*
Ἑλλάς, άδος, ἡ *Hellas,* the native name for *Greece.*
Ἕλλην, ηνος, ὁ *a Hellene,* the native word for *a Greek;* it is, however, a term wide enough to include all Greek-speaking (i.e., educated) non-Jews.
Ἑλληνικός, ή, όν *Greek;* ἡ Ἑλληνική (γλῶσσα), *the Greek language.*
Ἑλληνίς, ίδος, ἡ *Greek;* see Ἕλλην.
Ἑλληνιστής, οῦ, ὁ *a Hellenist, Grecian Jew,* a Greek-speaking Jew, i.e., one who can speak Greek only and not Hebrew (or Aramaic).
Ἑλληνιστί *in the Greek language.*
ἐλλογέω (ἐλλογάω) *I put down (set) to some one's account, reckon, impute.*
Ἐλμαδάμ, ὁ *Elmadam, father of Kosam, son of Er* [Heb.].
ἑλόμενος aor. mid. part. → αἱρέομαι.
ἐλπίζω *I hope, hope for;* the subst. following ἐν, εἰς, ἐπί w. dat. or acc., is the ground of the hope, that which makes hope possible.
ἐλπίς, ίδος, ἡ *hope.*
ἐλπιῶ fut. act. → ἐλπίζω.
Ἐλύμας, α, ὁ *Elymas,* the name of the sorcerer at Paphos (the form of the name is doubtful; some MSS read Ἑτοιμᾶς, *Son of the Ready*).
ἐλωΐ, ελωι *my God* (Aram., form of word is doubtful).
ἔμαθον aor. act. → μανθάνω.
ἐμαυτοῦ, ῆς *of myself.*
ἐμβαίνω *I embark.*
ἐμβαλεῖν aor. act. infin. → ἐμβάλλω.
ἐμβάλλω *I cast in, throw in.*
ἐμβάπτω act. and mid. *I dip in.*
ἐμβατεύω (*I enter on, take possession of*), hence a technical expression connected with the pagan Mysteries, *I enter, set foot on* (the inner shrine, after the first initiation). It indicates the final act in mystic ceremonial, the entrance on a new life in presence of the god.
ἐμβῆναι aor. act. infin. → ἐμβαίνω.
ἐμβιβάζω trans., *I embark, put on board.*
ἐμβλέπω *I look into (upon).*
ἐμβριμάομαι *I groan* (with the notion of coercion springing out of displeasure, anger, indignation,

antagonism), *I express indignant displeasure,* w. dat. of person w. whom it is felt, Matt 9:30; Mark 1:43; 14:5; absol. John 11:33, 38.

ἔμεινα aor. act. → μένω.

ἐμέω *I vomit.*

ἔμιξα aor. act. → μίγνυμι.

ἐμμαίνομαι *I am madly enraged with.*

Ἐμμανουήλ, ὁ *Emmanuel,* a Messianic title derived from Isa 7:14 = *God with us* [Heb.].

Ἐμμαοῦς (-ούς), ἡ *Emmaus (Ammaus),* a village not far from Jerusalem.

ἐμμένω (1) *I remain (abide) in,* Acts 28:30; (2) hence met., Heb 8:9; (3) w. dat., *I abide by, maintain,* Acts 14:22; Gal 3:10.

Ἐμμώρ (Ἐμμώρ), ὁ *Hamor, Emmor,* a man whose sons sold a field at Shechem to Jacob [Heb.].

ἐμνήσθην aor. pas. → μιμνήσκομαι.

ἐμός, ἡ, όν *my, mine* (predominates in John).

ἐμπαιγμονή, ῆς, ἡ *mockery.*

ἐμπαιγμός, οῦ, ὁ *mockery.*

ἐμπαίζω *I mock.*

ἐμπαίκτης, ου, ὁ *a mocker.*

ἐμπέπλησμαι perf. mid./pas. → ἐμπίμπλημι.

ἐμπεριπατέω *I walk among.*

ἐμπεσοῦμαι fut. mid. → ἐμπίπτω.

ἐμπί(μ)πλημι (ἐμπι[μ]πλάω) *I fill up, fill.*

ἐμπί(μ)πρημι (ἐμπρήθω) (1) *I burn, set on fire;* (2) pas. *I suffer inflammation* (from -πρήθω = *I cause to swell*), Acts 28:6 (var.).

ἐμπίπτω *I fall in, am cast in.*

ἐμπλέκω *I enfold, entangle.*

ἐμπλοκή, ῆς, ἡ *braiding.*

ἐμπνέω *I breathe of, breathe* (lit. *I breathe in*).

ἐμπορεύομαι (1) *I travel as a merchant, engage in trade;* (2) w. acc. *I traffic in, make gain* or *business of.*

ἐμπορία, ας, ἡ *trading, trade, trafficking, business.*

ἐμπόριον, ου, τό *a place of traffic, mart, market, market house.*

ἔμπορος, ου, ὁ *a merchant, trader.*

ἐμπρήθω see ἐμπί(μ)πρημι.

ἔμπροσθεν (1) prep., usually w. gen., *in front of, before the face of;* (2) adv., *in front, before the face;* sometimes made a subst. by the addition of the article.

ἐμπτύω *I spit upon.*

ἐμφανής, ές *manifest, visible.*

ἐμφανίζω (1) *I make visible (manifest);* (2) hence, act. *I report (inform) against,* Acts 24:1; 25:2, 15; (3) pas. (quasitechnical) *I appear before.*

ἔμφοβος, ον *full of fear, terrified.*

ἐμφυσάω *I breathe into, breathe upon.*

ἔμφυτος, ον *inborn, ingrown, congenital, natural.*

ἐμώρανα aor. act. → μωραίνω.

ἐμωράνθην aor. pas. → μωραίνω.

ἐν prep. w. dat., (1) of place, *in;* ἐν τοῖς, see ὁ; ἐν Χριστῷ, of mystic indwelling; (2) = εἰς, *into,* e.g., Matt 10:16; (3) of time, *in, during, at;* (4) of instrument, *(armed) with,* Luke 22:49; 1 Cor 4:21, etc.; (5) *amounting to,* Acts 7:14 (cf. Mark 4:8 twice); (6) *consisting in,* Eph 2:15; (7) *in the department of,* cf. 1 Cor 6:2; (8) *in the judgment of;* cf. 1 Cor 14:11; (9) Hebraistic use, Matt 10:32; Luke 12:8. For ἐν ᾧ, see ὅς.

ἐναγκαλίζομαι *I take (fold) in my arms.*

ἐνάλιος, ον of creatures, *living in the sea* (poetic).

ἔναντι prep. w. gen., *before, in the presence of.*

ἐναντίον prep. w. gen., (1) *before, in the presence of;* (2) *in the eyes of;* see also τοὐναντίον.

ἐναντιόομαι *oppose, be in opposition to* (Acts 13:45, var.).
ἐναντίος, α, ον *opposite, opposed, contrary;* ἐξ ἐναντίας (adv.), *opposite;* ὁ ἐξ ἐναντίας, *the adversary.*
ἐνάρχομαι *I begin (in).*
ἔνατος, η, ον *ninth.*
ἐνγ- see ἐγγ-
ἐνδεής, ές *in need, needy.*
ἔνδειγμα, ατος, τό *(a thing proved),* hence, *a plain token (sign, proof).*
ἐνδείκνυμι (in the mid. voice ἐνδείκνυμαι only), *I show forth.*
ἔνδειξις, εως, ἡ *a showing, proof, demonstration.*
ἕνδεκα *eleven.*
ἑνδέκατος, η, ον *eleventh.*
ἐνδέχομαι ἐνδέχεται, impers., *it is possible.*
ἐνδημέω *I am in my* δῆμος *(parish), I am at home.*
ἐνδιδύσκω (of clothing, *I put on* another); mid. *I put on* (myself); somewhat rare.
ἔνδικος, ον *just.*
ἐνδοξάζω *I glorify, acknowledge the glory belonging to* (cf. δόξα), *recognize as glorious (I make* ἔνδοξος*).*
ἔνδοξος, ον *glorious.*
ἔνδυμα, ατος, τό *a garment, dress.*
ἐνδυναμόω *I fill with δύναμις (power);* almost = δυναμόω.
ἐνδύνω *I slip in* (deviously).
ἔνδυσις, εως, ἡ *putting on* (of a garment).
ἐνδύω (1) *I put on, clothe* (another); mid. *I clothe* (myself), *dress;* (2) hence, met., of acquiring qualities; = ἐπενδύομαι, 2 Cor 5:3.
ἐνδώμησις, εως, ἡ *roofing, coping.* (So probably, from δῶμα = *roof,* but most interpret *building.*)
ἐνέβην aor. act. → ἐμβαίνω.
ἐνέγκαι aor. act. infin. → φέρω.
ἐνέγκας aor. act. part. → φέρω.
ἐνεγκεῖν aor. act. infin. → φέρω.
ἐνέδρα, ας, ἡ (1) *ambush;* (2) hence, *plot, treachery, fraud.*
ἐνεδρεύω *I lie in wait (ambush) for, seek to entrap* (hence, *I defraud, deceive*).
ἐνειλέω *I wrap up, roll up in* (something).
ἔνειμι *I am in (within);* τὰ ἐνόντα, probably *the contents* (of the dish), or perhaps *what you can* (but the words are obscure and may be a mistranslation of an Aram. original).
ἕνεκα (ἕνεκεν, εἵνεκεν) prep. w. gen., *for the sake of, on account of;* οὗ (neut.) εἵνεκεν, *on account of which, wherefore,* Luke 4:18; τίνος ἕνεκα, *on account of what, wherefore, why,* Acts 19:32.
ἐνέκοψα aor. act. → ἐγκόπτω.
ἐνέκρυψα aor. act. → ἐγκρύπτω.
ἐνέμεινα aor. act. → ἐμμένω.
ἐνενήκοντα *ninety.*
ἐνεός, ά, όν *speechless, dumb, unable to speak* (= ἄνεως).
ἐνέπαιξα aor. act. → ἐμπαίζω.
ἐνεπαίχθην aor. pas. → ἐμπαίζω.
ἐνέπεσον aor. act. → ἐμπίπτω.
ἐνεπλάκην aor. pas. → ἐμπλέκομαι.
ἐνέπλησα aor. act. → ἐμπίμπλημι.
ἐνεπλήσθην aor. pas. → ἐμπίμπλημι.
ἐνέπρησα aor. act. → ἐμπίμπρημι.
ἐνέργεια, ας, ἡ *working, action productive of* ἔργον (concr. *work*), *activity;* in the NT confined to superhuman activity.
ἐνεργέω (1) intrans., *I am at work, work;* (2) trans., *I work,* the acc. expressing "that which is worked," *effect.* In NT the word is generally connected with miraculous interventions; (3) pas. always w. nonpersonal subj., as ἐνεργεῖν always w. personal, *I am made operative (effective), I am made to produce my appropriate result, I am set in operation, I am made to work.* Mid. absent from NT.

ἐνέργημα, ατος, τό *a working.*
ἐνεργής, ές *effective, productive of due result.*
ἐνέστηκα perf. act. → ἐνίστημι.
ἐνεστηκώς perf. act. part. → ἐνίστημι.
ἐνεστώς perf. act. part. → ἐνίστημι.
ἐνετειλάμην aor. mid. → ἐντέλλομαι.
ἐνετράπην aor. pas. → ἐντρέπω.
ἐνέτυχον aor. act. → ἐντυγχάνω.
ἐνευλογέω *I bless* (of God); ἐν is considered to have instrumental force.
ἐνεχθείς aor. pas. part. → φέρω.
ἐνέχω (1) *I have a grudge against, I am angry (with);* (2) pas. or mid. *I am entangled, entangle myself* (var. in 2 Thess 1:4).
ἐνθάδε adv., *here, in this place.*
ἔνθεν adv., *hence, from this place.*
ἐνθυμέομαι *I meditate upon, reflect upon.*
ἐνθύμησις, εως, ἡ *inward thought, meditation;* plur. *thoughts.*
ἔνι, ἐνί Ionic form of ἐν), *is in (among);* οὐκ ἔνι, *there is* (or *can be*) *no room for.*
ἐνιαυτός, οῦ, ὁ *a year.*
ἔνιξα aor. act. → νίπτω.
ἐνίστημι only intrans., *I impend, am at hand, am present;* perf. part. ἐνεστηκώς (ἐνεστώς) as adj., *present.*
ἐνισχύω *I strengthen within, I fill with strength.*
ἐνκ- see ἐγκ-
ἐννέα *nine.*
ἐννεύω *I make a sign to by nodding.*
ἔννοια, ας, ἡ (*intelligence, thought*), *intention, purpose.*
ἔννομος, ον (1) *legal, statutory, duly constituted,* Acts 19:39; (2) *under the law, obedient to the law,* 1 Cor 9:21.
ἔννυχος, ον *in the night;* neut. plur. ἔννυχα as adv., *at night.*
ἐνοικέω *I dwell in, am settled (stationary) in.*
ἐνορκίζω w. double acc. *I adjure* some one *by, I solemnly appeal to* some one *by* (a strengthened ὁρκίζω).
ἑνότης, ητος, ἡ *oneness, unity.*
ἐνοχλέω *I disturb, torment* (Heb 12:15 is from the LXX, where ἐνοχλῇ appears to be a corruption for ἐν χολῇ, *in gall*).
ἔνοχος, ον *involved in,* hence, *liable,* generally w. dat. (or gen.) of the punishment.
ἐνπ- see ἐμπ-
ἐνστήσομαι fut. mid. → ἐνίστημι.
ἔνταλμα, ατος, τό *an injunction, ordinance.*
ἐνταφιάζω *I embalm, prepare for burial.*
ἐνταφιασμός, οῦ, ὁ *embalming, preparation* of corpse *for burial.*
ἐντέλλομαι *I give orders (injunctions, instructions, commands).*
ἐντελοῦμαι fut. mid. → ἐντέλλομαι.
ἐντέταλμαι perf. mid./pas. → ἐντέλλομαι.
ἐντεῦθεν adv., (1) *hence, from this place;* (2) ἐντεῦθεν καὶ ἐντεῦθεν, *on this side and on that,* cf. Rev 22:2.
ἔντευξις, εως, ἡ (lit. *approaching* the king, hence a technical term), *a petition.*
ἔντιμος, ον (*held precious*), hence, (1) *precious;* (2) *honored, honorable* in rank, etc., Luke 14:8.
ἐντολή, ῆς, ἡ *an ordinance, injunction, command.*
ἐντόπιος, α, ον *belonging to the place, native, resident.*
ἐντός prep. w. gen., *within, inside* (so also Luke 17:21); τὸ ἐντός, *the inside.*
ἐντραπήσομαι fut. pas. → ἐντρέπω.
ἐντρέπω (1) *I turn to confusion, put to shame,* e.g., 1 Cor 4:14; 2 Thess 3:14; Titus 2:8; (2) mid. w. acc.,

meaning *I reverence,* e.g., Mark 12:6; Heb 12:9.
ἐντρέφω *I nourish (sustain) on.*
ἔντρομος, ον *trembling.*
ἐντροπή, ῆς, ἡ *shame* (from ἐντρέπω).
ἐντρυφάω *I revel (in).*
ἐντυγχάνω (1) *I meet, encounter;* hence, (2) *I call (upon), I make a petition, I make suit, supplication,* cf. ἔντευξις.
ἐντυλίσσω *I wrap up, roll round, envelop.*
ἐντυπόω *I engrave.*
ἐνυβρίζω *I insult, outrage.*
ἔνυξα aor. act. → νύσσω.
ἐνυπνιάζομαι *I dream (see visions)* in my sleep.
ἐνύπνιον, ου, τό *a dream, vision.*
ἐνφ- see ἐμφ-
ἐνών pres. part. → ἔνειμι.
ἐνώπιον prep. w. gen., (1) *before the face of, in the presence of;* (2) *in the eyes of* (vernacular).
Ἐνώς, ὁ *Enos,* son of Seth, and father of Cainam [Heb.].
ἐνωτίζομαι *I take into my ear, give ear to* (from ἐν and οὖς).
Ἑνώχ, (Ἐνώχ, Ἐνώκ), ὁ *Enoch,* son of Jaret and father of Mathusala [Heb.]; Jude 14 refers to the apocryphal *Book of Enoch.*
ἐξ see ἐκ.
ἕξ *six.*
ἐξαγγέλλω *I announce publicly, proclaim.*
ἐξαγοράζω (1) *I buy out, buy away from, ransom;* (2) mid., *I purchase out, buy, redeem.*
ἐξάγω *I lead out,* sometimes to death, execution.
ἐξαιρέω (1) *I take out, remove;* (2) sometimes (mid.) *I choose,* sometimes *I rescue.*
ἐξαίρω *I remove.*
ἐξαιτέομαι (1) *I beg earnestly for;* (2) aor. = *I have procured to be given up to me.*
ἐξαίφνης (ἐξέφνης) adv., *suddenly.*
ἐξακολουθέω *I follow closely, adhere to.*
ἑξακόσιοι, αι, α *six hundred.*
ἐξαλείφω *I wipe away, obliterate.*
ἐξάλλομαι *I leap up* (for joy).
ἐξανάστασις, εως, ἡ *rising up and out, resurrection.*
ἐξανατέλλω *I rise (spring) up out* (of the ground).
ἐξανέστην aor. act. → ἐξανίστημι.
ἐξανέστησα aor. act. → ἐξανίστημι.
ἐξανίστημι (1) trans., *I raise up, cause to grow;* (2) intrans., *I rise up.*
ἐξαπατάω *I deceive.*
ἐξαπεστάλην aor. pas. → ἐξαποστέλλω.
ἐξαπέστειλα aor. act. → ἐξαποστέλλω.
ἐξάπινα adv., *suddenly.*
ἐξαπορέομαι *I am at my wits' end, I despair;* w. gen. *about,* 2 Cor 1:8.
ἐξαποστέλλω *I send away out, I send forth* (a person qualified for a task).
ἐξαποστελῶ fut. act. → ἐξαποστέλλω.
ἐξαρτίζω (1) *I fit up, equip, furnish, supply,* 2 Tim 3:17; (2) *I accomplish, finish,* Acts 21:5.
ἐξαστράπτω *I flash forth like lightning.*
ἐξαυτῆς adv., *immediately* (= ἐξ αὐτῆς τῆς ὥρας).
ἐξέβαλον aor. act. → ἐκβάλλω.
ἐξέβην aor. act. → ἐκβαίνω.
ἐξεβλήθην aor. pas. → ἐκβάλλω.
ἐξεγείρω *I raise up, arouse.*
ἐξεγερῶ fut. act. → ἐξεγείρω.
ἐξεδόμην aor. mid. → ἐκδίδομαι.
ἐξεῖλον aor. act. → ἐξαιρέω.
ἔξειμι *I go out (away), depart* (orig., *I shall go out*).
ἐξεκαύθην aor. pas. → ἐκκαίομαι.
ἐξεκόπην aor. pas. → ἐκκόπτω.
ἔξελε aor. act. imper. → ἐξαιρέω.
ἐξελέξω aor. mid. 2 sing. → ἐκλέγομαι.

ἐξελέσθαι aor. mid. infin. → ἐξαιρέω.
ἐξελεύσομαι fut. mid. → ἐξέρχομαι.
ἐξελήλυθα perf. act. → ἐξέρχομαι.
ἐξέλκω *I entice* (lit. *I draw out* of the right place, or *I draw aside* out of the right way).
ἐξέμαξα aor. act. → ἐκμάσσω.
ἐξενεγκεῖν aor. act. infin. → ἐκφέρω.
ἐξέπεσον aor. act. → ἐκπίπτω.
ἐξεπέτασα aor. act. → ἐκπετάννυμι.
ἐξεπλάγην aor. pas. → ἐκπλήσσομαι.
ἐξέπλευσα aor. act. → ἐκπλέω.
ἐξέπνευσα aor. act. → ἐκπνέω.
ἐξέραμα, ατος, τό *vomit, purge.*
ἐξεραυνάω (ἐξερευνάω) *I search diligently, I examine carefully (minutely).*
ἐξέρχομαι *I go out.*
ἐξεστακέναι perf. act. infin. → ἐξίστημι.
ἐξέστην aor. act. → ἐξίστημι.
ἐξέστησα aor. act. → ἐξίστημι.
ἔξεστι(ν) impers. *it is permitted (allowed),* sometimes followed by acc. + infin.; ἐξόν (ἐστιν) = ἔξεστιν, the ἔστιν being understood in Acts 2:29; 2 Cor 12:4.
ἐξέστραμμαι perf. mid./pas. → ἐκστρέφομαι.
ἐξετάζω (indicates precise and careful inquiry), *I examine, question, inquire at.*
ἐξετέθην aor. pas. → ἐκτίθημι.
ἐξέτεινα aor. act. → ἐκτείνω.
ἐξετράπην aor. pas. → ἐκτρέπομαι.
ἐξέφυγον aor. act. → ἐκφεύγω.
ἐξέχεα aor. act. → ἐκχέω.
ἐξεχύθην aor. pas. → ἐκχέω.
ἐξέωσαι aor. act. infin. → ἐξωθέω.
ἐξήγαγον aor. act. → ἐξάγω.
ἐξήγγειλα aor. act. → ἐξαγγέλλω.
ἐξήγειρα aor. act. → ἐξεγείρω.
ἐξηγέομαι (1) *(I interpret) I relate, expound, explain;* (2) *make declaration* (John 1:18).
ἐξῄεσαν imperf. 3 plur. → ἔξειμι.
ἑξήκοντα *sixty.*
ἐξῆλθον aor. act. → ἐξέρχομαι.
ἐξήνεγκα aor. act. → ἐκφέρω.
ἐξῆρα aor. act. → ἐξαίρω.
ἐξήραμμαι perf. mid./pas. → ξηραίνω.
ἐξήρανα aor. act. → ξηραίνω.
ἐξηράνθην aor. pas. → ξηραίνω.
ἑξῆς adv., *next in order;* ἡ ἑξῆς (understand ἡμέρα), *the next day, the following day;* τῷ ἑξῆς (Luke 7:11, var.), perhaps = τῷ ἑξῆς χρόνῳ, *at the period immediately following.*
ἐξῃτησάμην aor. mid. → ἐξαιτέομαι.
ἐξηχέω *I sound out (forth),* referring either to the clearness or to the loudness of the sound.
ἐξιέναι pres. infin. → ἔξειμι.
ἕξις, εως, ἡ *condition, state,* especially *good condition* of body or soul.
ἐξίστημι (ἐξιστάνω, ἐξιστάω) (lit. *I remove from a standing position*), (1) trans. (including ἐξέστακα), *I astonish, amaze;* (2) intrans., *I am astonished, amazed;* (3) *I am out of my mind, I am mad,* Mark 3:21; 2 Cor 5:13.
ἐξισχύω *I have strength for* (a difficult task).
ἐξιών pres. part. → ἔξειμι.
ἔξοδος, ου, ἡ (1) *going out, departure* from a place; (2) *death,* Luke 9:31; 2 Pet 1:15.
ἐξοίσω fut. act. → ἐκφέρω.
ἐξολεθρεύω (ἐξολοθρεύω) *I destroy utterly, annihilate, exterminate.*
ἐξομολογέω (1) *I consent fully, agree out and out,* Luke 22:6; (2) *I confess, admit, acknowledge* (cf. the early Hellenistic sense of the mid., *I acknowledge* a debt); (3) in certain

passages there is a difficulty as to the sense: in Matt 11:25 (Luke 10:21) the Vulgate (w. the Sahidic) renders by *confiteor,* but modern scholars prefer either *I give thanks* or *I praise.*

ἐξόν pres. act. part. → ἔξεστι.

ἐξορκίζω *I exorcise, cast out by appeal to a god.*

ἐξορκιστής, οῦ, ὁ *an exorcist, a caster out of evil spirits* by the use of names or spells.

ἐξορύσσω (1) *I dig out;* (2) hence, *I open up;* (3) *I gouge,* Gal 4:15.

ἐξουδενέω (ἐξουδενόω) see ἐξουθενέω.

ἐξουθενέω (ἐξουθενόω) *I set at naught, ignore, despise.*

ἐξουσία, ας, ἡ (1) *power, authority, weight,* especially *moral authority, influence;* in 1 Cor 11:10 the *authority* which the wearing of the veil gives the woman, making her sacrosanct; w. gen. indicates *over* any one; (2) in a quasipersonal sense, derived from later Judaism, of *a spiritual power,* 1 Pet 3:22, and hence of *an earthly power* (e.g., Luke 12:11 and often, in combination w. ἀρχή).

ἐξουσιάζω *I exercise (wield) power (authority),* w. gen., *over;* pas. 1 Cor 6:12, *I am ruled.*

ἐξουσιαστικός, ή, όν *authoritative* (Mark 1:27, var.).

ἐξοχή, ῆς, ἡ *projection, prominence;* οἱ κατ' ἐξοχήν, *the prominent persons, the chief men.*

ἐξυπνίζω *I wake* out of sleep.

ἔξυπνος, ον *awake* out of sleep.

ἔξω (1) prep. w. gen., *outside;* (2) adv., *without, outside;* in ὁ ἔξω, etc. the adv. is equivalent to an adj., τὰς ἔξω πόλλεις, *foreign cities,* Acts 26:11, ὁ ἔξω ἄνθρωπος, *the outer (physical) nature,* 2 Cor 4:16, especially οἱ ἔξω, *the outsiders, the non-Christians.*

ἕξω fut. act. → ἔχω.

ἔξωθεν (1) prep. w. gen., *outside* (Mark 7:15; Rev 11:2; 14:20, etc.); (2) adv., *from outside, from without;* τὸ ἔξωθεν, *the outside,* etc., οἱ ἔξωθεν = οἱ ἔξω; equivalent to ἔξω, both as adv. and as prep.

ἐξωθέω *I push out, thrust out;* εἰς αἰγιαλὸν ἐξῶσαι, *to drive the ship upon the beach,* Acts 27:39.

ἐξώτερος, α, ον *outmost.*

ἔοικα *I am like, resemble.*

ἑόρακα perf. act. → ὁράω.

ἑορτάζω *I take part in a festival, keep a feast* (allegorically).

ἑορτή, ῆς, ἡ *a festival, feast,* periodically recurring; ποιεῖν ἑορτήν, Acts 18:21 = ἑορτάζειν.

ἐπαγαγεῖν aor. act. infin. → ἐπάγω.

ἐπαγγελία, ας, ἡ *a promise;* cf. τέκνον (2).

ἐπαγγέλλομαι (1) *I promise;* (2) *I profess,* 1 Tim 2:10; 6:21.

ἐπάγγελμα, ατος, τό *a promise.*

ἐπάγω *I bring upon.*

ἐπαγωνίζομαι *I contend for.*

ἔπαθον aor. act. → πάσχω.

ἐπαθροίζομαι *I crowd upon* (some one), *press around.*

Ἐπαίνετος, ου, ὁ *Epaenetus,* a Christian in Rome.

ἐπαινέω *I praise, commend.*

ἔπαινος, ου, ὁ *praise.*

ἐπαίρω *I raise, lift up.*

ἐπαισχύνομαι *I am ashamed of.*

ἐπαιτέω *I beg, am a beggar.*

ἐπακολουθέω *I follow close after, I accompany, dog; I promote,* 1 Tim 5:10; hence, *I endorse* Mark 16:20.

ἐπακούω *I listen to, hear.*

ἐπακροάομαι *I listen to, hearken to.*

ἐπάν *whenever.*

ἐπαναγαγεῖν aor. act. infin. → ἐπανάγω.

ἐπάναγκες adv. used as adj., *necessary, inevitable, obligatory.*

ἐπανάγω (1) nautical, *I put out* (from the shore), (lit. *I take up* a

ship *on to* the high seas); (2) *I go up*, possibly *I go up again, return.*
ἐπαναμιμνῄσκω *I remind*, possibly *I remind again.*
ἐπαναπαήσομαι fut. pas. → ἐπαναπαύομαι.
ἐπαναπαύομαι *I rest upon.*
ἐπανελθεῖν aor. act. infin. → ἐπανέρχομαι.
ἐπανέρχομαι *I return.*
ἐπανίστημι intrans., *I rise against.*
ἐπανόρθωσις, εως, ἡ *setting straight (right) again.*
ἐπάνω (1) adv., *on the top, above;* (2) prep. w. gen., *on the top of, above, over, on;* met. of rule, *over*, Luke 19:17, etc.; *above, more than*, Mark 14:5; 1 Cor 15:6.
ἐπάξας aor. act. part. → ἐπάγω.
ἐπᾶραι aor. act. infin. → ἐπαίρω.
ἐπάρας aor. act. part. → ἐπαίρω.
ἐπάρατος, ον *accursed, cursed.*
ἐπαρκέω *I do service, render help.*
ἐπαρχεία, ας, ἡ *sphere of duty, province.*
ἐπάρχειος, ον *belonging to the province;* τῇ ἐπαρχείῳ (understand ἐξουσίᾳ), *the power over the province, the province* (a var. in Acts 25:1).
ἔπαυλις, εως, ἡ *a farm, estate.*
ἐπαύριον adv., *tomorrow.*
Ἐπαφρᾶς, ᾶ, ὁ *Epaphras, Epaphroditus*, a Colossian Christian, in captivity w. Paul in Rome (the pet form of Ἐπαφρόδιτος).
ἐπαφρίζω *I foam out* (a metaphor from the seaweed and refuse borne on the crest of waves).
Ἐπαφρόδιτος, ου, ὁ see Ἐπαφρᾶς.
ἐπέβαλον aor. act. → ἐπιβάλλω.
ἐπέβην aor. act. → ἐπιβαίνω.
ἐπεγείρω *I arouse, stimulate,*
ἐπέγνωκα perf. act. → ἐπιγινώσκω.
ἐπέγνων aor. act. → ἐπιγινώσκω.
ἐπεγνώσθην aor. pas. → ἐπιγινώσκω.
ἐπέδειξα aor. act. → ἐπιδείκνυμι.
ἐπεδόθην aor. pas. → ἐπιδίδωμι.
ἐπέδωκα aor. act. → ἐπιδίδωμι.
ἐπεθέμην aor. mid. → ἐπιτίθημι.
ἐπέθηκα aor. act. → ἐπιτίθημι.
ἐπεί (1) *after*, Luke 7:1 (var.), Acts 13:46 (var.); (2) *for, since;* (3) *otherwise*, Rom 11:6, 22; 1 Cor 5:10, etc.
ἐπειδή (1) *when*, Luke 7:1; (2) *since.*
ἐπειδήπερ *since.*
ἐπεῖδον *I looked upon, regarded.* aor. act. → ἐφοράω.
ἔπειμι in the part. ἐπιοῦσα, *coming on, next;* τῇ ἐπιούσῃ (understand ἡμέρᾳ), *next day.*
ἐπείπερ *since indeed*, var. in Rom 3:30.
ἐπειράσθην aor. pas. → πειράζω.
ἔπεισα aor. act. → πείθω.
ἐπεισαγωγή, ῆς, ἡ *bringing in, introduction, importation.*
ἐπεισελεύσομαι fut. mid. → ἐπεισέρχομαι.
ἐπεισέρχομαι *I come (in) upon.*
ἐπείσθην aor. pas. → πείθω.
ἔπειτα adv., *then, thereafter, afterwards.*
ἐπέκειλα aor. act. → ἐπικέλλω.
ἐπέκεινα prep. w. gen., *beyond.*
ἐπεκεκλήμην plup. mid./pas. → ἐπικαλέω.
ἐπεκλήθην aor. pas. → ἐπικαλέω.
ἐπεκτείνομαι *I strain after.*
ἐπελαβόμην aor. mid. → ἐπιλαμβάνομαι.
ἐπελαθόμην aor. mid. → ἐπιλανθάνομαι.
ἐπέμεινα aor. act. → ἐπιμένω.
ἐπενδύομαι *I put on* (as a garment).
ἐπενδύτης, ου, ὁ *a coat, outer wrap.*
ἐπενεγκεῖν aor. act. infin. → ἐπιφέρω.
ἐπέπεσον aor. act. → ἐπιπίπτω.
ἐπεποίθειν plup. act. → πείθω.
ἐπέρχομαι *I come upon*, sometimes with hostility.
ἐπερωτάω = ἐρωτάω simply, *I ask, question.*

ἐπερώτημα, ατος, τό = ἐρώτημα, *a request.*
ἔπεσα aor. act. → πίπτω.
ἐπέστειλα aor. act. → ἐπιστέλλω.
ἐπέστην aor. act. → ἐφίστημι.
ἐπεστράφην aor. pas. → ἐπιστρέφω.
ἐπέστρεψα aor. act. → ἐπιστρέφω.
ἐπέσχον aor. act. → ἐπέχω.
ἐπετράπην aor. pas. → ἐπιτρέπω.
ἐπέτυχον aor. act. → ἐπιτυγχάνω.
ἐπεφάνην aor. pas. → ἐπιφαίνω.
ἐπέχω (1) trans., *I hold forth;* (2) intrans. (νοῦν being understood), *I mark, pay attention (heed), note,* Acts 3:5; 1 Tim 4:16: *I delay,* Acts 19:22.
ἐπηγγειλάμην aor. mid. → ἐπαγγέλλομαι.
ἐπήγγελμαι perf. mid./pas. → ἐπαγγέλλομαι.
ἐπήγειρα aor. act. → ἐπεγείρω.
ἐπῆλθον aor. act. → ἐπέρχομαι.
ἐπῄνεσα aor. act. → ἐπαινέω.
ἔπηξα aor. act. → πήγνυμι.
ἐπῆρα aor. act. → ἐπαίρω.
ἐπηρεάζω *I insult, treat wrongfully, molest.*
ἐπήρθην aor. pas. → ἐπαίρω.
ἐπί prep., (1) w. gen. locally, *on, upon;* and so met. of that *on* which anything rests, e.g., ἐπ' ἀληθείας, *in truth;* of authority *over,* e.g., Matt 24:45; *concerning,* Gal 3:16; *in presence of,* e.g., Matt 28:14; *at, in,* Mark 12:26; *in (at) the time (period) of,* e.g., Mark 2:26; (2) w. dat. *on, upon; near,* e.g., Matt 24:33; *on the basis (ground) of,* e.g., Matt 4:4; *on account of,* e.g., Luke 5:5, ἐφ' ᾧ = (ἐπὶ τούτῳ, ὅ, τι), *in view of the fact that; over* (cf. under [1]), Luke 12:44; *against,* Luke 12:52; *in addition to,* e.g., 2 Cor 7:13; *in, at,* ἐπὶ τούτῳ, *meantime,* John 4:27; *for, with a view to,* cf. Acts 5:35; (3) w. acc. locally, *on, upon,* generally after verbs indicating motion, but afterwards more widely used, both lit. and met., ἐπὶ τὸ αὐτό, *in the same place, together, in all,* cf. Acts 1:15; 2:47; *near, to, towards* (after word expressing motion, and then more widely), both lit. and met.; *against; in addition to* (cf. under [2]), Phil 2:27; of number or degree attained, *as far as,* e.g., ἐπὶ πλεῖον, ἐφ' ὅσον; of charge, rule, or power *over; concerning,* e.g., Luke 23:28; *on account of, with a view to,* Mark 15:24; John 19:24; of time, *for, during,* e.g., Luke 4:25; of time, *about,* e.g., Luke 10:35.
ἐπιβαίνω (1) *I set foot on, I step on;* (2) *I mount* (a horse), *board* (a vessel).
ἐπιβάλλω (1) *I throw upon, cast over,* 1 Cor 7:35; Rev 18:19 (var.); (2) *I place upon;* (3) *I lay,* w. τήν χεῖρα (τὰς χεῖρας), either w. innocent, or w. hostile, intent; (4) intrans., *I strike upon,* Mark 4:37; (5) intrans., τὸ ἐπιβάλλον μέρος, *the share that falls to (belongs to) one,* Luke 15:12; (6) intrans., ἐπιβαλὼν ἔκλαιεν, *he set to and wept,* Mark 14:72.
ἐπιβαλῶ fut. act. → ἐπιβάλλω.
ἐπιβαρέω *I put a burden on, burden.*
ἐπιβάς aor. act. part. → ἐπιβαίνω.
ἐπιβέβηκα perf. act. → ἐπιβαίνω.
ἐπιβιβάζω *I place upon* (a horse, mule).
ἐπιβλέπω *I look with favor on.*
ἐπίβλημα, ατος, τό *something put on, a patch.*
ἐπιβουλή, ῆς, ἡ *a plot.*
ἐπιγαμβρεύω *I take to wife after.*
ἐπίγειος, ον (1) *on the earth, belonging to the earth* (as opposed to the sky); (2) in a spiritual sense, *belonging to the earthly sphere, earthly* (as opposed to heavenly); opp. to ἐπουράνιος in both senses.
ἐπιγίνομαι *I come on, supervene.*

ἐπιγινώσκω *I come to know* by directing my attention to (ἐπί) him or it, *I perceive, discern, recognize;* aor. *I found out.*
ἐπίγνωσις, εως, ἡ *knowledge* of a particular point (directed towards a particular object); *perception, discernment, recognition; intuition.*
ἐπιγνώσομαι fut. mid. → ἐπιγινώσκω.
ἐπιγραφή, ῆς, ἡ *an inscription.*
ἐπιγράφω *I write upon, inscribe.*
ἔπιδε aor. act. imper. → ἐφοράω.
ἐπιδείκνυμι *I show, display, point out, indicate; I prove, demonstrate,* Acts 18:28; Heb 6:17.
ἐπιδέχομαι *I welcome.*
ἐπιδημέω *I am resident* (temporarily, in a foreign city).
ἐπιδιατάσσομαι *I make an additional testamentary disposition, I furnish with additions.*
ἐπιδίδωμι (1) trans., *I hand in;* (2) intrans., *I give way* (to the wind), Acts 27:15.
ἐπιδιορθόω *I put besides into a state of order, I put in order.*
ἐπιδύω *I sink, set.*
ἐπιείκεια, ας, ἡ *considerateness, forbearance, fairness.*
ἐπιεικής, ές *forbearing, fair, reasonable.*
ἐπιζητέω *I seek after, search for, make inquiries about.*
ἐπιθανάτιος, ον *at the point of death, doomed to death.*
ἐπιθεῖναι aor. act. infin. → ἐπιτίθημι.
ἐπιθείς aor. act. part. → ἐπιτίθημι.
ἐπίθεσις, εως, ἡ *laying on.*
ἐπιθήσω fut. act. → ἐπιτίθημι.
ἐπιθυμέω *I desire, long;* ἐπιθυμίᾳ ἐπιθυμεῖν, Hebraistic, *to long eagerly,* Luke 22:15.
ἐπιθυμητής, οῦ, ὁ *a longer after, luster after.*
ἐπιθυμία, ας, ἡ *eager (passionate) desire, passion;* see ἐπιθυμέω.
ἐπιθῶ aor. act. subj. → ἐπιτίθημι.
ἐπικαθίζω *I sit.*
ἐπικαλέω (1) *I call (name) by a supplementary (additional, alternative) name;* (2) mid. *I call upon, appeal to, address.*
ἐπικάλυμμα, ατος, τό *a covering, pretext.*
ἐπικαλύπτω *I put a cover on, cover up.*
ἐπικατάρατος, ον *on whom a curse has been invoked, accursed.*
ἐπίκειμαι (1) w. dat. or w. ἐπί + dat. *I am placed upon, am laid upon, lie upon, am imposed; I press upon,* Luke 5:1; (2) absol. *I press hard,* Acts 27:20; *I am insistent, insist,* Luke 23:23.
ἐπικέκλημαι perf. mid./pas. → ἐπικαλέω.
ἐπικέλλω *I beach, run aground, drive* a ship *on to.*
Ἐπικούρειος, ου, ὁ *an Epicurean,* one who holds the tenets of Epicurus (341–270 B.C.).
ἐπικουρία, ας, ἡ *succor* (against foes), *help.*
ἐπικράνθην aor. pas. → πικραίνω.
ἐπικρίνω *I give decision, decide.*
ἐπιλαμβάνομαι *I lay hold of, take hold of, seize* (sometimes with beneficent, sometimes with hostile, intent).
ἐπιλανθάνομαι *I forget.*
ἐπιλέγομαι (1) mid. *I choose for myself,* Acts 15:40; (2) pas. *I am named.*
ἐπιλείπω *I fail, leave behind.*
ἐπιλείχω *I lick.*
ἐπιλέλησμαι perf. mid./pas. → ἐπιλανθάνομαι.
ἐπιλησμονή, ῆς, ἡ *forgetting,* in Jas 1:25 a Hebraistic gen. = *that forgets.*
ἐπίλοιπος, ον *remaining, i.e., left over.*
ἐπίλυσις, εως, ἡ *solution, explanation, interpretation.*

ἐπιλύω *I explain.*
ἐπιμαρτυρέω *I call to witness.*
ἐπιμέλεια, ας, ἡ *care, attention.*
ἐπιμελέομαι *I care for, attend to.*
ἐπιμελῶς adv., *carefully, attentively.*
ἐπιμένω (1) *I remain, tarry;* (2) w. dat. *I remain in, persist in.*
ἐπινεύω *I consent.*
ἐπίνοια, ας, ἡ *thought.*
ἔπιον aor. act. → πίνω.
ἐπιορκέω (ἐφιορκέω) *I take an oath, swear.*
ἐπίορκος, ου, ὁ *perjuring, a perjurer.*
ἐπιούσιος, ον *belonging to the morrow* (from ἡ ἐπιοῦσα [ἡμέρα]).
ἐπιπέπτωκα perf. act. → ἐπιπίπτω.
ἐπιπίπτω *I fall upon; I press upon,* Mark 3:10.
ἐπιπλήσσω *I reprove.*
ἐπιποθέω *I long for, strain after, desire greatly.*
ἐπιπόθησις, εως, ἡ *eager longing (desire).*
ἐπιπόθητος, ον *longed for, missed.*
ἐπιποθία, ας, ἡ *longing, eager desire.*
ἐπιπορεύομαι *I journey (to).*
ἐπι(ρ)ράπτω *I sew (on).*
ἐπι(ρ)ρίπτω *I throw (cast upon).*
ἐπισείω *urge on, incite* (a crowd).
ἐπίσημος, ον *notable, conspicuous.*
ἐπισιτισμός, οῦ, ὁ *provision, nourishment, food.*
ἐπισκέπτομαι (1) *I look out,* Acts 6:3; (2) *I visit.*
ἐπισκευάζομαι *I equip* (horses).
ἐπισκηνόω *I raise a tent (over).*
ἐπισκιάζω *I overshadow, envelop.*
ἐπισκοπέω (ἐπισκοπεύω) *I exercise oversight (care).*
ἐπισκοπή, ῆς, ἡ (1) *visitation* (of judgment), Luke 19:44; 1 Pet 2:12; (2) *oversight, supervision.*
ἐπίσκοπος, ου, ὁ *overseer, supervisor, ruler,* (used as an official title in civil life), especially used w. reference to the supervising function exercised by an elder or presbyter of a church or congregation, and therefore (at first) practically synonymous w. πρεσβύτερος.
ἐπισπάω mid. *I undo the effects of circumcision on myself* (lit. *I draw over*).
ἐπισπείρω *I sow above (over), I replant.*
ἐπίσταμαι *I know, understand.*
ἐπιστάς aor. act. part. → ἐφίστημι.
ἐπίστασις, εως, ἡ *plotting (conspiring) against.*
ἐπιστάτης, ου, ὁ *master, teacher.*
ἐπιστέλλω *I enjoin,* generally *in writing, I write.*
ἐπίστηθι aor. act. imper. → ἐφίστημι.
ἐπιστήμων, ον gen. **ονος** *knowing* by experience (personal acquaintance).
ἐπιστηρίζω *I prop up, uphold, support, confirm.*
ἐπιστολή, ῆς, ἡ *a letter, dispatch.*
ἐπιστομίζω *I muzzle, silence.*
ἐπιστρέφω (1) trans., *I turn (back) to (towards);* (2) intrans., *I turn (back* to [towards]); *I come to myself,* Luke 22:32.
ἐπιστροφή, ῆς, ἡ *a turning (to God).*
ἐπισυναγαγεῖν aor. act. infin. → ἐπισυνάγω.
ἐπισυνάγω *I collect, gather together.*
ἐπισυναγωγή, ῆς, ἡ *gathering (collecting) together, assembling.*
ἐπισυνάξαι aor. act. infin. → ἐπισυνάγω.
ἐπισυντρέχω *I run together to (towards).*
ἐπισφαλής, ές *dangerous.*
ἐπισχύω *I persist, insist.*
ἐπισωρεύω *I heap up.*
ἐπιταγή, ῆς, ἡ *instruction, command, order, authority* (often of a god).
ἐπιτάσσω *I give order, command.*

ἐπιτελέω *I complete, accomplish, perfect.*
ἐπιτήδειος, α, ον *necessary.*
ἐπιτίθημι *I place upon, lay on;* w. ὄνομα, *I add, give in addition.*
ἐπιτιμάω (1) *I rebuke, chide, censure;* (2) w. ἵνα, *I warn.*
ἐπιτιμία, ας, ἡ *punishment.*
ἐπιτρέπω *I allow, permit.*
ἐπιτροπεύω *I act as* ἐπίτροπος *(procurator) over,* var. Luke 3:1.
ἐπιτροπή, ῆς, ἡ *commission.*
ἐπίτροπος, ου, ὁ (1) (procurator) *a steward;* (2) (tutor) *a guardian* (appointed for an "infant" [under 14 perhaps] by the father or by a magistrate), Gal 4:2.
ἐπιτυγχάνω *I attain, obtain.*
ἐπιφαίνω *I appear* (as of a light in the heavens [cf. Acts 27:20] or from the heavens).
ἐπιφᾶναι aor. act. infin. → ἐπιφαίνω.
ἐπιφάνεια, ας, ἡ *appearing, manifestation* (of a conspicuous intervention from the sky on behalf of a worshipper).
ἐπιφανής, ές *manifest.*
ἐπιφαύσκω *I shine upon.*
ἐπιφαύσω fut. act. → ἐπιφαύσκω.
ἐπιφέρω *I bring forward (against).*
ἐπιφωνέω *I call out, shout;* w. dat. *against,* Acts 22:24.
ἐπιφώσκω *I draw near, dawn,* of the next day.
ἐπιχειρέω *I take in hand, I attempt.*
ἐπιχέω *I pour on.*
ἐπιχορηγέω *I supply, provide* (perhaps lavishly).
ἐπιχορηγία, ας, ἡ *supply, provision, equipment.*
ἐπιχρίω *I besmear, anoint.*
ἐπλάσθην aor. pas. → πλάσσω.
ἐπλήγην aor. pas. → πλήσσω.
ἔπλησα aor. act. → πίμπλημι.
ἐπλήσθην aor. pas. → πίμπλημι.
ἔπνευσα aor. act. → πνέω.
ἐποικοδομέω *I build upon (above)* a foundation.
ἐπονομάζω *I name, impose a name on.*
ἐποπτεύω *I am an eyewitness of, behold.*
ἐπόπτης, ου, ὁ *an eyewitness* (orig. of one initiated into the mysteries, but also found of *a surveyor, supervisor*).
ἔπος, ους, τό *a word;* ὡς ἔπος εἰπεῖν (a literary phrase), *one might almost say,* modifying a statement, Heb 7:9.
ἐπουράνιος, ον *heavenly, in heaven;* ἐν τοῖς ἐπουρανίοις, *in the heavenly sphere,* the sphere of spiritual activities (opp. ἐπίγειος).
ἐπράθην aor. pas. → πιπράσκω.
ἐπρίσθην aor. pas. → πρίζω.
ἑπτά *seven;* οἱ ἑπτά, *the seven* ("deacons" of Acts 6:3–6).
ἑπτάκις adv., *seven times;* ἑπτάκις τῆς ἡμέρας, *seven times in the day.*
ἑπτακισχίλιοι, αι, α *seven thousand.*
ἑπταπλασίων, ον gen. **ονος** *sevenfold.*
ἐπυθόμην aor. mid. → πυνθάνομαι.
Ἔραστος, ου, ὁ *Erastus,* steward of Corinth, a Christian.
ἐραυνάω *I search;* = ἐξεραυνάω, 1 Pet 1:11; (a form of ἐρευνάω not known before first c. A.D.).
ἐργάζομαι (1) *I am at work, I work;* (2) trans., *I produce by work, put in force, give operation to, realize,* e.g., Matt 7:23; w. cog. acc. ἔργον, ἔργα, Matt 26:10, etc.; w. acc. βρῶσιν, *I work for,* John 6:27.
ἐργασία, ας, ἡ *working, activity, work, service, trade, business, gains of business;* δὸς ἐργασίαν, *take pains to, see to it that you,* Luke 12:58; *performance, practice,* Eph 4:19.
ἐργάτης, ου, ὁ *a field laborer;* then, *a laborer, workman* in general.
ἔργον, ου, τό (1) *work, labor* (in

the physical, orig. in the agricultural, sphere); (2) moral *action, deed,* hence w. adjs. or gens. defining its character.

ἐρεθίζω *I stir up,* 2 Cor 9:2: *I arouse to anger, provoke,* Col 3:21.

ἐρείδω *I strike; I run aground* (of a ship).

ἐρεύγομαι *I utter, declare.* (lit. *I belch forth*)

ἐρημία, ας, ἡ *a desert place, a desert.*

ἔρημος, ου, ἡ adj., *desert;* hence, ἡ ἔρημος (understand χώρα), *the desert,* to the east and south of Palestine; of a person, *deserted, abandoned, desolate,* Gal 4:27.

ἐρημόω (1) *I make desolate, bring to desolation, destroy, waste;* (2) of a person, *I strip, rob.*

ἐρήμωσις, εως, ἡ *making into a desert, wasting, desolating, desolation.*

ἐρίζω *I strive.*

ἐριθεία, ας, ἡ *ambition, rivalry* (lit. the *seeking of followers and adherents by means of gifts, the seeking of followers*).

ἔριον, ου, τό *wool.*

ἔρις, ιδος, ἡ *strife.*

ἐρίφιον, ου, τό *a goat,* or *kid.*

ἔριφος, ου, ὁ *a goat.*

ἔριψα aor. act. → ῥίπτω.

Ἑρμᾶς, ᾶ, ὁ *Hermas,* a Roman Christian.

ἑρμηνεία, ας, ἡ *translation, interpretation.*

ἑρμηνευτής *translator, interpreter* (1 Cor 14:28, var.).

ἑρμηνεύω (1) *I translate;* (2) *I interpret* the meaning of, Luke 24:27 (var.).

Ἑρμῆς, οῦ, ὁ (1) *Hermes,* the messenger and herald of the Greek gods, or rather the corresponding Lycaonian deity; to him also corresponded the Lat. Mercurius, Acts 14:12; (2) *Hermes,* a Roman Christian.

Ἑρμογένης, ους, ὁ *Hermogenes,* a faithless Christian at Rome.

ἑρπετόν, οῦ, τό *a creeping creature, reptile,* especially *a serpent.*

ἔρραμαι perf. mid./pas. → ῥαίνω.

ἐρράντισμαι perf. mid./pas. → ῥαντίζω.

ἐρρέθην aor. pas. → λέγω.

ἔρρηξα aor. act. → ῥήγνυμι.

ἐρρίζωμαι perf. mid. → ῥιζόομαι.

ἔρριμμαι perf. mid./pas. → ῥίπτω.

ἔρριψα aor. act. → ῥίπτω.

ἐρρυσάμην aor. mid. → ῥύομαι.

ἐρρύσθην aor. pas. → ῥύομαι.

ἔρρωσθε perf. mid./pas. imper. 2 plur. → ῥώννυμι.

ἔρρωσο perf. mid./pas. imper. 2 sing. → ῥώννυμι.

ἐρυθρός, ά, όν *red.*

ἔρχομαι (1) *I go;* w. acc. of extent, ὁδόν; (2) *I come;* εἰς ἑαυτὸν ἐλθών, *having come to himself, having come to his right mind, "having reasoned with himself"* (Sahidic), Luke 15:17.

ἐρῶ fut. act. → λέγω. *I shall say;* w. acc. pers. ὑμᾶς εἴρηκα φίλους, *I have called you friends,* John 15:15, ἄρχοντα οὐκ ἐρεῖς κακῶς, *you shall not speak evilly of a leader,* Acts 23:5, cf. Rom 4:1 (var.); cf. εἶπον.

ἐρωτάω (1) *I ask* (a question), *I question;* (2) (= αἰτέω) *I request, make a request to, I pray.*

ἔσβεσα aor. act. → σβέννυμι.

ἐσήμανα aor. act. → σημαίνω.

ἐσθής, ῆτος, ἡ *clothing;* ἐσθήσεσι = ἔσθεσι, dat. plur. of ἐσθής.

ἐσθίω (ἔσθω) trans. and intrans., *I eat, I am eating; I take a meal;* aor. φαγεῖν, *to eat,* but in Rev 10:10 = καταφαγεῖν.

ἔσκυλμαι perf. mid./pas. → σκύλλω.

Ἐσλί (Ἐσλεί), ὁ *Esli (Eslei),* son of Naggai and father of Nahum [Heb.].

ἐσμυρνισμένος perf. mid./pas. part. → σμυρνίζω.

ἔσομαι fut. → εἰμί.

ἔσοπτρον, ου, τό *a mirror, looking*

glass (made of highly polished metal).

ἔσπαρμαι perf. mid./pas. → σπείρω.

ἑσπέρα, ας, ἡ *evening.*

ἑσπερινός *in the evening, belonging to the evening, evening* (Luke 12:38, var.).

Ἑσρώμ (Ἑσρών), ὁ *Hesrom, Hesron,* son of Phares, father of Aram [Heb.].

ἑσσόομαι *be worse off than, be inferior to* (2 Cor 12:13, var.).

ἐστάθην aor. pas. → ἵστημι.

ἑστάναι perf. act. infin. → ἵστημι.

ἕστηκα perf. act. → ἵστημι.

ἑστηκώς perf. act. part. → ἵστημι.

ἔστην aor. act. → ἵστημι.

ἔστησα aor. act. → ἵστημι.

ἐστράφην aor. pas. → στρέφω.

ἐστρωμένος perf. mid./pas. part. → στρώννυμι.

ἔστρωσα aor. act. → στρώννυμι.

ἔστω pres. imper. 3 sing. → εἰμί.

ἑστώς perf. act. part. → ἵστημι.

ἔστωσαν pres. imper. 3 plur. → εἰμί.

ἔσχατος, η, ον *last;* ἔσχατον, neut. acc. as adv., *at the last, finally;* ἐπ' ἐσχάτου, *at the end;* ἕως ἐσχάτου, *till the end.*

ἐσχάτως adv., ἐσχάτως ἔχειν, *to be at the extremity, to be "in extremis," to be at the last gasp.*

ἔσχηκα perf. act. → ἔχω.

ἔσχον aor. act. → ἔχω.

ἔσω adv., *within, inside,* w. verbs either of rest or of motion; ὁ ἔσω ἄνθρωπος, that part of man which is spiritual; οἱ ἔσω, *those within* (the church), *members of the church,* 1 Cor 5:12; prep. w. gen., *within, to within, inside,* Mark 15:16.

ἔσωθεν adv. (1) *from within, from inside;* (2) *within, inside;* τὸ ἔσωθεν, *the inner part, the inner element.*

ἐσώτερος, α, ον *inner;* τὸ ἐσώτερον, *the part that is within,* w. gen.

ἑταῖρος, ου, ὁ *companion, comrade.*

ἐταράχθην aor. pas. → ταράσσω.

ἐτάφην aor. pas. → θάπτω.

ἐτέθην aor. pas. → τίθημι.

ἔτεκον aor. act. → τίκτω.

ἑτερόγλωσσος, ον *speaking another language.*

ἑτεροδιδασκαλέω *I teach different things,* i.e., *different from the true* or *necessary teaching.*

ἑτεροζυγέω *I am yoked with one different from myself, unequally yoked.*

ἕτερος, α, ον (1) of two, *another, a second:* ἐν ἑτέρῳ (understand ψαλμῷ), Heb 5:6; ὁ ἕτερος, *the other, the second,* τῇ ἑτέρᾳ (understand ἡμέρᾳ), *on the second day,* Acts 20:15; 27:3; ἕτεροι, *others, another group;* (2) sometimes it does not differ from ἄλλος, being used of more than two, *other, different,* cf. Luke 8:6–8; 2 Cor 11:4; in Gal 1:6, 7 ἕτερος appears to mean *another of the same kind,* as contrasted w. ἄλλος, *another of a different kind.*

ἑτέρως adv., *differently.*

ἐτέχθην aor. pas. → τίκτω.

ἔτι adv. (1) of time, *still, yet; even now;* οὐκ ἔτι, *no longer,* and similarly w. other negatives; (2) of degree, *even; further, more, in addition.*

ἑτοιμάζω *I make ready, prepare.*

ἑτοιμασία, ας, ἡ (in LXX, *a stand, base,* but also) *readiness* (of bearer of good tidings).

ἕτοιμος, η, ον *ready, prepared;* ἐν ἑτοίμῳ ἔχοντες, *being ready,* 2 Cor 10:6, cf. ἑτοίμως.

ἑτοίμως adv., *readily;* ἑτοίμως ἔχειν, *to be ready.*

ἔτος (ἔτος), ους, τό *a year;* κατ' ἔτος (καθ' ἔτος), *annually;* ἀπὸ or ἐξ ἐτῶν followed by a number *(for),* lit. *from . . . years.*

ἐτύθην aor. pas. → θύω.

εὖ adv., *well;* as interj. *well done! bravo!*

Εὔα (Εὕα), ας, ἡ *Eva, Eve,* wife of Adam, the first man [Heb.].

εὐαγγελίζω *I bring good news, I preach good tidings,* normally mid., with or without an obj., expressing either the persons who receive the good news or the good news itself (the good news being sometimes expressed as a person, e.g., Acts 5:42).

εὐαγγέλιον, ου, τό *the good news* of the coming of the Messiah, *the gospel;* the gen. after it expresses sometimes the giver (God), sometimes the subj. (the Messiah, etc.), sometimes the human transmitter (an apostle).

εὐαγγελιστής, οῦ, ὁ *a missionary* (an occurrence on a pagan inscription = priest of Εὐάγγελος, i.e., of Ἑρμῆς, is found).

εὐαρεστέω *I give pleasure to, I please* (perhaps w. the added idea of *rendering good service to,* cf. ἀρέσκω).

εὐάρεστος, ον *well-pleasing* (especially to God).

εὐαρέστως adv., *in a well-pleasing way.*

Εὔβουλος, ου, ὁ *Eubulus,* a Christian with Paul in Rome.

εὖγε adv. interj., *well done! bravo!*

εὐγενής, ές (1) *of noble birth, of high birth;* (2) *noble* in nature, Acts 17:11.

εὐδία, ας, ἡ *fair weather, good weather.*

εὐδοκέω *I am well pleased,* w. acc. expressing *with,* Matt 12:18, etc.; *I think it good, am resolved* (a characteristic word of Jewish Gk.).

εὐδοκία, ας, ἡ (1) *goodwill (good pleasure), favor, feeling of complacency* of God to man; ἄνθρωποι εὐδοκίας (Hebraistic), *men with whom God is well pleased,* Luke 2:14; (2) *good pleasure, satisfaction, happiness, delight* of men, e.g., 2 Thess 1:11, though even in such passages there may be a latent reference to (divine) approval.

εὐεργεσία, ας, ἡ *good action, well doing, benefiting, kind service.*

εὐεργετέω *I do good deeds, perform kind service, benefit.*

εὐεργέτης, ου, ὁ *Benefactor,* an honorary title of kings and governors.

εὔθετος, ον *fitted, suitable;* absol. Heb 6:7.

εὐθέως adv., *immediately.*

εὐθυδρομέω *I run a straight course.*

εὐθυμέω *I keep up spirit, am of good courage.*

εὔθυμος, ον *in good spirits.*

εὐθύμως adv., *with good courage.*

εὐθύνω (1) *I make straight* (of the direction, not the surface, of a road); (2) *I steer,* Jas 3:4.

εὐθύς, εῖα, ύ gen. **έως** (1) *straight,* of direction, as opposed to crooked (σκολιός); (2) met. *upright.*

εὐθύς adv., *immediately;* characteristic of Mark.

εὐθύτης, ητος, ἡ *straightness, uprightness.*

εὐκαιρέω *I have a good (favorable) opportunity, I have leisure.*

εὐκαιρία, ας, ἡ *a good opportunity, an opportunity.*

εὔκαιρος, ον *opportune, timely, suitable;* in Mark 6:21 perhaps = *empty, holiday, festal.*

εὐκαίρως adv., *opportunely, in season, conveniently.*

εὔκοπος, η, ον *easy;* εὐκοπώτερόν ἐστιν, *it is easier.*

εὐλάβεια, ας, ἡ *caution, care;* then *anxiety, fear* (in a good sense); then almost *piety.*

εὐλαβέομαι *I am anxious,* **περί,** *about,* cf. εὐλάβεια).

εὐλαβής, ές (lit. *handling well*), hence, *cautious, circumspect;* hence, *God-fearing, pious.*

εὐλογέω *I bless* (lit. *I speak well of,*

opp. *I abuse, curse*); εὐλογημένος, of a man, *blessed* (by God; contrast εὐλογητός); εὐλογῶν (or ἐν εὐλογίᾳ) εὐλογῶ (Hebraistic), *I bless abundantly.*

εὐλογητός, ή, όν *blessed* (used only of God, as entitled to receive blessing from man).

εὐλογία, ας, ἡ *blessing.*

εὐμετάδοτος, ον *willingly sharing, ready to impart.*

Εὐνίκη, ης, ἡ *Eunice,* mother of Timothy.

εὐνοέω *I have goodwill.*

εὔνοια, ας, ἡ *goodwill.*

εὐνουχίζω *I make into a eunuch, emasculate, castrate.*

εὐνοῦχος, ου, ὁ (1) *a chamberlain, keeper of the bedchamber* of an Eastern potentate, *eunuch,* Acts 8; (2) hence, as such were castrated, *a eunuch, a castrated person.*

εὐξαίμην aor. mid. opt. → εὔχομαι.

Εὐοδία, ας, ἡ *Euodia, Evodia,* or rather *Euhodia,* a Christian woman of Philippi.

εὐοδόομαι *I have a happy (successful) journey;* hence, *I prosper,* w. the acc. in 1 Cor 16:2 expressing the concrete sign of prosperity.

εὐπάρεδρος, ον *constant in service, promoting fit waiting on.*

εὐπειθής, ές, gen. **οῦς** *compliant.*

εὐπερίστατος, ον *easily surrounding, easily encircling.*

εὐποιΐα (εὐποιία), ας, ἡ *good doing, doing of good.*

εὐπορέομαι *I am prosperous.*

εὐπορία, ας, ἡ *wealth, gain.*

εὐπρέπεια, ας, ἡ *glory* (with a notion of stateliness or majesty).

εὐπρόσδεκτος, ον *well-received, acceptable, welcome.*

εὐπροσωπέω *I look well, I make a fair show (a good outward appearance,* and so win good opinion).

Εὐρακύλων, ωνος, ὁ *Euraquilo,* an east-northeast wind (Acts 27:14, var.). See Εὐροκλύδων.

εὑρέθην aor. pas. → εὑρίσκω.

εὑρήσω fut. act. → εὑρίσκω.

εὑρίσκω *I find,* especially after searching; but in Phil 3:9 possibly *I surprise.*

Εὐροκλύδων, ωνος, ὁ *Euroclydon,* a southeast wind (Acts 27:14, var.). See Εὐρακύλων.

εὗρον aor. act. → εὑρίσκω.

εὐρύχωρος, ον *broad.*

εὐσέβεια, ας, ἡ *piety* (towards God), *godliness.*

εὐσεβέω *I am dutiful, pious;* w. acc. pers. *towards* one who has the right to it, man or God.

εὐσεβής, ές *pious, God fearing.*

εὐσεβῶς adv., *piously.*

εὔσημος, ον *with clear meaning.*

εὔσπλαγχνος, ον *tender-hearted, merciful.*

εὐσχημόνως adv., *becomingly, decorously.*

εὐσχημοσύνη, ης, ἡ *comeliness.*

εὐσχήμων, ον gen. **ονος** (1) *comely, seemly, decorous;* (2) *of honorable position* (in society).

εὐτόνως adv., *vehemently, powerfully.*

εὐτραπελία, ας, ἡ *versatility* (especially of speech); *facetiousness, raillery.*

Εὔτυχος, ου, ὁ *Eutychus,* a young hearer of Paul at Troas.

εὐφημία, ας, ἡ *good reputation.*

εὔφημος, ον *well reported of.*

εὐφορέω *I bear well, I bring a good harvest.*

εὐφραίνω *I cheer, make glad;* generally mid. or pas. *I am glad; I make merry, revel, feast.*

Εὐφράτης, ου, ὁ *the Euphrates,* boundary river of the province Syria.

εὐφροσύνη, ης, ἡ *gladness.*

εὐχαριστέω *I give thanks;* pas. 3 sing. *is received with thanks,* 2 Cor 1:11.

εὐχαριστία, ας, ἡ *thankfulness, gratitude.*
εὐχάριστος, ον *thankful.*
εὐχή, ῆς, ἡ *a prayer* comprising *a vow,* as was usual; *a prayer; a vow.*
εὔχομαι *I pray.*
εὔχρηστος, ον *useful, serviceable.*
εὐψυχέω *I am of good cheer.*
εὐωδία, ας, ἡ *a sweet smell.*
εὐώνυμος, ον *on the left-hand side, left;* ἐξ εὐωνύμων, *on the left* (lit. *well-named,* to avoid the evil omen attaching to the left).
ἔφαγον aor. act. → ἐσθίω.
ἐφάλλομαι *I leap upon.*
ἐφάνην aor. pas. → φαίνω.
ἐφάπαξ (ἐφ' ἅπαξ) adv., *once, once for all.*
Ἐφέσιος, α, ον *Ephesian, of Ephesus.*
Ἔφεσος, ου, ἡ *Ephesus,* a coast city, capital of the Roman province Asia.
ἐφέστηκα perf. act. → ἀφίστημι.
ἐφεστώς perf. act. part. → ἐφίστημι.
ἐφευρετής, ου, ὁ *a finder out, discoverer.*
ἔφη aor. or imperf. act. 3 sing. → φημί.
ἐφημερία, ας, ἡ *a class* of priests who served for a stated number of days.
ἐφήμερος, ον *for the day, for a day.*
ἐφικέσθαι aor. mid. infin. → ἀφίστημι.
ἐφικνέομαι *I reach as far as.*
ἐφιορκέω see ἐπιορκέω.
ἐφίστημι intrans. and pas., *I come upon (suddenly or unexpectedly) and stand by;* met. *I press forward,* 2 Tim 4:2.
ἐφνίδιος a phonetic spelling of αἰφνίδιος.
ἔφυγον aor. act. → φεύγω.
Ἐφραίμ (Ἐφραΐμ), ὁ *Ephraim,* a city of uncertain situation.
ἐφφαθά *be opened up* [Aram.]
ἐχάρην aor. pas. → χαίρω.
ἐχθές adv., *yesterday.*
ἔχθρα, ας, ἡ *enmity, hostility.*
ἐχθρός, ή, όν *an enemy.*
ἔχιδνα, ης, ἡ *a serpent, snake;* in Acts 28:3 probably *Coronella leopardinus,* a constrictor snake like a viper without poison fangs, which fixes its small teeth into the skin, but is harmless.
ἔχω (1) trans., *I hold, have, possess;* ἔσχον, generally, *I got, received, acquired,* ἔσχηκα, *I possessed;* ἔχω τι κατά (εἰς), *I have* a ground of complaint *against;* ἐν γαστρὶ ἔχειν, *to have* (a child) *in the womb;* w. double acc., the second being in the pred. (with or without εἰς), *to have* so and so *as . . ., to regard* so and so *as* (cf. Mark 11:32); w. obj. indicating time *to be* so and so days etc. *old;* (2) w. infin. *I am able;* (3) w. adv. equal to εἰμί w. corresponding adj.; intrans., κατὰ κεφαλῆς ἔχων, *having* a covering *over the head, with head covered,* 1 Cor 11:4; (5) Mid. *I am neighboring, I am next to,* e.g., Mark 1:38, τῇ ἐχομένῃ (understand ἡμέρα), *next day,* Luke 13:33, cf. Acts 13:44 (var.), etc.
ἐῶν pres. act. part. → ἐάω.
ἑώρακα perf. act. → ὁράω.
ἑώρων imperf. act. 3 plur. → ὁράω.
ἕως (1) conj., *until;* followed by the indic. where a def. time in the past is indicated; with or without οὗ or ὅτου, and followed by the subjun. aor. with or without ἄν or ἐάν, indicating an indef. time, *until . . . shall have,* e.g., ἕως ἂν πάντα γένηται, *until all shall have happened,* Matt 5:18; (2) prep. w. gen., *as far as, up to, as much as, until,* both in local and temp. connections, both w. nouns in gen. and w. advs. (or preps.).

Z

Ζαβουλών, ὁ *Zebulon,* one of the sons of Jacob, and founder of one of the twelve tribes [Heb.].

Ζακχαῖος, ου, ὁ *Zacchaeus,* a Jewish tax gatherer.
Ζάρα, Ζαρά, ὁ *Zara,* son of Judah and Thamar [Heb.].
ζαφθάνι (ζαφθανεί) (Why) *have you forsaken?* (Matt 27:46; Mark 15:34, var.); (Heb in contrast to the Aram. σαβαχθανεί).
Ζαχαρίας, ου, ὁ *Zechariah:* (1) a priest referred to in 2 Chr 24:20 as a son of Jehoiada, in most copies of Matt 23:35, and some of Luke 11:51, perhaps confused with Zechariah the prophet, who was son of Berechiah (Zech 1:1), but see also Βαραχίας; (2) another priest, father of John the Baptist [Heb].
ζάω *I live;* ἑαυτῷ ζῆν, *to be one's own master.*
ζβέννυμι see σβέννυμι.
Ζεβεδαῖος, ου, ὁ *Zebedee,* father of the disciples James and John.
ζεστός, ή, όν *boiling hot.*
ζεῦγος, ους, τό (1) *a yoke, team;* (2) hence, *a pair.*
ζευκτηρία, ας, ἡ *a band, a fastening.*
Ζεύς, gen. **Διός,** acc. **Δία, ὁ** *Zeus,* the Greek god of the sky in all its manifestations, corresponding to the Roman Jupiter and to the leading god of the native Lycaonians, etc.
ζέω *I burn* (in spirit); (lit. *I boil, I am boiling*).
ζηλεύω *I am zealous.*
ζῆλος, ου, ὁ (1) *eagerness, zeal, enthusiasm;* (2) *jealousy, rivalry.*
ζηλόω (1) intrans., *I am jealous;* (2) trans., *I am jealous of,* w. acc. of a person; *I am eager for, I am eager to possess,* w. acc. of a thing.
ζηλωτής, οῦ, ὁ *one who is eagerly devoted to* a person or thing, *a zealot.*
ζημία, ας, ἡ *loss.*
ζημιόω *I inflict loss (damage) upon, I fine, I punish,* sometimes w. the acc. of the penalty, even when verb is pas.
Ζηνᾶς acc. **ᾶν, ὁ** *Zenas,* a lawyer in Rome (pet form of Ζηνόδοτος or Ζηνόδωρος).
ζητέω *I seek, search for.*
ζήτημα, ατος, τό *a question, subject of inquiry.*
ζήτησις, εως, ἡ *questioning.*
ζιζάνιον, ου, τό plur. *darnel.*
Ζμύρνα see Σμύρνα.
Ζοροβάβελ (Ζοροβαβέλ), ὁ *Zerubbabel* (flourished sixth c. B.C.), son of Salathiel, according to one of three traditions, all of which agree on Davidic descent, and father Abiud and Resa [Heb.].
ζόφος, ου, ὁ *darkness, murkiness.*
ζυγός, οῦ, ὁ *a yoke;* hence met. (a Jewish idea) of a *heavy burden,* comparable to the heavy yokes resting on the bullocks' necks.
ζύμη, ης, ἡ *leaven, ferment,* both lit. and met.
ζυμόω *I leaven.*
ζωγρέω *I capture alive* or *I capture for life.*
ζωή, ῆς, ἡ *life,* both of physical (present) and of spiritual (particularly future) existence; sometimes, e.g., Mk 10:17, = Heb. *hayyim* (a plur. form) = *all the days you are alive* (nearer to βίος than ζωή), of a place in the New Age.
ζώνη, ης, ἡ *a girdle, belt, waistband;* because the purse was kept there, also *a purse.*
ζώννυμι (ζωννύω) *I gird, I put on the girdle,* especially as preparatory to active work; in John 21:18 there a *double entendre,* the second occurrence referring to *binding* by another.
ζωογονέω (ζῳογονέω) *I preserve alive* (lit. *bring to birth*).
ζῷον, ου, τό *an animal.*
ζωοποιέω (ζῳοποιέω) *I make* that which was dead *to live.*
ζῶσαι aor. mid. imper. 2 sing. → ζώννυμι.

ζώσω fut. act. → ζώννυμι.

Η

ἤ (1) *or,* both in rel. and interrog. clauses; in interrog. sentences we ought perhaps sometimes to accent ἦ (cf. εἶ) and regard simply as an interrog. particle, not to be translated; (2) *than,* sometimes almost otiose after πρίν; ἀλλ' ἤ (Luke 12:51; 2 Cor 1:13) should be ἄλλ' ἤ (i.e., ἄλλο ἤ), *nothing but;* ἤ γάρ in Luke 18:14 (var.) is corrupt.

ἤγαγον aor. act. → ἄγω.

ἤγγειλα aor. act. → ἀγγέλλω.

ἤγειρα aor. act. → ἐγείρω.

ἡγεμονεύω *I govern.*

ἡγεμονία, ας, ἡ *rule, authority.*

ἡγεμών, όνος, ὁ *a* (Roman) *governor.*

ἡγέομαι (1) *I lead;* ὁ ἡγούμενος (as subst.), *the leader;* (2) *I think, I am of opinion.*

ἠγέρθην aor. pas. → ἐγείρω.

ᾔδειν plup. act. → οἶδα.

ἡδέως adv., *gladly, pleasantly.*

ἤδη adv., *already; now at length, now after all this waiting* Rom 1:10.

ἥδιστα see ἡδέως.

ἡδονή, ῆς, ἡ *pleasure, a pleasure,* especially sensuous pleasure.

ἠδυνάμην aor. mid. → δύναμαι.

ἠδυνάσθην aor. pas. → δύναμαι.

ἠδυνήθην aor. pas. → δύναμαι.

ἡδύοσμον, ου, τό *mint, peppermint.*

ἤθελον imperf. → θέλω.

ἦθος, ους, τό *a habit.*

ἠκούσθην aor. pas. → ἀκούω.

ἥκω *I have come,* but other tenses are translated as if the pres. meant *I come.*

ἡλάμην aor. mid. → ἅλλομαι.

ἠλέγχθην aor. pas. → ἐλέγχω.

ἦλθα aor. act. → ἔρχομαι.

ἦλθον aor. act. → ἔρχομαι.

ἠλί (ἠλεί, Ἠλεί) *my God* (Heb., as contrasted w. the Aram. ἐλωί).

Ἠλί (Ἡλεί), ὁ *Heli,* the father of Joseph, husband of Mary, according to Luke [Heb.].

Ἠλίας (Ἡλίας, Ἠλείας, Ἡλείας), ου, ὁ *Elias, Elijah,* the prophet [Heb.].

ἡλικία, ας, ἡ *age, term of life; full age,* ἡλικίαν ἔχει, *he has come to maturity,* John 9:21, 23, cf. Eph 4:13; *stature,* only in Luke 19:3.

ἡλίκος, η, ον rel. and interrog. *of which size, of what size,* e.g., in Jas 3:5 ἡλίκον means *how small,* ἡλίκην, *how much.* Context determines the sense in each case.

ἥλιος, ου, ὁ *the sun;* μὴ βλέπων τὸν ἥλιον, equivalent to *stone-blind,* Acts 13:11.

ἧλος, ου, ὁ *a nail.*

ἤλπικα perf. act. → ἐλπίζω.

ἤλπισα aor. act. → ἐλπίζω.

ἡμάρτηκα perf. act. → ἁμαρτάνω.

ἡμάρτησα aor. act. → ἁμαρτάνω.

ἥμαρτον aor. act. → ἁμαρτάνω.

ἡμέρα, ας, ἡ *a day,* the period from sunrise to sunset; (ἡ) ἡμέρα κρίσεως, ἡ ἡμέρα ἐκείνη, ἡ ἡμέρα τοῦ κυρίου, *the judgment day,* coinciding with the end of the world, according to late Jewish belief; τῇ τρίτῃ ἡμέρᾳ, etc., *on the third day, after two days,* so διὰ τριῶν ἡμερῶν, Matt 26:61, etc.; νύκτα καὶ ἡμέραν, *through night as well as day;* νυκτὸς καὶ ἡμέρας, *by night as well as day,* imply merely *before dawn* as well as *during the day;* (τὸ) καθ' ἡμέραν, *day by day, each day;* πάσας τὰς ἡμέρας (vernacular phrase), *perpetually,* Matt 28:20.

ἡμέτερος, α, ον *our.*

ἤμην imperf. 1sing. → εἰμί.

ἡμιθανής, ές *half-dead.*

ἥμισυς, εια, υ, gen. **ἡμίσους** *half;* (τὸ) ἥμισυ, τὰ ἡμίσια (ἡμίσεια, elsewhere unparalleled; usual form ἡμίση), *the half.*

ἡμίωρον (ἡμιώριον), ου, τό *half an hour,* but see ὥρα.
ἠμφίεσμαι perf. mid./pas. → ἀμφιέννυμι.
ἦν imperf. 3 sing. → εἰμί.
ἤνεγκα aor. act. → φέρω.
ἠνέχθην aor. pas. → φέρω.
ἠνέῳγμαι perf. mid./pas. → ἀνοίγω.
ἠνέῳξα aor. act. → ἀνοίγω.
ἠνεῴχθην aor. pas. → ἀνοίγω.
ἡνίκα *when;* ἡνίκα ἄν, *whenever.*
ἠνοίγην aor. pas. → ἀνοίγω.
ἤνοιξα aor. act. → ἀνοίγω.
ἠνοίχθην aor. pas. → ἀνοίγω.
ἤντληκα perf. act. → ἀντλέω.
ἤπερ an intensified ἤ, *than.*
ἤπιος, α, ον *gentle.*
Ἤρ, ὁ *Er,* son of Joshua and father of Elmadam [Heb.].
ἦρα aor. act. → αἴρω.
ἤρεμος, ον *undisturbed.*
ἤρεσα aor. act. → ἀρέσκω.
ἤρθην aor. pas. → αἴρω.
ἦρκα perf. act. → αἴρω.
ἦρμαι perf. mid./pas. → αἴρω.
ἡρπάγην aor. pas. → ἁρπάζω.
Ἡρῴδης, ου, ὁ *Herod:* (1) *"Herod the King," "Herod the Great,"* Herod I (73–4 B.C.), Matt 2 *passim;* Luke 1:5; Acts 23:35; (2) *"Herod, the Tetrarch,"* son of (1), Herod Antipas, ruled 4 B.C.–A.D. 39; (3) *"Herod the King,"* Agrippa I, grandson of (1), brother of Herodias (10 B.C.–A.D. 44), ruled A.D. 37–44, Acts 12 *passim.*
Ἡρῳδιανοί, ῶν, οἱ *the Herodians, the partisans of Herod* (Antipas).
Ἡρῳδιάς, άδος, ἡ *Herodias* (died after A.D. 40), daughter of Aristobulus and granddaughter of Herod I, wife, first, of her uncle Herod, second, of his half brother, her uncle Herod Antipass.
Ἡρῳδίων, ωνος, ὁ *Herodion,* a Christian in Rome, a "relative" of Paul.
Ἠσαΐας, ου, ὁ *Esaias, Isaiah,* the prophet [Heb.].
Ἠσαῦ, ὁ *Esau,* elder son of Isaac the patriarch, brother of Jacob [Heb.].
ἡσσάομαι see ἡττάομαι.
ἡσσώθην aor. pas. → ἑσσόομαι.
ἥσσων (ἥττων), ον, gen. **ονος** *less; worse* (sometimes ἥττων under the influence of ἡττάομαι).
ἡσυχάζω *I am quiet, I keep quiet, I rest; I am silent.*
ἡσυχία, ας, ἡ *quietness; silence.*
ἡσύχιος, ον *quiet.*
ἤτοι *or of course.*
ἡττάομαι *I am defeated, I am worsted, I am made inferior.*
ἥττημα, ατος, τό *a defeat (failure).*
ἥττημαι perf. mid./pas. → ἡττάομαι.
ἥττων *see* ἥσσων.
ἤτω pres. imper. 3 sing. → εἰμί.
ηὐξήθην aor. pas. → αὐξάνω.
ηὔξησα aor. act. → αὐξάνω.
ἠχέω *I make a sound, give forth a sound, sound* (when struck).
ἤχθην aor. pas. → ἄγω.
ἦχος, ους, τό (1) *a sound;* (2) *a rumor,* Luke 4:37.
ἡψάμην aor. mid. → ἅπτω.

Θ

θα see μαρὰν ἀθά.
Θα(δ)δαῖος, ου, ὁ *Thaddaeus,* one of the twelve disciples (var. Λεββαῖος), (Aram. = *Theodotus* or some similar name).
θάλασσα, ης, ἡ (1) *the sea,* in contrast to the land (γῆ); τὸ πέλαγος τῆς θαλάσσης, *the depth of the sea,* Matt 18:6; (2) *a* particular *sea* or *lake,* e.g., *the sea of Galilee (Tiberias), the Red Sea.*
θάλπω (properly *I warm,* then) *I cherish.*
Θάμαρ, Θαμάρ, ἡ *Thamar, Tamar,* mother of Phares and Zara by Judah, son of Jacob [Heb.].

θαμβέω pas. *I am amazed* (almost *terrified*).
θάμβος, ους, τό *astonishment, amazement* (allied to terror or awe).
θανάσιμος, ον *deadly.*
θανατηφόρος, ον *death-bringing, deadly.*
θάνατος, ου, ὁ *death,* physical or spiritual; θάνατοι appears to mean *risks to life,* 2 Cor 11:23; ὁ δεύτερος θάνατος (ὁ θάνατος ὁ δεύτερος), spiritual death.
θανατόω *I put to death.*
θάπτω *I bury.*
Θάρα (Θαρά), ὁ *Thara, Terah,* the father of Abraham [Heb.].
θαρρέω *I am courageous, I am of good cheer,* a by form of θαρσέω.
θαρσέω *be of good cheer,* a by form of θαρρέω, only in the imper.
θάρσος, ους, τό *courage.*
θαῦμα, ατος, τό (1) concr., *a marvel, a wonder;* (2) abstr., *wonder.*
θαυμάζω (1) intrans., *I wonder;* cog. acc. θαυμάζειν θαῦμα μέγα, Rev 17:6, to *wonder very greatly;* (2) trans., *I wonder at, admire.*
θαυμάσιος, α, ον *wonderful.*
θαυμαστός, ή, όν *to be wondered at, wonderful.*
θεά, ᾶς, ἡ *a goddess.*
θεάομαι *I behold.*
θεατρίζω *I make a public show of, I expose to public shame.*
θέατρον, ου, τό (1) *a theatre,* a semicircular stone building, generally open to the sky; (2) *a spectacle,* 1 Cor 4:9.
θεῖναι aor. act. infin. → τίθημι.
θεῖον, ου, τό *brimstone, sulfur.*
θεῖος, α, ον *divine;* τὸ θεῖον, *the divine, the divine nature,* Acts 17:29.
θειότης, ητος, ἡ *divinity.*
θείς aor. act. part. → τίθημι.
θειώδης, ες *of brimstone, sulphureous.*
θέλημα, ατος, τό *an act of will, will;* plur. *wishes, desires;* τὸ θέλημα τοῦ Θεοῦ, *the will of God,* sometimes as a will to be recognized, sometimes as a will to be obeyed.
θέλησις, εως, ἡ *willing, will.*
θέλω (1) intrans., *I will;* οὐ θέλω, *I refuse;* θέλειν ἐν, *to fix one's will on, to stick resolutely to,* Col 2:18; followed by subj. with, or without, ἵνα, *I will that;* (2) trans., *I wish, desire.*
θεμέλιον, ου, τό *foundation,* θεμέλια, Acts 16:26.
θεμέλιος, ου, ὁ *a foundation.*
θεμελιόω *I found (lay a foundation),* lit., and met.
θεοδίδακτος, ον *taught by the god.*
θεομάχος, ον *fighting against the god.*
θεόπνευστος, ον *inspired by the god, due to the inspiration of the god.*
θεός, οῦ, ὁ (1) *a god* or *goddess,* John 10:34, 35; Acts 7:40; 14:11; 19:26, 37; 1 Cor 8:5; Gal 4:8; (2) *the god.* The word is an appellative. The Christian, like the Jew and many pagans, avoided *naming* his God, and referred to him as *the* god.
θεοσέβεια, ας, ἡ *reverence for the god.*
θεοσεβής, ές *devout, religious.*
θεοστυγής, ές *hating the god.*
θεότης, ητος, ἡ *deity, godhead.*
Θεόφιλος, ου, ὁ *Theophilus,* a friend of Luke of equestrian rank, to whom the Gospel and Acts are dedicated.
θεραπεία, ας, ἡ *care, attention* (Luke 12:42), especially *medical attention (treatment),* Luke 9:11; hence almost *healing* (Rev 22:2). In Luke 12:42 may, however, be taken as abstr. for concr., *the slaves.*
θεραπεύω *I care for, attend, serve, treat,* especially of a physician; hence, *I heal,* sometimes w. ἀπό, *of.*
θεράπων, οντος, ὁ *a servant, slave.*
θερίζω *I reap.*
θερισμός, οῦ, ὁ *reaping, harvest.*

θεριστής, οῦ, ὁ *a reaper, harvester.*
θερμαίνομαι *I warm myself.*
θέρμη, ης, ἡ *heat.*
θέρος, ους, τό *summer.*
Θεσσαλονικεύς, έως, ὁ *a man of Thessalonica.*
Θεσσαλονίκη, ης, ἡ *Thessalonica* (mod. *Saloniki*), an important city of the Roman province Macedonia.
θέτε aor. act. imper. 2 plur. → τίθημι.
Θευδᾶς, ᾶ, ὁ *Theudas,* a Jewish pretender of date about 4 B.C., otherwise unknown.
θεωρέω *I behold, look at.*
θεωρία, ας, ἡ *a sight.*
θήκη, ης, ἡ *a scabbard, a sheath.*
θηλάζω (1) *I give suck;* (2) *I suck.*
θῆλυς, εια, υ *female.*
θήρα, ας, ἡ *hunting, entrapping.*
θηρεύω *I hunt, I seek to catch* or *entrap.*
θηριομαχέω *I fight with wild beasts* (i.e., wild beasts in human form).
θηρίον, ου, τό properly *a wild beast,* hence, any *animal.*
θησαυρίζω *I store up, I treasure up, I save.*
θησαυρός, οῦ, ὁ *a storehouse* for precious things; hence, *a treasure, a store.*
θήσω fut. act. → τίθημι.
θιγγάνω *I touch.*
θλίβω (1) *I make narrow* (strictly *by pressure*), Matt 7:14; *I press upon,* Mark 3:9; (2) *I persecute, press hard.*
θλῖψις (θλίψις), εως, ἡ *persecution, affliction, distress.*
θνήσκω *I am dying;* perf. τέθνηκα, *I am dead;* τεθνηκώς, *dead.*
θνητός, ή, όν *mortal.*
θορυβάζω *I disturb greatly.*
θορυβέω *I disturb greatly, I terrify, I strike with panic.*
θόρυβος, ου, ὁ (1) *din, hubbub, confused noise,* Acts 21:34, cf. Mark 5:38; (2) *riot, disturbance.*
θραύω *I crush.*
θρέμμα, ατος, τό (lit. *a nursling*), hence plur., probably *cattle* (rather than *household, slaves*).
θρηνέω *I lament.*
θρῆνος, ου, ὁ *a dirge, lamentation* (Matt 2:18, var.).
θρησκεία, ας, ἡ *worship* as expressed in ritual acts, *religion* (underlying sense = *reverence* or *worship* of the gods).
θρησκός (θρῆσκος), όν *religious* (probably in a limited sense, refers probably to a careful observance of religious restrictions), Jas 1:26.
θριαμβεύω (properly, *I lead* one as my prisoner *in a triumphal procession*), hence, *I lead around, I make a show (spectacle) of.*
θρίξ (θρῖξ), τριχός, ἡ *a hair;* plur. *hair.*
θροέω *I disturb, agitate.*
θρόμβος, ου, ὁ *a clot.*
θρόνος, ου, ὁ *a* (king's) *throne, seat.*
θρύπτω *I break in pieces.*
Θυάτ(ε)ιρα, ων, τό *Thyatira,* a city of the old district Lydia, in the Roman province Asia.
θυγάτηρ, τρός, ἡ *a daughter;* hence (Hebraistic?), of any female *descendant,* however far removed, Luke 1:5; 13:16; even of one unrelated, *my young lady,* Mark 5:34, etc.
θυγάτριον, ου, τό *a little (young) daughter.*
θύελλα, ης, ἡ *a storm, tempest.*
θύϊνος, η, ον *of the sandarach* (so-called *citron*) *tree.*
θυμίαμα, ατος, τό *incense.*
θυμιατήριον, ου, τό (ordinarily *censer,* but) either the *altar of incense* (Exod 30:1–10), or the *shovel,* on which the high priest poured the coals, when he entered the Holy of Holies on the Day of Atonement (Lev 16:12).
θυμιάω *I burn incense.*
θυμομαχέω (lit. *I fight desperately*), hence, *I am furiously angry with.*

θυμόομαι *I am full of angry passion.*
θυμός, οῦ, ὁ *an outburst of passion, wrath.*
θύρα, ας, ἡ (1) *a door;* (2) met. *an opportunity,* Acts 14:27; 1 Cor 16:9, etc.
θυρεός, οῦ, ὁ the heavy oblong Roman *shield.*
θυρίς, ίδος, ἡ *a window sill.*
θυρωρός, οῦ, ὁ or ἡ *doorkeeper, porter.*
θυσία, ας, ἡ abstr. and concr., *sacrifice; a sacrifice.*
θυσιαστήριον, ου, τό *an altar* (for sacrifice).
θύω *I sacrifice,* generally an animal; hence, *I kill.*
Θωμᾶς, ᾶ, ὁ *Thomas,* also called Didymus, one of the Twelve.
θώραξ, ακος, ὁ *a breastplate, corslet, cuirass.*

I

Ἰάϊρος (Ἰάειρος), ου, ὁ *Jairus,* a Jewish ruler of the synagogue.
Ἰακώβ, ὁ *Jacob,* (1) the patriarch, son of Isaac; (2) father of Joseph, the husband of Mary, according to Matt 1:15, 16 [Heb.].
Ἰάκωβος, ου, ὁ *Jacobus, James,* (1) the Small, son of Alphaeus, and one of the Twelve, Matt 10:3; 27:56; Mark 2:13 (var.); 3:18; 15:40; 16:1; Luke 6:15; 24:10; Acts 1:13; (2) brother of Jesus, Matt 13:55; Mark 6:3; Acts 12:17; 15:13; 21:18; 1 Cor 15:7; Gal 1:19; 2:9, 12; Jas 1:1(?); Jude 1; (3) father(?) of Jude, Luke 6:16; Acts 1:13; (4) son of Zebedee, and brother of John, one of the Twelve, killed A.D. 44; (5) a late Egyptian(?) author, if not to be identified w. (2), Jas 1:1.
ἴαμα, ατος, τό *a healing, a curing.*
Ἰαμβρῆς, ὁ *Jambres,* a sorcerer at the court of the Pharaoh (var. Μαμβρῆς).
Ἰανναί, ὁ *Jannai,* an ancestor of Jesus, son of Joseph, and father of Melchi [Heb.].
Ἰάννης (Ἰαννῆς), ὁ *Jannes,* a sorcerer at the court of the Pharaoh (var. Ἰαμνῆς).
ἰάομαι *I heal,* generally of physical, sometimes of spiritual, disease.
Ἰάρετ, ὁ *Jareth,* son of Maleleel and father of Enoch. [Heb.]
ἴασις, εως, ἡ *healing.*
ἴασπις, ιδος, ἡ *jasper.*
Ἰάσων, ονος, ὁ *Jason,* a Christian of Thessalonica, perhaps the same as the "relative" of Paul in Rom 16:21.
ἰατρός, οῦ, ὁ *a physician.*
ἴδε *behold!* (orig. imper. of εἶδον and accented ἰδέ).
ἰδέα, ας, ἡ *appearance.*
ἴδετε aor. act. imper. 2 plur. → ὁράω.
ἴδιος (ἴδιος), α, ον *one's own, belonging to one, private, personal:* οἱ ἴδιοι, *one's own people, one's own family,* John 1:11; ὁ ἴδιος, possibly *his own* (son), Acts 20:28; τὰ ἴδια, *one's own home, one's own property,* John 1:11, etc.; ἰδίᾳ, κατ' ἰδίαν (καθ' ἰδίαν) *privately, apart, in private, by oneself, individually* (possibly understand ὁδόν).
ἰδιώτης, ου, ὁ (*unofficial*), hence, *an amateur, an unprofessional man, a layman.*
ἰδού interj., *behold! lo!* (orig. the imper. of εἰδόμην and accented ἰδοῦ, its excessive frequency is a Semitism).
Ἰδουμαία, ας, ἡ *Idumaea, Edom,* a district of Arabia, immediately south of Judaea.
ἱδρώς, ῶτος, ὁ *sweat, perspiration.*
ἰδών aor. act. part. → ὁράω.
Ἰεζάβελ, ἡ *Jezebel* (Zezabel, Old Lat. and Armenian), name given to a false prophetess of Thyatira, possibly borrowed from the name of Ahab's wife, queen of Israel (I Kgs 16:31, etc.).

Ἱεράπολις, εως, ἡ *Hierapolis,* a city of the Lycus valley in Phrygia, near Laodicea and Colossae.
ἱερατεία, ας, ἡ *the duty (office) of a priest.*
ἱεράτευμα, ατος, τό *act* or *office of priesthood.*
ἱερατεύω *I serve as priest.*
Ἱερεμίας (Ἱερεμίας), ου, ὁ *Jeremiah,* OT prophet (wrote about 603–586 B.C.) [Heb.].
Ἱεριχώ (Ἱερειχώ, Ἱερειχώ), ἡ *Jericho, Hiericus,* a city a little north of the Dead Sea.
ἱερεύς, έως, ὁ *a priest,* one who offers sacrifice to a god (in Jewish and pagan religions; of Christians only met.).
ἱερόθυτος, ον *slain as sacred, slain in sacrifice.*
ἱερόν, οῦ, τό *a temple,* either the whole building, or specifically the outer courts, open to worshippers; contrast ναός.
ἱεροπρεπής, ές *like those employed in sacred service.*
ἱερός, ά, όν *sacred.*
Ἱεροσόλυμα, ἡ or τά the Gk. form of the Heb. name *Jerusalem.* See Ἱερουσαλήμ.
Ἱεροσολυμ(ε)ίτης, ου, ὁ *an inhabitant of Jerusalem,* see Ἱερουσαλήμ.
ἱεροσυλέω *I rob temples.*
ἱερόσυλος, ου, ὁ *a robber of temples,* but possibly simply *sacrilegious.*
ἱερουργέω *I sacrifice.*
Ἱερουσαλήμ, ἡ *Jerusalem,* the capital of Palestine; hence, *Judaism,* Gal 4:25, and allegorically, *Christendom, the Christian Church,* Gal 4:26, etc. (Aram. form),
ἱερωσύνη, ης, ἡ the abstr. notion of the *priestly office* (earlier ἱερεωσύνη from ἱερεύς).
Ἰεσσαί, ὁ *Jesse,* son of Obed (Iobed), and father of King David [Heb.].
Ἰεφθάε, ὁ *Jephthah,* one of the Judges of Israel [Heb.].
Ἰεχονίας, ου, ὁ *Jechoniah,* son of Josiah and father of Salathiel [Heb.].
Ἰησοῦς, gen., dat. **οῦ,** acc. **οῦν** (1) Jesus, the Gk. form of Joshua, and the human name of our Savior (see Χριστός). The name is generally contracted thus, $\overline{\text{IC}}$, $\overline{\text{IHC}}$, in MSS, as a sign of sanctity; (2) according to certain manuscripts, one of the names of Barabbas, the robber, Matt 27:16, 17; (3) *Joshua,* Moses' successor as leader of the children of Israel, Acts 7:45; Heb 4:8; (4) an ancestor of our Lord, Luke 3:29; (5) *Jesus,* who was also called Justus, an early Christian, with Paul, Col 4:11. In these cases the name is not contracted.
ἱκανός, ή, όν (1) *considerable, sufficient,* of number, quantity, time: ἐξ ἱκανῶν χρόνων (var. ἱκανοῦ), *already for a long time,* Luke 23:8 (cf. 8:27); ἐφ' ἱκανόν, *for a sufficiently long time,* Acts 20:11; ἱκανόν ἐστιν, *enough* of this subject, Luke 22:38 (cf. 2 Cor 2:6); τὸ ἱκανὸν ποιεῖν τινι, *to satisfy one, to give him no ground of complaint,* Mark 15:15, τὸ ἱκανὸν λαμβάνω, *I get surety (security),* Acts 17:9; (2) of persons, *sufficiently strong* (*good,* etc.), *worthy, suitable,* w. various constructions.
ἱκανότης, ητος, ἡ *sufficiency, ability, power.*
ἱκανόω *I make sufficient, I make fit.*
ἱκετηρία, ας, ἡ *supplication, entreaty;* (orig. ἱκετηρίας ῥάβδος, the olive branch held in the hand of the suppliant).
ἰκμάς, άδος, ἡ *moisture.*
Ἰκόνιον, ου, τό *Iconium,* a Phrygian city of the Roman province Galatia (mod. Konia).
ἱλαρός, ά, όν *cheerful.*

ἱλαρότης, ητος, ἡ *cheerfulness.*

ἱλάσκομαι (1) w. dat. *I have mercy on, I show favor to;* (2) trans. w. obj. of sins, *I forgive.*

ἱλασμός, οῦ, ὁ *a propitiation* (of an angry god).

ἱλαστήριον, ου, τό (1) *a sin offering,* by which the wrath of the deity shall be appeased, *a means of propitiation,* Rom 3:25; (2) *the covering* of the ark, which was sprinkled with the atoning blood on the Day of Atonement (Heb. *kappōret*), Heb 9:5 (original idea, *propitiation* of an angry god).

ἵλεως, ων *propitious, forgiving,* Heb 8:12: ἵλεως σοι = ἵλεως εἴη σοι ὁ Θεός, *may the god be favorable to you, God be merciful to you, may God help you, God forbid!* Matt 16:22.

Ἰλλυρικόν, οῦ, τό *Illyricum,* a Roman province, afterwards called Dalmatia, bounded by Pannonia on the north, Macedonia on the south, Moesia on the east, and the Adriatic Sea on the west.

ἱμάς, άντος, ὁ *a thong, strap,* (1) for binding a man who is to be flogged, Acts 22:25; (2) for fastening a sandal or shoe.

ἱματίζω *I clothe, I provide clothing for.*

ἱμάτιον, ου, τό a long flowing *outer garment.*

ἱματισμός, οῦ, ὁ *raiment, clothing,* a collective word.

ἵνα (1) in statements: (a) indicating purpose, *in order that,* (b) indicating a command or wish, *that,* Mark 5:23; 6:25; 10:35, 51; John 17:24; 1 Cor 7:29; 2 Cor 8:7; Gal 2:10; Eph 5:33, (c) indicating consequence, *so that,* e.g., Rom 11:11, (d) a mere introduction to a noun clause, *that,* e.g., John 17:3; (2) in interrogations ἵνα τί; *why? wherefore?*

ἱνατί = ἵνα τί; see ἵνα.

Ἰόππη, ης, ἡ *Joppa,* a coast town of Judaea, west northwest of Jerusalem.

Ἰορδάνης, ου, ὁ *Jordan,* a great river flowing due south and bounding Galilee, Samaria, and Judaea on the east.

ἰός, οῦ, ὁ *poison;* hence, *rust,* Jas 5:3.

Ἰούδα see Ἰούδας.

Ἰουδαία, ας, ἡ *Judaea,* a Roman province, capital Jerusalem.

Ἰουδαΐζω *I live as a Jew* (in religion, ceremonially).

Ἰουδαϊκός, ή, όν *Jewish, Judaic.*

Ἰουδαϊκῶς adv., *in the manner of Jews* (religiously, ceremonially).

Ἰουδαῖος, α, ον *Jewish.*

Ἰουδαϊσμός, οῦ, ὁ *the Jewish religion, Judaism.*

Ἰούδας, α, ὁ (1) *Judah,* son of Jacob, the tribe founded by him, and the country occupied by it, Matt 1:2, 3; 2:6; Luke 1:39 (but some think Ἰούδα the name of the city, mod. *Yutta*); 3:33; Heb 7:14; 8:8; Rev 5:5; 7:5; (2) *Judas,* Iscariot (son of Simon), the disciple who betrayed Jesus; (3) *Jude,* the brother of Jesus, Matt 13:55; Mark 6:3; Jude 1(?); (4) *Jude,* an ancestor of Jesus, Luke 3:30; (5) *Jude* (son of James), the apostle, Luke 6:16; John 14:22; Acts 1:13; (6) *Judas,* a Galilean rebel about 4 B.C., Acts 5:37; (7) *Judas,* a resident of Damascus, Acts 9:11; (8) *Judas,* surnamed Barsabbas, a leading Christian and "prophet" sent by the Jerusalem church to Antioch, Acts 15:22–34, perhaps identical with (7); [Heb.].

Ἰουλία, ας, ἡ *Julia,* a Roman Christian, probably a slave or freedwoman of the Imperial household (Rom 16:15).

Ἰούλιος, ου, ὁ *Julius,* a Roman centurion on special service.

Ἰουνιᾶς, ᾶ, ὁ *Junias* a Roman Christian (Rom 16:7).

Ἰουνία, ας, ἡ *Junia,* a Roman Christian (Rom 16:15).

Ἰοῦστος, ου, ὁ *Justus,* (1) a surname of Joseph Barsabbas, one of the two nominated to fill Judas' place as apostle, Acts 1:23; (2) Titius *Justus,* a Corinthian Christian, Acts 18:7; (3) surname of Jesus, a Christian with Paul in Rome.

ἱππεύς, έως, ὁ *a horse soldier, a mounted soldier, a cavalryman.*

ἱππικός, ή, όν *pertaining to horses;* adj. used as collective subst., *cavalry.*

ἵππος, ου, ὁ *a horse.*

ἶρις, ιδος, ἡ *a rainbow.*

Ἰσαάκ, Ἰσάκ, ὁ *Isaac,* the patriarch [Heb.].

ἰσάγγελος, ον *like the angels.*

ἴσασι perf. act. 3 plur. → οἶδα.

ἴσθι pres. imper. → εἰμί.

Ἰσκαριώθ *Iscariot,* the surname of Judas the Betrayer, which would seem to indicate the place from which he came (var. Σκαριώθ).

Ἰσκαριώτης *Iscariot,* the grecized form of Ἰσκαριώθ (var. ἀπὸ Καρυώτου, *from Karyotes,* in John 6:71; 12:4; 14:22).

ἴσος (ἶσος), η, ον *equal, equivalent, identical;* τὰ ἴσα, *the equivalent,* Luke 6:34; ἴσα, adverbially, *on an equality,* Phil 2:6 (if text be sound).

ἰσότης, ητος, ἡ *equality; equality of treatment, fairness.*

ἰσότιμος, ον *equally privileged, equal.*

ἰσόψυχος, ον *likeminded.*

Ἰσραήλ (Ἰστραήλ), ὁ *Israel,* surname of Jacob, then the Jewish people, the people of God [Heb.].

Ἰσραηλ(ε)ίτης (Ἰστραηλείτης), ου, ὁ *an Israelite,* one of the chosen people Israel, a Jew.

Ἰσσαχάρ, ὁ *Issachar,* one of the sons of Jacob and founder of a tribe of Israel [Heb.].

ἴστε perf. ind or imper. 2 plur. → οἶδα.

ἵστημι (ἱστάνω) (1) trans. in act. tenses (including new perf. -έστακα), except 2 aor. and perf. (form ἕστηκα) and plup., *I make to stand, I set up; I weigh (pay),* Matt 26:15; (2) intrans. in 2 aor. and perf. (form ἕστηκα) and plup., also mid. and pas., *I am set up, I am made to stand, I stand, I take an erect position, I stand firm;* = ἀντιστῆναι, Eph 6:13. Form appearing first in third c. B.C..

ἱστορέω *I visit, see* (some person or object of importance).

ἰσχυρός, ά, όν *strong* (originally and generally of physical strength); *powerful.*

ἰσχύς, ύος, ἡ *strength* (absol.).

ἰσχύω *I have strength, I am strong, I am in full health and vigor* (opp. κακῶς ἔχω) Matt 9:12; and so *I am able,* sometimes followed by the infin. or εἰς w. acc. to indicate the purpose for which the strength is used, e.g., Matt 26:40; 5:13; w. acc. adverbially, qualifying the strength, τι ἰσχύει, *has any validity (value),* Gal 5:6, cf. Heb 9:17, πάντα ἰσχύω, *I have all strength (power),* Phil 4:13, πολὺ ἰσχύει, *has great power,* Jas 5:16.

ἴσως adv., *perhaps* (cf. Eng. *likely*).

Ἰταλία, ας, ἡ *Italy.*

Ἰταλικός, ή, όν *Italic,* the name of a cohort forming part of the Syrian army.

Ἰτουραῖος, α, ον *Ituraean,* an adj. applied to a district (χώρα), also called Trachonitic, about sixty miles east of the Sea of Galilee, and partly inhabited by the nomad tribe called Ituraeans (Ἰτουραῖοι).

ἰχθύδιον, ου, τό *a little fish.*

ἰχθύς, ύος, ὁ *a fish.*

ἴχνος, ους, τό *a track, footstep.*

Ἰωάθαμ (Ἰωαθάμ), ὁ *Joatham,* son of Ozias and father of Achaz [Heb.].

Ἰωακίμ (Ἰωακείμ), ὁ *Joakim* (Matt 1:11, var.) [Heb.]

Ἰωανάν, ὁ *Joanan, Johanan,* one of the ancestors of Jesus. [Heb.]

Ἰωάν(ν)α, ας, ἡ *Joanna, Johanna,* wife of Chuza, Herod's steward [Heb.].

Ἰωάν(ν)ης, Ἰωαν(ν)ᾶς, ου, ὁ *John:* (1) the Baptizer, son of Zacharias and Elizabeth; (2) son of Zebedee and brother of James; (3) the writer of the Apocalypse, by very many identified with (2); (4) also called Mark, cousin of Barnabas, generally regarded as author of the second Gospel, Acts 12, 13, 15; (5) the father of Simon Peter and Andrew, John 1, 21; (6) (var. Ἰωνάθας i.e., Jonathan, son of Annas, who succeeded Caiaphas) otherwise unknown, unless to be identified with Johanan ben Zacchai, president of the Great Synagogue after A.D. 70 [Heb.].

Ἰώβ, ὁ *Job,* the hero of the OT book of that name [Heb.].

Ἰωβήδ (Ὠβήδ), ὁ *Jobed, Obed,* son of Boaz and Ruth, father of Jesse, and grandfather of David [Heb.].

Ἰωδά, ὁ *Jodah,* an ancestor of Jesus [Heb.].

Ἰωήλ, ὁ *Joel,* the OT prophet [Heb.].

Ἰωνάθας (Ἰωναθάς), ου, ὁ *Jonathas* (Jonathan), Acts 4:6, var.; see Ἰωάννης.

Ἰωνάμ, ὁ *Jonam,* an ancestor of Jesus [Heb.].

Ἰωνᾶς, ᾶ, ὁ *Jonah,* the OT prophet [Heb.].

Ἰωράμ, ὁ *Joram,* son of Jehoshaphat and father of Ozias [Heb.].

Ἰωρ(ε)ίμ, ὁ *Jorim,* an ancestor of Jesus [Heb.].

Ἰωσαφάτ, ὁ *Jehoshaphat,* king of Judah, son of Asaph, father of Joram, an ancestor of Jesus [Heb.].

Ἰωσ(ε)ίας, ου, ὁ *Josiah,* king of Judah, son of Amos and father of Jechoniah [Heb.].

Ἰωσῆς, ἡ or ἦτος, ὁ *Joses,* son of Mary, sister of Mary, the mother of Jesus; see Ἰωσήφ (4) [Heb.].

Ἰωσήφ, ὁ *Joseph:* (1) son of Jacob the patriarch, John 4:5; Acts 7:9, 13, 14, 18; Heb 11:21, 22; Rev 7:8; (2) husband of Mary; (3) of Arimathaea, rich member of the Sanhedrin, Matt 27:57, 59; Mark 15:43, 45; Luke 23:50; John 19:38; (4) see Ἰωσῆς, which is a by form of Ἰωσήφ, and add Matt 13:55; 27:56; (5) an ancestor of Jesus, Luke 3:24; (6) another ancestor of Jesus, Luke 3:30; (7) also called Barsabbas and Justus, one of the two nominated to fill the place of the Betrayer Judas among the apostles, Acts 1:23; (8) another name of Barnabas of Cyprus, cousin of Mark, colleague of Paul.

Ἰωσήχ, ὁ *Josech,* an ancestor of Jesus [Heb.].

ἰῶτα, τό *yod,* the Heb. or rather Aram. letter which was smallest of all.

K

κἀγώ conj. or adv. contracted from καὶ ἐγώ, *I also, I too.*

καθά *as,* (i.e., καθ' ἅ, *according to which things*).

καθαίρεσις, εως, ἡ *taking down, razing, destroying.*

καθαιρέω (1) *I take down, pull down;* (2) *I depose,* Luke 1:52, cf. 2 Cor 10:4, w. gen. *I diminish* something *from,* Acts 19:27; (3) *I destroy,* Acts 13:19.

καθαίρω *I cleanse, purify.*

καθάπερ conj. or adv. (i.e., καθ' ἅπερ, *according to which things*), *even as.*

καθάπτω *I lay hold of, I fasten on to,* of a snake with short teeth harmless to the skin.

καθαρίζω *I make clean,* literally, ceremonially, or spiritually, according to context, ἀπό w. gen. being sometimes added, of the dirt removed. (Alternative spelling καθερίζω, perhaps = καθαιρίζω, but it occurs only in augmented and reduplicated forms and has been otherwise explained).

καθαριῶ fut. act. → καθαρίζω.

καθαρισμός, οῦ, ὁ *cleansing, purifying, purification,* literal, ceremonial, or moral.

καθαρός, ά, όν *clean, pure, unstained,* either Lat. or ceremonially or spiritually; καθαρὸς ἀπό, *unstained by.*

καθαρότης, ητος, ἡ *cleanness.*

καθέδρα, ας, ἡ *a seat, chair.*

καθέζομαι *I am sitting, I sit, I am seated.*

καθεῖλον aor. act. → καθαιρέω.

καθελῶ fut. act. → καθαιρέω.

καθελών aor. act. part. → καθαιρέω.

καθεξῆς adv., *in order, in succession;* ἐν τῷ καθεξῆς (understand χρόνῳ), *in the time immediately after, just after,* Luke 8:1; οἱ καθεξῆς, *those who followed,* Acts 3:24.

καθεύδω *I am sleeping (asleep), I sleep.*

καθηγητής, οῦ, ὁ *a leader, a teacher.*

καθῆκα aor. act. → καθίημι.

καθήκω impers. καθήκει, *it is fitting;* τὰ μὴ καθήκοντα (a technical phrase of the Stoic philosophy), *what is unfitting.*

κάθημαι *I am seated, I sit;* καθήμενος, *seated, sitting.*

καθημερινός, ή, όν *daily.*

καθῆψα aor. act. → καθάπτω.

καθίζω (1) trans., *I make to sit, I set;* (2) intrans. aor., *I sat down.*

καθίημι *I let down.*

καθίστημι (καθιστάνω) trans. (see ἵστημι), *I set, establish, appoint, constitute, make; I conduct,* Acts 17:15; καθίσταται, *shows itself, acts its part,* Jas 3:6.

καθό adv., *as, according as* (i.e., καθ' ὅ, *according to which thing*).

καθόλου adv., *at all* (i.e., καθ' ὅλου).

καθοπλίζω trans., *I arm completely, I arm head-to-toe.*

καθοράω *I see clearly.*

καθότι (1) *in proportion as, according as,* Acts 2:45; 4:35; (2) *because,* Luke 1:7; 19:9; Acts 2:24; 17:31 (i.e., καθ' ὅ, τι, neut. of ὅστις, cf. καθό, καθά),

κάθου pres. mid./pas. imper. 2 sing. → κάθημαι.

καθώς adv., *according to the manner in which, in the degree that, as.*

καθώσπερ adv., *according to the very manner in which, even as.*

καί *and;* sometimes modifying a following word, *even.*

Καϊάφας (Καϊαφᾶς), α, ὁ *Caiaphas,* Jewish high priest (Old Lat. and Sahidic = Καίφας).

Κάϊν (Καΐν, Καίν), ὁ *Cain,* son of Adam and Eve and brother of Abel [Heb.].

Καϊνάμ (Καϊνάν), ὁ *Cainam,* one of the ancestors of Jesus [Heb.].

καινός, ή, όν *fresh, new.*

καινότης, ητος, ἡ *freshness, newness.*

καίπερ *although.*

καιρός, οῦ, ὁ *fitting season, season, opportunity, occasion, time;* πρὸς καιρόν, *for a time.*

Καῖσαρ, ος, ὁ *Caesar,* a surname of the gens Iulia, which became practically synonymous with *the Emperor* for the time being; in the Gospels it refers always to Tiberius (A.D. 14–37) except in Luke 2:1 to Augustus (23 B.C.–A.D. 14), in Acts 17:7 to Claudius (A.D. 41–54), in Acts 25–28 and Phil 4:22 to Nero (A.D. 54–68).

Καισάρεια, ας, ἡ *Caesarea,*

(1) *Caesarea of Philip* (Luke 3:1), Matt 16:13; Mark 8:27, otherwise called *Caesarea Panias,* a city in Phoenice at the foot of Mount Hermon, by the source of the Jordan; (2) *Caesarea of Strato* (a king of Sidon) or *of Palestine,* on the coast of Palestine, about sixty miles north northwest of Jerusalem.

καίτοι *and yet.*

καίτοιγε *and yet.*

καίω trans., *I ignite, I light, I burn,* lit. and met.

κἀκεῖ adv., *and there, and yonder* (contraction of καὶ ἐκεῖ).

κἀκεῖθεν adv., *and thence, and from there* (contraction of καὶ ἐκεῖθεν).

κἀκεῖνος, η, ο *and he, and that* (contraction of καὶ ἐκεῖνος).

κακία, ας, ἡ (1) *evil* (i.e., trouble, labor, misfortune), Matt 6:34; (2) *wickedness,* Acts 8:22; (3) *vicious disposition, malice, spite.*

κακοήθεια, ας, ἡ *evil-mindedness,* the tendency to put the worst construction on everything.

κακολογέω *I speak evil of* (not so strong a word as βλασφημέω).

κακοπάθεια, ας, ἡ *experience of evil, suffering.*

κακοπαθέω *I am ill-treated.*

κακοποιέω *I do evil.*

κακοποιός, οῦ, ὁ *an evildoer;* in 1 Pet 4:15 probably *a sorcerer, magician,* or *poisoner.*

κακός, ή, όν *bad, evil,* in the widest sense.

κακοῦργος, ου, ὁ *a criminal* (lit. *an evil-worker*).

κακουχέω *I treat evilly.*

κακόω *I treat badly.*

κακῶς adv., *badly, evilly;* κακῶς ἔχω, see ἔχω.

κάκωσις, εως, ἡ *ill-treating, ill treatment.*

καλάμη, ης, ἡ *stubble.*

κάλαμος, ου, ὁ *a reed; a reed pen,* 3 John 13.

καλέω (1) *I call, summon, invite;* (2) *I call, name;* ἐπί, *after,* Luke 1:59.

καλλιέλαιος, ου, ἡ *a cultivated olive tree.*

κάλλιον see καλῶς.

καλοδιδάσκαλος, ον *a teacher of that which is noble (honorable).*

Καλοὶ Λιμένες, οἱ *Fair Havens.*

καλοποιέω *I do the noble (honorable) thing.*

καλός, ή, όν *beautiful,* as an outward sign of the inward *good, noble, honorable character; good, worthy, honorable, noble,* and seen to be so.

κάλυμμα, ατος, τό *a covering,* especially a covering of head and face, *a veil.*

καλύπτω *I veil, hide, conceal, envelop.*

καλῶς adv., *well, nobly, honorably; in a good place,* Jas 2:3: comp. κάλλιον; καλῶς ποιήσεις, especially w. aor. part., is idiomatic for *please,* 3 John 6, cf. Acts 10:33; Phil 4:14; 2 Pet 1:19.

κάμηλος, ου, ὁ or ἡ includes both *camel* and *dromedary.*

κάμινος, ου, ἡ *a furnace.*

καμμύω *I close.*

κάμνω (1) *I am weary,* Heb 12:3; (2) *I am ill,* Jas 5:15.

κάμπτω *I bend.*

κἄν *and if; even if* (= καὶ ἐάν).

Κανᾶ, ἡ *Cana,* a town in Galilee.

Καναναῖος, ου, ὁ *a Cananaean,* a (former) adherent of the party of Zealots (= ζηλωτής).

Κανανίτης, ου, ὁ *a Cananite.*

Κανδάκη, ης, ἡ *the Candace,* a dynastic name for queens of the Ethiopians in Abyssinia.

κανών, όνος, ὁ (1) *rule, regulation,* Gal 6:16; (2) *a measured (defined) area, province* (lit. *a level, ruler*).

καπηλεύω *I hawk, trade in, deal in for purposes of gain.*

καπνός, οῦ, ὁ *smoke.*
Καππαδοκία, ας, ἡ *Cappadocia,* a large Roman province in the central eastern part of Asia Minor.
καρδία, ας, ἡ (1) lit. *the heart,* as an organ of the body; (2) *mind* covers the nonphysical sense best: (a) *personality, character, inner life,* e.g., 1 Cor 14:25; 1 Pet 1:22, (b) *emotional state,* e.g., Rom 9:2, (c) *mind, intellect,* e.g., Rom 1:21, (d) *will, volition, intention,* e.g., Rom 2:5; (Heb. *lēb, lēbāb*).
Καρδιογνώστης, ου, ὁ *one who knows the inner life (character).*
καρπός, οῦ, ὁ (1) *fruit,* generally vegetable, sometimes animal (e.g., Luke 1:42; Acts 2:30); (2) met. *fruit, deed, action, result,* Matt 3:8; Luke 3:8; Jas 3:17–18, etc.; (3) *profit, gain,* Rom 1:13, etc.
Κάρπος, ου, ὁ *Carpus,* a Christian of Troas.
καρποφορέω act. and mid. *I bear fruit.*
καρποφόρος, ον *fruit-bearing.*
καρτερέω *I persevere, endure.*
Καρυώτου see Ἰσκαριώτης.
κάρφος, ους, τό *a dry stalk; a chip of wood.*
κατά prep. (1) w. gen., (a) *against,* Matt 12:30, (b) *down from,* Matt 8:32, κατὰ κεφαλῆς, *down over the head, on the head,* 1 Cor 11:4, (c) *throughout,* Luke 4:14; 23:5; Acts 9:31; 10:37, always w. ὅλος; ἡ κατὰ βάθους πτωχεία, *deep (abject) poverty,* 2 Cor 8:2, (d) in oaths, *by,* Matt 26:63; Heb 6:13, 16; (2) w. acc. (lit. *down along*), (a) *over against,* Acts 2:10; 16:7, (b) *among,* νόμος ὁ καθ' ὑμᾶς, *the law among you, your law,* Acts 18:15, cf. 17:28; 26:3; Eph 1:15; Col 4:7, etc., (c) w. distributive force, (τὸ) καθ' ἡμέραν, *daily, day by day, each day,* κατὰ ἑορτὴν *at each feast,* Matt 27:15; Mark 15:6, κατὰ ἑκατόν, *by hundreds,* Mark 6:40, ungrammatically εἷς κατὰ (καθ') εἷς, Mark 14:19, (John 8:9, contrast Eph 5:33), τὸ δὲ καθ' εἷς (καθεῖς), *singly, with reference to each individual,* Rom 12:5, etc., (d) *according to, by way of,* Matt 2:16, καθ' ὅσον, etc.; in titles of Gospels, κατά practically indicates the author, (e) various adv. phrases: τὸ κατ' ἐμέ, *as far as in me lies,* w. πρόθυμος, Rom 1:15, cf. τὸ κατὰ σάρκα, Rom 9:5, etc.; κατ' ἰδίαν (καθ' ἰδίαν), *privately, by oneself, individually* (opp. δημοσίᾳ), Matt 14:13, etc.; κατὰ μόνας, *alone,* Mark 4:10; Luke 9:18; κατὰ πρόσωπον, in a Hebraistic periphrasis, *in the presence of,* Luke 2:31; Acts 3:13, cf. 25:16.
καταβαίνω *I go down, I come down,* either from the sky or from higher land.
καταβάλλω (1) mid. *I lay,* of a foundation, Heb 6:1 (cf. καταβολή); (2) met. *I cast down,* 2 Cor 4:9.
καταβαρέω *I burden, oppress.*
καταβαρύνω *I weigh down, make heavy.*
κατάβασις, εως, ἡ *descent.*
κατάβηθι aor. act. imper. 2 sing. → καταβαίνω.
καταβῆναι aor. act. infin. → καταβαίνω.
καταβιβάζω *I bring down, I cause to go down.*
καταβολή, ῆς, ἡ (1) *foundation,* only in Matt 13:35 (var.) without κόσμου; (2) *depositing, sowing, deposit,* σπέρματος, technically used of the act of conception, Heb 11:11.
καταβραβεύω of the umpire in a contest, *I decide against, take part against, condemn* (perhaps with the idea of *unjust assumption, officialism*).

καταγαγεῖν aor. act. infin. → κατάγω.
καταγγελεύς, έως, ὁ *a reporter, announcer, proclaimer, herald, setter forth.*
καταγγέλλω *I announce.*
καταγελάω *I laugh at, ridicule.*
καταγινώσκω *I condemn;* κατεγνωσμένος, *reprehensible,* Gal 2:11.
κατάγνυμι *I break.*
καταγράφω *I write (down).*
κατάγω *I lead down, I bring down,* either from a high place on land to a lower (or actually to the seacoast), or from the high seas to land.
καταγωνίζομαι *I subdue* (in warfare).
καταδέω *I bind up.*
κατάδηλος, ον *quite clear.*
καταδικάζω *I condemn.*
καταδίκη, ης, ἡ *sentence of condemnation, condemnation.*
καταδιώκω *I hunt down.*
καταδουλόω *I enslave.*
καταδυναστεύω *I overpower, quell; I treat harshly.*
κατάθεμα, ατος, τό *an accursed thing.*
καταθεματίζω *I curse.*
καταθέσθαι aor. mid. infin. → κατατίθημι.
καταισχύνω *I shame, disgrace, bring to shame, put to utter confusion.*
κατακαίω *I burn down.*
κατακαλύπτομαι *I veil myself, I cover my head.*
κατακαῦσαι aor. act. infin. → κατακαίω.
κατακαύσω fut. act. → κατακαίω.
κατακαυχάομαι *I boast against.*
κατάκειμαι *I recline* (at table); more often, *I keep my bed, I am lying ill* (in bed).
κατακλάω *I break up.*
κατακλείω *I shut up.*
κατακληροδοτέω *I distribute by lot, give as an inheritance* (var. for κατακληρονομέω in Acts 13:9).
κατακληρονομέω *I give as a rightful inheritance.* See κατακληροδοτέω.
κατακλίνω *I cause to recline* at table; mid. (and pas.) *I recline* at table.
κατακλύζω *I flood over, overwhelm.*
κατακλυσμός, οῦ, ὁ *a flood.*
κατακολουθέω *I follow after.*
κατακόπτω *I beat.*
κατακρημνίζω *I throw down a precipice.*
κατάκριμα, ατος, τό *punishment following condemnation, penal servitude.*
κατακρίνω *I condemn.*
κατάκρισις, εως, ἡ *condemnation.*
κατακύπτω *I stoop down, I look down.*
κατακυριεύω *I exercise lordship over, I overpower.*
καταλαλέω *I speak evil of.*
καταλαλιά, ᾶς, ἡ *evil-speaking, backbiting, detraction.*
κατάλαλος, ου, ὁ *speaking against; a backbiter.*
καταλαμβάνω (1) act., (a) *I seize tight hold of, arrest, catch, capture, appropriate,* Mark 9:18; (John 8:3, 4); Rom 9:30; 1 Cor 9:24; Phil 3:12, 13; (b) *I overtake,* John 1:5; 6:17 (var.); 12:35; 1 Thess 5:4; (2) mid. aor. *I perceived, comprehended.*
καταλέγω *I enter in a list, register.*
καταλείπω *I leave behind; I desert, abandon.*
καταλέλειμμαι perf. mid./pas. → καταλείπω.
καταλιθάζω *I stone down, stone to death, overwhelm with stones.*
καταλλαγή, ῆς, ἡ *reconciliation.*
καταλλάσσω *I reconcile.*
κατάλοιπος, ον *left behind;* οἱ κατάλοιποι, *the rest, the remainder.*

κατάλυμα, ατος, τό *an inn, lodging.*

καταλύω (1) trans., *I break up, overthrow, destroy,* both lit. and met., ὁ καταλύων, *you would-be destroyer (of),* Matt 27:40; (2) *I unyoke, unharness* a carriage horse or pack animal; hence, *I put up, I lodge, I find a lodging,* Luke 9:12; 19:7; (lit. *I loosen thoroughly*).

καταμανθάνω *I understand, take in a fact about.*

καταμαρτυρέω *I give evidence against.*

καταμένω *I wait,* Acts 1:13; *I stay,* πρός, *with,* 1 Cor 16:6.

καταναλίσκω *I consume utterly.*

καταναρκάω (properly a medical term, *I stupefy*), hence, *I burden, encumber.*

κατανεύω *I nod, make a sign.*

κατανοέω *I understand, take in a fact about, take knowledge of, take notice of, perceive; I detect,* Luke 20:23; *I master,* Acts 7:31.

καταντάω (1) *I come down,* either from high land to lower (or actually to the sea coast), or from the high seas to the coast; hence met., *I reach* (my destination), Acts 26:7; Eph 4:13; Phil 3:11; (2) of property, *I come down (descend)* by inheritance to an heir, 1 Cor 10:11; 14:36.

κατάνυξις, εως, ἡ *deep sleep, torpor, insensibility.*

κατανύσσομαι met. *I am pierced, stung.*

καταξιόω *I deem (count) worthy.*

καταπατέω lit. and met. *I trample down.*

κατάπαυσις, εως, ἡ *resting, rest* (in OT of *the rest* attained by the settlement in Canaan).

καταπαύω (1) trans., *I cause to rest, bring to rest;* w. gen. *I cause to refrain,* Acts 14:18; (2) intrans., *I rest,* Heb 4:4, 10.

καταπέτασμα, ατος, τό *curtain* (lit. *that which is spread out downwards, that which hangs down*), of that which separated the Holy of Holies from the outer parts of the temple at Jerusalem, also of an outer curtain at the entrance to the Holy Place in the same temple; the latter is strictly denoted by κάλυμμα; yet Heb 9:3 speaks of the former as τὸ δεύτερον καταπέτασμα.

καταπιεῖν pres. infin. → καταπίνω.

καταπίμπρημι *I burn to ashes;* 2 Pet 2:6, var.

καταπίνω (1) *I drink up, swallow, gulp down; I gobble* (orig. of liquids, extended to solids); (2) pas. lit. and met. *I drown, am drowning.*

καταπίπτω *I fall down.*

καταπλέω *I sail down* (from the high seas to the shore).

καταπονέω *I ill treat;* pas. *I am getting the worse.*

καταποντίζω mid. *I am submerged, I drown.*

κατάρα, ας, ἡ *cursing; a curse.*

καταράομαι *I curse;* κατηραμένοι, *having become the subjects of a curse,* Matt 25:41.

καταργέω (1) *I make idle (inactive), I make of no effect, I annul, abolish, bring to naught;* (2) w. ἀπό, *I discharge, sever, separate from.*

καταριθμέω *I number.*

καταρτίζω (1) *I fit (join) together,* Mark 1:19; Matt 4:21; met. *I compact together,* 1 Cor 1:10; (2) act. and mid. *I prepare, I perfect,* for his (its) full destination or use, *I bring into its proper condition* (whether for the first time, or after a lapse).

κατάρτισις, εως, ἡ *restoration.*

καταρτισμός, οῦ, ὁ *bringing to a condition of fitness, perfecting.*

κατασείω *I shake* (the hand) up and *down, I wave;* intrans., *I beckon* for silence.

κατασκάπτω *I dig down.*
κατασκευάζω *I build, construct, prepare, make.*
κατασκηνόω *I encamp, take up my quarters, tabernacle, dwell.*
κατασκήνωσις, εως, ἡ *a dwelling.*
κατασκιάζω *I overshadow.*
κατασκοπέω *I spy out.*
κατάσκοπος, ου, ὁ *a spy.*
κατασοφίζομαι *I circumvent by trickery.*
καταστέλλω *I restrain, quiet.*
κατάστημα, ατος, τό *demeanor, deportment* (a man's outward bearing, including *gait, posture, expression of countenance, dress,* etc., involving the idea of *calmness* and *composure*).
καταστήσω fut. act. → καθίστημι.
καταστολή, ῆς, ἡ *garb, clothing.*
καταστρέφω *I overturn.*
καταστρηνιάω *I exercise my youthful vigor against.*
καταστροφή, ῆς, ἡ *destruction,* material or spiritual.
καταστρώννυμι *I scatter on the ground.*
κατασύρω *I drag (down).*
κατασφάζω *I slaughter.*
κατασφραγίζω *I seal* and thus close.
κατάσχεσις, εως, ἡ abstr., (permanent) *possession.*
κατάσχω aor. act. subj. → κατέχω.
κατατίθημι (1) *I lay down, deposit;* (2) mid. χάριν, χάριτα, *I lay down* or *deposit a favor,* with the view of receiving one in return, *I seek favor.*
κατατομή, ῆς, ἡ *a cutting up, spoiling* (a wordplay w. περιτομή).
κατατρέχω *I run down.*
καταφάγομαι fut. mid. → κατεσθίω.
καταφέρω (1) *I bring down,* ψῆφον, *the pebble* into the urn, i.e. *I give my vote;* αἰτίωμα, *I bring a charge against;* (2) *I oppress;* καταφερόμενος, *being gradually oppressed, becoming oppressed,* Acts 20:9, κατενεχθείς, *being borne down, overcome,* Acts 20:9.
καταφεύγω *I flee for refuge* (implying that the refuge is reached); aor. indicates moment of arrival.
καταφθείρω *I destroy, I corrupt.*
καταφιλέω *I kiss affectionately.*
καταφρονέω *I despise, scorn,* and show it by active insult.
καταφρονητής, οῦ, ὁ *a despiser.*
καταχέω *I pour (down) over.*
καταχθείς aor. pas. part. → κατάγω.
καταχθόνιος, ον *under the earth, subterranean.*
καταχράομαι *I use to the full, I use up.*
καταψύχω *I cool, I refresh.*
κατεάγην aor. pas. → κατάγνυμι.
κατέαξα aor. act. → κατάγνυμι.
κατεάξω fut. act. → κατάγνυμι.
κατέβην aor. act. → καταβαίνω.
κατέγνωσμαι perf. mid./pas. → καταγινώσκω.
κατέδραμον aor. act. → κατατρέχω.
κατέθηκα aor. act. → κατατίθημι.
κατείδωλος, ον *full of images* of gods.
κατείλημμαι perf. mid./pas. → καταλαμβάνω.
κατείληφα perf. act. → καταλαμβάνω.
κατεκάην aor. pas. → κατακαίω.
κατεκλίθην aor. pas. → κατακλίνομαι.
κατεκρίθην aor. pas. → κατακρίνω.
κατελαβόμην aor. mid. → καταλαμβάνω.
κατέλαβον aor. act. → καταλαμβάνω.
κατελήμφθην aor. pas. → καταλαμβάνω.
κατελθεῖν aor. act. infin. → κατέρχομαι.

κατέλιπον aor. act. → καταλείπω.
κατέμαθον aor. act. → καταμανθάνω.
κατέναντι adv. and prep. w. gen., *opposite, in front (of).*
κατενεχθείς aor. pas. part. → καταφέρω.
κατενύγην aor. pas. → κατανύσσομαι.
κατενώπιον prep. w. gen., *before the face of.*
κατεξουσιάζω *I have (exercise) power (authority) over.*
κατέπεσον aor. act. → καταπίπτω.
κατεπέστην aor. act. → κατεφίσταμαι.
κατέπιον aor. act. → καταπίνω.
κατέπλευσα aor. act. → καταπλέω.
κατεπόθην aor. pas. → καταπίνω.
κατέπρησα aor. act. → καταπίμπρημι.
κατεργάζομαι *I work out; I produce, accomplish.*
κατέρχομαι *I come down* from sky to earth, or from high land to lower land (or to the coast), or from the high seas to the shore; part. qualitative in Jas 3:15.
κατεσθίω (κατέσθω) *I eat up, I eat till it is finished* (cf. καταπίνω); aor. καταφαγεῖν.
κατεστάθην aor. pas. → καθίστημι.
κατέσταλμαι perf. mid./pas. → καταστέλλω.
κατέστειλα aor. act. → καταστέλλω.
κατέστησα aor. act. → καθίστημι.
κατεστρώθην aor. pas. → καταστρώννυμι.
κατέσχον aor. act. → κατέχω.
κατευθύνω (1) *I make straight,* 1 Thess 3:11; (2) met. *I put in the right way, I direct.*
κατευλογέω *I bless.*
κατέφαγον aor. act. → κατεσθίω.
κατέφθαρμαι perf. mid./pas. → καταφθείρω.
κατεφίσταμαι aor. intrans., *I set upon, I rise up against.*
κατέφυγον aor. act. → καταφεύγω.
κατέχω (1) *I hold fast, bind, arrest;* (2) *I take possession of, lay hold of,* Luke 14:9; (3) *I hold back, detain, restrain,* Luke 4:42; Rom 1:18; 2 Thess 2:6, 7; Phlm 13; (4) *I hold a ship* (supply τὴν ναῦν), *keep its heading,* Acts 27:40.
κατήγαγον aor. act. → κατάγω.
κατήγγειλα aor. act. → καταγγέλλω.
κατηγγέλην aor. pas. → καταγγέλλω.
κατηγορέω *I accuse, charge; I prosecute.*
κατηγορία, ας, ἡ *a charge, an accusation.*
κατήγορος, ου, ὁ *a prosecutor, an accuser.*
κατήγωρ, ορος, ὁ *an accuser* (an abbreviated vulgar form of κατήγορος).
κατῆλθον aor. act. → κατέρχομαι.
κατηλλάγην aor. pas. → καταλλάσσω.
κατήνεγκα aor. act. → καταφέρω.
κατήραμαι perf. mid./pas. → καταράομαι.
κατήφεια, ας, ἡ *a downcast countenance* as a sign of sorrow, *gloominess, gloom, dejection.*
κατήχθην aor. pas. → κατάγω.
κατηχέω *I instruct orally.*
κατιόω *I rust;* pas. *I am rusted.*
κατισχύω (1) *I have strength against, I prevail against,* Matt 16:18; (2) *I prevail,* Luke 23:23; (3) *I have strength, I am able,* w. infin., Luke 21:36.
κατίωμαι perf. mid./pas. → κατιόομαι.
κατοικέω *I dwell in* (implying a more permanent settlement than

παροικέω), *I settle in, I am established in* (permanently).
κατοίκησις, εως, ἡ *dwelling, abode.*
κατοικητήριον, ου, τό *a habitation, dwelling place.*
κατοικία, ας, ἡ *dwelling, habitation.*
κατοικίζω *I take up a dwelling,* but probably κατῴκισεν is an itacistic error for κατῴκησεν (from κατοικέω), as κατοικίζω is properly trans.
κατοπτρίζω mid. for act., *I mirror, reflect;* elsewhere mid. = *I gaze upon myself in a mirror.*
κάτω adv., (1) *down, below,* also *downwards;* (2) compar. κατωτέρω, *lower, under, less,* of a length of a time, Matt 2:16.
κατῴκησα aor. act. → κατοικέω.
κατῴκισα aor. act. → κατοικίζω.
κατώτερος, α, ον compar. adj., *lower,* Hebraistic, w. ref. to Sheol.
κατωτέρω adv. *lower, below.*
Καῦδα *Cauda* (mod. *Gaudho*), an island twenty-three miles south of the western end of Crete (var. Κλαῦδα).
καυήσομαι fut. pas. → καίω.
καυθήσωμαι fut. pas. → καίω.
καῦμα, ατος, τό *burning heat, heat.*
καυματίζω trans., *I burn, I scorch.*
καῦσις, εως, ἡ *burning.*
καυσόω trans., *I burn* (perhaps by internal heat).
καυστηριάζω (καυτηριάζω) *I cauterize, I burn with a hot iron;* hence met., *I sear.*
καύσων, ωνος, ὁ *the East wind* of Palestine, *the Simoom,* which blows from February to June.
καυχάομαι *I boast; I glory (exult) proudly.*
καύχημα, ατος, τό *a boasting, a ground of boasting (glorying, exultation).*
καύχησις, εως, ἡ *boasting; glorying, exultation.*
Καφαρναούμ, ἡ *Capharnahum* (the form *Capernaum* appears to be a conscious alteration made in Syria not earlier than the fourth c.), perhaps mod. *Tell Ḥum.*
Κεγχρεαί (Κεγχρειαί), ῶν, αἱ *Cenchreae,* the harbor town of Corinth on the Saronic Gulf.
κέδρος (Κεδρών), ὁ *a cedar;* in John 18:1 τῶν Κέδρων is probably due to a popular misunderstanding of the orig. name τοῦ Κεδρών (*Kidron,* 1 Kgs 2:37, etc.), especially as cedars grew in the vicinity.
κεῖμαι *I have been placed (put, laid),* hence, *I lie;* a perf. used instead of the perf. pas. of τίθημι, the former sense explains the constr. w. εἰς and acc.
κειρία, ας, ἡ a kind of *girdle* made of cords; *a bandage.*
κείρω *I shear, I cut the hair of;* mid. *I cut my own hair, I have my hair cut.*
Κείς see Κίς.
κέκαυμαι perf. mid./pas. → καίω.
κεκέρασμαι perf. mid./pas. → κεράννυμι.
κέκληκα perf. act. → καλέω.
κέκλικα perf. act. → κλίνω.
κεκόρεσμαι perf. mid./pas. → κορέννυμι.
κέκραγα perf. act. → κράζω.
κέκρικα perf. act. → κρίνω.
κέκρυμμαι perf. mid./pas. → κρύπτω.
κέλευσμα, ατος, τό *a word of command, a call.*
κελεύω *I command, I order.*
κενοδοξία, ας, ἡ *vainglory.*
κενόδοξος, ον *vainglorious.*
κενός, ή, όν (1) *empty;* (2) met. *empty* (in moral content), *vain, ineffective, foolish, worthless;* εἰς κενόν, *in vain, to no purpose;* (3) *false, unreal, pretentious, hollow,* Eph 5:6; Col 2:8; Jas 2:20.

κενοφωνία, ας, ἡ *a worthless utterance.*
κενόω (1) *I empty,* Phil 2:7; (2) *I deprive of content; make unreal.*
κέντρον, ου, τό *a goad.*
κεντυρίων, ωνος, ὁ *a centurion,* an officer commanding about a hundred infantry in the Roman army (Lat., = Gk. ἑκατοντάρχης).
Κενχρεαί (Κενχρειαί) see Κεγχρεαί.
κενῶς adv., *falsely.*
κεραία (κερέα), ας, ἡ *a little hook, an apostrophe* on letters of the alphabet, distinguishing them from other like letters, or *a separation stroke* between letters.
κεραμεύς, έως, ὁ *a potter.*
κεραμικός, ή, όν *of clay, made by a potter.*
κεράμιον, ου, τό *an earthenware pitcher.*
κέραμος, ου, ὁ *a tile;* οἱ κέραμοι, practically *the roof.*
κεράννυμι *I mix.*
κέρας, ατος, τό (1) *a horn;* (2) as a symbol of strength, κέρας σωτηρίας, *a powerful support of salvation,* Luke 1:69; (3) a dwarfed *column* set upon or at the corner of an altar, with ritual significance, Rev 9:13.
κεράτιον, ου, τό *a husk (pod) of the carob* (siliqua graeca).
κερδαίνω *I gain;* ὕβριν καὶ ζημίαν, *I gain injury and loss,* i.e. *I gain by shunning injury and loss, I do not suffer (I am spared) injury and loss,* Acts 27:21.
κερδήσω fut. act. → κερδαίνω.
κέρδος, ους, τό *gain.*
κερέα see κεραία.
κέρμα, ατος, τό *a small coin;* plur. *small change.*
κερματιστής, ου, ὁ properly *a changer of* large into smaller *coins, a moneychanger.*
κεφάλαιον, ου, τό (1) *the chief matter, the main point,* Heb 8:1; (2) *a sum* of money, Acts 22:28.
κεφαλαιόω var. for κεφαλιόω in Mark 12:4, q.v.
κεφαλή, ῆς, ἡ (1) *head,* κατὰ κεφαλῆς ἔχων, see κατά; (2) met. κεφαλὴ γωνίας, *a corner stone,* uniting two walls, Mark 12:10 and pars.; *head, ruler, lord,* 1 Cor. 11:3, etc.
κεφαλιόω *I wound in the head.*
κεφαλίς, ίδος, ἡ *a roll* (lit. *little head,* then the *knob* at the end of the wooden core of a roll of papyrus).
κημόω *I muzzle* (from κημός, *a muzzle*).
κῆνσος, ου, ὁ *poll tax* [Lat. *census*].
κῆπος, ου, ὁ *a garden.*
κηπουρός, οῦ, ὁ *keeper of a garden.*
κηρίον, ου, τό *a honeycomb.*
κήρυγμα, ατος, τό *a proclamation.*
κῆρυξ (κήρυξ), υκος, ὁ *a herald, proclaimer.*
κηρύσσω *I proclaim, herald, preach.*
κῆτος, ους, τό *a sea monster, a huge sea fish.*
Κηφᾶς, ᾶ, ὁ *Cephas* (Aram. for *rock*), the new name given to Simon, the disciple.
κιβωτός, οῦ, ἡ (properly *a wooden box*), hence, *the Ark,* in which Noah sailed.
κιθάρα, ας, ἡ *a harp.*
κιθαρίζω intrans. and trans., *I play on the harp, I harp,* w. acc. of the tune.
κιθαρῳδός, οῦ, ὁ *a harpist.*
Κιλικία, ας, ἡ *Cilicia,* a Roman province between the Taurus range of mountains and the coast in the southeast corner of Asia Minor, linked up with the province of Syria.
κινδυνεύω *I am in danger,* sometimes w. infin. *of . . . .*
κίνδυνος, ου, ὁ *danger, peril, risk.*
κινέω trans., *I move; I stir, excite.*
κίνησις, εως, ἡ *moving, stirring.*

κιννάμωμον, ου, τό *cinnamon* (a Semitic word).

Κίς, Κείς, ὁ *Kish,* father of Saul, king of Israel [Heb.].

κίχρημι *I lend.*

κλάδος, ου, ὁ *a branch* of a tree.

κλαίω *I weep;* w. acc. or ἐπί w. acc. *I weep for, mourn.*

κλάσις, εως, ἡ *breaking.*

κλάσμα, ατος, τό *a fragment.*

Κλαῦδα see Καῦδα.

Κλαυδία, ας, ἡ *Claudia,* a Christian woman in Rome; if historical, probably a freedwoman of the imperial household.

Κλαύδιος, ου, ὁ (1) *Claudius,* the fourth of the Roman Emperors, Tiberius Claudius Caesar Augustus Germanicus, who ruled A.D. 41–54; (2) *Claudius* Lysias, a tribune at Jerusalem.

κλαυθμός, οῦ, ὁ *weeping.*

κλάω *I break.*

κλείς, κλειδός, ἡ *a key.*

κλείω *I shut.*

κλέμμα, ατος, τό *a theft.*

Κλεοπᾶς (Κλεόπας), ᾶ, ὁ *Cleopas,* one of the two companions of the risen Jesus from Jerusalem to Emmaus.

κλέος, ους, τό *glory, fame.*

κλέπτης, ου, ὁ *a thief.*

κλέπτω *I steal;* ὁ κλέπτων, *the stealer,* Eph 4:28.

κληθήσομαι fut. pas. → καλέω.

κλῆμα, ατος, τό *a branch.*

Κλήμης, εντος, ὁ *Clement,* a fellow worker of Paul in Rome [Lat. = *Clemens*].

κληρονομέω *I inherit, I obtain (possess) by inheritance.*

κληρονομία, ας, ἡ *an inheritance, an heritage,* regularly the gift of God to His chosen people, in OT the Promised Land, in NT a possession viewed in one sense as present, in another as future.

κληρονόμος, ου, ὁ *an heir, an inheritor;* cf. κληρονομία.

κλῆρος, ου, ὁ (1) *a lot;* (2) *a portion* assigned, Acts1:17; 8:21; 26:18; Col 1:12; hence, a portion of the people of God assigned to one's care, *a congregation,* 1 Pet 5:3.

κληρόω lit. *I choose by lot, I appoint by lot;* hence, *I assign;* mid. *I assign to myself, choose;* pas. *I am assigned, I am chosen* as God's portion (κλῆρος), Eph 1:11.

κλῆσις, εως, ἡ *a calling, invitation, summons* of God to the religious life; sometimes, e.g. Phil 3:14; 2 Thess 1:11; Heb 3:1, it may include a reference to the final issue of this invitation.

κλητός, ή, όν *called, invited, summoned* by God to the religious life.

κλίβανος, ου, ὁ *an oven, a furnace.*

κλίμα, ατος, τό a small geographical division, district, or *territory,* a portion of a χώρα (q.v.).

κλινάριον, ου, τό *a couch* or *litter* of a sick person.

κλίνη, ης, ἡ *a couch, a bed,* alike a mere mat (e.g. Matt 9:2, 6), and a more elaborate structure (e.g. Mark 4:21); possibly *a bier* in Rev 2:22.

κλινίδιον, ου, τό *a couch* or *litter* of a sick person.

κλίνω (1) trans., (a) *I rest, recline* (even in John 19:30); *I bend, incline,* (b) *I cause to give ground, I make to yield,* Heb 11:34; (2) intrans. of the day, *declines, approaches its end,* Luke 9:12; 24:29.

κλισία, ας, ἡ properly *a dining couch;* hence, *a group of diners.*

κλοπή, ῆς, ἡ *thieving, theft.*

κλύδων, ωνος, ὁ *rough water, roughness of water;* κλύδωνι θαλάσσης *a rough sea,* Jas 1:6.

κλυδωνίζω *I toss as in a storm at sea.*

Κλωπᾶς, ᾶ, ὁ *Clopas,* husband of one Mary, who stood by the cross.

κνήθω *I rub, tickle;* κνηθόμενοι τὴν ἀκοήν, *with ears itching* with eagerness to hear pleasant things, 2 Tim 4:3.

Κνίδος, ου, ἡ *Cnidus,* a town on the coast of Caria (southwest Asia Minor) near the island of Cos.

κοδράντης, ου, ὁ *a quadrans,* the smallest Roman copper coin, a quarter of an *assarion,* the sixteenth part of a *sestertius.*

κοιλία, ας, ἡ *belly, abdomen,* a general term covering any organ in the abdomen, e.g. stomach, womb; ἐκ κοιλίας μητρός, *from birth.*

κοιμάομαι pas. w. act. sense, *I fall asleep, I am asleep,* sometimes of the sleep of death (e.g. Matt 27:52).

κοίμησις, εως, ἡ *sleeping,* followed by constituent gen. τοῦ ὕπνου, *which is slumber.*

κοινός, ή, όν (1) *common, shared;* (2) Heb. use (in contrast to ἅγιος), *profane; dirty, unclean, unwashed,* Mark 7:2; Acts 10:14, 28; 11:8; Rom 14:14; Heb 10:29; Rev 21:27.

κοινόω (cf. κοινός), (1) *I make unclean, I pollute;* (2) mid. *I regard (treat) as unclean,* Acts 10:15; 11:9.

κοινωνέω (1) *I share, communicate, contribute, impart,* Rom 12:13; Gal 6:6; (2) *I share in, I have a share of, I have fellowship with,* w. gen. or dat.

κοινωνία, ας, ἡ (1) *contributory help,* Acts 2:42; Rom 15:26; 2 Cor 8:4; 9:13; Heb 13:16; (2) *sharing in,* Phil 1:5; 3:10; Phlm 6, cf. (3); (3) spiritual *fellowship,* a *fellowship* in the spirit, 1 Cor. 1:9; 10:16; 2 Cor 6:14; 13:13; Gal 2:9; Phil 2:1; 1 John 1:3, 6, 7 (lit. *partnership,* frequently outside NT, of the marriage relationship).

κοινωνικός, ή, όν *willing to share.*

κοινωνός, οῦ, ὁ and **ἡ** *a sharer; a partner.*

κοίτη, ης, ἡ (1) *a bed,* Luke 11:7; (2) *a marriage bed,* Heb 13:4; κοίτην ἔχειν ἐκ, *to conceive seed from,* Rom 9:10; plur. *repeated* (immoral) *sexual intercourse,* Rom 13:13.

κοιτών, ῶνος, ὁ *bedchamber;* ὁ ἐπὶ τοῦ κοιτῶνος, *chamberlain.*

κόκκινος, η, ον *crimson,* dyed with Kermes, the female coccus of the Kermes oak.

κόκκος, ου, ὁ *a grain.*

κολάζω *I punish;* mid. *I cause to be punished.*

κολακεία, ας, ἡ *flattery,* with a view to advantage or gain.

κόλασις, εως, ἡ *punishing, punishment,* perhaps with the idea of *deprivation,* 1 John 4:18.

κολαφίζω *I strike with the fist;* hence, *I maltreat violently.*

κολλάω (lit. *I glue*); hence, mid. and pas. *I join myself closely, I cleave, I adhere* (to), *I keep company* (with), of friendly intercourse; of inanimate objects, Luke 10:11.

κολλούριον (κολλύριον), ου, τό *eye salve.*

κολλυβιστής, οῦ, ὁ *a money-changer,* who changed heathen into Jewish money, for payment into the Temple treasury (from κόλλυβος, *a commission paid on exchange*).

κολλύριον earlier spelling of κολλούριον.

κολοβόω (lit. *I maim, mutilate*), *I cut short, shorten, abbreviate.*

Κολοσσαί, ῶν, αἱ *Colossae,* a town of the Roman province Asia, in the Lycus valley, near Laodicea and Hierapolis.

κόλπος, ου, ὁ (1) sing. and plur. *bosom;* the overhanging fold of the garment used as a pocket, Luke 6:38; (2) *a bay, gulf,* Acts 27:39.

κολυμβάω (properly *I dive*); hence, *I swim.*

κολυμβήθρα, ας, ἡ (lit. a *diving* or *swimming place*), *a pool.*

κολωνία, ας, ἡ *a colony*, a city settlement of Roman (soldier) citizens; *a garrison city*.
κομάω *I wear the hair long, I allow the hair to grow long*.
κόμη, ης, ἡ *hair, long hair*.
κομίζω (1) act. *I convey, bring*, Luke 7:37; (2) mid. *I receive back, I receive* what has belonged to myself but has been lost, or else promised but kept back, or *I get* what has come to be my own by earning, *I recover*.
κομψότερον compar. adv. *better* (of sick persons).
κονιάω *I whitewash*.
κονιορτός, οῦ, ὁ *dust*.
κοπάζω *I cease, drop*.
κοπετός, οῦ, ὁ *beating of the breast* or *head* in lamentation, *lamentation*.
κοπή, ῆς, ἡ *slaughter*.
κοπιάω (1) *I grow weary*, Matt 11:28; John 4:6; Rev 2:3; (2) *I toil, work with effort* (of bodily and mental labor alike).
κόπος, ου, ὁ (1) *trouble;* κόπους (κόπον) τινι παρέχειν, *to give trouble to one, to annoy one;* (2) *toil, labor, laborious toil*, involving weariness and fatigue.
κοπρία, ας, ἡ *manure*.
κόπριον, ου, τό *manure*.
κόπτω (1) *I cut, I cut of*, Matt 21:8; Mark 11:8; (2) mid. *I beat my breast* or *head* in lamentation, *I lament, mourn*, sometimes w. acc. (ἐπί w. acc.) of person whose loss is mourned.
κόραξ, ακος, ὁ *a raven*.
κοράσιον, ου, τό *a little girl, a young girl; a girl* (colloquial).
κορβᾶν (κορβάν) *a gift consecrated to God* [Aram.].
κορβανᾶς, ᾶ, ὁ *the temple treasure*.
Κόρε (Κορέ), ὁ *Korah* (Num 16:1ff.) [Heb.].
κορέννυμι *I fill, sate, glut, feed full*.
Κορίνθιος, ου, ὁ *Corinthian, of Corinth*.
Κόρινθος, ου, ἡ *Corinth*, in northeast Peloponnese, the capital of the Roman province Achaia.
Κορνήλιος, ου, ὁ *Cornelius*, a centurion of the Roman army, stationed at Caesarea (2).
κόρος, ου, ὁ *a (dry) measure*, equivalent to ten Attic μέδιμνοι or 120 gallons [Heb.].
κοσμέω *I put into order; I decorate, deck, adorn*.
κοσμικός, ή, όν *earthly, worldly* (belonging to the present, earthly world as opposed to the heavenly and future).
κόσμιος, ον *orderly, virtuous*.
κοσμίως *in an orderly, virtuous manner; modestly*.
κοσμοκράτωρ, ορος, ὁ *ruler of this world*, i.e., of the world as asserting its independence of God; used of the angelic or demonic powers controlling the sublunary world, cf. ἀρχή, ἐξουσία, στοιχεῖον.
κόσμος, ου, ὁ (1) *the universe, the world*, the sum total of created things; (2) a Jewish conception; the word has acquired a bad sense in Isaiah (e.g. 13:11), the sum of the fierce surrounding heathen nations, the powers of the heathen world, at once destructive and corruptive. Hence, *the world* as apart from God its Creator, the world as self-sufficient, consequently running counter to its Creator, and thus evil in its tendency, cf. John, 1 John (e.g. 2:15), Jas (e.g. 4:4), 2 Pet 2:20; (3) sometimes seems not different from, *the* inhabited *world;* (4) *adornment*, 1 Pet 3:3.
Κούαρτος, ου, ὁ *Quartus*, a Christian, brother of Erastus the Corinthian. Cf. ἀδελφός.
κουμ (κούμ, κοῦμι) *arise* [Aram.].
κουστωδία, ας, ἡ concr., *a guard* [Lat. *custodia*].
κουφίζω *I lighten*.

κόφινος, ου, ὁ a stiff wicker *basket.*
κράβαττος (κρά[β]βατος), ου, ὁ *a bed, mattress, mat* of a poor man (spelled κράβακτος in Egyptian documents).
κράζω *I cry aloud, shriek.*
κραιπάλη, ης, ἡ *excessive drunkenness, carousing, surfeiting.*
κρανίον, ου, τό *the skull.*
κράσπεδον, ου, τό *the fringe, the edge.*
κραταιόω *I strengthen,* pas. *I become strong.*
κραταιός, ά, όν *strong, powerful.*
κρατέω *I lay hold of, take possession of, obtain,* w. gen. and (much oftener) w. acc.
κράτιστος, η, ον *most excellent,* an official epithet, used in addressing a Roman of high rank, and in the second c. one of equestrian (as distinguished from senatorial) rank.
κράτος, ους, τό *might, rule, power,* divine except in Heb 2:14.
κραυγάζω *I cry aloud, shout.*
κραυγή, ῆς, ἡ (1) *a shout, cry, clamor;* (2) *outcry, clamoring* against another, Eph 4:31.
κρέας, κρέως and **κρέατος,** acc. plur. **κρέα, τό** *flesh; pieces of flesh, kinds of flesh.*
κρείττων (κρείσσων), ον gen. **ονος** *better.*
κρεμάννυμι *I hang, I suspend;* mid. *I am hanging, I hang.*
κρεπάλη see κραιπάλη.
κρημνός, οῦ, ὁ *a crag, precipice.*
Κρής, ητός, ὁ *a Cretan, an inhabitant of Crete.*
Κρήσκης, εντος, ὁ *Crescens,* a Christian, coadjutor of Paul.
Κρήτη, ης, ἡ *Crete;* see Κυρήνη.
κριθή, ῆς, ἡ *barley.*
κριθήσομαι fut. pas. → κρίνω.
κρίθινος, η, ον *made of barley.*
κρίμα, ατος, τό (1) *a judgment, a verdict;* sometimes implying *an adverse verdict, a condemnation;* (2) *a case at law, a lawsuit,* 1 Cor 6:7.
κρίνον, ου, τό *a lily* growing wild, variously identified with the red anemone, the white lily, the sword lily.
κρίνω (1) *I judge,* whether in a law court or privately; sometimes w. cog. nouns κρίμα, κρίματι, κρίσιν, emphasizing the notion of the verb; (2) *I decide, I think (it) good,* w. infin. Acts 3:13; 15:19, etc. (cf. Acts 27:1).
κρίσις, εως, ἡ *judging, judgment;* generally *divine judgment; accusation,* Jude 9.
Κρίσπος (Κρῖσπος), ου, ὁ *Crispus,* ruler of the synagogue at Corinth, converted and baptized by Paul.
κριτήριον, ου, τό (1) *a law court,* Jas 2:6; (2) *a law case* before an arbiter.
κριτής, ου, ὁ *a judge.*
κριτικός, ή, όν *able to judge.*
κρούω *I beat* a door with a stick, to gain admittance.
κρυβῆναι aor. pas. infin. → κρύπτω.
κρύπτη (κρυπτή), ης, ἡ *a hidden place,* cf. κρυπτός.
κρυπτός, ή, όν *hidden, secret;* τὰ κρυπτά, as subst. *the hidden (secret) things (parts), the inward nature (character);* ἐν [τῷ] κρυπτῷ, *in the secret place, in the hidden sphere, inwardly.*
κρύπτω *I hide, conceal.*
κρυσταλλίζω *I am clear as crystal.*
κρύσταλλος, ου, ὁ *crystal.*
κρυφαῖος, α, ον *hidden, secret;* ἐν τῷ κρυφαίῳ = ἐν τῷ κρυπτῷ.
κρυφῆ (κρυφῇ) adv., *in secret, secretly.*
κτάομαι (1) *I acquire, win, get, purchase, buy;* (2) *I possess,* 1 Thess 4:4.
κτῆμα, ατος, τό *a piece of landed property, a field,* Acts 5:1; plur. *posses-*

sions, property, possibly *landed property, property in land* in Mark 10:22; Matt 19:22, as it is in Acts 2:45.

κτῆνος, ους, τό *a beast of burden* (generally, a horse or mule), either for riding or for carrying loads on its back, or for yoking to a cart or carriage.

κτήτωρ, ορος, ὁ *a possessor, owner.*

κτίζω *I create, found, make,* always of God.

κτίσις, εως, ἡ (1) abstr., *creation;* (2) concr., *creation, creature, institution* (often of the *founding* of a city). Always of Divine work.

κτίσμα, ατος, τό *a created thing, a creature,* of God.

κτίστης, ου, ὁ *creator,* God, (often of the *founder* of a city).

κυβεία, ας, ἡ (lit. *playing with dice, gaming*), hence, *trickery, sleight.*

κυβέρνησις, εως, ἡ (lit. *steering, piloting*), *governing, government,* supposed to refer to such duty as was, later at least, performed by any presbyter or by that presbyter who was ἐπίσκοπος.

κυβερνήτης, ου, ὁ *a steersman, a pilot.*

κυκλεύω *I encircle, invest, enclose.*

κυκλόθεν adv. and prep. w. gen., *in a circle round, round about.*

κύκλῳ dat. of κύκλος, *a circle;* as adv., *in a circle, round about.*

κυκλόω *I encircle, invest, surround.*

κυλισμός, οῦ, ὁ *rolling, wallowing.*

κυλίω trans., *I roll;* mid. intrans., *I roll* (myself).

κυλλός, ή, όν *maimed.*

κῦμα, ατος, τό *a wave.*

κύμβαλον, ου, τό *a cymbal.*

κύμινον, ου, τό *cummin,* a plant used as a spice (a Semitic word).

κυνάριον, ου, τό *a house dog,* possibly with a touch of contempt.

Κύπριος, ου, ὁ *Cypriote, belonging to Cyprus.*

Κύπρος, ου, ἡ *Cyprus.*

κύπτω *I stoop.*

Κυρηναῖος, ου, ὁ *belonging to Cyrene.*

Κυρήνη, ης, ἡ *Cyrene,* a district west of Egypt on the Mediterranean coast, forming with Crete a Roman province.

Κυρήνιος, ου, ὁ Publius Sulpicius *Quirinius* (died A.D. 21), who conducted two censuses of the province Syria, one in 8, 7, or 6 B.C., Luke 2:2, as plenipotentiary of the Emperor, and another as *legatus pro praetore* in A.D. 7, Acts 5:37.

κυρία, ας, ἡ *a lady;* voc. *my lady,* an address of courtesy.

κυριακός, ή, όν *of the Lord* (κύριος), *special to the Lord;* δεῖπνον, supper (dinner) for church members, combined with the Eucharist; ἡμέρα, Sunday. (In constitutional law the word means *imperial.*)

κυριεύω *I rule;* w. gen. *I rule over, lord it over, master.*

κύριος, ου, ὁ (1) *an owner* of property, particularly of slaves (δοῦλοι), *a lord, master* (cf. 1 Pet 3:6); plur. οἱ κύριοι, *master and mistress,* Matt 15:27(?), Luke 19:33; Acts 16:16, 19, and perhaps elsewhere; (2) weaker sense, in the voc., as a polite address, κύριε, *sir!,* κύριοι, *gentlemen, sirs,* Acts 16:30, cf. κυρία; (3) of divine beings, κύριος, *Lord,* without article, generally refers to God, whereas ὁ κύριος, *the Lord,* generally refers to Jesus, the Messiah (cf. Acts 2:34). In this sense the word connotes that these Divine Beings are absolute rulers (kings) of the whole world, and that we are their slaves (subjects). As the term was also applied to oriental sovereigns and to the Roman Emperors (particularly frequently in Nero's case) in the same sense, it focused the deadly rivalry between the two powers (cf. Acts 25:26).

κυριότης, ητος, ἡ (1) abstr., *lordship*, 2 Pet 2:10; (2) concr., *divine* or *angelic lordship, domination, dignity*, Eph 1:21; Col 1:16; Jude 8, usually with reference to a celestial hierarchy.

κυρόω *I ratify, confirm.*

κύων, κυνός, dat. pl. **κυσί, ὁ** *a dog;* universally despised in the east, and thus the name is applied contemptuously to persons, Phil 3:2; Rev 22:15 (cf. Matt 15:26).

κῶλον, ου, τό *a limb;* plur. *bodies.*

κωλύω *I prevent, debar, hinder;* w. infin. *from* doing so and so.

κώμη, ης, ἡ *a village.*

κωμόπολις, εως, ἡ a city which in constitution has only the status of a village.

κῶμος, ου, ὁ *a revel, a reveling,* such as took place at the gathering of the grapes.

κώνωψ, ωπος, ὁ *a gnat, mosquito,* referred to proverbially as something small.

Κῶς, Κῶ, ἡ *Cos,* an island in the Aegean Sea, southwest of Asia Minor.

Κωσάμ, ὁ *Cosam,* son of Elmadam and father of Addei [Heb.].

κωφός, ή, όν *dumb.*

Λ

λαβεῖν aor. act. infin. → λαμβάνω.

λάβοι aor. opt. 3 sing. → λαμβάνω.

λαβών aor. act. part. → λαμβάνω.

λαγχάνω (1) *I obtain (receive) by lot, my lot (turn) is;* (2) *I cast lots,* John 19:24.

Λάζαρος, ου, ὁ (Ἐλεάζαρος in old Western documents) *Lazarus, Eliezer,* (1) the beggar, Luke 16:20ff.; (2) the brother of Martha and Mary, of Bethany, John 11, 12.

λαθεῖν aor. act. infin. → λανθάνω.

λάθρα (λάθρᾳ) adv., *secretly.*

λαῖλαψ, απος, ἡ *a sudden storm, a squall.*

λακάω *I burst apart, burst open, burst asunder with a loud noise,* Acts 1:18. (The form λάσκω was previously believed to be the source of ἐλάκησεν.)

λακτίζω *I kick.*

λαλέω (*I talk, chatter* in classical Gk., but in NT a more dignified word) *I speak; I say.*

λαλιά, ᾶς, ἡ (in classical Gk. *babble, chattering*) *speech, talk; manner of speech.*

λαμά *why* [Heb.].

λαμβάνω (1) *I receive, get;* πρόσωπον λαμβάνειν τινός (Hebraistic), lit. *to receive the face of, to accept the person of,* i.e. *to favor specially;* (2) *I take;* συμβούλιον λαβεῖν, *to deliberate,* Matt 12:14; (3) = παραλαμβάνω, John 1:12.

Λάμεχ, ὁ *Lamech,* son of Methuselah and father of Noah [Heb.].

λαμπάς, άδος, ἡ *a lamp, a lantern.*

λαμπρός, ά, όν *shining, glossy, bright.*

λαμπρότης, ητος, ἡ *brightness.*

λαμπρῶς adv., *sumptuously.*

λάμπω *I shine.*

λανθάνω *I am hidden (concealed), I lie hid, I escape notice,* sometimes w. acc. of person from whom concealment takes place, Acts 26:26; 2 Pet 3:8; w. parts. (classical constr.), I do so and so *unconsciously, unknown to myself, I shut my eyes to* so and so, Heb 13:2.

λαξευτός, ή, όν *hewn* out of the rock.

Λαοδίκεια, ας, ἡ *Laodicea,* a city in the Lycos valley in the Roman province Asia, near Colossae and Hierapolis.

Λαοδικεύς, έως, ὁ *a Laodicean, an inhabitant of Laodicea.*

λαός, οῦ, ὁ (1) *a people,* characteristically of God's chosen people, first the Jews, then the Christians;

(2) sometimes, but rarely, *the people, the crowd,* e.g. Luke 9:13; 20:6.

λάρυγξ, γγος, ὁ *the throat.*

Λασαία (Λασέα), ας, ἡ *Lasaea,* a city in Crete, about the middle of the south coast.

λάσκω see λακάω.

λατομέω *I hew* (of stone).

λατρεία, ας, ἡ *service* rendered to God, perhaps simply *worship.*

λατρεύω *I serve,* especially God, perhaps simply *I worship.*

λάχανον, ου, τό *a vegetable.*

λάχω aor. act. subj. → λαγχάνω.

λαχών aor. act. part. → λαγχάνω.

Λεββαῖος, ου, ὁ *Lebbaeus,* a pet name, a var. for Thaddaeus, one of the twelve disciples of Jesus. The full form of the name is not known.

λεγιών (λεγεών), ῶνος, ἡ properly a division of the Roman army, numbering about 6,000 infantry with additional cavalry (cf. Matt 26:53); hence, *a very large number* [Lat. *legio*].

λέγω (denoting speech in progress), (1) *I say, speak; I mean; I mention, tell;* (2) *I call, name,* especially in the pas., e.g. Matt 1:16; John 1:38, but also act., e.g. Mark 10:18; (3) *I tell, I command,* e.g. Matt 5:34, 39; Rom 2:22.

λεῖμμα, ατος, τό *a remnant, a remainder.*

λεῖος, α, ον *smooth.*

λείπω (earlier, *I leave behind, abandon*), (1) *I am wanting;* τὰ λείποντα, *what is defective,* Tit. 1:5; (2) mid. e.g. w. gen. *I come behind* (in a race), *I am left behind in, I fall short of* (some standard), *I am wanting in.*

λειτουργέω *I act in the public service, I render service, I minister,* in the widest sense, Rom 15:27, of some special public religious service, Acts 13:2; but also of the service of priests and Levites, Heb 10:11.

λειτουργία, ας, ἡ *public service* in the widest sense, 2 Cor 9:12; Phil 2:30; *service* as of priest or Levite ritual, Luke 1:23; Phil 2:17; Heb 8:6; 9:21.

λειτουργικός, ή, όν *given to serving (ministration), ministering.*

λειτουργός, οῦ, ὁ *minister, servant,* of an official character; of priests and Levites, Heb 8:2.

λεμά *why;* see λαμά [Aram.].

λέντιον (λεντίον), ου, τό *a towel* [loan word from Lat. *linteum*].

λεπίς, ίδος, ἡ *a scale, a scaly substance* thrown off from the body.

λέπρα, ας, ἡ *leprosy.*

λεπρός, οῦ, ὁ *a leprous person, a leper.*

λεπτός, ου, τό *small, light;* neut. subs. *a small piece of money,* probably *the smallest piece of money* = a half quadrans (see κοδράντης).

Λευί (Λευεί, Λευίς, Λευείς), ὁ *Levi,* (1) an ancestor of Jesus, Luke 3:24; (2) another ancestor of Jesus, Luke 3:29; (3) third son of Jacob, the patriarch, and founder of a tribe named after him, Heb 7:5, 9; Rev 7:7; (4) son of Alphaeus, and called also Matthew, a revenue officer and one of the twelve disciples of Jesus [Heb.].

Λευίτης (λευείτης), ου, ὁ *a Levite,* properly a man of the tribe of Levi; hence, *a priest's assistant, an under priest;* as the members of that tribe were charged with this duty.

Λευιτικός (λευειτικός), ή, όν *belonging to the tribe of Levi, levitical.*

λευκαίνω *I whiten.*

λευκοβύσσινος *of white fine linen* (var. for βύσσινον λευκόν; see βύσσινος).

λευκός, ή, όν *white.*

λέων, οντος, ὁ *a lion;* ἐκ τῆς φυλῆς Ἰούδα applied to Jesus, Rev 5:5 (after Gen 49:9); in 2 Tim

4:17 used proverbially for very great danger.

λήθη, ης, ἡ *forgetfulness.*

λῆμψις (λῆψις), εως, ἡ *a receiving.*

λήμψομαι fut. mid. → λαμβάνω.

ληνός, οῦ, ἡ *a winepress;* hence met., Rev 14:19; 19:15.

λῆρος, ου, ὁ *folly, nonsense, idle talk.*

λῃστής, οῦ, ὁ *a robber, brigand, bandit.*

λίαν adv., *very; very much, exceedingly.*

λίβα acc. → λίψ.

λίβανος, ου, ὁ *frankincense, incense* (Semitic word).

λιβανωτός, οῦ, ὁ *a censer.*

Λιβερτῖνος, ου, ὁ *a freedman,* one of the class of manumitted slaves [Lat. *libertinus*]. A synagogue at Jerusalem appears to have been reserved for them.

Λιβύη, ης, ἡ *Libya, Africa* (in the mod. sense).

λιθάζω *I stone.*

λίθινος, η, ον *made of stone.*

λιθοβολέω *I stone, I cast stones (at).*

λίθος, ου, ὁ *a stone;* met. of Jesus as the chief stone in a building, etc., Acts 4:11, etc.

λιθόστρωτος, ου, τό *paved with stone;* neut. subs. *stone pavement.*

λικμάω *I crush to powder.*

λιμήν, ένος, ὁ *a harbor, port.*

λῖμμα (λίμμα) see λεῖμμα.

λίμνη, ης, ἡ *a lake.*

λιμός, οῦ, ὁ and **ἡ** *a famine.*

λίνον, ου, τό *flax; linen.*

Λίνος, ου, ὁ *Linus,* a Christian in Rome.

λιπαρός, ά, όν (lit. *fat*) *rich, sumptuous.*

λίτρα, ας, ἡ *a* Roman *pound,* of about twelve ounces, 327½ grams.

λίψ, λιβός, acc. **λίβα, ὁ** *the southwest wind,* and thus the quarter from which it comes.

λογεία (λογία), ας, ἡ *a collection, collecting* (of money), particularly of an irregular local contribution for religious purposes (from λογεύω, "I collect").

λογίζομαι (properly of an accountant, bookkeeper, *I count, reckon up*), (1) *I reckon, count, put down* to one's account, τι or τινί τι, Rom 4:6; 1 Cor. 13:5; 2 Cor 5:19; 2 Tim 4:16; also w. εἴς τι = *as something, as of some value,* e.g. Acts 19:27; Rom 4:3; Gal 3:6; (2) *I number, class* amongst, Mark 15:28; Luke 22:37; (3) *I reckon up accounts, I weigh arguments, I deliberate,* Mark 11:31 (var.); (4) hence, *I consider, weigh,* John 11:50; 2 Cor 10:11; Phil 4:8; Heb 11:19; (5) *I think, I judge,* often; (6) *I decide, determine,* 2 Cor 10:2.

λογικός, ή, όν (1) *reasonable, rational,* Rom 12:1; (2) *metaphorical,* as contrasted w. lit., 1 Pet 2:2 (so perhaps also in Rom 12:1).

λόγιον, ου, τό plur. *oracles, divine responses* or *utterances* (it can include the entire OT scriptures); in Rom 3:2 mainly of the promises in the OT; in Heb 5:12 probably of Jesus' teaching.

λόγιος, α, ον *eloquent.*

λογισμός, οῦ, ὁ *reasoning, thinking.*

λογομαχέω *I battle with (for) words.*

λογομαχία, ας, ἡ *a battling with (for) words, a battle of words.*

λόγος, ου, ὁ (speech in progress); (1) *a word, an utterance, speech, discourse, saying,* frequently of God through his messengers; the gen. expresses either this origin or the subj. of the word; διὰ λόγου, *by spoken word, by word of mouth;* ὁ λόγος, the Gospel news, e.g. Luke 1:2; Acts 14:25; (2) *the personalized Word* or *Divine utterance,* a conception of Palestinian or Alexandrian theology, referred by the Fourth Evangelist to Jesus the Messiah, John 1:1, 14; (3) *an account,* Acts

20:24; 1 Pet 4:5; hence, (4) *reason, a reason,* 1 Pet 3:15; κατὰ λόγον, *rightly, deservedly,* Acts 18:14; (5) *analogy,* ἐπέχειν λόγον τινος, *to correspond to, be analogous to, be instead of* something, Phil 2:16.

λόγχη, ης, ἡ *a long lance.*

λοιδορέω *I revile* a person *to his face, I abuse insultingly.*

λοιδορία, ας, ἡ *reviling, abuse.*

λοίδορος, ου, ὁ *a railer, reviler, abuser.*

λοιμός, οῦ, ὁ (1) *a pestilence;* (2) *a pestilent fellow,* Acts 24:5.

λοιπός, ή, όν (1) *left, left behind,* οἱ λοιποί, *the remainder, the rest, the others;* (2) adv. phrases, acc. neut., λοιπόν, τὸ λοιπόν, *for the rest, now, already;* temp. gen., τοῦ λοιποῦ (supply χρόνου), *henceforth.*

Λουκᾶς, ᾶ, ὁ *Lucas, Luke,* Christian physician and writer of the Third Gospel and Acts, an abbreviated pet form either of Λουκανός, as the Old Latin Bible gave in the title of the Third Gospel, or of Λουκίος, as some moderns have thought.

Λούκιος, ου, ὁ *Lucius,* (1) of Cyrene, an early Christian, in the church of Antioch, Acts 13:1, by some identified with the evangelist Luke; (2) a Christian with Paul at Corinth, by some identified with (1), Rom 16:21.

λουτρόν, οῦ, τό *a bath* (of the water, not the vessel), *water for washing, washing.*

λούω *I wash, bathe* (the body, literally or merely ceremonially); mid. of *washing, bathing oneself.*

Λύδδα, ας, ἡ *Lydda, Diospolis, Lod* (mod. *Ludd*), a city on the way to Joppa within a day's journey of Jerusalem.

Λυδία, ας, ἡ *Lydia,* a lady resident of Philippi, native of Thyatira in Lydia (Asia Minor), and engaged in the clothing trade.

Λυκαονία, ας, ἡ *Lycaonia, the country of the Lykaones,* a district of Asia Minor, comprised within the Roman province Galatia and including the cities Derbe and Lystra.

Λυκαονιστί *in the Lycaonian language.*

Λυκία, ας, ἡ *Lycia,* a small Roman province on the south coast of Asia Minor.

λύκος, ου, ὁ *a wolf,* or perhaps *a jackal;* often applied to persons of wolfish proclivities.

λυμαίνομαι *I ravage, harry, devastate.*

λυπέω *I pain, grieve, vex.*

λύπη, ης, ἡ *pain, grief.*

Λυσανίας, ου, ὁ *Lysanias,* tetrarch of Abilene.

Λυσίας, ου, ὁ Claudius *Lysias,* a Roman tribune of the soldiers in Jerusalem.

λύσις, εως, ἡ *dissolution, release.*

λυσιτελέω impers. 3 sing. *it is advantageous to, it profits.*

Λύστρα, dat. **Λύστροις,** acc. **Λύστραν, ἡ** and **τό** *Lystra,* a Lycaonian city in the southern part of the Roman province Galatia.

λύτρον, ου, τό *the purchasing money* for manumitting slaves, *a ransom, the price of ransoming;* especially *the sacrifice by which expiation is effected, an offering of expiation.*

λυτρόω (orig., *I deliver* captives from robbers or enemies in war *by payment, I manumit* or *liberate* a slave from slavery), *I ransom, liberate, deliver.*

λύτρωσις, εως, ἡ (in OT *ransoming from imprisonment for debt,* or *from slavery, release from national misfortune,* etc.), *liberation, deliverance, release* (cf. λυτρόω).

λυτρωτής, οῦ, ὁ *a redeemer, one who pays a ransom, a liberator.*

λυχνία, ας, ἡ *a lamp stand.*
λύχνος, ου, ὁ *a lamp.*
λύω (1) *I unloose, loose, loosen, untie, release,* Mark 1:7, etc.; thus *I break* (in a phrase where the time order of the two processes is inverted), Rev 5:2; (2) met. *I break, destroy, set at naught, contravene;* sometimes merely, *I declare* a law *to be not binding,* John 5:18; *I break up* a meeting, Acts 13:43; *I annul,* 1 John 4:3 (var.).
Λωΐς (Λωίς), ΐδος, ἡ *Lois,* grandmother of Timothy.
Λώτ (Λώθ), ὁ *Lot,* nephew of Abraham [Heb.].

M

Μάαθ (Μαάθ), ὁ *Maath, Mahath,* an ancestor of Jesus [Heb.].
Μαγαδάν (Μαγδαλά), ἡ *Magadan (Magdala).* The reading and the site are uncertain. Two views are held with regard to the latter, (1) that it was in the Decapolis near Gerasa; (2) that it was at Megdel on the western bank of the Sea of Galilee.
Μαγδαληνός, ἡ, όν *a Magdalene, of Magdala,* a place identical with mod. Megdel, near Tiberias; see Μαγαδάν (2). Fem. subs. Μαγδαληνή, surname of Mary from Magdala; see Μαρία (2).
Μαγεδών *Magedon,* the second part of the name, Ἂρ Μαγεδών *(Har Magedon),* perhaps *Megiddo.*
μαγεία (μαγία), ας, ἡ *sorcery, magic.*
μαγεύω *I practice sorcery* or *magic.*
μαγία see μαγεία.
μάγος, ου, ὁ *a sorcerer, a magician, a wizard.*
Μαγώγ, ὁ *Magog,* sometimes as name of a people, sometimes as name of a country in OT (Gen 10:2; Ezek 38:2; 39:6), probably the Scythians; hence, used in apocalyptic literature [Heb.].
Μαδιάμ, ὁ *Madiam, Midian,* generally taken to mean or to include the peninsula of Sinai [Heb.].
μαθεῖν aor. act. infin. → μανθάνω.
μαθητεύω *I make disciples, I make into disciples;* followed by dat. of instrument, Matt 13:52.
μαθητής, οῦ, ὁ *a learner, disciple, pupil.*
μαθήτρια, ας, ἡ *a woman disciple.*
Μαθθαῖος (Ματθαῖος), ου, ὁ *Matthaeus, Matthew,* a revenue officer, then one of the twelve disciples of Jesus.
Μαθθάν (Ματθάν), ὁ *Matthan,* son of Eleazar and father of Jacob, an ancestor of Jesus [Heb.].
Μαθθάτ (Ματθάτ), ὁ *Matthat,* son of Levi and father of Jorem, an ancestor of Jesus [Heb.].
Μαθθίας (Ματθίας), ου, ὁ *Matthias,* elected one of the Twelve in room of the deceased Judas.
Μαθουσαλά (Μαθουσάλα), ὁ *Methuselah,* son of Enoch and father of Lamech [Heb.].
μαίνομαι *I am raving mad, I speak as a madman.*
μακαρίζω *I deem (declare) happy.*
μακάριος, α, ον *happy, to be envied.*
μακαρισμός, οῦ, ὁ *felicitation, regarding as happy* or *enviable.*
Μακεδονία, ας, ἡ *Macedonia,* a Roman province north of Achaia (Greece) [Heb.].
Μακεδών, όνος, ὁ *a Macedonian,* an inhabitant of the Roman province Macedonia.
μάκελλον, ου, τό *meat market* [Lat. *macellum*].
μακράν adv., sometimes used adjectivally, *at a distance, far away.*
μακρόθεν adv., *from a (long) distance,* often in the tautological expression ἀπὸ μακρόθεν =

μακρόθεν, ἀπὸ μακράν (cf. Luke 18:13).

μακροθυμέω *I defer my anger, I am longsuffering,* i.e. the opp. of short- or quick-tempered.

μακροθυμία, ας, ἡ *longsuffering.*

μακροθύμως adv., *with longsuffering, patiently.*

μακρός, ά, όν (1) *long;* acc. neut. plur. as adv. *long,* Mark 12:40; Luke 20:47; (2) *distant.*

μακροχρόνιος, ον *long-timed, long-lived.*

μαλακία, ας, ἡ *weakness, illness.*

μαλακός, ή, όν (1) *soft,* (τὰ) μαλακά, as subs., *soft material;* (2) of persons, *soft, voluptuous, effeminate.*

Μαλελεήλ, ὁ *Maleleel, Malelehel,* one of the ancestors of Jesus [Heb.].

μάλιστα adv., *most of all, especially* (superl., see μᾶλλον).

μᾶλλον adv., *more, rather* (comp., see μάλιστα).

Μάλχος, ου, ὁ *Malchus,* a slave of the high priest at Jerusalem (Aram. *Malchu*).

μάμμη, ης, ἡ *a grandmother.*

μαμωνᾶς, ᾶ, ὁ *riches, money, possessions, property* (Aram., w. cog. words in Heb. and Punic).

Μαναήν, ὁ *Manaen,* probably a member of Herod Antipas' court (grecized form of Aram. *Menahem*).

Μανασσῆς (Μανασσῆ), ῆ, ὁ *Manasseh,* (1) son of Joseph, founder of a tribe of Israel, Rev 7:6; (2) son of Hezekiah and father of Amon (Amos) [Lat.].

μανθάνω *I learn;* w. adjs. or nouns, *I learn* to be so and so, 1 Tim 5:13; w. acc. of person who is the object of knowledge, Eph 4:20; aor. sometimes to *ascertain,* Acts 23:27; Gal 3:2.

μανία, ας, ἡ *raving madness.*

μάννα, τό *manna,* the supernatural food eaten by the Israelites in the desert; of spiritual food, Rev 2:17 [Lat.].

μαντεύομαι *I practice soothsaying,* suggesting the fraud involved in the practice.

μαραίνω pas. *I die, I wither* (like the grass).

μαράνα θά (μαρὰν ἀθά) Aram., early Christian (eucharistic?) formula meaning, *Lord, come!* or *Our Lord hath come* or *Our Lord cometh (will come, is at hand).*

μαρανθήσομαι fut. pas. → μαραίνομαι.

μαργαρίτης, ου, ὁ *a pearl.*

Μάρθα, ας, ἡ *Martha,* sister of Mary and Lazarus of Bethany.

Μαρία (Μαριάμ), ας, ἡ *Mary, Miriam* (the former is the grecized form), (1) the mother of Jesus; (2) of Magdala, which epithet is always attached (except John 20:11, 16 where it is unnecessary; (3) sister of Martha and Lazarus, Luke 10:39, 42; John 11; 12:3; (4) mother of James and Joseph (or Joses), Matt 27:56; Mark 15:40, and presumably in Mark 15:47; 16:1; Luke 24:10; wife of Clopas, John 19:25. Also referred to in Matt 27:61; 28:1; (5) mother of John Mark, Acts 12:12; (6) a Christian in Rome, Rom 16:6.

Μᾶρκος, ου, ὁ *Marcus, Mark,* who also had the Heb. name John, son of Mary ([5] above), nephew of Barnabas, coadjutor of Barnabas, Saul (Paul), and Peter.

μάρμαρος, ου, ὁ *marble.*

μαρτυρέω *I witness, I bear witness, I give evidence, I testify,* w. dat. pers. or quality, in one's favor, in favor of; w. acc. cog., μαρτυρίαν, ὁμολογίαν, practically otiose; in the pas., *I am witnessed to, I am borne witness to,* sometimes w. nom. and dependent infin. (impers.,

3 John 12), corresponding to the act.; Rev 1:2; 22:16, 18, 20.

μαρτυρία, ας, ἡ *witness, evidence, testimony.*

μαρτύριον, ου, τό *witness, evidence* (of recovery, Matt 8:4; Mark 1:44; Luke 5:14; so of other occurrences or thoughts); ἡ σκηνὴ τοῦ μαρτυρίου, *the tent* of the congregation, *the tent* of meeting of God with His people, because it contained the ark and the tablets *of the testimony* to the covenant between God and his people, cf. Exod 25:9, 10.

μαρτύρομαι (properly, *I call [summon] to witness,* and then, absol.) *I testify, I protest, I asseverate; I conjure, solemnly charge,* 1 Thess 2:12; Eph 4:17.

μάρτυς, μάρτυρος, dat. pl. **μάρτυσιν, ὁ** *a witness, eyewitness* or *ear witness.* In Acts 22:20; Rev 2:13 it approaches the ecclesiastical sense of *martyr,* i.e. one who gives public testimony to his faith before a tribunal, and suffers the penalty.

μασάομαι *I gnaw.*

μασθός see μαστός.

μαστιγόω *I flog, scourge,* the victim being strapped to a pole or frame, see μάστιξ.

μαστίζω *I flog, scourge,* see μάστιξ.

μάστιξ, ιγος, ἡ (1) *a scourge, lash,* of leathern thongs with pieces of metal sewn up in them, Acts 22:24; Heb 11:36; (2) met. *severe pains (sufferings)* sent by God.

μαστός (μασθός), οῦ, ὁ *a breast,* especially *a nipple* of a woman's breast.

ματαιολογία, ας, ἡ *vain speaking, foolish talking.*

ματαιολόγος, ου, ὁ *speaking vain things.*

ματαιόομαι pas., *I am made vain, ineffective, godless.*

μάταιος, α, ον *vain, unreal, ineffectual, unproductive;* practically *godless.*

ματαιότης, ητος, ἡ *vanity, emptiness, unreality, purposelessness, ineffectiveness, instability.*

μάτην adv., *in vain, in an unreal way.*

ματθ. see μαθθ.

Ματταθά, ὁ *Mattathah,* an ancestor of Jesus [Heb.].

Ματταθίας, ου, ὁ *Mattathias,* an ancestor of Jesus [Heb.].

μάχαιρα, ης, ἡ *a sword;* met. of the spirit, Eph 6:17.

μάχη, ης, ἡ (earlier, *a battle, conflict,* perhaps in Jas 4:1); hence in the sphere of words, etc., *strife, contention, quarrel.*

μάχομαι *I engage in battle, I fight;* hence, *I strive,* John 6:52.

μεγαλεῖος, α, ον neut. subs. *greatness;* plur. τὰ μεγαλεῖα, *the mighty deeds.*

μεγαλειότης, ητος, ἡ *(divine) majesty* or *magnificence.*

μεγαλοπρεπής, ές *magnificent, superb, transcendent.*

μεγαλύνω (1) *I enlarge, lengthen,* Matt 23:5; (2) *I increase, magnify.*

μεγάλως adv., *greatly;* compar. μεῖζον.

μεγαλωσύνη, ης, ἡ *(divine) majesty;* in Heb 1:3; 8:1, a sort of substitute for the divine Name.

μέγας, μεγάλη, μέγα *large, great,* in the widest sense; see μειζότερος, μείζων, μέγιστος.

μέγεθος, ους, τό *greatness.*

μεγιστάν, ᾶνος, ὁ *a great one, a lord, a courtier, a satrap.* (The word has an oriental flavor and belongs to late Gk..)

μέγιστος, η, ον (elative superl., practically obsolete and only literary), *very great;* see μέγας (positive), μείζων (comp. and superl.).

μεθερμηνεύω *I translate* (from one language into another).

μέθη, ης, ἡ *deep drinking, drunkenness.*

μεθίστημι (μεθιστάνω) *I cause to change its place, I move out of its place, I translate, transfer, remove.*

μεθοδεία, ας, ἡ *scheming, craftiness* (from μέθοδος, *a way of search after something, an inquiry; a method*).

μεθύσκω *I intoxicate;* pas., *I become intoxicated with wine, I become drunk.*

μέθυσος, ου, ὁ *a drunkard* (orig., *tipsy*).

μεθύω *I am intoxicated with wine, I am drunk.*

μεῖζον adv. *all the more* (neut. sing. of μείζων, comp. of μέγας); see μεγάλως.

μειζότερος, α, ον *greatest,* Matt 13:32; 23:11; 1 Cor 13:13, etc. (superl. of μέγας).

μείζων, ον, ον *greater,* 3 John 4 (compar. of μέγας). See also adv. μεῖζον.

μεῖναι aor. act. infin. → μένω.

μεῖνον aor. act. imper. → μένω.

μέλας, αινα, αν, gen. **ανος, αίνης, ανος** *black;* τὸ μέλαν, *ink,* 2 Cor 3:3; 2 John 12; 3 John 13.

Μελεά, ὁ *Meleah,* one of the ancestors of Jesus [Heb.].

μέλει impers., *it is a care, it is an object of anxiety,* w. dat. of the person; pers., διὸ μελήσω, wherefore *I will take care,* true text in 2 Pet 1:12.

μελετάω *I devise, plan; practice, exercise myself in.*

μέλι, ιτος, τό *honey.*

μελίσσιος, ον *belonging to bees, coming from bees.*

Μελίτη (Μελιτήνη), ης, ἡ *Malta.*

μέλλω (1) w. infin. *I am about to, I intend;* (2) absol., in pres. part., *coming, future;* so τὸ μέλλον, *the future,* εἰς τὸ μέλλον (supply ἔτος), *next year,* Luke 13:9, τὰ μέλλοντα, *the things that are to be (come to pass).* See μέλει.

μέλος, ους, τό *a bodily organ, limb, member* (wider in sense than κῶλον).

Μελχί (Μελχεί), ὁ *Melchi,* one of the ancestors of Jesus [Heb.].

Μελχισέδεκ (Μελχισεδέκ), ὁ *Melchisedek,* king and priest of Salem (Gen 14:18–20) [Heb.].

μεμάθηκα perf. act. → μανθάνω.

μεμβράνα, ης, ἡ *a parchment leaf,* perhaps for notes [Lat. *membrana*].

μεμενήκειν plup. act. → μένω.

μεμίαμμαι perf. mid./pas. → μιαίνω.

μέμιγμαι perf. mid./pas. → μίγνυμι.

μέμνημαι perf. mid./pas. → μιμνήσκομαι.

μέμφομαι *I blame.*

μεμψίμοιρος, ον *blaming one's lot* or *destiny, discontented.*

μέν an untranslatable particle, generally answered by δέ (sometimes by ἀλλά, πλήν), each of the two introducing a clause intended to be contrasted with the other. (The μέν is very often omitted as compared with classical Gk..) Other uses are (1) μέν followed by καί (e.g. Luke 8:5), where an additional detail is given, not explicitly contrasted with the earlier, (2) μέν followed by no contrasting particle in the following clause (e.g. πρῶτον almost *at the very first,* Rom 1:8; 1 Cor 11:18), and (3) μὲν οὖν, for the most part in narrative passages, where the μέν brings the accompanying noun or pron. into relief, without any contrast being expressed by a following δέ (e.g. Acts 1:6), (a) where what has preceded is summed up on the way to the relation of some new detail, or (b) where it acts as the introduction to a further occurrence; but see μενοῦν for another use.

Μεννά, ὁ *Menna,* one of the ancestors of Jesus [Heb.].

μενοῦν (μὲν οὖν), μενοῦνγε (μὲν οὖν γε) *nay more, nay rather,* especially in an answer, strengthening or correcting).

μέντοι (1) *indeed, really,* Jas 2:8; (2) *yet, however, nevertheless.*

μένω *I remain, abide, wait;* w. acc. *I wait for, await.*

μερίζω *I divide into parts, I divide, I part, I share, I distribute;* mid. *I go shares, I share* (with others; in this case with Paul, Apollos, Cephas), *I take part in a partitioning,* 1 Cor. 1:13; *I distract,* 1 Cor. 7:34.

μέριμνα, ης, ἡ *care, worry, anxiety.*

μεριμνάω *I am overanxious;* w. acc. *I am anxious about, I care for.*

μερίς, ίδος, ἡ (1) *a part, division* of a country, Acts 16:12 (a sense amply attested outside); (2) *a share, portion.*

μερισμός, οῦ, ὁ (1) *a distributing, a distribution,* Heb 2:4; (2) *a parting, dividing, severance, separation.*

μεριστής, οῦ, ὁ *a divider, arbitrator, distributor.*

μέρος, ους, τό *a part, portion;* τὰ μέρη, territorially, *the region;* adv, phrases are ἀπὸ μέρους, ἐκ μέρους, *in part, partly,* ἀνὰ μέρος, κατὰ μέρος, *part by part, each part separately, in detail; a party,* Acts 23:9.

μεσημβρία, ας, ἡ (lit. *midday,* hence, the position of the sun at midday), *the south.*

μεσιτεύω *I mediate, interpose;* but probably in Heb 6:17 rather *I am surety, I give bail.*

μεσίτης, ου, ὁ (1) *a mediator, intermediary,* 1 Tim 2:5; (2) *a go-between, arbiter, agent* of something good, Gal 3:19, 20; Heb 8:6; 9:15; 12:24.

μεσονύκτιον, ου, τό *midnight,* the middle of the period between sunset and sunrise.

Μεσοποταμία, ας, ἡ *Mesopotamia, the Country between the* (two) *Rivers,* i.e. the Euphrates and the Tigris.

μέσος, η, ον *middle, in the middle,* sometimes followed by the gen. of the whole area referred to; adv. (with or without gen.) are μέσον (acc. neut.), ἀνὰ μέσον (elliptical in 1 Cor. 6:5), κατὰ μέσον, ἐν [τῷ] μέσῳ, *in the middle, before them all,* ἐκ μέσου, *from the midst.*

μεσότοιχον, ου, τό *mid-wall.*

μεσουράνημα, ατος, τό *mid-heaven, the middle of heaven.*

μεσόω *I am in the middle* of my course.

Μεσσίας, ου, ὁ *Messiah, the Anointed One* [Heb.], generally translated into Gk. as Χριστός.

μεστός, ή, όν *full;* met. (cf. πλήρης) almost *tainted, diseased with,* Matt 23:28; Rom 1:29.

μεστόω *I fill.*

μετά prep. (1) w. gen. *with, in company with;* merely, *in connection with,* Luke 1:58; (2) w. acc., (a) *behind, beyond, after,* of place, (b) *after,* of time, w. nouns, neut. of adjs., or τό w. infin.

μεταβαίνω *I change my place (abode), I leave, I depart, I remove.*

μεταβάλλω mid. *I change my mind.*

μεταβέβηκα perf. act. → μεταβαίνω.

μεταβήσομαι fut. mid. → μεταβαίνω.

μετάγω (usually *transfer, transport,* and met., to a better mind), *I turn about, I change the position of.*

μεταδίδωμι (lit. *I offer by way of change, I offer so that a change* of owner is produced), *I share;* sometimes merely, *I impart.*

μεταδοῦναι aor. act. infin. → μεταδίδωμι.

μετάθεσις, εως, ἡ (1) *change,*

transformation, Heb 7:12; 12:27; (2) *removal,* Heb 11:5.

μεταίρω *I change my position, remove.*

μετακαλέω mid. *I summon to myself, I send for.*

μετακινέω trans., *I move away, I dislodge.*

μεταλαβεῖν aor. act. infin. → μεταλαμβάνω.

μεταλαμβάνω (1) *w. gen. I take a share (part) of, I share in, I partake of;* (2) w. acc. *I take after (later)* or *I take instead,* Acts 24:25.

μετάλημψις, εως, ἡ *partaking of, sharing in.*

μεταλλάσσω *I transform, alter.*

μεταμέλομαι (lit. *I change* one *care* or *interest* for another), *I change my mind* (generally for a better).

μεταμορφόω *I change a form* (involving a change of inmost nature; contrast the creatures described in Ovid's *Metamorphoses);* mid. w. acc. *I assume* something *through a change,* 2 Cor 3:18.

μετανοέω *I change* my *mind, I change the inner man* (particularly with reference to acceptance of the will of God by the νοῦς (mind) instead of rejection); w. ἀπό or ἐκ, the giving up definitely of the courses denoted by the following words is indicated.

μετάνοια, ας, ἡ *a change of mind, a change in the inner man;* ἀπό indicates what is given up in this change, Heb 6:1.

μεταξύ prep. w. gen., *between;* μεταξὺ σοῦ καὶ αὐτοῦ μόνου, *privately* (Aram. idiom), Matt 18:15; μεταξὺ ἀλλήλων, *in their mutual intercourse,* Rom 2:15; adv. w. ὁ in the sense *the next, the next after* (because *between* the present and the one after that), Acts 13:42, ἐν τῷ μεταξύ (supply χρόνῳ), *meantime, meanwhile,* John 4:31.

μεταπέμπομαι *I send for, summon.*

μεταστήσας aor. act. part. → μεθίστημι.

μεταστραφήσομαι fut. pas. → μεταστρέφω.

μεταστρέφω *I turn, change.*

μετασχηματίζω *I change the outward appearance (the dress, the form of presentation)* of something; *I transfer by a fiction, adapt.*

μετατίθημι (1) *I transfer,* Acts 7:16; Heb 11:5; mid. *I go over* to another party, *I desert,* Gal 1:6; (2) *I change,* Heb 7:12.

μετατρέπω trans., *I turn, change.*

μετέβην aor. act. → μεταβαίνω.

μετέθηκα aor. act. → μετατίθημι.

μετέπειτα adv., *thereafter.*

μετεστάθην aor. pas. → μεθίστημι.

μετέστησα aor. act. → μεθίστημι.

μετέσχηκα perf. act. → μετέχω.

μετέσχον aor. act. → μετέχω.

μετετέθην aor. pas. → μετατίθημι.

μετετράπην aor. pas. → μετατρέπω.

μετέχω *I have a share of, I participate in, I share.*

μετεωρίζομαι *I am μετέωρος,* i.e. *suspended in midair, anxious,* Luke 12:29.

μετήλλαξα aor. act. → μεταλλάσσω.

μετῆρα aor. act. → μεταίρω.

μετοικεσία, ας, ἡ *transportation, deportation,* followed by gen. of reference, βαβυλῶνος.

μετοικίζω *I transport.*

μετοικιῶ fut. act. → μετοικίζω.

μετοχή, ῆς, ἡ *sharing, partnership.*

μέτοχος, ου, ὁ *a sharer, partner;* w. gen. *in* something.

μετρέω *I measure.*

μετρητής, οῦ, ὁ *a measure,* about 39.39 liters or 8¾ gallons.

μετριοπαθέω *I feel moderately,* with

particular reference to displeasure at men's sin.

μετρίως adv., *moderately;* οὐ μετρίως, *greatly, exceedingly.*

μέτρον, ου, τό *a measure,* whether lineal (e.g. Rev 21:15) or cubic (e.g. Luke 6:38); ἐκ μέτρου (Aram. idiom?), *in scanty measure.*

μετῴκισα aor. act. → μετοικίζω.

μέτωπον, ου, τό *forehead.*

μέχρι, μέχρις conj. with or without οὗ, the ἄν (ἐάν) being omitted in NT examples, w. aor. subj., *until . . .* shall have . . .; prep. w. gen., *as far as; until.*

μή negative particle, *not, that . . . not (lest),* etc., used generally, instead of οὐ, the negative of fact (expressed by the indic.), where there is some indefiniteness about the action or occurrence referred to (expressed by other moods), either because it is in the future, or because it is in an interrog. clause (a feature of everyday language), or because it is in an indef. rel., or a cond., opt., or final clause, etc. Sometimes w. indic. to be translated by *perhaps,* Luke 11:35; Col 2:8 (cf. Heb 3:12); Gal 4:11 (but also w. subjun. as in classical Gk., Matt 25:9, var.). οὐ μή, (1) w. indic. fut. or, far more often, w. subjun. aor., in a statement, a very emphatic negative, *assuredly not.* It occurs for the most part in passages coming from the OT and sayings of Christ (both from Semitic originals), where words of decisive tone are especially in place. In this constr. the prohibition refers to the future, "do not" (in future), as contrasted w. μὴ ποίει, meaning "desist from"; the latter is sometimes durative; (2) w. subjun. aor. in interrog. clause, *not,* Luke 18:7; John 18:11. μή ποτε, see μήποτε; μή που, see μήπου.

μήγε see εἰ δὲ μήγε under εἰ.

μηδαμῶς adv., *not at all.*

μηδέ *nor . . . either,* generally after a preceding μή.

μηδείς, μηδεμία, μηδέν (1) adj., *no,* in agreement w. nouns; (2) each gender used as a noun, *no person, nothing.* Its use with respect to that of οὐδείς corresponds to that of μή with respect to that of οὐ. See also μηδέν; (also another Hellenistic orthography μηθείς, Acts 27:33).

μηδέν adv. (neut. sing. of μηδείς), *not at all, in no way.*

μηδέποτε adv., *not at any time.*

μηδέπω adv., *not yet.*

Μῆδος, ου, ὁ *a Mede, a Median,* from east of Assyria.

μηθείς, μηθέν see μηδείς, μηδέν.

μηκέτι adv., *no longer.*

μῆκος, ους, τό *length.*

μηκύνω *I lengthen.*

μηλωτή, ῆς, ἡ *sheep's* (sometimes *pig's*) *hide, sheepskin.*

μήν, μηνός, ὁ noun, *a* (lunar) *month.*

μήν adv., expressing emphasis, mostly in the formulae of oaths, *assuredly, in very truth.*

μηνύω (1) *I reveal, make known;* in a law court, *I lay information, I inform,* John 11:57; Acts 23:30; (2) *I make known, I point out,* Luke 20:37; 1 Cor 10:28.

μήποτε *lest at any time, lest;* then weakened, *whether perhaps, whether at all;* in a principal clause, *perhaps* (= μή ποτε).

μήπου *lest anywhere* (= μή που).

μήπω adv., *not yet.*

μήπως *lest in any way* (= μή πως).

μηρός, οῦ, ὁ *thigh.*

μήτε (= μή τε) *nor;* μήτε . . . μήτε, *neither . . . nor,* sometimes also oftener than twice (e.g. Jas 5:12)

μήτηρ, τρος, ἡ *a mother;* sometimes also of one who is *as a* *mother,* who takes the place of a mother, Mark 3:34, 35, etc.; John 19:27; Rom 16:13; Gal 4:26; 1 Tim 5:2; Rev 17:5.

μήτι (μή strengthened by the addition of the acc. neut. of τις [indef.] as adv.); (1) w. εἰ; thus εἰ μήτι = εἰ μή, *if not, unless,* Luke 9:13, εἰ μήτι ἄν, *unless in a given case,* 1 Cor 7:5; (2) in questions, expecting a negative answer, cf. Matt 7:16, *can it be that* suggesting impossibility.

μήτιγε a modified μήτι, in elliptical constr., *not to speak of.*

μήτις = μή τις.

μήτρα, ας, ἡ *the womb.*

μητρολῴας (μητραλῴας), ου, ὁ *a person who murders his mother, a matricide.*

μιαίνω met. *I stain, pollute, defile.*

μίασμα, ατος, τό *a pollution, a defilement.*

μιασμός, οῦ, ὁ *pollution, defilement.*

μίγμα (μῖγμα, μεῖγμα), ατος, τό *a mixture.*

μίγνυμι *I mix.*

μικρόν neut. sing. of μικρός, as adv. or noun, *a little,* both of space and of time as well as of size, degree; in John 14:19, etc., understand ἐστιν or ἔσται after μικρόν.

μικρός, ά, όν (1) *small;* superl. μικρότερος, *smallest,* in Mark 15:40 possibly *junior;* (2) of time, *short;* see μικρόν.

Μίλητος, ου, ἡ *Miletus,* a city on the coast of the Roman province Asia.

μίλιον, ου, τό *a Roman mile,* measuring 1478.5 meters [Lat. *milium, a thousand double paces*].

μιμέομαι *I imitate.*

μιμητής, οῦ, ὁ *an imitator.*

μιμνήσκομαι (μιμνῄσκομαι) mid. and pas., *I remember;* the pas. forms sometimes have pas. sense, from act. μιμνήσκω, *I call to mind, I recall, I mention,* Acts 10:31; Rev 16:19.

μισέω *I hate.*

μισθαποδοσία, ας, ἡ (lit. *repayment of price* or *payment of price due*), *reward,* Heb 10:35; 11:26; in the sense, *due punishment,* Heb 2:2.

μισθαποδότης, ου, ὁ *a rewarder,* (see μισθαποδοσία).

μίσθιος, ου, ὁ *a paid worker, a hired servant, a hireling* (contrasted with a slave).

μισθόομαι *I hire, engage.*

μισθός, οῦ, ὁ (1) *pay, wages, salary;* (2) *reward, recompense.*

μίσθωμα, ατος, τό *a rented apartment* or *flat.*

μισθωτός, οῦ, ὁ *hired, engaged* for wages.

Μιτυλήνη (Μυτιλήνη), ης, ἡ *Mitylene,* the capital of the island of Lesbos in the northern Aegean sea

Μιχαήλ, ὁ *Michahel, Michael,* an archangel.

μνᾶ, ᾶς, ἡ *a mina,* a semitic word for the Gk. money unit worth about one hundred δραχμαί.

Μνάσων, ωνος, ὁ *Mnason,* an early Christian, native of Cyprus, resident at a place between Caesarea and Jerusalem.

μνεία, ας, ἡ *remembrance, recollection, mention; commemoration,* Rom 12:13 (var.).

μνῆμα, ατος, τό *a tomb, monument.*

μνημεῖον, ου, τό *a tomb, monument.*

μνήμη, ης, ἡ *memory,* or *mention.*

μνημονεύω *I remember; I hold in remembrance; I make mention of,* Heb 11:22.

μνημόσυνον, ου, τό *reminder, memorial; a remembrance offering,* Acts 10:4.

μνησθήσομαι fut. pas. → μιμνήσκομαι.

μνήσθητι aor. pas. imper. 2 sing. → μιμνήσκομαι.

μνηστεύω *I betroth.*

μογγιλάλος, ον *speaking with a hoarse voice;* var. for μογιλάλος in Mark 7:32.

μογιλάλος, ον (lit. *speaking with difficulty*), hence, *dumb.*

μόγις adv., *with difficulty; scarcely, hardly.*

μόδιος, ου, ὁ a dry measure, the chief corn unit, nearly two English gallons [Lat. *modius*].

μοιχαλίς, ίδος, ἡ (1) *an adulteress* (i.e., a married woman who commits adultery), Rom 7:3; 2 Pet 2:14; (2) Heb., extended to those who worship any other than the true God (Yahweh).

μοιχάομαι *I commit adultery,* not only of a married woman but of a married man (see Matt 19:9, var.; Mark 10:11).

μοιχεία, ας, ἡ *adultery.*

μοιχεύω *I commit adultery* (of a man with a married woman, but also (Luke 16:18) of a married man).

μοιχός, οῦ, ὁ *an adulterer,* i.e., a man who is guilty with a married woman.

μόλις adv., *with difficulty, hardly.*

Μολόχ, ὁ *Moloch,* a god worshipped by several Semitic peoples (Heb., name is properly an appellation = king).

μολύνω *I soil, stain, pollute,* lit. and morally.

μολυσμός, οῦ, ὁ *staining, contamination, pollution.*

μομφή, ῆς, ἡ (lit. *blame, fault finding*), *a complaint, fault.*

μονή, ῆς, ἡ (1) abstr., μονὴν ποιεῖσθαι, *to stay, to dwell,* John 14:23; (2) concr., *lodging, dwelling place, room.*

μονογενής, ές *only-born, only,* of children.

μόνον *only,* acc. sing. neut. of μόνος, used as adv.

μόνος, η, ον *alone;* κατὰ μόνας = κατ' ἰδίαν, *by himself.*

μονόφθαλμος, ον *one-eyed, with one eye only.*

μονόω *I leave alone (solitary).*

μορφή, ῆς, ἡ *form,* implying essential character as well as outline. It suggests unchangeableness, as contrasted with σχῆμα (= figure, fashion). In Phil 2:6 the reference is to the preincarnate Christ with divine attributes.

μορφόω *I form, shape* (of the development of the embryo into the fully formed child).

μόρφωσις, εως, ἡ a mere *form, outline.*

μοσχοποιέω *I make* a model of *a calf.*

μόσχος, ου, ὁ *a calf.*

μουσικός, οῦ, ὁ *a musician,* but probably in some narrower sense in Rev 18:22.

μόχθος, ου, ὁ *struggle, hardship,* involved in continued *labors.*

μυελός, ου, ὁ *marrow.*

μυέω (*I initiate* into the Mysteries), hence, *I habituate.*

μῦθος, ου, ὁ *an idle tale, fable, fanciful story.*

μυκάομαι *I roar.*

μυκτηρίζω (properly, *I turn up the nose* as a sign of contempt), *I sneer at, disdain.*

μυλικός, ή, όν *belonging to a mill.*

μύλινος, η, ον *a millstone.*

μύλος, ου, ὁ *a mill.*

Μύρα, ων, τό *Myra,* a port in Lycia, southwest Asia Minor.

μυριάς, άδος, ἡ a group of *ten thousand, a ten thousand.*

μυρίζω *I anoint.*

μύριοι (μυρίοι), αι, α *ten thousand;* also used for a very large number.

μυρίος, α, ον *innumerable, countless.*

μύρον, ου, τό *anointing oil; ointment* (a Semitic word).
Μύρρα see Μύρα.
Μυσία, ας, ἡ *Mysia,* a country in the northwest of the Roman province Asia (and of Asia Minor).
μυστήριον, ου, τό *a secret,* Mark 4:11 and pars.; also (1) a symbol containing *a secret* meaning, Rev 17:5, cf. Eph 5:32; (2) the meaning of such a symbol, Rev 1:20; 17:7; (3) as the counterpart of ἀποκάλυψις, *secret* to be revealed, *the secret purpose* of God in His dealings with man, *a Divine secret,* especially the inclusion of the Gentiles as well as the Jews in the scope of the Messiah's beneficent reign; (4) the sum of the Christian faith, 1 Tim 3:9, 16.
Μυτιλήνη see Μιτυλήνη.
μυωπάζω *I half close the eyes, I blink.*
μώλωψ, ωπος, ὁ *a welt* or *bruise* left on the body by scourging.
μωμάομαι *I calumniate, slander.*
μῶμος, ου, ὁ *a blemish* (a "Hebraic" sense peculiar to biblical Gk.; the classical sense is *blame*).
μωραίνω (1) *I make foolish, I turn to foolishness;* (2) *I taint,* and thus *make useless,* Matt 5:13; Luke 14:34 (from μωρός).
μωρία, ας, ἡ *foolishness.*
μωρολογία, ας, ἡ *foolish talking.*
μωρός, ά, όν (1) adj., *foolish;* (2) noun, *a fool.*
Μωϋσῆς (Μωυσῆς), έως, ὁ *Moses* (the form nearer Heb. found in oldest Latin Bible and Vulgate), *Moyses,* the lawgiver of the Hebrews, thus regarded as the author of the Pentateuch, where the laws are preserved (cf. 2 Cor 3:15, etc.).

N

Ναασσών, ὁ *Naasson,* son of Aminadab and father of Salmon (Sala), and one of the ancestors of Jesus [Heb.].
Ναγγαί, ὁ *Naggai,* one of the ancestors of Jesus [Heb.].
Ναζαρά (Ναζαρέτ), ἡ *Nazareth,* a city of Galilee, where Jesus lived before His ministry. (The former is the Gk. form, declined, while the latter is the native form, not declined).
Ναζαρηνός, οῦ, ὁ *of Nazareth, a Nazarene.*
Ναζωραῖος, ου, ὁ commonly interpreted to mean, *of Nazareth, Nazarene,* the ω being nearer to the Syr. form *Natsoreth.*
Ναθάμ, ὁ *Nathan,* son of David, and an ancestor of Jesus [Heb.].
Ναθαναήλ, ὁ *Nathanael, Nathanahel,* of Cana in Galilee, an early disciple.
ναί *yes,* sometimes made a subs. by prefixing the article τό.
Ναιμάν, ὁ *Naaman,* commander in chief of the army of a king of Syria in the ninth c. B.C. (2 Kgs 5).
Ναΐν (Ναϊν, Ναϊμ), ἡ *Nain,* a city southwest of the Sea of Galilee.
ναός, οῦ, ὁ *a temple, a shrine,* that part of the temple where the god himself resides (contrast ἱερόν); so also figuratively.
Ναούμ, ὁ *Naum, Nahum,* an ancestor of Jesus [Heb.].
νάρδος, ου, ἡ *spikenard,* a perfume made originally from the *Nardo-stachys Jatamansi* growing on the Himalayas [Heb., borrowed into Persian and Sanskrit].
Νάρκισσος, ου, ὁ *Narcissus,* a resident in Rome in Nero's time.
ναυαγέω (1) *I am shipwrecked;* so (2) figuratively, *I come to ruin.*
ναύκληρος, ου, ὁ *a captain (master)* of a ship.
ναῦς, acc. **ναῦν, ἡ** *a ship, a vessel,* Acts 27:41 only (literary, almost

obsolete, rare in the vernacular; see πλοῖον).
ναύτης, ου, ὁ *a sailor.*
Ναχώρ, ὁ *Nachor,* one of the ancestors of Jesus [Heb.].
νεανίας, ου, ὁ *a young man, a man in his prime* (used even of a man of 40).
νεανίσκος, ου, ὁ *a youth.*
Νεάπολις = Νέα Πόλις, see νέος.
νεῖκος, ους, τό see νῖκος.
νεκρός, ά, όν (1) adj., *dead, lifeless;* hence met.; (2) noun, *a dead body, a corpse,* ἐκ [τῶν] νεκρῶν, *from among the dead.*
νεκρόω lit. and met. *I make (cause) to be dead; I make as dead.*
νέκρωσις, εως, ἡ (1) *putting to death,* 2 Cor 4:10; (2) *dead* or *lifeless condition,* Rom 4:19.
νεομηνία (νουμηνία), ας, ἡ *a new moon* (the Ionic form νεομηνία probably not used by NT writers).
νέος, α, ον (1) *young;* (2) *new, fresh;* Νέα πόλις, *Neapolis, New City,* the harbor town of Philippi.
νεότης, ητος, ἡ *youth, youthfulness.*
νεόφυτος, ον (lit. *newly planted*), *newly converted* to Christianity.
νεύω *I nod, make a sign.*
νεφέλη, ης, ἡ *a cloud.*
Νεφθαλείμ (Νεφθαλίμ), ὁ *Naphthali,* son of Jacob, founder of a tribe which occupied territory.
νέφος, ους, τό (lit. *a cloud*), hence, *a dense crowd.*
νεφρός, οῦ, ὁ *a kidney* (as a general emotional centre).
νεωκόρος, ου, ὁ (lit. *temple sweeper*), *temple warden;* an honorary title.
νεωτερικός, ή, όν *associated with youth (younger men), youthful.*
νή *by,* w. an acc. of adjuration.
νήθω *I spin* (a vulgar and late form of νέω).
νηπιάζω *I am childish (infantile).*
νήπιος, α, ον *an infant, a child.*
Νηρεύς, έως, ὁ *Nereus,* a Christian in Rome.
Νηρί (Νηρεί), ὁ *Nerei,* an ancestor of Jesus [Heb.].
νησίον, ου, τό *a little island, an islet.*
νῆσος, ου, ἡ *an island.*
νηστεία, ας, ἡ *fasting.*
νηστεύω *I fast.*
νῆστις, ιδος, acc. pl. **νήστεις, ὁ** and **ἡ** *fasting, without food.*
νηφάλιος, α, ον *sober, not intoxicated* (with wine).
νήφω (lit. *I am sober*), *I am calm (vigilant).*
Νίγερ, ὁ *Niger,* another name of Symeon, a Christian at Antioch.
Νικάνωρ, ορος, ὁ *Nicanor,* one of the original seven "deacons" in the church at Jerusalem.
νικάω *I conquer* (transferred from battle to other conflicts).
νίκη, ης, ἡ *victory.*
Νικόδημος, ου, ὁ *Nicodemus,* a rich Jewish follower of Jesus, and member of the Sanhedrin.
Νικολαΐτης, ου, ὁ *a Nicolaitan, a follower of Nicolaus* (a heretic at Ephesus).
Νικόλαος, ου, ὁ *Nicolaus,* a Jewish proselyte of Antioch, one of the original seven "deacons" in the church at Jerusalem.
Νικόπολις, εως, ἡ *Nicopolis,* probably the city near Actium in Epirus, northwest Greece.
νῖκος, ους, τό *victory* (a later variety of νίκη, dating from about the middle of first c. B.C.).
Νινευίτης (Νινευείτης), ου, ὁ *a Ninevite, an inhabitant of Nineveh* or *Ninus,* a city on the Tigris in Assyria.
νιπτήρ, ῆρος, ὁ *a basin.*
νίπτω *I wash;* mid. *I wash my own* (hands, etc.).
νοέω *I understand, conceive, apprehend;* aor. possibly *realize,* John 12:40; Eph 3:4.

νόημα, ατος, τό *a thought; a design.*
νόθος, η, ον *a bastard, an illegitimate son.*
νομή, ῆς, ἡ (1) *pasture;* (2) ἔχειν νομήν, *to spread,* 2 Tim 2:17.
νομίζω *I think, suppose.*
νομικός, ή, όν (1) adj., *connected with law, about law,* Tit. 3:9; (2) noun, *a lawyer, one learned in the Law* (i.e. in the Gospels), *one learned in the* OT *scriptures* (like γραμματεύς), *a scribe; a jurist,* Tit. 3:13.
νομίμως adv., *in a legitimate way, according to law and regulation.*
νόμισμα, ατος, τό *a coin.*
νομοδιδάσκαλος, ου, ὁ (1) *a teacher of the Law, one learned in the Law* (i.e. the OT), = γραμματεύς, νομικός; (2) *a teacher of laws,* probably with reference to heretics of ascetic tendency, 1 Tim 1:7.
νομοθεσία, ας, ἡ *legislation* (at Sinai), *enactment of the Law.*
νομοθετέω (1) *I ordain, lay down, give the sanction of law to, enact,* Heb 8:6; (2) *I base legally, I regulate, I direct.*
νομοθέτης, ου, ὁ *a legislator.*
νόμος, ου, ὁ (1) *the Law,* and so sometimes = the body of moral and ceremonial enactments forming the basis of Judaism; especially as set forth in the OT; *the Old Testament;* but also ὁ νόμος καὶ οἱ προφῆται, Matt 7:12, etc., as a description of the content of the OT, though as strictly interpreted the phrase excludes the "writings" (namely Psalms, Proverbs, Job, Song of Songs, Ruth, Ecclesiastes, Esther, Daniel, Ezra, Nehemiah, Chronicles); (2) *power to legislate, a sense of law, something with legislative authority,* e.g. Rom 7:23; 8:2; Gal 6:2; (3) *a law, an ordinance,* Rom 7:2; Jas 1:25; 2:8.
νοσέω *I am diseased,* hence of mental or spiritual disease.
νόσημα, ατος, τό *a disease, a trouble.*
νόσος, ου, ἡ *a disease, a malady.*
νοσσιά (νοσσία), ᾶς, ἡ *a nestling, a young bird in the nest* (syncopated from νεοσσία).
νοσσίον, ου, τό *a nestling, a young bird in the nest;* see νοσσιά.
νοσσός, οῦ, ὁ *a nestling, a young bird, a young one.*
νοσφίζω mid. *I separate for myself, I set apart for myself, I annex, appropriate for my own benefit, purloin, peculate.*
νότος, ου, ὁ *the south wind;* hence, *the south.*
νουθεσία, ας, ἡ *a warning, admonition.*
νουθετέω *I admonish, warn.*
νουμηνία see νεομηνία.
νουνεχῶς adv., *reasonably, sensibly.*
νοῦς, νοός, ὁ *the intellectual faculty* of the natural man, applicable to God or Christ (Rom 11:34; 1 Cor 2:16), employed in practical judgment, capable of being good or evil, and of being regenerated, *the mind, the reason, the reasoning faculty* (a non-Semitic Gk. term, meaning in Plato *reason, intuition,* sometimes in the LXX taking the place of the commoner καρδία as a rendering of Heb. *lēb*).
Νύμφα (Νυμφᾶς), ας, ἡ *Nympha,* a woman's name, if we read Νύμφαν and αὐτῆς in Col 4:15, as we probably should; otherwise, Νυμφᾶν will be the acc. of the masc. name Νυμφᾶς, a pet form of Νυμφόδωρος, *Nymphas, Nymphodorus.*
νύμφη (νύνφη), ης, ἡ (1) *a bride;* hence, in the symbolism of Rev, the New Jerusalem, the Lamb's Bride; (2) *a daughter-in-law,* Matt 10:35; Luke 12:53.

νυμφίος, ου, ὁ *a bridegroom;* name applied to the Messiah, Mark 2:19, 20 and pars.

νυμφών, ῶνος, ὁ *a wedding chamber;* οἱ υἱοὶ νυμφῶνος (a Semitism), *the wedding guests,* the Messiah being spoken of as bridegroom, Mark 2:19 and pars., cf. νυμφίος.

νῦν, adv. *now, at present,* sometimes w. article preceding, τὸ νῦν, τὰ νῦν, governed at times by preps., ἀπό, ἕως, ἄχρι.

νυνί, adv. *now* (orig. a more emphatic νῦν).

νύξ, νυκτός, ἡ (1) *night;* νυκτός, διὰ νυκτός, *by night, sometime during the night,* see also ἡμέρα; (2) met. 1 Thess 5:5, etc.

νύσσω *I prick.*

νυστάζω *I sleep, slumber;* met. 2 Pet 2:3.

νυχθήμερον, ου, τό *a night and a day* (not necessarily more than the latter part of a night and the earlier part of the succeeding day).

Νῶε, ὁ *Noah* [Heb.].

νωθρός, ά, όν (1) *blunt, dull;* (2) hence spiritually, *sluggish, remiss, slack.*

νῶτος, ου, ὁ *the back.*

Ξ

ξαίνω *I comb, clean* (of the preparation of wool to make thread).

ξενία, ας, ἡ *a lodging,* or rather, abstr., *hospitality.*

ξενίζω (1) *I entertain* a stranger; (2) *I startle, bewilder,* Acts 17:20; 1 Pet 4:4, 12.

ξενοδοχέω *I receive (entertain) strangers.*

ξένος, η, ον (1) adj., *foreign,* Acts 17:18; *strange, unusual,* Heb 13:9; 1 Pet 4:12; (2) noun, *a stranger, a foreigner* (either one belonging to another community in the same country, or to another country); *a resident alien,* without city rights, Acts 17:21; Eph 2:19; Heb 11:13; w. gen. *a stranger to,* Eph 2:12; *a host (guest) friend,* the word indicating the reciprocal relationship, which was a sacred one, Rom 16:23.

ξέστης, ου, ὁ properly a Roman dry measure, rather less than a pint; referred to rather as a household *utensil* than as a measure [Lat. *sextarius*].

ξηραίνω *I dry up; parch.*

ξηρός, ά, όν *dry;* ἡ ξηρά, *dry land,* as opposed to sea, etc.; *dried up, withered, parched;* in generalizing neut., Luke 23:31.

ξύλινος, η, ον *made of wood.*

ξύλον, ου, τό *wood, a piece of wood;* hence, *a club, a staff,* Mark 14:43, 48 and pars.; *the trunk of a tree,* used to support the crossbar of a cross in crucifixion, Acts 5:30, etc.; *a tree,* Luke 23:31, ζωῆς, the fruit of which gives life, Rev 2:7; 22:2, 14, 19.

ξυράω *I shave,* mid. and pas. *I have* my head *shaved.*

Ο

ὁ, ἡ, τό the def. article, by which the following word is defined more precisely or exactly than it would be (but it is often omitted, for example, after a prep., even where a definite place is intended, cf. ἐν οἴκῳ, *in the house,* Mark 2:1, ἐν ἀγορᾷ, *in the marketplace,* Luke 7:32, ἐν συναγωγῇ, *in church,* John 6:59; 18:20). It is thus found (1) w. common nouns, e.g. ὁ ἀγρός, *the* field (ἀγρός, *a* field), (in Tit. 2:13 the absence of τοῦ before σωτῆρος shows that Christ Jesus is our great God and Savior), and (2) sometimes also w. proper nouns, where it was equivalent to pointing out a man, and was popular in origin; w. the voc., commonest where translated from Semitic; (3) w. adjs., e.g. ὁ ἄλλος, *the* other (ἄλλος, *an* other), ὁ αὐτός, *the same* (αὐτός, *he, self*), ὁ πᾶς, πᾶς ὁ, *the whole* (πᾶς, *every*); (4) w. numerals, e.g. ὁ εἷς *the* one (εἷς, *one*), ὁ πρῶτος, *the* first, *the* former (πρῶτος, *first*); (5) w. parts., e.g. τοῖς καθημένοις, *those* seated, Matt 4:16, cf. instances where a part. may be regarded as understood, e.g. Σαῦλος ὁ καὶ Παῦλος, *Saul who was also called Paul, Saul, otherwise Paul,* Acts 13:9; (6) w. the infin., making it a subs., and so capable of being governed by preps.; see below also; (7) w. advs., e.g. τὸ πέραν, *the other side* (πέραν, *beyond*), τὸ νῦν, τὰ νῦν (8) w. interjections, e.g. τὸ ἀμήν, ἡ οὐαί (9) w. a clause or phrase, e.g. τὸ οὐ φονεύσεις, *the command Thou shalt do no murder,* Matt 19:18. The gen. sing. neut. τοῦ w. the infin. is used in three special ways (like ἵνα), (a) as in classical Gk., indicating purpose, final, telic, *in order that;* never in Paul, (b) indicating consequence, epexegetic, *so that, so as to, with the result that,* e.g. Rom 1:24; 7:3; 8:12; 1 Cor. 10:13; Rev 12:7, (c) introducing a noun clause, indicating content, in no way different from τό, Matt 21:32; Luke 17:1; Acts 10:25; Jas 5:17. Orig. a demons. pron., as in τοῦ γένος ἐσμέν, *we are descended from Him,* Acts 17:28, cf. ὁ μέν . . . ὁ δέ (ἄλλος δέ), *the one . . . the other.* But in the following phrases some word is understood, ὁ τινός, *the son of* so and so, cf. Matt 4:21, ἡ τινός, *the daughter (wife) of* so and so, ἐν τοῖς τινός, *in the house of* so and so, Luke 2:49.

ὀγδοήκοντα *eighty.*

ὄγδοος, η, ον *eighth.*

ὄγκος, ου, ὁ (properly *bulk, mass*), hence, *a burden.*

ὅδε, ἥδε, τόδε *this here, this;* also as pron..

ὁδεύω *I am on a journey.*

ὁδηγέω *I lead, guide.*

ὁδηγός, οῦ, ὁ *a guide.*

ὁδοιπορέω *I am on a journey, I journey.*

ὁδοιπορία, ας, ἡ *journeying, traveling, travel.*

ὁδοποιέω *I journey* (a Latinism[?], = *iter facere;* in careful Gk. it would mean, *I build* or *pave a road*).

ὁδός, οῦ, ἡ (1) *a road;* (2) *a journey;* hence met., *a way of life, a course of conduct,* and ἡ ὁδός, *the way* of life, *Christianity,* Acts 9:2, etc.

ὀδούς, ὀδόντος, ὁ *a tooth.*

ὀδυνάομαι pas. *I suffer acute pain,* physical or mental.

ὀδύνη, ης, ἡ *acute* mental *pain.*

ὀδυρμός, οῦ, ὁ *mourning, grieving.*

Ὀζίας (Ὀζείας), ου, ὁ *Ozeias, Uzziah,* son of Joram and father of Joatham, and king of Judah from about 785 to 746 B.C., an ancestor of Jesus [Heb.].

ὄζω intrans., *I smell, am fetid.*

ὅθεν adv., (1) local, *whence, from which place;* (2) inferential, *wherefore.*

ὀθόνη, ης, ἡ *a sheet,* made of fine linen (a word of Semitic origin).

ὀθόνιον, ου, τό *a bandage, a wrapping* (see ὀθόνη).

οἶδα (1) *I know* a fact; perhaps, *I remember,* 1 Cor 1:16; 2 Cor 12:3; w. infin. *I know how to;* (2) *I know (am acquainted with)* a person.

οἰκεῖος, ου, ὁ (from οἶκος, *household, family*), *of one's family, intimate,* 1 Tim 5:8; hence met.

οἰκετεία, ας, ἡ *household* of slaves.

οἰκέτης, ου, ὁ *a household slave, a slave.*

οἰκέω *I dwell,* lit. and met.; w. acc. *I inhabit.*

οἴκημα, ατος, τό *a prison* (euphemism for δεσμωτήριον).

οἰκητήριον, ου, τό *a dwelling place,* lit. and met.

οἰκία, ας, ἡ *a house* (strictly *the whole house,* see οἶκος); of Heaven, John 14:2; also met. *property, belongings,* Mark 12:40 and pars.; *household,* John 4:53; of the body, 2 Cor 5:1, 2.

οἰκιακός, οῦ, ὁ *a member of one's household.*

οἰκοδεσποτέω *I am master/mistress of a house.*

οἰκοδεσπότης, ου, ὁ *a master of a house, a head of a house.*

οἰκοδομέω *I build* (a house); hence met.

οἰκοδομή, ῆς, ἡ (1) abstr., *building, the operation (process) of building,* sometimes transitional, without being strictly concr., 1 Cor 3:9; 2 Cor 5:1; Eph 2:21; 4:12, 16, 29 (here perhaps = *improvement*); (2) met. *upbuilding, edification;* (3) concr., *a building,* Mark 13:1, 2; Matt 24:1.

οἰκοδόμος, ου, ὁ *a house builder, a builder.*

οἰκονομέω *I am a steward, I do the work of a steward.*

οἰκονομία, ας, ἡ *household management, stewardship, the office of a steward;* hence met. of any position of trust or the duties of that position, *provision, arrangement, dispensation* (even God being sometimes regarded as steward).

οἰκονόμος, ου, ὁ (1) *a steward* (commonly a superior slave of tried character, who looked after the accounts of a household; hence met. 1 Cor iv 1, 2; Tit. 1:7; 1 Pet 4:10; (2) apparently, *City Steward* or *Treasurer,* Rom 16:23; (3) perhaps not to be separated from (1), *a guardian, a legal guardian,* Gal 4:2. In any case he manages the property of the "infant" till the age of 25, perhaps.

οἶκος, ου, ὁ (strictly *a set of rooms,* see οἰκία), (1) *a house,* the material building; οἶκος τοῦ θεοῦ, the Temple at Jerusalem, Mark 2:26, etc. (referred to in Matt 23:38); (2) hence met., *a household, family;* οἶκος Ἰσραήλ, Ἰακώβ, Δαυείδ (Hebraic, note the omission of the article).

οἰκουμένη, ης, ἡ (properly pres. part. pas. of οἰκέω, w. γῆ understood, *the land that is being inhabited, the land in a state of habitation*), *the inhabited world,* i.e., *the Roman world,* for all outside it was regarded as of no account.

οἰκουργός, όν *a house worker, a housekeeper,* var. for οἰκουρός in Titus 2:5.

οἰκουρός, όν *staying at home; a housekeeper,* see οἰκουργός.

οἰκτιρήσω fut. act. → οἰκτίρω.

οἰκτίρω (οἰκτείρω) *I pity.*

οἰκτιρμός, οῦ, ὁ *pity, mercy;* the frequency of the plur. is due to Hebraic influence (the corresponding Heb. word has the same meaning in the plur.).

οἰκτίρμων, ον *pitiful, merciful.*

οἶμαι, οἴομαι *I think;* w. infin. the underlying idea is that of purpose, Phil 1:17.

οἰνοπότης, ου, ὁ *an excessive wine drinker.*

οἶνος, ου, ὁ *wine;* met. Rev (except 6:6; 18:13), where almost otiose.

οἰνοφλυγία, ας, ἡ *sottishness,* steeping of oneself in wine.

οἴομαι see οἶμαι.

οἷος, α, ον rel. and indir. interrog., *such as, of what kind (character);* οὐχ οἷον δὲ ὅτι, Rom 9:6, is equivalent to a strong negative, *not of course* (lit. *it is not so that*). Prop-early correlative to τοιοῦτος, the combined expression meaning *of such a kind as*, 1 Cor 15:48; by itself.

οἴσω fut. act. → φέρω.

ὀκνέω *I shrink (from), I hesitate, I am afraid.*

ὀκνηρός, ά, όν *timid; slothful;* ἐμοὶ οὐκ ὀκνηρόν, a kind of epistolary formula, *I do not hesitate.*

ὀκταήμερος, ον *eight days old.*

ὀκτώ *eight.*

ὄλεθρος, ου, ὁ *ruin, doom, destruction.*

ὀλιγοπιστία, ας, ἡ *smallness of belief (faith).*

ὀλιγόπιστος, ον *of little faith (belief).*

ὀλίγος (ὀλίγος), η, ον (1) especially in the plur., *few;* (2) in the sing., *small;* hence, of time, *short,* of degree, *light, slight, little;* πρὸς ὀλίγον, *to a slight degree,* 1 Tim 4:8, *for a short time,* Jas 4:14; ἐν ὀλίγῳ, *in brief compass, in brief, in few words, briefly* (cf. 1 Pet 5:12), Eph 3:3; Acts 26:28 (perhaps = *in very short time*); ὀλίγον (acc. neut.), adverbially, of space, *a little,* Mark 1:19; Luke 5:3, of time, *for a short (little) time,* Mark 6:31; 1 Pet 1:6 (but more probably, *to a little amount*), 5:10; Rev 17:10.

ὀλιγόψυχος, ον *pusillanimous, of small courage.*

ὀλιγωρέω *I hold in low esteem, I make light* of.

ὀλίγως adv., *slightly, just.*

ὀλοθρευτής, οῦ, ὁ *the destroying angel* (cf. Num 16:41ff.).

ὀλοθρεύω ὁ ὀλοθρεύων, *the Destroyer, the destroying angel* (cf. Exod 12:23, and ὀλοθρευτής).

ὁλοκαύτωμα, ατος, τό *a burnt offering.*

ὁλοκληρία, ας, ἡ *perfect (unimpaired) health.*

ὁλόκληρος, ον *complete* (in every part), *entire, whole* (properly a word of Gk. ritual, of either victim for sacrifice or priest, *free from bodily defect*).

ὀλολύζω *I howl* (onomatopoeic).

ὅλος, η, ον *whole, all;* δι' ὅλου, *throughout, for its whole extent, quite, entirely,* John 19:23.

ὁλοτελής, ές *complete, rounded off.*

Ὀλυμπᾶς, ᾶ, ὁ *Olympas,* a Christian man in Rome (probably a pet form of Ὀλυμπιόδωρος).

ὄλυνθος, ου, ὁ *an unripe fig.*

ὅλως adv., (1) *entirely, altogether, at all;* (2) *actually,* 1 Cor 5:1; *absolutely,* 1 Cor. 6:7; 15:29.

ὄμβρος, ου, ὁ *a rainstorm.*

ὁμείρομαι *I long for,* w. gen. (perhaps a nursery word, derived from a word indicating "remembrance").

ὁμιλέω *I consort with, associate with, commune with;* particularly, *I talk (converse) with,* Acts 20:11.

ὁμιλία, ας, ἡ *intercourse, companionship, conversation.*

ὅμιλος, ου, ὁ *a crowd, throng* (var. in Rev 18:17).

ὁμίχλη, ης, ἡ *a mist, fog.*

ὄμμα, ατος, τό *an eye.*

ὀμνύω (ὄμνυμι) *I swear, I take an oath;* sometimes w. cog. acc. or w. dat.; w. acc., or w. κατά w. gen., of the power invoked or appealed to, *by,* Jas 5:12; Heb 6:13, 16.

ὁμοθυμαδόν adv., *with one mind, with one accord.*

ὁμοιάζω *I am like.*

ὁμοιοπαθής, ές *of like feelings,* almost, *of like nature.*

ὅμοιος, α, ον *like.*

ὁμοιότης, ητος, ἡ *resemblance;* understand ἡμῶν in Heb 4:15, cf. 7:15.

ὁμοιόω *I make like, liken; I compare.*

ὁμοίωμα, ατος, τό (orig., *a thing made like* something else), *likeness,* or rather *form.*

ὁμοίως adv., *in a similar way, similarly, in the same way.*

ὁμοίωσις, εως, ἡ *making like; likeness* (cf. Gen 1:26).

ὁμολογέω (orig., *I agree with the statement* of another), (1) *I promise,* Matt 14:7; Acts 7:17; (2) *I confess;* (3) *I publicly declare,* cf. 1 John 2:23, 4:3, sometimes w. the Aram. and Syr. constr., ἐν w. dat. equivalent to an acc., Matt 10:32; Luke 12:8, of confessing allegiance to Jesus before an earthly law court; w. cog. acc. 1 Tim 6:12; (4) a Hebraism, *I praise, celebrate,* Heb 13:15 (cf. ἐξομολογέομαι).

ὁμολογία, ας, ἡ *a confession* (the act rather than the contents or substance) of faith in Christ; 1 Tim 6:12 refers either to that at baptism or to that at ordination; 1 Tim 6:13 is referred by Pelagius to John 18:37, not inappropriately.

ὁμολογουμένως adv., *admittedly.*

ὀμόσαι aor. act. infin. → ὀμνύω.

ὁμότεχνος, ον *of the same trade.*

ὁμοῦ adv., *together.*

ὁμόφρων, ον *of one mind (intent, purpose).*

ὅμως adv., *nevertheless.*

ὀναίμην aor. opt. → ὀνίνημι.

ὄναρ, τό *a dream.*

ὀνάριον, ου, τό *an ass* (a conversational diminutive).

ὀνειδίζω *I reproach.*

ὀνειδισμός, οῦ, ὁ *a reproaching, a reproach.*

ὄνειδος, ους, τό *a reproach.*

Ὀνήσιμος, ου, ὁ *Onesimus,* a slave of Philemon, a Christian of Colossae (orig. adj., *useful,* hence the play upon words in Phlm 10, 11, and very common as slave name).

Ὀνησίφορος, ου, ὁ *Onesiphorus,* a Christian of the province of Asia. (An Onesiphorus, probably intended to be the same person, comes into the *Acts of Paul*).

ὀνικός, ή, όν *connected with an ass;* μύλος ὀνικός, an upper millstone so heavy that it requires an ass to turn it (in contrast to the ordinary hand mill).

ὀνίνημι trans., *I profit;* pas. w. gen. *I have joy of.*

ὄνομα, ατος, τό (1) *a name;* but as, according to Heb. notions, the name is something inseparable from the person to whom it belongs, something of his essence, and therefore in the case of the God specially sacred, it is often used Hebraistically in the sense of (2) *person, personality, power, authority, character* (cf. Acts 1:15; Rev 3:4; 11:13); in some passages it is in consequence best left untranslated altogether; εἰς τὸ ὄνομά τινος is a vernacular phrase, however [see (4)]; (3) *a title of rank (dignity),* Eph 1:21; Phil 2:9; (4) *account, reason, pretext,* Mark 9:41; 1 Pet 4:16; similarly εἰς ὄνομα, Matt 10:41, 42 = *as;* (5) *reputation,* Rev 3:1.

ὀνομάζω *I name, give a name to.*

ὄνος, ου, ὁ and **ἡ** *an ass.*

ὄντως adv., *really, actually.*

ὄξος, ους, τό *vinegar of wine* (Num 6:3), *vinegar,* the drink of field laborers and private soldiers.

ὀξύς, εῖα, ύ (1) *sharp;* (2) *swift, express,* Rom 3:15.

ὀπή, ῆς, ἡ *a crevice* (in a rock); *a cave.*

ὄπισθεν adv. and prep. w. gen., *behind;* in Rev 5:1 the reverse (outer) side of the papyrus roll, where the fibers are vertical, is referred to; this was seldom written on, and only from motives of economy.

ὀπίσω adv. and prep. w. gen. *behind; after;* εἰς τὰ ὀπίσω (Mark 13:16) = ὀπίσω (Matt 24:18), cf. Luke 9:62.

ὁπλίζω trans., *I arm;* mid. *I arm myself;* especially of defensive armor (breastplate, shield, etc.).
ὅπλον, ου, τό especially plur. ὅπλα, *defensive armor* (Rom 13:12), but also *offensive armor, weapons, arms* (John 18:3); sometimes met.
ὁποῖος, α, ον rel. and indir. interrog., corresponding to τοιοῦτος, *of which kind; of what kind, what sort of.* This word was dying out in NT times.
ὁπότε adv., *when,* Luke 6:3 (var. ὅτε); (in classical Gk. *whenever*).
ὅπου adv., *where,* also *to what place;* ὅπου ἄν (ἐάν), *wherever,* also *to whatever place.*
ὀπτάνομαι *I appear, I am seen (by), I let myself be seen (by).*
ὀπτασία, ας, ἡ *a vision; an appearance.*
ὀπτός, ή, όν *broiled.*
ὀπώρα, ας, ἡ *autumn;* hence, *fruit.*
ὅπως *in order that; that* (especially after ἐρωτάω), w. the subjun., with or without ἄν.
ὅραμα, ατος, τό (lit., *something seen*), *a sight, a vision.*
ὅρασις, εως, ἡ *a sight, a vision;* ὁράσει, *in appearance,* Rev 4:3.
ὁρατός, ή, όν *to be seen, visible.*
ὁράω *I see;* hence, like γεύω, widened in sense to mean, *I experience* (Luke 3:6, etc.); ὅρα (ὅρατε) μή, *see that* you do *not . . ., beware of* doing so and so; *beware lest.*
ὀργή, ῆς, ἡ *anger, wrath, passion; the settled feeling of anger* (cf. Eph 4:31), particularly, τοῦ θεοῦ, of God, *the hostility* to sin; ἡ μέλλουσα (ἐρχομένη) ὀργή also refers to the divine wrath, and has a definite eschatological reference; occasionally also without epithet, of the divine wrath, e.g. Rom 3:5; 5:9; 9:22; 13:5; 1 Thess 2:16.
ὀργίζομαι *I am angry.*
ὀργίλος, η, ον *irascible.*
ὀργυιά, ᾶς, ἡ *a fathom* (six feet).
ὀρέγομαι mid. *I hanker after, I seek (long) for, I am eager for, I aspire to.*
ὀρεινός (ὀρινός), ή, όν, ἡ *hilly, mountainous;* ἡ ὀρεινὴ (supply γῆ), *the mountain (mountainous) country (region), the highlands.*
ὄρεξις, εως, ἡ *eagerness, strong desire.*
ὀρθοποδέω (strictly, *I am an* ὀρθόπους [*a man with straight feet*], and therefore πρός = *with reference to;* but it is possible that we ought to take it) *I go straight,* πρός, *to.*
ὀρθός, ή, όν *straight, erect* (perhaps with reference to recovery of health), Acts 14:10; met. *that goes in the right direction,* Heb 12:13.
ὀρθοτομέω perhaps, *I cut* (or *carve*) *according to rule* (and thus, *I define* according to the norm of the Gospel); if the metaphor be from drawing furrows (understanding τὴν γῆν), then it may be, *I cultivate, I am occupied with.*
ὀρθρίζω *I rise early, I come in the morning.*
ὀρθρινός, ή, όν *belonging to the morning;* hence, equivalent to adv., *in the morning, early.*
ὄρθρος, ου, ὁ *dawn, early morning, daybreak.*
ὀρθῶς adv., *rightly.*
ὁρίζω (lit. *I bound, I fix a limit*); hence, *I fix, determine, define; I fix upon, appoint, designate.*
ὀρινός see ὀρεινός.
ὅριον, ου, τό plur. ὅρια (fines), *territory, district.*
ὁρκίζω *I adjure,* w. double acc., of the one adjured and of the one in the name of whom he is adjured.
ὅρκος, ου, ὁ *an oath* (see ὀμνύω).
ὁρκωμοσία, ας, ἡ *the swearing of an oath, the taking of an oath.*
ὁρμάω *I rush.*

ὁρμή, ῆς, ἡ *a sudden movement, an impulse,* communicated by the hand, Jas 3:4; *inclination,* hostile *intention, instigation.*

ὅρμημα, ατος, τό *a mighty impulse (impetus).*

ὄρνεον, ου, τό (orig., *a little bird*), *a bird.*

ὄρνιξ *a bird* (var. for ὄρνις in Luke 13:34).

ὄρνις, ιθος, ἡ *a bird;* fem., *a hen.*

ὁροθεσία, ας, ἡ (orig., *a laying down [fixing] of a boundary*), *a boundary.*

ὅρος, ου, ὁ *a boundary, limit* (var. in Freer ending of Mark).

ὄρος, ους, τό *a mountain.*

ὀρύσσω *I dig.*

ὀρφανός, ή, όν *orphaned; an orphan;* hence, *friendless,* John 14:18.

ὀρχέομαι *I dance.*

ὅς, ἥ, ὅ rel. pron., *who, which;* ὃς ἄν (ἐάν) w. subjun., *whosoever;* ὅς is sometimes equal to the classical ὅστις, Matt 10:26; 24:2; Luke 12:2; Acts 19:35, etc.; it is frequently attracted into the case of its antecedent, the latter being sometimes omitted; sometimes the attraction is inverse, i.e., the antecedent is attracted into the case of the rel., e.g. Matt 21:42; Luke 12:48; Acts 10:36; 1 Cor. 10:16; sometimes the demons. pron. is pleonastically added in the rel. clause (a colloquial Gk. use) the frequency of which is probably suggested by Semitic usage, e.g. Mark 1:7; 7:25 (cf. 13:19); Luke 3:16; John 1:27; Acts 15:17; 1 Pet 2:24 (var.); Rev 3:8; 7:2, 9; 13:8, 12; 20:8 (either a Heb. or an Aram. source is generally presumed); ὃς μέν . . . ὃς δέ, *the one . . . the other,* or *one . . . another;* ἀφ' οὗ, ἀφ' ἧς, *since* (where ἡμέρας or ὥρας can be supplied) 2 Pet 3:4; ὅ ἐστιν can introduce rel. clauses containing interpretations, whatever be the gender and number of the antecedent, e.g. Mark 12:42; 15:22; ἐν ᾧ, *in that, because,* Rom 2:1; 8:3; Heb 2:18; *wherefore,* Heb 6:17; *as long as, while,* Mark 2:19; Luke 5:34; John 5:7; *until,* Luke 19:13 (= εἰς ὅ) ἐφ' ᾧ, see ἐπί; ἐφ' ὃ πάρει, *to the task for which you have come,* Matt 26:50 (a command, not a question); ἄχρι, ἕως, μέχρις οὗ (lit. *up to the point at which*), *until;* ἀνθ' ὧν, οὗ εἵνεκεν, οὗ χάριν, *on account of which, wherefore;* ὅ, as cog. acc., Rom 6:10; Gal 2:20.

ὁσάκις adv., always w. ἐάν and subjun., *as often as, as many times as.*

ὅσιος, α, ον (1) *holy, pious* (implying the right relation to God); τὰ ὅσια, *the pieties, the pious deeds,* Acts 13:34; (2) ὁ ὅσιος, *the Holy One,* i.e. the Messiah. (Heb. *ḥāsîd* means not only *godly, pious,* but also *beloved of Yahweh*).

ὁσιότης, ητος, ἡ *holiness, piety.*

ὁσίως adv., *religiously, piously.*

ὀσμή, ῆς, ἡ *odor;* generally met. in connection w. εὐωδίας (from OT), originally of the sweet smelling odor of sacrifice, and then widely used.

ὅσος, η, ον rel. and indir. interrog. adj. (orig. correlative to τοσοῦτος, cf. Heb 10:25), *as great as; how great;* of time, *as long as,* Mark 2:19; ὅσος ἐάν (ἄν) generalizes, *however great,* plur. *as many as;* ὅσοι = πάντες οἵ, *how many, as many as;* ἐφ' ὅσον, *as long as,* e.g. Matt 9:15; *to the degree that, inasmuch as,* e.g. Matt 25:40; Rom 11:13; καθ' ὅσον, *in proportion as,* Heb 3:3; 7:20; 9:27; ὅσον ὅσον, *a little* (cf. Eng. *so so*).

ὅσπερ, ἥπερ, ὅπερ *just the one who, which indeed* (= ὅς περ, etc.).

ὀστέον (ὀστοῦν), έου (οῦ), τό *a bone.*

ὅστις, ἥτις, ὅ τι either generic, *who,* as other like persons, *which,* as other like things, or essential, *who,* by his/her very nature, *which,* by its very nature. Rare except in the nom. There is a tendency (seen in the Ionic dialect and also in colloquial Gk.) to weaken ὅστις to the sense of ὅς, cf. Matt 27:62; Luke 2:4; 10:42, but examples are very rare; ὅστις ἄν (ἐάν) = ἐάν τις, w. subjun., *whosoever* (it is doubtful whether the ἄν should be omitted, cf. Matt 10:33; Jas 2:10); ὅ, τι, short for τί ὅ, τι (= τί γέγονεν ὅτι, John 14:22), *why,* Mark 2:16 (var.); 9:11, 28 (var.); John 8:25 (but in this passage ὅτι can be read, "do you reproach me *that* . . ."); examples of τί ὅ, τι (or ὅτι) are Mark 2:16 (var.), Luke 2:49; ἕως ὅτου, *until* the time at *which, until.*

ὀστράκινος, η, ον *made of pottery, of earthenware.*

ὄσφρησις, εως, ἡ *sense of smell.*

ὀσφύς, ύος, ἡ sing. and plur., *the loins, the middle,* mentioned in two connections, first as the quarter from which comes the male seed (Hebraism Acts 2:30, etc.), and second as the part of the body round which the girdle is placed, when the flowing robes are girt higher with a view to travel or work (cf. Luke 12:35); hence also met., 1 Pet 1:13 (the negation of mental slackness is referred to).

ὅταν *whenever, as often as,* followed by the indic., in case of repeated events in the past (thus it is incorrectly used = *when* in Rev 8:1, etc.), but also like ἐάν w. pres. and fut. indic., usually w. variations in the reading, Mark 11:25; 13:7; Luke 11:2; 13:28; John 7:27; followed by subjun., where frequency in the future is referred to, the subjun. pres. being strictly equivalent to the Lat. pres. subjun. or fut. indic. (conative, continuous, or iterative), while the subjun. aor. (punctiliar) corresponds to the fut. perf. indic. In Mark 11:19 perhaps *when.*

ὅτε *when, at which time,* used especially w. all tenses of the indic.; only once w. subjun., *the time when,* Luke 13:35 (var.).

ὅτι most often, either (1) *because, for,* or, (2) after a verb or other word of saying (perhaps under influence of Aram. in Mark) or thinking, *that,* introducing a noun clause; an ellipsis of δῆλον in 1 Tim 6:7; 1 John 3:20; so ὡς ὅτι pleonastically, 2 Cor 5:19; 11:21; 2 Thess 2:2, where the expressions are equivalent to ὡς w. the part.; ὅτι sometimes also introduces a piece of direct speech, e.g. John 10:36, and so perhaps in Mark 2:16; 9:11, 28; John 8:25 (see under ὅστις); ὅτι w. infin., Acts 27:10, is due to forgetfulness; οὐχ ὅτι = οὐ λέγω ὅτι, *not that,* John 6:46; 7:22; 2 Cor 1:24; Phil 4:11, etc., with which cf. οὐχ οἷον ὅτι, *it is not so that, it is by no means the case that,* Rom 9:6. A Hebraistic weakening of the force of causal ὅτι is seen in Matt 8:27; Mark 1:27, (var.); 4:41; Luke 4:36; 8:25; John 2:18 (14:22); Heb 2:6, etc. In Mark 8:24 ὅτι is a mistranslation of an Aram. word which should have been rendered οὗς. ὅτι orig. a development of ὅ, τι, neut. of ὅστις.

οὐ (οὐκ, οὐχ) *not,* the proper negative for a denial of a fact, used generally w. the indic., as μή is w. other moods, but sometimes w. the part., it being closely related to the indic. and coming also under the rule that οὐ negatives a single word rather than a clause; οὐ w.

fut. indic. in a question is equivalent to an imper.; for οὐχ ὅτι see ὅτι; οὐ . . . πᾶς is Heb. = οὐδείς, Luke 1:37, etc.; for οὐ μή see under μή. Regularly οὐκ before smooth breathings and οὐχ before rough breathings.

οὔ interj., *no!* an accented form of οὐ.

οὗ, rel. adv., *where;* also *to the place where.*

οὐά an interj. expressing real or ironical wonder.

οὐαί adv., *woe,* w. dat. or acc., sometimes in Rev made a noun, ἡ οὐαί (= ἡ κραυγὴ οὐαί?); expresses rather a statement than a wish or imprecation, *distress comes (will come) upon.*

οὐδαμῶς adv., *in no way, in no respect, not at all.*

οὐδέ *nor . . . either, nor . . . at all; not even.*

οὐδείς (οὐθείς), οὐδεμία, οὐδέν adj. and noun, *no; no one* (masc. or fem.), *nothing* (neut.).

οὐδέποτε adv., *not at any time, never.*

οὐδέπω adv., *not yet either, not yet, not as yet, never before.*

οὐθείς later form of οὐδείς, occurring first in 378 B.C. and with more or less frequency until its disappearance before 200 A.D..

οὐκ see οὐ.

οὐκέτι adv., *no longer, no more.*

οὐκοῦν interog. adv., *so then?*

οὖν adv. or conj., *therefore,* properly in causal connection, but also freely of a mere temp. connection, continuing a narrative, *then,* for example, in the combined expression μέν οὖν (see under μέν); it sometimes indicates the return to the narrative after some digression, John 4:45; 6:24; 1 Cor 8:4; 11:20; ἄρα οὖν is a strengthened οὖν.

οὔπω adv., *not yet.*

οὐρά, ᾶς, ἡ *a tail.*

οὐράνιος, ον *in heaven, belonging to heaven, heavenly, from heaven.*

οὐρανόθεν adv., *from heaven, from the sky.*

οὐρανός, οῦ, ὁ *the sky. the heaven;* as later Jewish cosmology conceived of a series of heavens one above the other (sometimes three, sometimes seven), the plur. is sometimes used, where we should use the sing., and numbers are even attached to individual strata (e.g. 2 Cor 12:2). Heaven was conceived as the special realm and abode of the Deity, hence the word is constantly used in connection with Him, and almost as equivalent to the divine name; cf. the practical equivalence of ἡ βασιλεία τῶν οὐρανῶν, the kingdom (rule) *from heaven,* of *divine* origin, a phrase which may be in origin purely eschatological (so Matthew) w. ἡ βασιλεία τοῦ θεοῦ, God Himself being the ruler, Matt 12:28; 19:24 (var.); 21:31, 43; Mark; Luke; Paul.

Οὐρβανός, οῦ, ὁ *Urbanus,* a Christian in Rome, fellow worker of Paul.

Οὐρίας, ου, ὁ *Uriah,* husband of Bathsheba, the mother of Solomon [Heb.].

οὖς, ὠτός, τό *an ear.*

οὐσία, ας, ἡ *property.*

οὔτε adv., οὔτε . . . οὔτε, *neither . . . nor;* οὐ . . . οὔτε . . . οὔτε, *not . . . neither . . . nor;* sometimes the other clause is positive, e.g. John 4:11; 3 John 10.

οὗτος, αὕτη, τοῦτο demons. adj. and pron., *this; he, her, it;* αὕτη (Hebraistic) = τοῦτο, Matt 21:42; τοῦτ' ἔστιν, *which means, meaning, actually, in reality* (cf. 1 Pet 3:20); ἐκ τούτου, *for this reason,* John 6:66 (possibly, *from* *that time onwards*),19:12, *by this mark, by this means,* 1 John 4:6; ἐν τούτῳ, *for this reason,* John 16:30; Acts 24:16, *by this mark, by this means,* 1 John 3:19; ἐπὶ τούτῳ, *meantime,* John 4:27; τούτου χάριν, *on this account;* κατὰ ταῦτα, *in the same way,* Luke 6:23 var., 17:30 var.; καὶ τοῦτο, *and that too; especially;* καὶ ταῦτα, *and indeed.* A special sense = *as it is called,* Heb 9:11.

οὕτω, οὕτως adv., *in this way (manner), thus, so, under these circumstances;* used sometimes w. εἶναι, γίνεσθαι, where a part of τοιοῦτος would be expected (cf. ἔχω), Matt 1:18; 19:10, etc.

οὐχ see οὐ.

οὐχί *not; no, not so,* a more emphatic form of οὐ (οὐκ, οὐχ), also used in a question, expecting a positive answer.

ὀφειλέτης, ου, ὁ (1) *a debtor, one who owes, one who is indebted;* (2) *one who has sinned against* another (an Aramaism, see ὀφείλημα), *a sinner,* Luke 13:4.

ὀφειλή, ῆς, ἡ *a debt, what is owing (due);* the mutual obligation of married life, 1 Cor 7:3.

ὀφείλημα, ατος, τό (1) *a debt;* (2) in Aram. the same word indicates a debt and a sin; hence, *a sin* (probably as that for which we owe reparation to God or to another person).

ὀφείλω *I owe;* w. infin. *I ought.*

ὄφελον *I would that* (orig. an aor. of ὀφείλω, w. augment dropped).

ὄφελος, ους, τό *advantage, gain.*

ὀφθαλμοδουλία (-εία), ας, ἡ *enslavement to the eye,* the subjection that waits upon a glance of a master's eye.

ὀφθαλμός, οῦ, ὁ (1) *an eye;* (2) ὀφθαλμὸς πονηρός (a Semitic idiom), *envy, ill will,* Matt 20:15; Mark 7:22; (3) met. "the mind's *eye,*" Eph 1:18.

ὀφθείς aor. pas. part. → ὁράω.

ὀφθήσομαι fut. pas. → ὁράω.

ὄφις, εως, ὁ *a serpent.*

ὀφρύς, ύος, ἡ (properly *the brow*); hence, *the brow, a ridge* (of a mountain).

ὀχετός, οῦ, ὁ *a drain pipe, a sewer line* Mark 7:19 (var.).

ὀχλέω *I trouble, torment, worry.*

ὀχλοποιέω *I gather a crowd.*

ὄχλος, ου, ὁ *a crowd* of men, *a mob, a multitude;* the plur. much affected by Matthew (Semitism?) does not differ in meaning from the sing. (cf. 4:25).

ὀχύρωμα, ατος, τό *a bulwark, a bastion;* hence, met.

ὀψάριον, ου, τό (conversational diminutive of ὄψον, *seasoning* [especially *fish*] taken as a relish with bread); hence, *a relish;* then especially, *a fish.*

ὀψέ adv., *late;* sometimes prep. w. gen., either *late on* or *after.*

ὀψία, ας, ἡ *early evening,* of a period never earlier than sunset.

ὄψιμος, ου, ὁ *late* in the year (opp. to πρόϊμος).

ὄψιος, α, ον *late,* Mark 11:11 (var.).

ὄψις, εως, ἡ (1) *the face;* (2) *the features, the outward appearance,* John 7:24.

ὄψομαι fut. mid. → ὁράω.

ὀψώνιον, ου, τό especially plur. ὀψώνια, (*rations;* then) soldier's *pay,* Luke 3:14, cf. 1 Cor 9:7; *pay, wages, salary, reward* in general, Rom 6:23; 2 Cor 11:8; *charges,* 1 Cor 9:7.

Π

παγιδεύω *I ensnare, I entrap.*

παγίς, ίδος, ἡ *a snare* (especially for catching birds; perhaps a net thrown over one); hence, met., of moral snares.

Πάγος see Ἄρειος.

παθεῖν aor. act. infin. → πάσχω.

πάθημα, ατος, τό properly colorless, *an experience;* but most commonly, *an evil experience, evil treatment, suffering,* e.g. τὰ εἰς Χριστὸν παθήματα, *the sufferings destined for Messiah,* 1 Pet 1:11.

παθητός, ή, όν *capable of suffering.*

πάθος, ους, τό (properly *experience, feeling*); hence, *passion, lustfulness, lust* (as a state or condition).

παιδαγωγός, οῦ, ὁ *a boy leader,* a slave or freedman who attends and guards a boy to and from (sometimes also in) school, and looks after his moral character especially, *a tutor.*

παιδάριον, ου, τό either *a boy* or *a slave* (formerly a diminutive).

παιδεία (παιδία), ας, ἡ *discipline.*

παιδευτής, οῦ, ὁ *one who disciplines, a trainer;* almost *a chastiser,* Heb 12:9.

παιδεύω (1) *I discipline, educate, train;* (2) more severely, *I chastise.*

παιδία see παιδεία.

παιδιόθεν adv., *from childhood, from early boyhood.*

παιδίον, ου, τό (1) *a little boy, a child* (from birth onwards); hence affectionately, of those grown up; (2) *a slave* (cf. the use of *boy* in parts of Africa), Luke 11:7.

παιδίσκη, ης, ἡ *a female slave, a maidservant, a maid.*

παίζω *I play, I sport* (includes singing and dancing).

παῖς, παιδός, ὁ and **ἡ** (1) *a male child, a boy;* (2) *a* male *slave, a servant* (cf. παιδίον); thus *a servant of* God, especially as a title of the Messiah (from Isa. 41–53) Acts 4:27, 30; (3) *a* female *child, a girl,* Luke 8:51, 54.

παίω *I strike.*

πάλαι adv., *long ago,* almost weakened to *already* in Mark 15:44.

παλαιός, ά, όν *old;* ὁ παλαιὸς ἄνθρωπος (perhaps Hebraism), one's *former character (personality).* The word and its derivatives bear a derogatory sense.

παλαιότης, ητος, ἡ *oldness.*

παλαιόω *I make old, I antiquate; I wear out; I treat as past,* Heb 8:13; pas. *I fall to the past,* Heb 8:13.

πάλη, ης, ἡ *wrestling, a wrestling bout;* hence, *a struggle, a conflict.*

παλιγγενεσία, ας, ἡ (1) *rebirth,* an eschatological term (used by Pythagoreans and Stoics, found in Josephus of the rebirth of the fatherland after the exile, and in Philo of the rebirth of the earth after the flood), in Matt 19:28 for the current conception of the Messianic renewal of the world or of the people Israel, (2) *rebirth* of the individual life following on or typified in baptism, Tit. 3:5.

πάλιν adv., *again,* properly of a return over the same course in the reverse direction, but also used of a repetition of the same journey in the same direction; it may also be used of any number of times; in Mark 15:13 perhaps an unsuitable mistranslation of an Aram. word of much wider signification, *further, thereupon;* εἰς τὸ πάλιν = πάλιν, 2 Cor 13:2.

παλινγενεσία see παλιγγενεσία.

παμπληθεί adv., *all together* (in unison); lit., *with the whole crowd.*

Παμφυλία, ας, ἡ *Pamphylia,* a Roman province on the south coast of Asia Minor.

πανδοχεῖον, ου, τό *an inn, khan, hotel.*

πανδοχεύς, έως, ὁ *an innkeeper, landlord, hotel manager.*

πανήγυρις, εως, ἡ *a festival assembly.*

πανοικεί (πανοικί) adv., *with all (his) household.*

πανοπλία, ας, ἡ *armor.*

πανουργία, ας, ἡ (1) *cleverness,* usually with the idea that it is evil; (2) *cunning, craftiness,* Luke 20:23.

πανοῦργος, ον *crafty* (playfully used).

πανπληθεί see παμπληθεί.

πανταχῆ (πανταχῇ) adv., *everywhere.*

πανταχόθεν adv. *from every direction;* var. for πάντοθεν in Mark 1:45.

πανταχοῦ adv., *everywhere.*

παντελής, ές εἰς τὸ παντελές, *utterly, at all,* Luke 13:11; in Heb 7:25 either *entirely,* or, more probably, *for ever, finally.*

πάντη adv., *in every way.*

πάντοθεν adv., *from all sides, from all quarters; on all sides.*

παντοκράτωρ, ορος, ὁ *ruler of all, ruler of the universe;* the LXX introduced κύριος (θεὸς) παντοκράτωρ as a translation of *Lord of Hosts.*

πάντοτε adv., *at all times, always.*

πάντως adv., *entirely; in any case;* (after a negative) *at all; assuredly, to be sure.*

παρά prep. (1) w. acc. *by, beside, near,* without difference between "where?" (properly παρὰ τίνι) and "to what place?"; not w. persons; (*not in accordance with,* opp. κατά) *against, contrary to,* Rom 1:26; 11:24; 2 Cor 8:3 *(over); differently from,* Gal 1:8 (cf. 1 Cor 3:11); *more than,* sometimes w. comp., Luke 13:2, 4; Rom 1:25; 12:3; 14:5; *less,* 2 Cor 11:24; οὐ παρὰ τοῦτο . . . , *this is no reason that etc.,* 1 Cor 12:15; (2) w. gen. *from the side of, from,* only w. persons; οἱ παρ' αὐτοῦ, *his family, his relations,* Mark 3:21 (in papyri generally = *his agents, his representatives*), τὰ παρ' ἑαυτῆς, *her money, her wealth,* Mark 5:26, cf. Luke 10:7; Phil 4:18; (3) w. dat. *by, beside,* answering the question "where?" with the exception of John 19:25 only of persons, not of immediate proximity, but *in the house of* any one, Luke 19:7; John 1:39; Acts 10:6, *among* a people, Rev 2:13; *in the eyes of,* e.g. παρὰ τῷ θεῷ, *in the judgment of,* Rom 12:16, etc.

παραβαίνω (1) *I fall away, take a false* step, Acts 1:25; (2) *I overstep, transgress.*

παραβάλλω *I cross over, I strike across.*

παράβασις, εως, ἡ *transgression; a transgression.*

παραβάτης, ου, ὁ (lit. *an overstepper*), *a transgressor, a lawbreaker.*

παραβιάζομαι *I urge, press.*

παραβολεύομαι *I expose myself* (to danger).

παραβολή, ῆς, ἡ *a similitude, allegory, parable, emblematic allusion;* in Heb 11:19 ἐν = *as.*

παραβουλεύομαι *I am careless, I have no concern* (w. dat.); var. for παραβολεύομαι Phil 2:30.

παραγγελία, ας, ἡ *a command, an injunction; a precept, rule* of living, 1 Thess 4:2.

παραγγέλλω *I command, I charge;* παπαγγελίᾳ παραγγέλλειν (Hebraism), *to charge strictly,* Acts 5:28.

παραγίνομαι (1) *I come on the scene, I appear, I come;* (2) w. words expressing destination, *I present myself at, I arrive at, I reach.*

παράγω (1) *I pass by,* Matt 20:30; Mark 15:21, etc.; (2) *I vanish, disappear,* 1 Cor 7:31, in which sense the pas. is used, 1 John 2:8, 17 (the verb being originally trans.); (3) *I depart,* Matt 9:9, 27 (var. in both passages, and therefore this meaning is questionable); (4) almost, *I walk,* Mark 1:16; 2:14; 15:21(?)

παραδειγματίζω *I put to open shame.*

παράδεισος, ου, ὁ *paradise* (lit. *an enclosed orchard* or *garden with fruit trees*), a quarter of heaven conceived by the later Jews to be in or just above the "third heaven."

παραδέχομαι *I receive (welcome) favorably.*

παραδίδωμι *I hand over, I pledge; I hand down, deliver; I betray.*

παράδοξος, ον *unexpected;* hence, *wonderful.*

παράδοσις, εως, ἡ orig. abstr., *handing over,* generally concr., *that which is handed down, a tradition* (whether of written or of oral teaching).

παραδώσω fut. act. → παραδίδωμι.

παραζηλόω *I make jealous, I provoke to jealousy.*

παραθαλάσσιος, α, ον *by the sea (lake), on the coast.*

παραθεῖναι aor. act. infin. → παρατίθημι.

παραθεωρέω *I look past, overlook, neglect.*

παραθήκη, ης, ἡ *a deposit* (properly of money or valuables deposited with a friend for safe-keeping, while the owner is abroad).

παραθήσω fut. act. → παρατίθημι.

παράθου aor. mid. imper. → παρατίθημι.

παραινέω *I admonish, advise.*

παραιτέομαι (1) *I beg* from another, Mark 15:6 (var.), Heb 12:19 (cf. (2)); (2) *I beg off from, I seek to turn away* (from myself) *by entreaty;* hence, *I give an excuse, I excuse myself, I beg to be excused,* Luke 14:18, 19; Heb 12:25; *I decline, refuse, object to,* Acts 25:11; 1 Tim 4:7; 5:11; 2 Tim 2:23; Tit. 3:10.

παρακαθέζομαι *I sit beside.*

παρακαθίζω *I sit down beside,* var. for παρακαθέζομαι in Luke 10:39.

παρακαλέω (1) *I ask, beseech;* (2) *I exhort;* (3) *I comfort.*

παρακαλύπτω *I conceal, veil.*

παράκειμαι *I rest with.*

παρακέκλημαι perf. mid./pas. → παρακαλέω.

παράκλησις, εως, ἡ *an appeal,* which according to circumstances may be either hortatory, *exhortation,* or consolatory, *consolation;* in Luke 2:25 it seems to have a quasi-technical sense, with reference to the coming of the Messiah.

παράκλητος, ου, ὁ *helper; consoler* (corresponding to the name Menahem given to the Messiah); orig. pas. in sense, *one called in* for support, *one summoned* as support, but this idea drops into the background; in the technical legal sense it never occurs, but in writings prior to the NT has the general sense, *one who speaks in favor of another, an intercessor, helper;* it tends thus to have an act. sense, and was borrowed by Heb. and Aram.

παρακοή, ῆς, ἡ *disobedience.*

παρακολουθέω *I accompany, follow closely,* both lit. and met., *I investigate; I result* Mark 16:17 (var.).

παρακούω (1) *I hear carelessly* or *incidentally,* or *I pretend not to hear,* Mark 5:36; (2) *I refuse to hear; I disobey.*

παρακύπτω *I stretch forward the head to catch a glimpse* (especially through a window or door, sometimes inwards, oftener outwards; fig. it implies a rapid, hasty, and cursory glance), *I look, peep, peer in (at); I look down.*

παραλαμβάνω *I take* from, *I receive* from, or, *I take* to, *I receive* (apparently not used of money, see ἀπέχω); *I take with* me.

παραλέγομαι *I coast along, sail along.*

παραλήμψομαι fut. mid. → παραλαμβάνω.

παράλιος, ου, ἡ *on the seacoast, on the seaboard;* ἡ παράλιος (supply χώρα), *the coast country.*

παραλλαγή, ῆς, ἡ *a variation;* hence, *a periodic change* of a heavenly body.

παραλογίζομαι *I deceive, beguile.*

παραλυτικός, οῦ, ὁ *a paralytic,* a more colloquial word than παραλελυμένος, the medical term (cf. Luke 5:24).

παραλύω pas., παραλελυμένος, *one who has become loosened (unstrung), one whose power of movement has gone, paralyzed, a paralytic.*

παραμένω *I remain beside, I stand by;* hence equivalent to, *I serve* (as a free man), cf. perhaps Phil 1:25; Jas 1:25; *I remain in* office, Heb 7:23; *I persevere* in the law, Jas 1:25.

παραμυθέομαι *I encourage, comfort, console.*

παραμυθία, ας, ἡ *encouragement, comfort, consolation.*

παραμύθιον, ου, τό *consolation.*

παρανομέω *I contravene a statute (law).*

παρανομία, ας, ἡ *a breach of a statute (law).*

παραπικραίνω absol. *I embitter, provoke, irritate.*

παραπικρασμός, οῦ, ὁ *embitterment, provocation, irritation.*

παραπίπτω *I fall back* (into the unbelieving and godless ways of the old time).

παραπλεῦσαι aor. act. infin. → παραπλέω.

παραπλέω *I sail past* (without stopping there).

παραπλήσιος, ια, ιον *coming near, resembling, similar,* neut. sing. as adv. *nearly.*

παραπλησίως adv., *correspondingly, in like manner.*

παραπορεύομαι *I go past,* Mark 11:20; 15:29 (= Matt 27:39); *I go,* apparently a colloquial or incorrect use, Mark 2:23 (var.); 9:30 (var.).

παράπτωμα, ατος, τό *a falling away, a lapse, a slip, a false step, a trespass.*

παραρρέω (lit. *I flow past, I glide past*), hence, *I am lost, I perish,* or merely, *I drift away (I fall away) from duty* (or *the way of salvation*).

παράσημος, ον *a figurehead.*

παρασκευάζω *I prepare;* mid. *I prepare, make preparations,* 1 Cor 14:8.

παρασκευή, ῆς, ἡ *the day of preparation, the day before the Sabbath, Friday.*

παραστήσω fut. act. → παρίστημι.

παρασχών aor. act. part. → παρέχω.

παρατείνω *I prolong.*

παρατηρέω act. and mid. (1) *I watch carefully, keep my eye on* (as a cat does a mouse); absol. *I watch my opportunity,* Luke 20:20; (2) *I observe, keep,* Gal 4:10.

παρατήρησις, εως, ἡ *a watching for.*

παρατίθημι (1) *I set* (especially a meal) *before, I serve;* (2) act. and mid., *I deposit* with, *I entrust* to.

παρατυγχάνω *I come by chance, I am by chance* in a certain place.

παραυτίκα adv. w. force of adj., *present, immediate.*

παραφέρω *I turn aside, I cause (suffer) to pass by,* Mark 14:36; Luke 22:42; *I carry away, remove,* lit. or met.

παραφίημι *I set aside, neglect;* Luke 11:42, var.

παραφρονέω *I am out of my senses.*

παραφρονία, ας, ἡ *madness.*

παραχειμάζω *I spend the winter, I winter.*
παραχειμασία, ας, ἡ *spending the winter, wintering.*
παραχρῆμα adv., *immediately.*
πάρδαλις, εως, ἡ *a leopard.*
παρέβαλον aor. act. → παραβάλλω.
παρέβην aor. act. → παραβαίνω.
παρεγενόμην aor. mid. → παραγίνομαι.
παρεδόθην aor. pas. → παραδίδωμι.
παρεδρεύω *I have my seat beside, I attend.*
παρέδωκα aor. act. → παραδίδωμι.
παρεθέμην aor. mid. → παρατίθημι.
παρέθηκα aor. act. → παρατίθημι.
παρειμένος perf. mid./pas. part. → παρίημι.
πάρειμι *I am present; I have come, arrived* (hence w. εἰς, πρός).
παρεῖναι aor. act. infin. → πάρειμι or παρίημι.
παρεισάγω *I introduce from the side.*
παρείσακτος, ον *introduced (imported) from the side.*
παρεισδύω (παρεισδύνω) *I creep in.*
παρεισενέγκας aor. act. part. → παρεισφέρω.
παρεισέρχομαι *I come in from the side.*
παρεισῆλθον aor. act. → παρεισέρχομαι.
παρειστήκειν plup. act. → παρίστημι.
παρεισφέρω *I bring in (import) from the side, I smuggle.*
παρεκλήθην aor. pas. → παρακαλέω.
παρεκτός (1) adv. used as adj., *outside, without, left over;* (2) prep., *apart from.*
παρέλαβον aor. act. → παραλαμβάνω.
παρελεύσομαι fut. mid. → παρέρχομαι.
παρεληλυθέναι perf. act. infin. → παρέρχομαι.
παρεληλυθώς perf. act. part. → παρέρχομαι.
παρελθεῖν aor. act. infin. → παρέρχομαι.
παρεμβάλλω *I throw (raise) up beside.*
παρεμβαλῶ fut. act. → παρεμβάλλω.
παρεμβολή, ῆς, ἡ *a camp,* either a fixed camp, occupied possibly for centuries, *a fort, castle,* like that at Jerusalem, or a marching camp, according to context; hence, *the army* occupying such, Heb 11:34.
παρέμεινα aor. act. → παραμένω.
παρένεγκε aor. act. imper. → παραφέρω.
παρενοχλέω *I trouble,* or perhaps, *I trouble further.*
παρέπεσον aor. act. → παραπίπτω.
παρεπίδημος, ου, ὁ *a stranger* settled in a town or region for a time without making it his permanent residence, *a sojourner;* so in a spiritual sense of those who are on the earth for a time, whose real home is heaven.
παρεπίκρανα aor. act. → παραπικραίνω.
παρέρχομαι trans. and intrans., *I pass by, I pass;* sometimes practically, *I pass out of sight, I disappear;* w. acc. (cf. παραβαίνω) *I transgress;* intrans., *I approach, come up to,* Luke 12:37; 17:7; Acts 24:7 (var.).
πάρεσις, εως, ἡ *overlooking, suspension, remission* of punishment for (from παρίημι).
παρέστηκα perf. act. → παρίστημι.
παρεστηκώς perf. act. part. → παρίστημι.
παρέστην aor. act. → παρίστημι.
παρέστησα aor. act. → παρίστημι.

παρεστώς perf. act. part. → παρίστημι.

παρέσχον aor. act. → παρέχω.

παρέτεινα aor. act. → παρατείνω.

παρέχω act. and mid. *I offer, provide, confer, afford, give, bring, show, cause;* κόπους (κόπον) τινί παρέχειν, *to cause one trouble.*

παρήγγειλα aor. act. → παραγγέλλω.

παρηγορία, ας, ἡ *a consolation.*

παρῆλθον aor. act. → παρέρχομαι.

παρῃτημένος perf. mid./pas. part. → παραιτέομαι.

παρθενία, ας, ἡ *maidenhood, virginity.*

παρθένος, ου, ἡ *a maiden, a virgin;* hence (Rev 14:4), extended to men who have not known women; in 1 Cor 7:25–38, the word must have its usual sense, and refer to women living in merely spiritual wedlock with men. In Matt 1:23 παρθένος is an inaccurate translation (due to LXX) of a Heb word in Isa. 7:14 meaning *a female adolescent, a young woman of marriageable age,* whether married or not, rightly translated by Theodotion and Aquila νεᾶνις.

Πάρθος, ου, ὁ *a Parthian,* an inhabitant of the country beyond the eastern boundary of the Roman Empire between the Caspian Sea and the Persian Gulf.

παρίημι (1) *I let pass, neglect, omit,* Luke 11:42; (2) *I slacken, weary,* Heb 12:12.

παρίστημι (παριστάνω) (1) in the trans. tenses, *I cause to come to and stand beside; I bring; I present, offer, commend; I introduce* (one person to another); *I prove by argument,* Acts 24:13; (2) in the intrans. tenses, *I come up to and stand by,* sometimes with the idea of thus providing support (cf. 2 Tim 4:17).

Παρμενᾶς, ᾶ, acc. **ᾶν, ὁ** *Parmenas,* one of the original seven "deacons" at Jerusalem (a pet form of Παρμενίδης).

πάροδος, ου, ἡ *way-by, passage.*

παροικέω *I sojourn (in),* as a resident stranger.

παροικία, ας, ἡ *a sojourn* in a foreign city or land; so also in the spiritual sense (cf. παρεπίδημος), 1 Pet 1:17.

πάροικος, ου, ὁ adj. and noun, *a stranger, sojourner,* in a land not his own, *a non-citizen,* with limited rights; so, met., of the Christian resident on the earth, whose real home is in heaven, Eph 2:19; 1 Pet 2:11; (= μέτοικος).

παροιμία, ας, ἡ *a veiled speech* in which particularly high thoughts are concealed, *a cryptic saying, an allegory; a proverb,* 2 Pet 2:22 (from παρά and οἶμος *beside the common way*).

πάροινος, ου, ὁ *one given too much to wine, an excessive drinker.*

παροίχομαι *I have passed.*

παρομοιάζω *I resemble.*

παρόμοιος, ον *like, similar.*

παροξύνω *I arouse to anger, I provoke.*

παροξυσμός, οῦ, ὁ (1) *irritation of mind, sharp feeling, indignation;* (2) *spurring, incitement,* Heb 10:24.

παροργίζω *I provoke to anger.*

παροργιῶ fut. act. → παροργίζω.

παροργισμός, οῦ, ὁ (generally act. *provocation*), *the state of feeling provocation, wrath.*

παροτρύνω *I urge on.*

παρουσία, ας, ἡ (in ordinary Gk. = *presence; arrival;* also, technical term with reference to *the visit* of a king or some other official, *a royal visit*), (1) *presence,* as opposed to "absence," 1 Cor 16:17; 2 Cor 7:6, 7 (cf. 10:10); Phil 1:26; 2:12; (2) a technical eschatological term, representing a word used by Jesus Himself, *the presence, coming, arrival, advent* of the glorified Messiah, to be followed by a permanent residence with His people (so, in 2 Thess 2:9, of that of the Lawless One).

παροψίς, ίδος, ἡ *a bowl, dish.*

παρρησία, ας, ἡ *boldness, freedom, liberty,* shown especially *in speech;* ἐν παρρησίᾳ, μετὰ παρρησίας, *quite openly* (opp. to "secretly").

παρρησιάζομαι *I speak boldly, I am bold of speech.*

παρῴχημαι perf. mid./pas. → παροίχομαι.

πᾶς, πᾶσα, πᾶν, gen. **παντός, πάσης, παντός** (1) adj. (a) in the sing. without the article, *every, every kind of;* (b) in the sing. w. the article preceding or following, *the whole, all the;* (c) in the plur. without the article, *all;* (d) in the plur. w. the article following, *all the;* (2) pron. (a) masc. *every one,* neut. *everything;* (b) πάντες, *all, everybody,* πάντα, *all things;* (c) οὐ πᾶς, etc., *not all,* i.e. *only some,* e.g. Matt 19:11; John 13:10; Rom 10:16, but also (like πᾶς . . . οὐ) Hebraistic, especially when words intervene between οὐ and πᾶς, etc. (translation Gk.), = *none, no,* Matt 24:22; Mark 13:20; Luke 1:37; Acts 20:25; Rom 3:20; Gal 2:16; 2 Pet 1:20; 1 John 2:21; Rev 7:16; 21:27; 22:3; πάντες οὐ = οὐ πάντες, 1 Cor 15:51; (3) with preps. (a) διὰ παντός, *continually, continuously, always;* (b) κατὰ πάντα, *in everything, in every respect,* Acts 3:22; 17:22, etc.

πάσχα, τό *the feast of Passover, the paschal meal,* which took place on the night of full moon after the spring equinox, i.e., the night between 14th and 15th Nisan. On the afternoon of 14th Nisan before sunset the *paschal lamb,* also called τὸ πάσχα (so met., 1 Cor 5:7), was sacrificed [Heb., Aram.].

πάσχω *I am acted upon* in a certain way, *I experience* certain treatment, e.g. Matt 17:15 (var.); hence (by a development from the original use), *I experience ill treatment, etc., I suffer,* e.g. Matt 17:12.

Πάταρα, ων, τό *Patara,* a town on the coast of the Roman province Lycia.

πατάσσω *I strike* (as, with a sword).

πατέω trans. and intrans., *I tread; I trample upon.*

πατήρ, πατρός, ὁ (1) *father* in the strict sense, e.g. Matt 2:22; (2) any male *ancestor,* e.g. Matt 3:9; (3) *The Father,* used of God as the creator of all beings (cf. Eph 3:14, 15), the fountain and origin of all life, and, among other beings, of our Lord Jesus Christ, who is in a special sense ὁ υἱός, *the Son,* of the Father (cf. especially John). He is sometimes spoken of as the Heavenly Father, the Father in the Heavens (e.g. Matt 5:16), as distinguished from earthly fathers. Other epithets, such as τῆς δόξης, τῶν οἰκτιρμῶν, τῶν φώτων, are attached to the Name, some of them under the influence of Heb., expressing not only that He is the author of these signs or qualities, but that they bear a likeness to Him; thus πατὴρ τῆς δόξης = *glorious Father.*

Πάτμος, ου, ὁ *Patmos,* a small rocky island in the Aegean sea, southwest of Ephesus.

πατριά, ᾶς, ἡ a group of persons united by descent from a common father or ancestor, *a family, a tribe.*

πατριάρχης, ου, ὁ *a ruler of a family* (or *tribe*), given as an honorary title to David (Acts 2:29) as ancestor of the race of Jewish kings.

πατρικός, ή, όν *belonging to the fathers (ancestors).*

πατρίς, ίδος, ἡ *native city, native town, native place.*

Πατροβᾶς (Πατρόβας), ᾶ, ὁ *Patrobas,* a Christian in Rome.

πατρολῴας, ου, ὁ *a parricide, a murderer of his father.*

πατροπαράδοτος, ον *handed down by (from) one's ancestors, inherited.*

πατρῷος, α, ον *belonging to ancestors, ancestral.*

Παῦλος, ου, ὁ *Paulus, Paul,* (1) the third part (cognomen) of the full Roman name of the Apostle, the other two parts of which (Gaius Iulius?) are now unknown; (2) the third part (cognomen) of the full name of the proconsul of Cyprus, the first part of which seems to be unknown, Acts 13:7.

παύω (1) act. *I cause to cease,* 1 Pet 3:10; (2) mid. *I cease.*

Πάφος, ου, ἡ *Paphos,* a city at the western end of Cyprus.

παχύνω *I thicken;* used w. καρδία, of obtuseness of mind, *it has become obtuse.*

πέδη, ης, ἡ *a fetter.*

πεδινός, ή, όν *level, low-lying.*

πεζεύω *I go by land.*

πεζῇ adv. *on foot* or *by land.*

πεζός, ή, όν *going on foot* or *by land.*

πειθαρχέω *I obey* one in authority.

πειθός, ή, όν *persuasive.*

πειθώ, οῦς, dat. sg. **πειθοῖ, ἡ** *persuasiveness,* 1 Cor. 2:4, var.

πείθω (1) *I urge, I apply persuasion, I seek to persuade, I exercise suasion;* (2) 2 perf. and plup., *I trust,* ἐπί, *in;* (3) mid. or pas. *I am persuaded* (I admit suasion to myself); hence, *I believe;* hence also, w. dat., *I obey.*

Πειλᾶτος see Πιλᾶτος.

πεῖν aor. act. infin. → πίνω.

πεινάω *I hunger,* either lit. or met.; w. acc. *I hunger for.*

πεῖρα, ας, ἡ *an attempt, a trial;* πεῖραν λαμβάνειν, *to have experience of.*

πειράζω (1) *I make trial of, try, test, explore;* God *tests* man by means of suffering or in some other way, man *tests* God by seeking how far it is possible to go on disobeying Him, without provoking his anger; (2) a secondary neutral or evil sense, *I tempt,* Matt 4:1; Mark 1:13; Luke 4:2; 1 Cor 7:5; Jas 1:13 (second occurrence), 14; if trial fails, the result is moral evil; the agency of Satan is interposed, the same process being carried on for God's good purpose and Satan's evil purpose; thus ὁ πειράζων comes to indicate the intermediary, *the Tempter,* Matt 4:3; 1 Thess 3:5; (3) w. inf. *I try, attempt.*

πειράομαι *I try, attempt.*

πειρασμός, οῦ, ὁ (1) *trial, probation, testing, being tried;* (2) *temptation,* Mark 14:38 and pars., Matt 6:13; Luke 4:13; (3) in Gal 4:14 the reading τὸν πειρασμόν (without ὑμῶν or other addition) has been taken, on the analogy of modern popular Gk. usage, *the devil, the demonic power* as the cause of the Apostle's infirmity. (From πειράζω, q.v.)

πεισθήσομαι fut. pas. → πείθω.

πεισμονή, ῆς, ἡ *persuasion,* both *the act of persuasion* and *the being persuaded.*

πέλαγος, ους, τό *the open sea;* in Matt 18:6 the use of the two words for sea produces a more impressive effect.

πελεκίζω *I behead* with an axe.

πέμπτος, η, ον *fifth.*

πέμπω *I send.*

πένης, ητος, ὁ *poor.*

πενθερά, ᾶς, ἡ *a mother-in-law.*

πενθερός, οῦ, ὁ *a father-in-law.*
πενθέω *I mourn.*
πένθος, ους, τό *mourning, sorrow.*
πενιχρός, ά, όν *poor.*
πεντάκις adv., *five times.*
πεντακισχίλιοι, αι, α *five thousand.*
πεντακόσιοι, αι, α *five hundred.*
πέντε *five.*
πεντεκαιδέκατος, η, ον *fifteenth.*
πεντήκοντα *fifty.*
πεντηκοστή, ῆς, ἡ (orig. supply ἡμέρα; lit. *the fiftieth day* from 14th Nisan, the date of the Passover Feast), *Pentecost,* a Feast of the Jews, *Whitsuntide.*
πέπεισμαι perf. mid./pas. → πείθω.
πέποιθα perf. act. → πείθω.
πεποίθησις, εως, ἡ *confidence, trust.*
πέπονθα perf. act. → πάσχω.
πέπραγμαι perf. mid./pas. → πράσσω.
πέπρακα perf. act. → πιπράσκω.
πέπραμαι perf. mid./pas. → πιπράσκω.
πέπραχα perf. act. → πράσσω.
πεπρησμένος perf. mid./pas. part. → πίμπραμαι.
πέπτωκα perf. act. → πίπτω.
πέπωκα perf. act. → πίνω.
περ enclitic intensifying particle. See its compound forms: διόπερ, ἐάνπερ, εἴπερ, ἐπειδήπερ, ἐπείπερ, ἤπερ, καθάπερ, καίπερ, ὅσπερ, ὥσπερ.
περαιτέρω adv., (compar. of πέρα, *beyond*), *further, beyond that.*
πέραν prep. w. gen., *beyond, on the other side of, across;* sometimes elliptically used, πέραν = (ἀπὸ) τῆς πέραν, Mark 3:8 (Matt 4:25), πέραν = τῆς πέραν, Mark 10:1; τὸ πέραν, as subs., *the other side, the country beyond.*
πέρας, ατος, τό (1) *a boundary, limit;* (2) *an end,* Heb 6:16.
Πέργαμος (Πέργαμον), ου, ἡ (τό) *Pergamum,* an important city of the Roman province Asia.
Πέργη, ης, ἡ *Perga,* a city on the river Cestrus in the Roman province Pamphylia.
περί prep. (1) w. gen., most often, *concerning, about* (in such phrases as "to speak, know, care, etc., about"); at the beginning of a clause, *with regard to,* e.g. 1 Cor 7:1; *on account of* (w. κρίνεσθαι, ἐνκαλεῖν, ἐπωτᾶν, etc.), whence it often passes into the meaning *for* and becomes identical with ὑπέρ, e.g. Matt 26:28; 1 Cor 1:13 (ὑπέρ is nearly always a textual variant in such cases); so w. verbs of feeling (= ἐπί w. acc. or dat.), *over;* περί αὐτοῦ, *with him,* Luke 2:27, seems incorrect (= περὶ αὐτόν, αὐτῷ, ἐν αὐτῷ); (2) w. acc., local and temp., *about,* οἱ περὶ αὐτόν Mark 4:10; Luke 22:49, *his disciples,* but οἱ περὶ Παῦλον, Acts 13:13, *Paul and his company* (according to the classical idiom); used to indicate the circumstances of the action or of the effort, e.g. w. ἐπιθυμίαι, Mark 4:19; Paul in his later epistles uses it = *concerning, touching,* e.g. Phil 2:23.
περιάγω (1) trans., (a) *I carry about,* (b) *I go about;* (2) intrans., *I go about.*
περιαιρέω (1) *I strip off, I strip from, I take away;* (2) *I cast off, cut adrift,* Acts 27:40; in Acts 28:13, if the text be right, the word must be rendered in the same way, *I cast off, I cast loose.*
περιάπτω *I light, ignite.*
περιαστράπτω *I flash (gleam) around* like lightning.
περιάψας aor. act. part. → περιάπτω.
περιβάλλω *I cast around,* Luke 19:43 (var.); *I wrap* a garment

about, I put on; hence mid., *I put on* to myself, *I clothe myself, I dress.*
περιβαλῶ fut. act. → περιβάλλω.
περιβέβλημαι perf. mid./pas. → περιβάλλω.
περιβλέπομαι *I look round for, look for, survey.*
περιβόλαιον, ου, τό *a wrapper, mantle.*
περιδέω *I bind (tie) around.*
περιέβαλον aor. act. → περιβάλλω.
περιέδραμον aor. act. → περιτρέχω.
περιεζωσάμην aor. mid. → περιζώννυμι.
περιεζωσμένος perf. mid./pas. part. → περιζώννυμι.
περιέθηκα aor. act. → περιτίθημι.
περιελεῖν aor. act. infin. → περιαιρέω.
περιελθών aor. act. part. → περιέρχομαι.
περιελών aor. act. part. → περιαιρέω.
περιέπεσον aor. act. → περιπίπτω.
περιεργάζομαι *I am active around, I am a busybody.*
περίεργος, ου, ὁ (1) *inquisitive, prying, a busybody;* (2) *curious, magical,* Acts 19:19.
περιέρχομαι intrans. and trans., (1) *I go round, I move about* (περιερχόμενοι, *strolling,* Acts 19:13); (2) *I make a circuit, tack,* Acts 28:13 (var.).
περιέστησα aor. act. → περιΐστημι.
περιεστώς perf. act. part. → περιΐστημι.
περιέσχον aor. act. → περιέχω.
περιέτεμον aor. act. → περιτέμνω.
περιετμήθην aor. pas. → περιτέμνω.
περιέχω (1) *I contain* (of a book *containing* subject matter); hence, impers., *it stands (has its content) thus,* 1 Pet 2:6; (2) *I encompass, surround; I get hold of, seize.*
περιζώννυμι *I gird round;* mid. *I gird myself,* generally for active work or travel.
περιζώσομαι fut. mid. → περιζώννυμαι.
περιῆλθον aor. act. → περιέρχομαι.
περιθείς aor. act. part. → περιτίθημι.
περίθεσις, εως, ἡ *a putting around* (or *on*).
περιίστημι (περιΐστημι) (1) in intrans. tenses, *I surround;* (2) *I stand clear of, avoid,* 2 Tim 2:16; Tit. 3:9.
περικάθαρμα, ατος, τό *a rinsing* of a dirty vessel.
περικαλύπτω *I veil round, I cover over; I conceal.*
περίκειμαι *I am placed around* something; *I have had* something *placed around* me, Acts 28:20; Heb 5:2.
περικεφαλαία, ας, ἡ *a helmet.*
περικρατής, ές *mastering, gaining control over.*
περικρύβω *I conceal, hide* (*entirely,* by putting something *around* it).
περικυκλόω *I encircle, invest.*
περιλάμπω *I shine around.*
περιλείπω *I leave behind.*
περίλυπος, ον *deeply pained (grieved).*
περιμένω *I await* the happening of something.
πέριξ adv., *round about, in the neighborhood.*
περιοικέω *I dwell around (near).*
περίοικος, ου, ὁ *neighboring; a neighbor.*
περιούσιος, ον *of (for) one's own (special, private) possession.*
περιοχή, ῆς, ἡ *a clause, sentence, short passage.*
περιπατέω (1) *I walk;* (2) hence Hebraistically in an ethical sense, *I conduct my life, I live.*

περιπείρω *I pierce round about (on all sides).*
περιπίπτω *I fall into, I fall in with, I meet with, I come upon accidentally, I chance upon, I light upon.*
περιποιέομαι *I make my own, I acquire (get) for myself, I gain for myself;* in Luke 17:33 perhaps, *I preserve alive.*
περιποίησις, εως, ἡ *acquiring, obtaining, possessing, possession, ownership.*
περιρέραμμαι perf. mid./pas. → περιραίνω.
περι(ρ)ραίνω *I sprinkle round about, I sprinkle over.*
περι(ρ)ρήγνυμι *I rend all round, I tear of.*
περιρήξας aor. act. part. → περιρήγνυμι.
περισπάω *I distract, trouble greatly.*
περισσεία, ας, ἡ *surplus, superabundance, superfluity.*
περίσσευμα, ατος, τό *what is in excess; overflow, superabundance, superfluity.*
περισσεύω (1) intrans., *I exceed* the ordinary (the necessary), *I abound, I overflow; I am left over;* hence met.; (2) trans., *I cause to abound,* Matt 13:12; Luke 15:17; 2 Cor 4:15(?); 9:8; Eph 1:8; 1 Thess 3:12.
περισσός, ή, όν adj. and adv., *over and above, excessive, abundant, overflowing; superfluous.* Practically a synonym for πλείων (cf. Matt 5:37), especially in the comp. περισσότερος; ἐκ περισσοῦ, *superabundantly, exceedingly.*
περισσοτέρως adj. and adv., *more exceedingly, to a greater degree;* see περισσός.
περισσῶς adv., *exceedingly,* so perhaps Acts 26:11; but usually *more* (cf. περισσός), with reference to what precedes.
περιστερά, ᾶς, ἡ *a dove.*
περιτέμνω *I cut round* the foreskin, *I circumcise.*
περιτέτμημαι perf. mid./pas. → περιτέμνω.
περιτίθημι *I place around; I put about (upon), I clothe with.*
περιτομή, ῆς, ἡ *circumcision* (see περιτέμνω); οἱ ἐκ περιτομῆς, *the party of circumcision, the party advocating circumcision,* the rigorist Christian Jews; sometimes met. (as in OT), of that *chastening* of the heart (mind) which leads to heartier service to God, e.g. Rom 2:29.
περιτρέπω *I turn round, I turn, change.*
περιτρέχω *I run round (around).*
περιφέρω *I carry around (about); I swing round,* Eph 4:14.
περιφρονέω *I lightly esteem; I despise.*
περίχωρος, ου, ἡ *neighboring;* ἡ περίχωρος (supply γῆ), *the neighboring country, the neighborhood, surroundings.*
περίψημα, ατος, τό *that which is scraped off round* anything, *a scraping.*
περπερεύομαι *I show myself off; I am boastful (a braggart).*
Περσίς, ίδος, ἡ *Persis,* name of a Christian lady in Rome.
πέρυσι adv., *the previous year, last year.*
πεσεῖν aor. act. infin. → πίπτω.
πεσοῦμαι fut. mid. → πίπτω.
πεσών aor. act. part. → πίπτω.
πετεινός, ή, όν *flying;* neut. πετεινόν, *a bird.*
πέτομαι *I fly.*
πέτρα, ας, ἡ *rock, solid rock, native rock,* rising up through the earth, which trips up the traveler, Rom 9:33; 1 Pet 2:8; in Matt 16:18, of such faith as Peter has just shown; in 1 Cor 10:4, allegorically interpreted.

Πέτρος, ου, ὁ *Petros, Peter* (a Gk. name meaning "rock," a translation of the Aram. name Κηφᾶς, given to Symeon (Simon) by our Lord).

πετρώδης, ους, τό *rocky.*

πήγανον, ου, τό *rue,* a plant used for flavoring, garnishing dishes, etc.

πηγή, ῆς, ἡ *a spring, a fountain; a well,* John 4:6.

πήγνυμι *I fix, pitch; I erect.*

πηδάλιον, ου, τό *a helm, rudder.*

πηλίκος, η, ον *how large, how great.*

πηλός, οῦ, ὁ *mud; clay.*

πήρα, ας, ἡ *a bag* (to hold food, etc.), *a wallet, a traveling bag,* perhaps especially *a collecting bag* (such as beggar-priests of pagan cults carried).

πηρόω *I maim, disable, cripple.*

πῆχυς, εως, ὁ *the forearm;* hence, *a cubit,* about a foot and a half; used as a measurement of time in Matt 6:27 (Luke 12:25), to indicate any extension.

πιάζω *I take hold of, seize, apprehend, catch, arrest, grasp* (a Doric form; contrast πιέζω).

πίε aor. act. imper. → πίνω.

πιέζω *I press down.*

πιεῖν aor. act. infin. → πίνω.

πιθανολογία, ας, ἡ *persuasive speech.*

πιθός see πειθός.

πικραίνω *I make bitter (tart, sour);* mid. *I am embittered, I show quick temper.*

πικρανῶ fut. act. → πικραίνω.

πικρία, ας, ἡ *bitterness, sourness;* hence met., *an embittered (resentful) spirit,* which refuses reconciliation, Eph 4:31.

πικρός, ά, όν *bitter,* lit. and met.

πικρῶς adv., *bitterly.*

Πιλᾶτος, ου, ὁ *Pilatus, Pilate,* the third name (cognomen) of the procurator of Judaea, whose first name (praenomen) is unknown.

πίμπλημι *I fill.*

πίμπρημι *I cause to swell;* pas., *I become inflamed, I am swollen.*

πινακίδιον, ου, τό *a little* waxed *tablet,* on which to write with iron pen.

πίναξ, ακος, ἡ *a flat dish.*

πίνω *I drink.*

πίομαι fut. mid. → πίνω.

πιότης, ητος, ἡ *fatness.*

πιπράσκω *I sell.*

πίπτω *I fall.*

Πισιδία, ας, ἡ *Pisidia,* a country of Asia Minor, being the southwestern part of the Roman province Galatia.

Πισίδιος, α, ον *Pisidian,* or rather, *near Pisidia;* see Ἀντιόχεια.

πιστεύω (1) *I believe,* w. various constructions; w. dat., *I believe* a person, or a statement made by a person (to be true); εἰς (ἐπί) w. acc., ἐν (ἐπί) w. dat., *I place (repose) my trust* on either God or the Messiah, *I rely* on them, *I commit my life* to them, *I believe in, I believe on, I cast myself upon* them as stable and trustworthy, with energy of faith; ἐν is sometimes = *in the sphere of,* Mark 1:15 (cf. Rom 1:9; 2 Cor 8:18; 10:14; 1 Thess 3:2, etc.); (2) w. acc. and dat., *I entrust* (so in pas. constr., 1 Thess 2:4; 1 Tim 1:11).

πιστικός, ή, όν probably = *genuine, pure.*

πίστις, εως, ἡ (1) *faith, belief, trust,* generally of the leaning of the entire human personality upon God or the Messiah in absolute trust and confidence in His power, wisdom, and goodness. The older meaning, *intellectual conviction* of certain truths, is often present. (In Eph 1:15 [shorter text] εἰς = *among*); (2) w. the article, *the faith* (in Luke 18:8 perhaps *the necessary faith* or *the faith that perseveres*), *the*

Christian faith, Acts 6:7; 13:8; 16:5; 24:24; Gal 1:23; 3:23; 6:10; Eph 4:13; Jude 3, 20, etc.; (3) as a psychological faculty, Heb 11:1; (4) *integrity, faithfulness, trustworthiness, loyalty,* Matt 23:23; Rom 1:17(?); Gal 5:22; 2 Tim 4:7; (5) *a guarantee,* Acts 17:31.

πιστός, ή, όν *faithful, trusty, trustworthy, reliable;* οἱ πιστοί, *the Christians.*

πιστόω *I make sure, I convince, I give assurance to;* pas. *I show myself faithful, I am convinced.*

πλανάω (1) *I cause to wander;* hence, in the moral sense, *I cause to err;* (2) pas. *I wander;* hence, *I err.*

πλάνη, ης, ἡ *wandering from the way,* and so met., *error* (perhaps sometimes actively, *deceit*).

πλανήτης, ου, ὁ *wandering* (probably of shooting stars).

πλάνος, ον adj., *misleading, deceiving;* as subst. *a deceiver.*

πλάξ, πλακός, ἡ *a tablet.*

πλάσμα, ατος, τό *a molded thing; a created thing, a creature.*

πλάσσω *I mold* out of clay; *I create.*

πλαστός, ή, όν *made up, fictitious.*

πλατεῖα, ας, ἡ *a public square* (supply ὁδός); generally taken as *an open street, a street.*

πλάτος, ους, τό *breadth.*

πλατύνω *I broaden, I make broad;* met., of the growth of tenderness and love, 2 Cor 6:11, 13.

πλατύς, εῖα, ύ *broad.*

πλέγμα, ατος, τό *plaiting, braiding, dressing* the hair.

πλεῖστος, η, ον superl. of πολύς, *very large;* plur. *very many (numerous);* adv. τὸ πλεῖστον, *at the most,* 1 Cor 14:27.

πλείων (πλέων), πλεῖον (πλέον) gen. **ονος** comp. of πολύς, *larger; more; a considerable number of,* Acts 21:10, etc.; οἱ πλείονες, *the majority,* 1 Cor 15:6; ἐπὶ πλεῖον, as adv., *more, to a greater extent.*

πλέκω *I plait.*

πλεονάζω (1) intrans., *I abound, I increase;* (2) trans., *I make to abound, I cause to increase,* 1 Thess 3:12.

πλεονεκτέω *I take advantage of, I overreach, I defraud* (sometimes with reference to adultery and the injury thus done to the husband).

πλεονέκτης, ου, ὁ *a greedy, covetous, rapacious, acquisitive, self-aggrandizing person; a defrauder, one who tramples on the rights of others.*

πλεονεξία, ας, ἡ *covetousness, greediness, rapacity, entire disregard of the rights of others,* a word act. in meaning and wide in scope.

πλευρά, ᾶς, ἡ *a side* of a human being.

πλέω *I travel by sea, I sail, voyage.*

πληγή, ῆς, ἡ *a blow,* especially, caused by the lash, *a stripe, a stroke.*

πλῆθος, ους, τό *a multitude, a crowd, a large number.*

πληθύνω (1) trans., *I multiply, I increase;* (2) intrans., *I multiply, I go on increasing,* Acts 6:1.

πλήθω see πίμπλημι.

πλήκτης, ου, ὁ *a striker; a pugnacious person.*

πλήμμυρα (πλημμύρα), ης, ἡ *a flooding, flood.*

πλήν (1) conj., (a) *however, nevertheless,* Matt 26:39 (Luke 22:42); Matt 11:22, 24; 26:64, etc., (b) *but,* Luke 12:31; 23:28, (c) πλὴν ὅτι, *except that, save that,* Acts 20:23, (d) *only, in any case,* ending the discussion and calling special attention to the essential, especially in Paul, e.g. 1 Cor 11:11; Eph 5:33; (2) prep. w. gen., *except, apart from.*

πλήρης, ες *full* (sometimes, from about the beginning of our era, indeclinable, and used for any case sing. or plur., a usage perhaps derived from commercial life; e.g. Mark 4:28[?]; John 1:14, where πλήρης agrees with δόξαν, and there should be no parenthesis, Acts 6:5 [var.]).

πληροφορέω (lit. *I carry full*), (1) *I complete, carry out fully,* 2 Tim 4:5, 17; Luke 1:1(?); (2) *I fully convince,* Rom 4:21; 14:5; perhaps *I satisfy fully,* Col 4:12; (3) *I fully believe,* Luke 1:1(?).

πληροφορία, ας, ἡ *full assurance, conviction (confidence).*

πληρόω (1) *I fill, I fill up,* e.g. Luke 2:40; 3:5; John 12:3; (2) much oftener, *I fill up to the full, I fulfill, I give fullness (completion) to, I accomplish, carry out,* of prophecies or other statements which are absolutely and completely confirmed by reality (actual occurrence), or of duties; *I preach fully,* Rom 15:19, cf. Col 1:25; in Eph 1:23 the Messiah *is being fulfilled (completed)* by the Church.

πλήρωμα, ατος, τό (1) *a fill, fullness; full complement; supply, supplement,* Mark 2:21; Matt 9:16; (2) *fullness, filling, fulfillment, completion.* (Indicates the result of the activity denoted by πληρόω.)

πλήσας aor. act. part. → πίμπλημι.

πλησθῆναι aor. pas. infin. → πίμπλημι.

πλησθήσομαι fut. pas. → πίμπλημι.

πλησίον adv. and prep. w. gen., *near* (John 4:5), used as adj. and (especially w. article ὁ) noun, *neighboring, neighborly; a neighbor.*

πλησμονή, ῆς, ἡ *repletion, satiety.*

πλήσσω *I strike.*

πλοιάριον, ου, τό *(a little boat),* hence, *a boat.*

πλοῖον, ου, τό *a boat;* hence, *a ship* (the old word ναῦς having become almost obsolete), Acts 20:13, etc.

πλόος, πλοῦς, ὁ *a voyage.*

πλούσιος, α, ον *rich, wealthy;* hence, met., of other than material wealth.

πλουσίως adv., *richly; lavishly.*

πλουτέω *I am rich (wealthy);* w. εἰς and acc. the person on whom the wealth is lavished is indicated; w. ἐν, *I abound in,* 1 Tim 6:18.

πλουτίζω *I enrich.*

πλοῦτος, ου, ὁ and **τό** *wealth,* material or spiritual.

πλύνω *I wash.*

πνεῦμα, ατος, τό (from πνέω, has as its earliest meanings *breath* and *wind,* and it is from the former that the characteristic use is derived), (1) *wind,* John 3:8; Heb 1:7; (2) *breath,* what distinguishes a living from a dead body, the life principle, Matt 27:50; Luke 8:55; 23:46; John 6:63; 19:30; Acts 7:59; 2 Thess 2:8; Jas 2:26; Rev 11:11; 13:15; (3) the breath was often in early times identified with the life or soul itself. Heb. employed three words for the breath-soul, *nefesh, ruah, neshamah,* of which the first and second are the more important, indicating respectively the personal soul and the invading spirit. (1) *Nefesh,* orig. *breath,* (a) refers predominantly to the emotional life; (b) is a strong pers. or refl. pron.; or (c) is equivalent to *person.* (2) *Ruah,* orig. *wind,* indicates also especially, (a) supernatural influences acting on man from without; (b) the normal breath-soul, the principle of life (like *nefesh*) or of its energies, directly derived from the wind at the bidding of God; (c) the resultant psychical life, like *nefesh,* "heart," the inner life in general. It is distinguished from *nefesh* by its association with Yahweh. Normal human nature was regarded as animated by the same divine *ruah* to which its highest inspiration is due. In the Gk. OT *nefesh* is represented by ψυχή (q.v.) and *ruah* by πνεῦμα (a purely Hebraistic usage of the word). In the NT πνεῦμα refers nearly always to supernatural influences. Sometimes it is employed of the *higher nature* in man, e.g. Rom 1:9, and is hardly to be distinguished from the result of the influence of the divine πνεῦμα. Sometimes, e.g. Rom 8:16; 2 Cor 7:1, it denotes a normal element in human nature. But the Christian is essentially the product of the divine πνεῦμα, which is mediated to us by the Messiah. Parallel to the divine πνεῦμα are the unclean, evil spirits, the spirits of demons, etc., which act in a corresponding way on the spirit of man. πνεῦμα ἅγιον, *holy breath, spirit of holiness,* adopted originally from Isa 63:10–11; Ps 51:11, practically synonymous w. πνεῦμα θεοῦ, etc., gradually tends to become personalized. The first step in the process is reached by affixing the def. article and making it τὸ Πνεῦμα τὸ Ἅγιον (τὸ Ἅγιον Πνεῦμα). Each operation of *the* Holy Spirit is most commonly represented as due to *a* holy spirit.

πνευματικός, ή, όν *having the characteristics of* πνεῦμα, *spiritual,* with general reference to the higher nature of man as directly in touch with and influenced by the divine, but sometimes (like πνεῦμα) associated with the demonic world, τὰ πνευματικὰ τῆς πονηρίας, *the spiritual hosts of evil,* Eph 6:12; *supernatural,* 1 Cor 10:3.

πνευματικῶς adv., *spiritually, in a spiritual way; from a spiritual point of view.*

πνέω *I blow;* τῇ πνεούσῃ (supply αὔρᾳ, *breeze*).

πνίγω *I choke, throttle, strangle;* hence, *I drown,* Mark 5:13.

πνικτός, ή, όν *strangled* (i.e. killed without letting out the blood).

πνοή, ῆς, ἡ (1) *breath,* Acts 17:25; (2) *gust, breeze, wind,* Acts 2:2.

ποδήρης, ους, ὁ *a tunic* or *robe reaching the feet* (properly an adj. in the expression χιτὼν ποδήρης).

πόθεν interrog. adv., *whence? from what place?* also indir. interrog.; hence, *how?* e.g. Mark 12:37; John 1:48.

ποία *a green herb* (a possible interpretation of the word in Jas 4:14; others regard it as the fem. of ποῖος).

ποιέω (1) *I make, manufacture, construct;* (2) *I do, act, cause;* μετά τινος (Hebraistic idiom), *on some one's behalf,* Luke 1:72; Acts 14:27, etc.; w. an obj. indicating time, *I spend,* e.g. Jas 4:13; ὁδὸν ποιεῖν, Mark 2:23 (var.), which ought to mean *to construct (pave) a road,* is incorrectly used for ὁδὸν ποιεῖσθαι (cf. μνείαν ποιεῖσθαι, Eph 1:16), *to journey* (cf. Luke 13:22); w. καλῶς, see under καλῶς.

ποίημα, ατος, τό (concr.), *creation, workmanship, handiwork;* plur. *pieces of work.*

ποίησις, εως, ἡ *doing.*

ποιητής, οῦ, ὁ (1) *a "maker," a poet,* Acts 17:28 (the reference is to Epimenides' *Minos*); (2) *a doer, a carrier out.*

ποικίλος, η, ον *multicolored, particolored;* hence, *varied, various* (plurality as well as difference seems sometimes to be suggested).

ποιμαίνω *I shepherd, I tend, I herd;* hence, *I rule.*

ποιμανῶ fut. act. → ποιμαίνω.

ποιμήν, ένος, ὁ *a shepherd;* hence

met., of the feeder, protector, and *ruler* of a flock of men.

ποίμνη, ης, ἡ *a flock; herd* (of goats perhaps, in 1 Cor 9:7).

ποίμνιον, ου, τό *a little flock;* hence, of men.

ποῖος, α, ον properly direct interrog., *of what sort?,* then often weakened to *what?* simply; also indir. interrog.; ποίας (local gen., supply ὁδοῦ), *by what way.*

πολεμέω *I war, carry on war.*

πόλεμος, ου, ὁ *a war;* also, *a battle,* Luke 14:31, etc.

πόλις, εως, ἡ strictly *a* free *city, city-state* of the Gk. (particularly the Athenian) type, comprising not only the city in the mod. sense, but territory (often considerable) around it. The word is used rather of the citizens than of the locality (cf. the examples below). Its constitution commonly consisted of an ἐκκλησία (assembly of free citizens) and a βουλή (an advisory and deliberative council, in NT times a mere honorary corporation). Examples are: Matt 8:34; 12:25; Mark 1:33; ἡ ἁγία πόλις (cf. Ἱερο- in Ἱεροσόλυμα), *the holy city,* i.e. Jerusalem, as containing the temple of Yahweh.

πολιτάρχης, ου, ὁ *a politarch, a city magistrate* (a special, characteristically Macedonian, title of the chief magistrates [five or six in number] of Thessalonica and a few other cities).

πολιτεία, ας, ἡ (1) *commonwealth, polity; citizen body,* Eph 2:12; (2) (the Roman) *citizenship, citizen's rights, franchise,* Acts 22:28.

πολίτευμα, ατος, τό (properly, *that which one does as citizen*), *the constitution; citizenship, franchise; the state, the community, the commonwealth.* The word sometimes means *a colony* of foreigners, whose organization is a miniature copy of the πολιτεία at home, and this gives excellent sense in Phil 3:20.

πολιτεύομαι (a characteristic Gk. idea), *I live the life of a citizen; I live as a member of a* (citizen) *body; I fulfill corporate duties;* in Phil 1:27 some take simply of *manner of life.*

πολίτης, ου, ὁ *a citizen; a fellow citizen,* Luke 19:14; Heb 8:11.

πολλάκις adv., *often, frequently.*

πολλαπλασίων, ον *manifold, many times over.*

πολυλογία, ας, ἡ *much speaking, loquaciousness, volubility.*

πολυμερῶς adv., *in many portions* (one at one time, another at another, and so on).

πολυποίκιλος, ον *much varied, very varied.*

πολύς, πολλή, πολύ, gen. **πολλοῦ, πολλῆς** a word indicating quantity and number, not size, sing. *much,* plur. *many;* οἱ πολλοί, *the majority;* πολλῷ, before a comp., *much;* πολλά, as adv., *much* (often in Mark, an exact translation of Aram.), like the more regular πολύ; πολλοῦ, *for much, at a great price,* Matt 26:9; w. sing. words indicating time, *long* is the most suitable Eng. rendering; πολλάς (supply πληγάς), Luke 12:47. The καί following, Acts 25:7, is superfluous according to our idiom. (Compar. πλείων and superl. πλεῖστος, q.v.)

πολύσπλαγχνος, οῦ ον *full of tender feeling* (a Hebraistic idiom, the bowels [σπλάγχνα, q.v.] being regarded as the seat of compassion and pity, etc.).

πολυτελής, ές *expensive, costly;* hence, *precious, valuable,* 1 Pet 3:4.

πολύτιμος, ον *costly, expensive;* hence, *valuable, precious,* 1 Pet 1:7.

πολυτρόπως adv., *in many ways, under many aspects* (with reference probably to different laws or injunctions).

πόμα, ατος, τό *drink.*

πονηρία, ας, ἡ the active exercise of vicious propensity, *malignity, wickedness;* plur. *iniquities,* Mark 7:22; Acts 3:26.

πονηρός, ά, όν *evil, wicked, malicious,* particularly as active; especially, ὁ πονηρός (even Matt 6:13; Luke 11:4 [var.], according to the almost unanimous opinion of the early Church), *the evil one,* i.e. Satan, the devil (a Hebraism); many passages like these, being in the oblique cases, are unfortunately ambiguous, but Matt 13:19; 1 John 2:13, 14; 5:18 are absolutely certain examples of the masc., and in many other passages there is a strong probability; τὸ πονηρόν, *the evil* in the world, *all that is wicked,* e.g. Rom 12:9.

πόνος, ου, ὁ *labor, toil; trouble.*

Ποντικός, ή, όν *belonging to Pontus* (q.v.).

Πόντιος, ου, ὁ *Pontius,* the second or gentile name of Pilate.

πόντος, ου, ὁ *the (open) sea,* Rev 18:17 var.

Πόντος, ου, ὁ *Pontus,* a Roman province in the north of Asia Minor, bordering on the Black Sea, governed along with Bithynia.

Πόπλιος, ου, ὁ the Gk. form of the Lat. name *Publius* (originally the same in form as the Gk. form); a governor of Malta.

πορεία, ας, ἡ *a journey.*

πορεύομαι *I travel, journey;* sometimes weakened to the sense, *I go; I depart* this life, *I die,* Luke 13:33(?); 22:22; Hebraistic, of manner of life, 1 Pet 4:3, etc.

πορθέω *I devastate, lay waste;* hence, *I bring destruction upon, I destroy.*

πορισμός, οῦ, ὁ *a means of gain, a way of making a living, a livelihood, a living.*

Πόρκιος, ου, ὁ *Porcius,* the middle (gentile) name of the procurator Festus.

πορνεία, ας, ἡ *fornication,* the practice of consorting with πόρναι or πόρνοι, habitual *immorality.*

πορνεύω *I practice fornication,* especially of men consorting with πόρναι.

πόρνη, ης, ἡ *a prostitute.*

πόρνος, ου, ὁ *a male prostitute;* the weaker sense, one who consorts with πόρναι, *a fornicator,* is generally adopted for NT.

πόρρω adv., *far, at a distance;* comp. adv. πορρώτερον *farther.*

πόρρωθεν adv., *from a long distance,* Heb 11:13; hence (cf. ἔξωθεν), *at a long distance, far away,* Luke 17:12.

πορφύρα, ας, ἡ *a purple* robe, *purple; a red colored cloak,* such as common soldiers wore, Mark 15:17, 20.

πορφυρόπωλις, ιδος, ἡ *a* woman *dealer in purple dyed* garments.

πορφυροῦς (πορφύρεος), ᾶ, οῦν *dyed with purple,* Rev 17:4; 18:16; *dyed scarlet,* John 19:2, 5 (see πορφύρα).

ποσάκις adv., *how many times?, how often?*

πόσις, εως, ἡ *drinking;* hence, concr., *drink,* as perhaps in all NT passages (certainly in John 6:55).

πόσος, η, ον *how great?, how large?;* in plur., *how many?;* πόσῳ, before compar. (cf. Matt 12:12), *by how much?, how much?*

ποταμός, οῦ, ὁ *a river.*

ποταμοφόρητος, ον *river-borne, carried off by a river.*

ποταπός, ή, όν (*from what country?, in what country born?,* and then) *of what sort?, how fashioned?* (hence, practically, *how great?,* 1 John 3:1).

πότε interrog. adv., *at what time?, when?;* ἕως πότε, *till what time?, till when?, how long?* Also in indir. interrog. clauses.

ποτέ indef. temp. particle, *at any time, ever, at some time; at one time,* especially w. past tenses; for μή ποτε, see μήποτε.

πότερον adv., *whether.*

ποτήριον, ου, τό *a wine cup.*

ποτίζω *I cause to drink, I make to drink, I give drink to.*

Ποτίολοι, ων, ὁ *Puteoli* (now Pozzuoli), the great harbor for traffic with Alexandria, etc., on the Bay of Naples.

πότος, ου, ὁ *a drinking bout.*

ποῦ interrog. adv., *where?;* also used (for the obsolete ποῖ) in the sense, *to what place?*

που adv., (1) *anywhere,* Acts 27:29; *somewhere,* Heb 2:6, etc.; (2) *about,* Rom 4:19; for δή που and μή που, see also δήπου, μήπου.

Πούδης, εντος, ὁ *Pudens,* a Christian man in Rome [Lat.].

πούς, ποδός, ὁ *a* (human) *foot.*

πρᾶγμα, ατος, τό (1) *a deed, action;* (2) used more vaguely, *a matter, an affair;* πρᾶγμα ἔχειν πρός τινα, *to have something against one, to have ground for a lawsuit against one,* 1 Cor 6:1; ἐν τῷ πράγματι, *in the matter in hand* (i.e. sins of the flesh), rather than generically, *in business,* 1 Thess 4:6.

πραγματεία, ῶν, ἡ *business, business transaction;* pl., *affairs, pursuits.*

πραγματεύομαι *I do business, I trade.*

πραθῆναι aor. pas. infin. → πιπράσκω.

πραιτώριον, ου, τό (1) *the official residence of the procurator,* which in Jerusalem was the palace of Herod on the west side of the city; (2) pers., *the imperial guard, the praetorian guard,* or perhaps, *the law officers of the Crown,* Phil 1:13 [From Lat. *praetorium,* meaning orig., *the quarters (residence) of the general.*]

πράκτωρ, ορος, ὁ (usually, *a collector of revenue,* but in Luke) *an officer (usher) of the court.*

πρᾶξις, εως, ἡ (1) abstr., *conduct; function,* Rom 12:4; (2) concr., in plur. *doings, deeds.*

πραότης *see* πραΰτης.

πρασιά, ᾶς, ἡ *a vegetable* or *flower bed;* πρασιαὶ πρασιαί, colloquial type of phrase, *like vegetable* or *flower beds,* referring to the rectangular arrangement of the groups.

πράσσω (referring rather to the purpose, motive of an action than to the actual doing), (1) trans., *I act, do;* (2) trans., *I exact, extort,* Luke 3:13; 19:23; (3) intrans., *I fare;* εὖ πράξετε, *you shall fare well,* Acts 15:29, τί πράσσω, *how I fare,* Eph 6:21.

πραϋπαθία (πραϋπάθεια), ας, ἡ *meekness (gentleness) of spirit.*

πραΰς, πραεῖα, πραΰ *meek, gentle.*

πραΰτης, ητος, ἡ *meekness, gentleness.*

πρέπω *I suit;* generally impers., or w. neut. pron. as subj., **πρέπει** = πρέπον ἐστίν, *it is becoming, it is fitting.*

πρεσβεία, ας, ἡ *an embassy, delegation.*

πρεσβεύω *I am an ambassador* (especially, *I am on embassy to the Emperor*).

πρεσβυτέριον, ου, τό (1) amongst the Jews, *a college of elders,* who supervised the worship, etc., of the synagogue; hence, *the Sanhedrin* at Jerusalem; (2) the Christian analogue, *a college of elders* of a particular church.

πρεσβύτερος, α, ον (1) of age simply, *the elder* of two, Luke

15:25; *old, aged,* Acts 2:17; 1 Tim 5:1; plur. our (their, etc.) *ancestors,* Matt 15:2; Mark 7:3, 5; Heb 11:2; (2) a title of honor applied among the Jews to various classes of dignitary, because such offices were originally conferred on the old, e.g. *a member of the Sanhedrin,* Matt 16:21, etc., [τοῦ Ἰσραήλ], Acts 4:8, τῶν Ἰουδαίων, Acts 25:15, τοῦ λαοῦ, Matt 21:23, etc.; *magistrates* of a particular city, Luke 7:3; (3) among the Christians, *an elder of* a congregation or church, Acts 11:30, etc., τῆς ἐκκλησίας, Acts 20:17; Jas 5:14, one of whom was commonly appointed ἐπίσκοπος; hence the two words are practically identical in meaning, the former indicating status, the latter function; (4) *an elder* of the twenty-four in the heavenly assembly, Rev 4:4, etc. (The title was applied in Egypt (a) to holders of a communal office in civil life, who were responsible for the peace of the village, and received a small salary, (b) to priests of pagan temples.)

πρεσβύτης, ου, ὁ *an old man.*

πρεσβῦτις, ιδος, ἡ *an old woman.*

πρηνής, ές gen. **οῦς** *swollen up, inflamed* (a medical term, denoting a disease, and corresponding to πίμπρημι, q.v.).

πρησθείς aor. pas. part. → πίμπραμαι.

πρίζω *I saw, I saw through.*

πρίν used either with or without ἤ *(than)* and w. the infin. following (once w. ἄν and subjun., Luke 2:26, once w. the opt., Acts 25:16), *before.*

Πρίσκα (Πρῖσκα), Πρίσκιλλα, ης, ἡ *Prisca, Priscilla,* a Roman lady, probably of good birth, wife of the Jewish Christian Aquila. The former is the more correct and formal name, the latter a diminutive and more familiar form.

πρό prep. w. gen., (1) of place, *before, in front of;* (2) of time, *before, earlier than;* found even w. article and the infin. = πρίν; πρὸ ἓξ ἡμερῶν τοῦ πάσχα, *six days before,* etc., John 12:1, πρὸ ἐτῶν δεκατεσσάρων, *fourteen years before,* 2 Cor 12:2.

προαγαγεῖν aor. act. infin. → προάγω.

προάγω (1) trans., *I lead forth,* Acts 16:30; in the judicial sense, into court, Acts 12:6, w. ἐπί w. gen. of the person who is to try the case, Acts 25:26; (2) intrans. and trans., *I precede, I go before;* so pres. part. *preceding, previous,* Heb 7:18; *I lead forwards* to a definite goal, 1 Tim 1:18; (3) intrans., *I go too far,* 2 John 9.

προαιρέομαι mid. *I choose deliberately.*

προαιτιάομαι *I make a prior accusation.*

προακούω *I hear beforehand.*

προαμαρτάνω *I sin previously.*

προαύλιον, ου, τό *a forecourt,* a courtyard in the front part of a building.

προβαίνω *I go forward, move forward, advance;* met. *I advance* (in years), Luke 1:7, 18; 2:36.

προβάλλω (1) trans., *I put forward;* (2) *I put forth shoots, I sprout, burst into leaf,* Luke 21:30.

προβάς aor. act. part. → προβαίνω.

προβατικός, ή, όν *connected with sheep;* προβατική (supply πύλη) *the Sheep Gate* of Jerusalem; if κολυμβήθρᾳ be read, προβατικῇ agrees with it.

προβάτιον, ου, τό lit. *a little sheep;* the diminutive (of πρόβατον) is here used to express tender affection.

πρόβατον, ου, τό *a sheep.*

προβέβηκα perf. act. → προβαίνω.

προβιβάζω *I instruct.*

προβλέπομαι mid. *I provide; I resolve on.*
προγίνομαι *I happen (come about) previously.*
προγινώσκω (properly, *I get to know (I learn) beforehand*), (1) *I know previously;* (2) *I designate before* (to a position or function), 1 Pet 1:20.
πρόγνωσις, εως, ἡ *foreknowledge.*
πρόγονος, ου, ὁ or **ἡ** *an ancestor.*
προγράφω (1) *I write previously (aforetime),* Rom 15:4; Jude 4; *I write above (already),* Eph 3:3; (2) *I evidently portray* or *I placard, advertise,* Gal 3:1.
πρόδηλος, ον *perfectly clear (evident).*
προδίδωμι *I give previously.*
προδότης, ου, ὁ (1) *a betrayer;* (2) *traitorous, treacherous,* 2 Tim 3:4.
προδραμών aor. act. part. → προτρέχω.
πρόδρομος, ου, ὁ *a forerunner.*
προέγνων aor. act. → προγινώσκω.
προέδραμον aor. act. → προτρέχω.
προέδωκα aor. act. → προδίδωμι.
προεθέμην aor. mid. → προτίθημι.
προεῖδον aor. act. → προοράω.
προεῖπον aor. act. → προλέγω, *I said beforehand (previously).*
προείρηκα perf. act. → προλέγω, *I have previously said; I have said above.*
προέλαβον aor. act. → προλαμβάνω.
προελεύσομαι fut. mid. → προέρχομαι.
προελθών aor. act. part. → προέρχομαι.
προελπίζω *I hope before* another, *I am the first to hope.*
προενάρχομαι *I begin earlier (previously).*
προεπαγγέλλομαι *I promise beforehand.*
προέρχομαι (1) intrans., *I go in front (before);* sometimes w. acc. of distance covered, Acts 12:10; (2) trans., *I precede,* Mark 6:33; Luke 22:47.
προεστώς perf. act. part. → προΐστημι.
προετοιμάζω *I prepare beforehand.*
προευαγγελίζομαι *I proclaim the good news beforehand.*
προέχω *I excel, surpass;* pas. in Rom 3:9.
προήγαγον aor. act. → προάγω.
προηγέομαι *I lead in front, I give a lead to.*
προῆλθον aor. act. → προέρχομαι.
προήλπικα perf. act. → προελπίζω.
προημάρτηκα perf. act. → προαμαρτάνω.
προῄρημαι perf. mid./pas. → προαιρέομαι.
πρόθεσις, εως, ἡ (1) οἱ ἄρτοι τῆς προθέσεως, lit. *the loaves of the laying out* (*before* God), i.e. *the loaves laid out,* grecized in Heb 9:2, ἡ πρόθεσις τῶν ἄρτων [Heb.]; (2) *deliberate purpose (plan, scheme).*
προθεσμία, ας, ἡ *a term* (or *age, date*) *previously indicated (fixed, laid down).*
προθυμία, ας, ἡ *eagerness, zeal, enthusiasm.*
πρόθυμος, ον *eager;* in Rom 1:15 τὸ κατ᾽ ἐμὲ πρόθυμον may be = ἡ ἐμὲ προθυμία, *my good will,* but perhaps it is better to read πρόθυμος (supply εἰμί) with some authorities.
προθύμως adv., *eagerly.*
προϊδών aor. act. part. → προοράω.
πρόϊμος, ου, ὁ *early* in the year (understand ὑετός or some other word meaning *rain);* reference is to that beginning in October; opposed to ὄψιμος. (Not πρώϊμος, but from πρό.)
προΐστημι (προίστημι) in intrans. tenses, *I take up a position (stand) in front; I take the lead, I rule;* hence, w. gen. *I lead, supervise,*

manage; also *I practice, exercise* a calling or profession.

προκαλέομαι mid. *I call forth, challenge.*

προκαταγγέλλω *I announce beforehand.*

προκαταρτίζω *I prepare (arrange) beforehand.*

προκατέχω *I possess* or *occupy previously;* Rom 3:9, var..

πρόκειμαι *I am set (placed, put) before, I am already there.*

προκηρύσσω *I proclaim previously.*

προκοπή, ῆς, ἡ *progress, advance.*

προκόπτω *I advance, progress, make progress* (originally of the pioneer cutting his way through brushwood).

πρόκριμα, ατος, τό *prejudgment* (favorable or unfavorable).

προκυρόω *I make valid beforehand.*

προλαμβάνω (1) *I take before* another (perhaps); *I am in a hurry to take, I take eagerly, I seize,* 1 Cor 11:21; (2) προέλαβεν μυρίσαι, *has by anticipation anointed* (perhaps an Aramaism), Mark 14:8; (3) *I catch, capture, overtake* (*before* he can escape).

προλέγω *I tell (say) beforehand.*

προμαρτύρομαι *I call (*God) *beforehand to witness.*

προμελετάω *I practice beforehand, I prepare, I get up.*

προμεριμνάω *I am anxious beforehand.*

προνοέω act. and mid., *I take thought for beforehand, I provide for.*

πρόνοια, ας, ἡ *forethought, foresight;* πρόνοιαν ποιοῦμαι = προνοέω.

προοράω *I see beforehand, I foresee, I see previously,* Acts 21:29; mid. *I pay regard to, set before me,* Acts 2:25.

προορίζω *I foreordain* (lit. *I bound [limit] beforehand*).

προπαθών aor. act. part. → προπάσχω.

προπάσχω *I suffer previously.*

προπάτωρ, ορος, ὁ *a forefather.*

προπέμπω (1) *I send in front (forth, forward), set forward, start on their way* (in Tit. 3:13, of being provided with necessaries for the journey); (2) *I convoy, I escort on* (*his,* etc.) *way,* as a mark of affection and respect, Acts 15:3; 20:38; 21:5; Rom 15:24; 3 John 6.

προπετής, ές, gen. **οῦς** *impulsive, rash, reckless* (of thoughtless haste).

προπορεύομαι *I journey in front, I go before.*

πρός prep. (1) w. gen., *on the side of, in the interests of, for* (literary), Acts 27:34; (2) w. dat., *close to, close by, near, at;* (3) w. acc. (of persons, places, things), (a) *to,* w. verbs of coming, sending, bringing, saying, (b) *near,* after the verb "to be," etc. (instead of παρά τινι), (c) *near,* instead of παρά, Acts 5:10, *into the house of,* Acts 11:3, (d) of time, *near,* Luke 24:29; *for* (a time), and no longer, Luke 8:13; John 5:35; Heb 12:10, etc., (e) of hostile or friendly relations, *with,* μάχεσθαι, εἰρήνην ἔχειν, etc.; τί πρὸς ἡμᾶς; *what have we to do with it?* Matt 27:4; John 21:22; *with reference to, of,* Mark 12:12, cf. 10:5; Matt 19:8; Luke 12:41; 18:1; 20:19; John 13:28, etc., (f) w. ἀγαθός, ὠφέλιμος, δυνατός, etc., *for,* 2 Cor 10:4; Eph 4:29; 1 Tim 4:8, where it indicates also the destination, purpose, result, e.g. Luke 14:32; 19:42; John 4:35; 11:4 (cf. John 5:16, 17); Acts 3:10, (g) *in conformity with, according to,* Luke 12:47; 1 Cor 12:7; 2 Cor 5:10; *with respect to,* Heb 1:7, 8, (h) *in comparison with,* Rom 8:18.

προσάββατον, ου, τό *the day before the Sabbath,* i.e. from 6:00 p.m. on Thursday to 6:00 p.m. on Friday.

προσαγαγεῖν aor. act. infin. → προσάγω.

προσαγορεύω *I designate as* by addressing by a certain title; *I recognize as.*

προσάγω (1) *I lead to, I bring to;* characteristically, *I bring* a subj. *into the presence of* a king, *I present to, I introduce,* 1 Pet 3:18; (2) intrans., *I approach,* Acts 27:27 (var.).

προσαγωγή, ῆς, ἡ *access, entrée,* or perhaps a metaphor from the concr. sense *landing stage.*

προσαιτέω *I beg, I am a beggar.*

προσαίτης, ου, ὁ *a beggar.*

προσαναβαίνω *I go up to, I come up to.*

προσαναλίσκω *I spend in addition.*

προσαναπληρόω *I fill up by adding, make up, supply.*

προσανατίθεμαι (1) *I add, contribute;* (2) *I consult with, turn (have recourse) to.*

προσανεθέμην aor. mid. → προσανατίθεμαι.

προσανέχω *I rise up toward,* w. dat., Acts 27:27, var.

προσαπειλέομαι *I add a threat* (or *threats*) to the warning.

προσαχέω *I sound near,* Acts 27:27 (Doric form for προσηχέω, var.).

προσδαπανάω *I spend in addition.*

προσδέομαι *I need (have need of)* something *additional.*

προσδέχομαι (1) *I await, expect;* (2) *I receive, welcome* (orig. *to* my house), e.g. Luke 15:2; Rom 16:2; Phil 2:29; (3) *I accept,* Acts 24:15.

προσδοκάω *I expect, wait for, await.*

προσδοκία, ας, ἡ *expectation, waiting.*

προσδραμών aor. act. part. → προστρέχω.

προσεάω *I permit* to go straight *onwards.*

προσεγγίζω *I come near to, I approach.*

προσεθέμην aor. mid. → προστίθημι.

προσέθηκα aor. act. → προστίθημι.

προσεκλίθην aor. pas. → προσκλίνομαι.

προσελαβόμην aor. mid. → προσλαμβάνομαι.

προσελεύσομαι fut. mid. → προσέρχομαι.

προσελήλυθα perf. act. → προσέρχομαι.

πρόσελθε aor. act. imper. → προσέρχομαι.

προσενέγκαι aor. act. infin. → προσφέρω.

προσενεχθείς aor. pas. part. → προσφέρω.

προσενήνοχα perf. act. → προσφέρω.

προσέπεσον aor. act. → προσπίπτω.

προσέπηξα aor. act. → προσπήγνυμι.

προσεργάζομαι *I produce in addition, I gain.*

προσέρηξα aor. act. → προσρήγνυμι.

προσέρχομαι *I come up to, I come to; I come near (to), I approach; I consent (to),* 1 Tim 6:3.

προσέσχηκα perf. act. → προσέχω.

προσέσχον aor. act. → προσέχω.

προσέταξα aor. act. → προστάσσω.

προσετέθην aor. pas. → προστίθημι.

προσευχή, ῆς, ἡ (1) *prayer* (to God); τοῦ θεοῦ, *to God,* Luke 6:12; (2) *a place for prayer,* Acts 16:13 (used by Jews, perhaps where there was no synagogue).

προσεύχομαι *I pray;* w. acc., *I pray for;* sometimes w. Hebraistic tautology, προσευχῇ or διὰ προσευχῆς is added.

προσέχω (1) *I attend to, pay attention*

to, w. dat., Acts 8:6; 16:14, etc. (τὸν νοῦν was originally added, *I direct the mind*), cf. (3); (2) w. ἐμαυτῷ, or absol., *I attend to myself, I pay attention for myself,* Hebraism for *I am cautious, I beware, I take care for (of) myself,* Luke 17:3; Acts 5:35, w. ἀπό governing the thing *of* which one has to beware, Matt 7:15; Luke 12:1, etc.; so w. μή, *lest;* (3) supply ἐμαυτόν, *I attach myself to, I join,* Acts 8:10; 1 Tim 4:1; *I devote myself to* (by way of enjoyment or of work), 1 Tim 1:4; 3:8; 4:13; Tit. 1:14; Heb 7:13.

προσῆλθον aor. act. → προσέρχομαι.

προσηλόω *I nail to.*

προσήλυτος, ου, ὁ (lit. *that has come to*), *a proselyte,* i.e., a non-Jew, who has been circumcised and has adopted the Jews' religion.

προσήνεγκα aor. act. → προσφέρω.

προσηνέχθην aor. pas. → προσφέρω.

προσήχθην aor. pas. → προσάγω.

προσθεῖναι aor. act. infin. → προστίθημι.

προσθείς aor. act. part. → προστίθημι.

πρόσθες aor. act. imper. → προστίθημι.

προσθῶ aor. act. subj. → προστίθημι.

πρόσκαιρος, ον *for an occasion, transitory.*

προσκαλέομαι *I call to myself.*

προσκαρτερέω (1) *I continue all the time, I continue steadfast, I persist,* either of remaining in a place, or of persisting in a certain course of action; (2) *I attach myself assiduously to,* Acts 8:13; 10:7; (3) w. a lifeless subj., *I continue near (at hand),* Mark 3:9.

προσκαρτέρησις, εως, ἡ *constant attendance, persistence, perseverance, constancy.*

προσκέκλημαι perf. mid./pas. → προσκαλέομαι.

προσκεφάλαιον, ου, τό *a pillow* or *a cushion.*

προσκληρόω *I allot (assign) to* (as disciples), Acts 17:4, where, if the pas. has a mid. force, we may translate, *threw in their lot with.*

προσκλίνω mid. *I attach myself to, follow.*

πρόσκλισις, εως, ἡ *inclination;* possibly, *taking sides, party spirit.*

προσκολλάω (lit. *I glue* one thing *to* another), *I join (unite) closely;* fut. pas. probably as mid., *I cleave (to).*

πρόσκομμα, ατος, τό (lit. *striking against,* generally in the Hebraistic gen., after λίθος, a stone or loose boulder in the way, *against* which the traveler may *strike* his foot), *an obstacle, a cause of stumbling; stumbling;* hence especially met.

προσκοπή, ῆς, ἡ *causing of stumbling* (met.).

προσκόπτω *I strike against;* intrans., Matt 7:27, etc., also absol., *I stumble,* John 11:9, 10; Rom 14:21; *I stumble at,* 1 Pet 2:8. Sometimes met. (cf. πρόσκομμα).

προσκυλίω *I roll to (up to).*

προσκυνέω *I go down on my knees to; I do obeisance to; I worship.*

προσκυνητής, οῦ, ὁ *a worshipper.*

προσλαλέω *I speak to.*

προσλαμβάνομαι (1) *I take to myself;* (2) *I take aside, take along* Mark 8:32; Matt 16:22; Acts 17:5; 18:26; (3) *I welcome,* Acts 28:2; Rom 14:1, etc.

προσλέγω *I answer, reply;* Mark 16:14, var.

πρόσλημψις, εως, ἡ *taking to one's self; assumption* into God's favor.

προσμεῖναι aor. act. infin. → προσμένω.

προσμένω *I remain;* w. dat., *I abide in, I remain in, I persist in.*

προσορμίζομαι *I come into harbor, I anchor at* a place.

προσοφείλω *I owe besides (in addition).*

προσοχθίζω *I entertain anger (disgust, abhorrence).*

πρόσπεινος, ον either *inclined to hunger* or *very hungry.*

προσπήγνυμι *I fix to* anything.

προσπίπτω *I fall upon; I fall at (beside).*

προσποιέομαι (1) *I pretend;* (2) *I take notice.*

προσπορεύομαι *I come to.*

προσρήσσω (προσρήγνυμι) *I burst upon, break in pieces.*

προστάσσω (1) *I instruct, command;* (2) *I appoint,* Acts 17:26.

προστάτις, ιδος, ἡ *protectress, patroness* (a development of the political sense of προστάτης, *a political sponsor* of resident aliens).

προστέταγμαι perf. mid./pas. → προστάσσω.

προστῆναι aor. act. infin. → προΐστημι.

προστίθημι *I place (put) to, I add;* mid. w. infin. (perhaps a Hebraistic idiom), best translated by representing the verb in the infin. by the indic., and adding the word *besides,* etc., thus: προσέθετο πέμψαι, *besides (in addition, further) he sent,* Luke 20:11.

προστρέχω *I run (run up) to* a person.

προσφάγιον, ου, τό *a relish, delicacy,* or *tidbit* eaten with bread (commonly it would be fish).

πρόσφατος, ον (from πρός and the root of φόνος, therefore orig. *newly slaughtered, fresh-killed*), *now for the first time made, new.*

προσφάτως adv., *freshly, recently.*

προσφέρω (1) *I bring to;* (2) characteristically, *I offer* (of gifts, sacrifices, etc.).

προσφιλής, ές *lovable, amiable.*

προσφορά, ᾶς, ἡ *an offering* (especially to God).

προσφωνέω w. acc. *I call, I summon;* w. dat. *I call (out) to; I address, I give a speech to,* Acts 22:2, cf. absol. Acts 21:40.

πρόσχυσις, εως, ἡ *pouring upon* the altar (as was done in later times, not in that of Moses).

προσψαύω *I touch, handle.*

προσωπολημπτέω *I favor specially* (from προσωπολήμπτης, Hebraistic, later than LXX).

προσωπολήμπτης, ου, ὁ *a special favorer* of one more than of another, *a respecter of persons* (from πρόσωπον and λαμβάνειν, Hebraistic, later than LXX; see under the latter).

προσωπολημψία, ας, ἡ *favoritism, partiality* (a Hebraistic expression, later than LXX).

πρόσωπον, ου, τό (1) *the* human *face;* often Hebraistically otiose, e.g. πρὸ προσώπου σου practically = πρὸ σοῦ, Matt 11:10; πρόσωπον πρὸς πρόσωπον (Hebraistic), *face to face;* (2) hence applied to God, from His having been originally conceived as in human form, *presence* (cf. Acts 5:41); (3) *appearance, outward aspect* (Matt 16:3), Luke 12:56, etc.; *surface,* Luke 21:35; (4) for the practically synonymous Hebraistic expressions βλέπειν εἰς πρόσωπον, θαυμάζειν πρόσωπον, λαμβάνειν πρόσωπον, *to show special favor to,* see under λαμβάνω; (5) by Hebraistic pleonasm (cf. (1) above), πρὸ προσώπου τῆς εἰσόδου αὐτοῦ, *before his entrance,* Acts 13:24; (6) *person* in a rather loose sense as a possessor of dignity or honor; *pride,* Jas 1:11.

προτείνω *I stretch forward, I put into a tense posture.*

πρότερος, α, ον (becoming replaced by πρῶτος), *first of two, former, previous, earlier;* acc. as adv. (τὸ) πρότερον, *on the former of two occasions,* e.g. Gal 4:13; *on a previous occasion; at first, formerly, previously,* sometimes used practically as an adj., as the latter was dying out (see πρῶτος), 1 Tim 1:13.

προτίθεμαι (1) *I add (to);* (2) *I set before myself, I purpose openly;* but perhaps, (3) *I offer, I provide.*

προτρέπομαι *I encourage.*

προτρέχω *I run forward.*

προϋπάρχω *I am (previously), I exist before, I have been already.*

πρόφασις, εως, ἡ *ostensible reason* for which a thing is done (i.e., commonly, the false reason), *pretence; excuse, pretext;* προφάσει, *under color, under pretence.*

προφέρω *I bring forth (out), produce.*

προφητεία, ας, ἡ the quality or action of a προφήτης, *declaration* of the will of God, whether with special reference to the future, in which case it may be translated *prophecy,* or not.

προφητεύω I do the duty of a προφήτης, *I declare* the will of God, sometimes with regard to what is to happen in the future, in which case it may be rendered, *I prophesy.*

προφήτης, ου, ὁ a man specially endowed to *tell forth (declare)* the will of God in speech, whether as touching the present or as regards the future, *a prophet;* the adoption of a literary form as seen in the prophetical books of the OT is a later stage of a prophet's activity; Epimenides is so styled (in Tit. 1:12), perhaps as related to the Cretans in the same way as the prophets of Israel were to Israel.

προφητικός, ή, όν belonging to a προφήτης or to προφῆται, *prophetic.*

προφῆτις, ιδος, ἡ *a prophetess.*

προφθάνω *I anticipate, I forestall.*

προχειρίζομαι *I appoint, elect* (for an important duty).

προχειροτονέω *I appoint beforehand.*

Πρόχορος, ου, ὁ *Prochorus,* one of the seven original "deacons" at Jerusalem.

πρύμνα, ης, ἡ *the stern* of a ship.

πρωΐ adv., *early, in the morning* (in John 20:1, even of the period before dawn).

πρωΐα, ας, ἡ *early morning.*

πρώϊμος see πρόϊμος.

πρωϊνός, ή, όν (from πρωΐ) *belonging to the morning, morning;* opp. ἑσπερινός.

πρῷρα (πρῴρα), ης, ἡ *the prow, the bow* of a ship.

πρωτεύω *I hold the first (chief) place, I am the head.*

πρωτοκαθεδρία, ας, ἡ *the chief (most honorable) seat (chair, stall).*

πρωτοκλισία, ας, ἡ *the chief (most honorable) reclining place* on the dining couches at a dinner table.

πρῶτον adv., *in the first place, first;* τὸ πρῶτον, *at first, at the beginning.*

πρῶτος, η, ον *first* (of time, then of status), strictly of more than two, being a superl., but also used where there are two elements only, as πρότερος, the true comp., was dying out in NT times, Acts 1:1; Heb 8:7, 13; 9:1, 2, 6, 8, etc.; οἱ πρῶτοι, *the chief men,* Mark 6:21; Luke 19:47, etc., cf. ὁ πρῶτος, an official title, equivalent to *the governor,* Acts 28:7; πρῶτος μου, John 1:15, 30, either = πρότερός μου, *earlier than I* (cf. 15:18), or,

w. μου as possessive gen., *my chief, my lord.*

πρωτοστάτης, ου, ὁ *one who stands in the front rank,* hence, *a leader, ringleader.*

πρωτοτόκια, ων, τό pl. *one's rights as firstborn.*

πρωτότοκος, ον *firstborn, earliest born, eldest.*

πρώτως adv., *for the first time* (var.).

πταίω of incipient falling, *I trip, stumble,* lit. or met.

πτέρνα, ης, ἡ *heel.*

πτερύγιον, ου, τό *the gable, roof projection of the temple roof, pinnacle;* or possibly (see ἱερόν), *the wall* surrounding the temple precinct.

πτέρυξ, υγος, ἡ *a wing.*

πτηνός, ή, όν, τό *winged;* hence as neut. subs., *a bird.*

πτοέω *I scare, I strike with panic.*

πτόησις, εως, ἡ *fear, terror* (or other violent excitement).

Πτολεμαΐς, ΐδος, ἡ *Ptolemais,* a coast city of Phoenicia, midway between Tyre and Caesarea.

πτύξας aor. act. part. → πτύσσω.

πτύον, ου, τό *a winnowing fan,* a simple wooden pitchfork.

πτύρω *I frighten, terrify.*

πτύσμα, ατος, τό *spittle.*

πτύσσω *I roll up, close.*

πτύω *I spit.*

πτῶμα, ατος, τό *a corpse.*

πτῶσις, εως, ἡ *falling, fall.*

πτωχεία, ας, ἡ (strictly *beggary,* but rather merely) *poverty.*

πτωχεύω *I live the life of a poor man.*

πτωχός, ή, όν (strictly *a beggar;* weakened afterwards), *poor; a poor man;* met. (Matt 5:3; Luke 6:20; Rev 3:17), not of those who are poor in material things, but of the humble devout persons, who feel the need of God's help.

πυγμή, ῆς, ἡ *the fist;* meaning of Mark 7:3 (var.) still uncertain ("turning the closed fist of one hand about the hollow of the other," or "as far as the elbow," or paraphrased by "diligently," "carefully").

πυθόμενος aor. mid. part. → πυνθάνομαι.

πύθων, ωνος, ὁ *a ventriloquist* (the utterance being supposed to be due to the presence of a familiar spirit [πύθων] within the body of the speaker).

πυκνός, ή, όν (spissus, *thick*); hence) *frequent;* acc. plur. neut. πυκνά as adv., *frequently, often* (cf. regular comp. of adv., Acts 24:26).

πυκτεύω *I am a boxer, I box.*

πύλη, ης, ἡ *a gate.*

πυλών, ῶνος, ὁ *entrance passage, gateway; gate* (properly, *the passage which led from the street through the front part of the house to the inner court,* closed by a heavy πύλη at the streetward end).

πυνθάνομαι *I enquire.*

πῦρ, ός, τό *fire; a fire,* both lit., and met., and eschatologically (as an instrument of punishment in the conception of later Judaism, *the fire* of the Divine wrath which burns in Gehenna).

πυρά, ᾶς, ἡ *a fire.*

πύργος, ου, ὁ *a tower.*

πυρέσσω *I have fever, I suffer from fever.*

πυρετός, οῦ, ὁ *a fever;* medical writers use the plur. (Acts 28:8), where we should use the sing., because of recurring attacks of fever.

πύρινος, η, ον *as of fire,* i.e., probably, *fire colored.*

πυρόω (1) *I equip with fire,* Eph 6:16 (of flaming darts), *I refine by fire,* Rev 1:15; 3:18, *I burn with fire, I fire,* 2 Pet 3:12; (2) mid. or pas. met., of strong passion or feeling, *I burn with fleshly lust,* 1 Cor 7:9; *I blaze with anger,* 2 Cor 11:29.

πυρράζω *I am red (ruddy).*

πυρρός, ά, όν *red.*

Πύρρος, ου, ὁ *Pyrrhus,* father of the Christian Sopater of Beroea.

πύρωσις, εως, ἡ (1) *burning;* (2) met. *trial* as it were *by fire, fiery test,* 1 Pet 4:12.

πωλέω (*I advertise, put up for sale), I sell.*

πῶλος, ου, ὁ (*the young* of various animals), hence particularly, *the foal (colt) of an ass.*

πώποτε adv., *ever yet, yet at any time,* only used after a negative word.

πωρόω (from πῶρος, *a kind of marble,* then, *a bony formation on the joints,* and a *callus* or *ossification* uniting two portions of a fractured bone; thus πωρόω, *I petrify* and *I cover with a callus,* and *I deaden, I dull) I make (render) obtuse (dull, dead); I bind (intellectually* or *morally).*

πώρωσις, εως, ἡ (orig., *petrifaction, hardness;* then the result of this, as met. applied to organs of feeling), *insensibility, numbness, obtuseness, dulling* of the faculty of perception, *deadness;* intellectual (moral) *blindness.*

πώς indef., enclitic, *in some way, in any way;* εἴ πως, *if in any way;* see μήπως.

πῶς (1) *how?, in what manner?,* also in indir. interrog.; πῶς γάρ . . . *why, how* . . .; (2) = ὡς, ὅτι, *that* (variant readings sometimes occur), Matt 12:4; Mark 12:26, 41; Luke 6:4; 14:7; Acts 11:13; 1 Thess 1:9.

P

Ῥαάβ, ἡ *Rahab,* a Canaanite woman, who rescued the Hebrew spies at Jericho, by tradition wife of Salmon (Matt 1:4, 5) [Heb.].

ῥαββί (ῥαββεί) *my master,* a title given by pupils to their teacher [Aram.].

ῥαββουνί (ῥαββουνεί) *my master* (Aram., a fuller form of (ῥαββεί).

ῥαβδίζω *I flog (beat) with a rod (staff),* a Roman punishment.

ῥάβδος, ου, ἡ *a staff, rod.*

ῥαβδοῦχος, ου, ὁ (lit. *a rod holder, holder of rods*), *a lictor, an attendant (orderly),* of certain Roman magistrates, *a tipstaff.*

Ῥαγαύ, ὁ *Ragau,* an ancestor of Jesus [Heb.].

ῥᾳδιούργημα, ατος, τό *a moral wrong, a crime.*

ῥᾳδιουργία, ας, ἡ *(ease in working; so unscrupulousness);* hence, *fraud, wickedness.*

Ῥαιφάν (Ῥεφάν, Ῥομφάν), ὁ *Rephan, Rompha,* probably a corruption of the Assyrian name for the planet Saturn (= Chiun, Amos 5:26).

ῥακά (ῥαχά) *empty foolish* [Aram.].

ῥάκος, ους, τό *a piece of cloth.*

Ῥαμά, ἡ *Rama,* a place in Ephraim, two hours north of Jerusalem.

ῥαντίζω (1) *I sprinkle* and thus purify; (2) mid. *I sprinkle (purify) myself,* Mark 7:4.

ῥαντισμός, οῦ, ὁ *sprinkling,* as a symbolic purification (cf. Exod 24:6–8).

ῥαπίζω *I slap, strike.*

ῥάπισμα, ατος, τό *a slap, a blow on the cheek with the open hand.*

ῥαφίς, ίδος, ἡ *a sewing needle* (= classical βελόνη, used by Luke).

ῥαχά see ῥακά.

Ῥαχάβ, ἡ another spelling of Ῥαάβ [Heb.].

Ῥαχήλ, ἡ *Rachel,* younger wife of the patriarch Jacob [Heb.].

Ῥεβέκκα, ας, ἡ *Rebecca,* wife of the patriarch Isaac [Heb.].

ῥέδη, ης, ἡ *a carriage* (*reda,* a word of Keltic origin).

ῥέραμμαι perf. mid./pas. → ῥαίνω.

ρεράντισμαι perf. mid./pas. → ραντίζω.

ρεύσω fut. act. → ῥέω.

Ῥεφάν see Ῥαιφάν.

ῥέω *I flow.*

Ῥήγιον, ου, τό *Regium,* a city in the southwest corner of Italy opposite Sicily (mod. Reggio).

ῥῆγμα, ατος, τό *a breaking up, collapse.*

ῥήγνυμι (ῥήσσω) (1) *I break; I rend, tear;* in Mark 9:18; Luke 9:42, it either = σπαράσσω, of convulsions, or *I throw on the ground;* (2) intrans., *I break forth into joy,* Gal 4:27.

ρηθείς aor. pas. part. → λέγω.

ῥῆμα, ατος, τό (1) *a spoken word, an utterance,* the concr. expression of λόγος; hence, perhaps Hebraistic, (2) a subject as spoken about, a subject of speech, *a matter, a thing, a fact,* Matt 18:16; Luke 1:37; 2:15, etc.; (3) in a solemn sense, of a divine *word,* Luke 3:2; Eph 6:17, etc.; (4) the Christian *teaching, the gospel,* 1 Pet 1:25 (cf. Rom 10:8ff.), (the first = the promise to deliver Israel); (5) the Christian confession, "Jesus is Lord," which leads to salvation, and precedes baptism, Eph 5:26, cf. Rom 10:9; 1 Cor 12:3; Phil 2:11.

ρῆξον aor. act. imper. → ρήγνυμι.

Ῥησά, ὁ *Resa,* an ancestor of Jesus [Heb.].

ῥήσσω see ῥήγνυμι.

ῥήτωρ, ορος, ὁ *a rhetorician, a professional public speaker;* hence, *a barrister,* acting as counsel for the prosecution.

ῥητῶς adv., *in so many words, expressly, explicitly.*

ῥίζα, ης, ἡ *a root;* hence met., *a source.*

ῥιζόω *I root, I fix by the root.*

ῥιπή, ῆς, ἡ *a glance* (indicating instantaneousness), *flash* of an eye.

ῥιπίζω (from ῥιπίς, a fire fan; hence, *I fan* either a fire or a person), *I raise* with the wind.

ῥίπτω (ῥιπτέω) *I throw, cast; I shake, toss;* ἐρριμμένοι, *sunk powerless,* Matt 9:36; in Acts 22:23, *I toss about,* a sign of excitement and uncontrollable rage.

ρίψον aor. act. imper. → ρίπτω.

Ῥοβοάμ, ὁ *Rehoboam,* son of Solomon, and King of Israel [Heb.].

Ῥόδη, ης, ἡ (lit. *Rose*), *Rhoda,* a maidservant in the house of John Mark's mother at Jerusalem.

Ῥόδος, ου, ἡ *Rhodes,* an island in the Aegean sea, southwest of Asia Minor.

ῥοιζηδόν adv., *with thunderous crash (roar);* properly expressing the whizzing sound produced by rapid motion through the air.

Ῥομφά see Ῥαιφάν.

ῥομφαία, ας, ἡ (properly a long Thracian sword), *a sword, scimitar;* met. in Luke 2:35 of acute suffering.

ῥοπή, ῆς, ἡ *an inclination, movement;* 1 Cor 15:52, var.

Ῥουβήν, ὁ *Reuben,* eldest son of the patriarch Jacob and founder of a tribe [Heb.].

Ῥούθ, ἡ *Ruth,* wife of Boes (Boaz) and mother of Iobed (Obed) [Heb.].

Ῥοῦφος, ου, ὁ *Rufus,* a Christian man in Rome (Rom 16:3), probably to be identified with the brother of Alexander and son of Simon of Cyrene mentioned in Mark 15:21.

ῥύμη, ης, ἡ *a street* or *lane* in a town or city.

ῥύομαι *I rescue* (from danger or destruction).

ῥυπαίνω *I make dirty, I stain;* mid. and pas., *I am filthy* (morally), *I am stained* (by sin); (var.).

ῥυπαρεύομαι mid. *I am filthy;*

hence morally, *I am stained with sin* (var.).

ῥυπαρία, ας, ἡ *defilement.*

ῥυπαρός, ά, όν *shabby, soiled;* hence morally, *filthy, corrupt, sinful,* Rev 22:11.

ῥύπος, ου, ὁ *filth, dirt.*

ῥύσις, εως, ἡ *flowing;* ῥύσις αἵματος, *hemorrhage.*

ῥυτίς, ίδος, ἡ *a wrinkle* of age.

Ῥωμαϊκός, ή, όν *Roman* (language), *Latin,* var.

Ῥωμαῖος, ου, ὁ *Roman; a Roman;* the plur., according to context, suggests either the imperial people (e.g. John 11:48) or citizens of the Roman Empire (e.g. Acts 16:21).

Ῥωμαϊστί adv., *in the Latin language.*

Ῥώμη, ης, ἡ *Rome,* the famous city on the Tiber, the capital of the Roman Empire.

ῥώννυμι *I make strong;* perf. mid. imper., a formula of correspondence, at the end of a letter, ἔρρωσο, ἔρρωσθε, farewell.

Σ

σαβαχθανί (σαβαχθανεί) *thou hast forsaken* [Aram.].

Σαβαώθ (σαβαώθ) (Lord of) *Sabaoth, hosts, armies* [Heb.].

σαββατισμός, οῦ, ὁ *a resting* as *on the Sabbath.*

σάββατον, ου, τό sing. and plur., *the Sabbath,* a night and day which lasted from about 6:00 p.m. on Friday till about 6:00 p.m. on Saturday (Semitic); πρώτη (μία) [τῶν] σαββάτων ([τοῦ] σαββάτου), *Sunday, the first day after the Sabbath, the day following the Sabbath,* i.e., from about 6:00 p.m. on Saturday till about 6:00 p.m. on Sunday; [Heb.].

σαγήνη *a fishing net.*

Σαδδουκαῖος (Σαδδυκαῖος), ου, ὁ *a Sadducee, a Zadokite priest,* a member of the aristocratic party among the Jews, from whom the high priests were almost invariably chosen.

Σαδώκ, ὁ *Zadok,* an ancestor of Jesus [Heb.].

σαίνω *I draw aside, allure* from the right path (properly of dogs, *I wag the tail, fawn;* then met. *I fawn upon, beguile*), 1 Thess 3:3; perhaps the var. σιαίνεσθαι, *to be disturbed (troubled),* ought to be read instead.

σάκκος, ου, ὁ *sackcloth, sacking,* a rough mourning dress held together by string, and hanging on the bare body (a Semitic word).

Σαλά, ὁ *Sala,* the name of two of the ancestors of Jesus (var. in Luke 3:32) [Heb.].

Σαλαθιήλ, ὁ *Salathiel,* son of Jechonias and father (according to one tradition) of Zerubbabel [Heb.].

Σαλαμίς, ῖνος, ἡ *Salamis,* a city at the eastern end of Cyprus.

Σαλίμ, Σαλείμ, ὁ *Salim,* a place eight Roman miles south of Scythopolis in the extreme north of Samaria.

σαλεύω *I shake,* lit., and met.; *I dislodge.*

Σαλήμ, ἡ *Salem,* doubtless identical with Jerusalem.

Σαλμών, ὁ *Salmon,* son of Naasson and father of Boes (Boaz); var. in Luke 3:32.

Σαλμώνη, ης, ἡ *Salmone,* a promontory on the east of Crete.

σάλος, ου, ὁ *a rough sea, surf.*

σάλπιγξ, ιγγος, ἡ *a bugle, a war trumpet,* used for signals and commands; hence in eschatological passage as signal for Judgment or Resurrection.

σαλπίζω *I sound the bugle, I give a blast of the bugle;* the subj. is sometimes omitted, so that the word becomes practically impers..

σαλπιστής, οῦ, ὁ *a bugler, trumpeter.*

Σαλώμη, ης, ἡ *Salome,* wife of Zebedee and mother of James and John, the disciples.

Σαλωμών see Σολομών.

Σαμάρεια, ας, ἡ *Samaria,* a small district of Palestine, bounded by Galilee on the north, and by Judaea on the south, and taking its name from the city of Samaria, the ancient capital of the kingdom of (northern) Israel.

Σαμαρίτης (Σαμαρείτης), ου, ὁ *a Samaritan, an inhabitant of Samaria.*

Σαμαρῖτις (Σαμαρεῖτις), ιδος, ἡ *a Samaritan woman.*

Σαμοθρᾴκη, ης, ἡ *Samothrace,* an island south of the province of Thrace.

Σάμος, ου, ἡ *Samos,* an island in the Aegean sea off the coast of Asia Minor, near Ephesus and Miletus.

Σαμουήλ, ὁ *Samuhel, Samuel,* an OT prophet [Heb.].

Σαμψών, ὁ *Sampson, Samson,* one of the Judges of Israel [Heb.].

σανδάλιον, ου, τό *a sandal, an open work shoe, a shoe.*

σανίς, ίδος, ἡ *a plank, board.*

Σαούλ, ὁ (1) *Saul,* the first king of Israel, Acts 13:21; (2) *Saul,* the Heb. name of the Apostle to the Gentiles (see Σαῦλος).

σαπρός, ά, όν *crumbling, decayed, decaying, rotten;* hence, *old and worn out, stale, worthless;* met. *corrupt,* Eph 4:29.

Σάπφιρα (Σάπφειρα), ης, ἡ *Sapphira,* wife of Ananias, an early Christian (perhaps from an Aram. word meaning *beautiful*).

σάπφιρος (σάπφειρος), ου, ἡ *a sapphire; lapis lazuli* (Semitic).

σαργάνη, ης, ἡ *a mat basket,* a large basket of flexible material closed by sewing and usually employed to hold slices of salt fish (raisins and figs are also mentioned).

Σάρδεις, εων, ἡ *Sardis,* an ancient city of Lydia in the province of Asia.

σάρδιον, ου, τό *sardius, sard,* a quartz of a deep red color.

σαρδόνυξ, υχος, ὁ *sardonyx.*

Σάρεπτα, ων, τό *Sarepta,* a town in the district of Sidon in Phoenicia.

σαρκικός, ή, όν generally ethical, *belonging to* σάρξ (q.v.), belonging to the natural life of man as a creature of flesh, *with the characteristics of* σάρξ, *fleshly, unspiritual, carnal.*

σάρκινος, η, ον material, *made of flesh, consisting of flesh.*

σάρξ, σαρκός, ἡ (in general used Hebraistically), (1) *flesh,* all the solid part of the body of man or beast except the bones, plur. (Hebraistic), e.g. Luke 24:39 (var.), Rev 17:16; σὰρξ καὶ αἷμα, a Hebraistic periphrasis for *human nature, a human being;* (2) hence, the substance (material) of the body, *the body;* μία σάρξ, *one body,* of husband and wife; it is contrasted sometimes w. πνεῦμα, sometimes w. ψυχή; (3) (Hebraistic) *mankind, humanity* as such, without any necessary connotation of frailty, e.g. Rom 3:20; 1 Cor. 1:29; Gal 2:16; (4) *the animal (sensuous) nature* of man, the sphere of present existence, e.g. John 1:13; Rom 9:3; 1 Cor 10:18; Heb 12:9; (5) in reference to fleshly (physical) weakness, helplessness, 1 Cor 15:50 (corruptible); 2 Cor 4:11 (mortal); 7:5; 10:3; Eph 6:12; intellectual weakness, Rom 6:19; Gal 1:16; Col 2:18; cf. also 2 Cor 11:18; Gal 6:12, 13; Phil 3:3, 4; (6) in an ethical sense, characteristic of Paul, applied to part of human nature, generally as ruling instead of being, as it ought to be, in subjection; the two aspects are, (a) a general relation is implied between *the flesh* and sin, Rom 7:5; 8:3–9, 12, 13; 2 Cor 10:2; Gal 4:29; Col 2:11, 13, (b) *the flesh* is in some sense active in the production of evil, its desires (or lusts) are evil; in the physical nature it is the immediate enemy of the higher life, e.g. Rom 7:7–25; 8:12; 13:14; Gal 5:13, 16, 17, 19, 24; Eph 2:3; Col 2:23.

σαρόω *I sweep.*

Σάρρα, ας, ἡ *Sarah,* wife of Abraham [Heb.].

Σαρών, ῶνος, ὁ *Sharon,* the maritime plain between Carmel and Joppa.

σατάν (σατανᾶς), ᾶ, ὁ both with and without the article, a representation of the word which is also translated ὁ διάβολος, *the enemy, Satan, the devil,* the chief of the evil spirits (Aram., lit. *adversary*).

σάτον, ου, τό a large measure equivalent to nearly three English gallons [Aram.].

Σαῦλος, ου, ὁ the grecized form of the Heb. name Σαούλ of the Apostle to the Gentiles.

σβέννυμι (ζβέννυμι) *I extinguish, put out;* met. 1 Thess 5:19.

σβέσω fut. act. → σβέννυμι.

σεαυτοῦ, ῆς *of thyself (yourself).*

σεβάζομαι *I reverence, worship.*

σέβασμα, ατος, τό *an object of worship, a thing worshipped.*

Σεβαστός, ή, όν (official Gk. equivalent of Augustus), *Augustus,* the name meaning "worthy to be reverenced (worshipped)," given to Octavian by the Senate in Jan. 27 B.C., and retained by most of his successors, e.g. by Nero, to whom it refers in Acts 25:21, 25, where it is of course used by non-Christians; in Acts 27:1 σπεῖρα Σεβαστή is the official equivalent of a *cohors Augusta* (a *cohors I Augusta* had its headquarters in Batanaea in northeast Palestine).

σέβομαι *I reverence, worship* generally in Acts of god-fearing, uncircumcised Gentiles who joined the Jewish synagogues (contrast Acts 13:43).

σειρός *a pit* (properly *a pit, excavation* for the storage of grain); var. σειρά, *a chain, fetter.*

σεισμός, οῦ, ὁ *an earthquake.*

σείω *I shake.*

Σεκοῦνδος (Σέκουνδος), ου, ὁ *Secundus,* a Christian of Thessalonica [Lat.].

Σελεύκεια, ας, ἡ *Seleucia,* on the Syrian coast, the harbor of Syrian Antioch.

σελήνη, ης, ἡ *the moon.*

σεληνιάζω *I bring under the influence of the moon;* pas. *I am epileptic* (the state of an epileptic being attributed to the moon [σελήνη]).

Σεμεΐν (Σεμεειν), ὁ *Semein,* an ancestor of Jesus [Heb.].

σεμίδαλις, εως, ἡ *the finest wheaten meal.*

σεμνός, ή, όν *grave, worthy of respect.*

σεμνότης, ητος, ἡ *gravity, dignified behavior.*

Σέργιος, ου, ὁ *Sergius,* the middle (gentile) name of the proconsul of Cyprus.

Σερούχ, ὁ *Seruch,* an ancestor of Jesus [Heb.].

σέσηπα perf. act. → σήπω.

σέσωκα perf. act. → σῴζω.

Σήθ, ὁ *Seth,* third son of Adam [Heb.].

Σήμ, ὁ *Shem,* a son of Noah [Heb.].

σημαίνω *I indicate by a word; I point out in a letter (by letter),* Acts 25:27 (a technical term for the speech of a communicator of an oracle).

σημεῖον, ου, τό *a sign, an outward (visible) indication* of secret power or truth; *a miracle* regarded from that point of view.

σημειόομαι *I mark (notify) for myself, I take note of;* hence, with an idea of disapprobation added.

σήμερον adv. *today, this day;* ἡ σήμερον (supply ἡμέρα), noun, *today, this day.*

σήπω trans., *I cause to rot;* 2 perf. σέσηπα, *I have rotted, I am rotten.*

σής, σητός, ὁ *a moth.*

σητόβρωτος, ον *moth-eaten.*

σθενόω *I strengthen.*

σιαγών, όνος, ἡ *a cheek.*

σιγάω *I am silent.*

σιγή, ῆς, ἡ *silence.*

σιδηροῦς (σιδήρεος), ᾶ, οῦν *made of iron.*

σίδηρος, ου, ὁ *iron.*

Σιδών, ῶνος, ἡ *Sidon,* a great coast city of Phoenicia; in Mark 7:31 perhaps an error for *Saidan* = Bethsaida.

Σιδώνιος, α, ον *belonging to Sidon, Sidonian;* hence, as subst., *a Sidonian;* ἡ Σιδωνία (supply χώρα), *the region* or *territory of Sidon,* Luke 4:26.

σικάριος, ου, ὁ *an assassin, a murderer* (from Lat. *sica,* a stiletto); with reference to a fanatical Jewish political faction, accustomed to assassinate their opponents.

σίκερα, τό *an intoxicating drink, a strong fruit wine* [Aram.].

Σίλας (Σιλᾶς), α (ᾶ), ὁ *Silas,* a Jewish prophet and evangelist, a Roman citizen and a helper of Paul. The name is generally regarded as a pet form (used in Acts only) of Σιλουανός, and Silas is in consequence identified with him.

Σιλουανός, οῦ, ὁ *Silvanus* [Lat., *Siluanus*]; see Σίλας.

Σιλωάμ, ὁ *Siloam, Shiloah,* a spring (the only spring) within the walls, in the southeast corner of Jerusalem. The name is Aram. and really a subs. (= *discharge* or *gushing forth* of water).

σιμικίνθιον, ου, τό *an* artisan's working *apron* [Lat., *semicinctium*].

Σίμων, ωνος, ὁ *Simon,* (1) the Apostle, son of Jonas (John) and brother of Andrew; (2) the Cananaean (former Zealot), one of the disciples; (3) a brother of Jesus; (4) a Pharisee, a former leper, at Bethany; (5) a native of Cyrene, Mark 15:21; Matt 27:32; Luke 23:26; (6) father of Judas Iscariot; (7) Simon Magus, a sorcerer in Samaria; (8) a tanner at Joppa. (See also Συμεών.)

Σινᾶ (Σινά) *Sinai,* a mountain in Arabia; according to Hebrew allegorical methods of interpretation identified with Hagar, concubine of Abraham, Gal 4:25 (Arabic *hadjar = rock, stone,* and thus comes the equation Hagar = Sinai).

σίναπι, εως, τό *mustard.*

σινδών, όνος, ἡ *a fine light dress* worn over the underclothing, or *a nightgown,* or *a sheet* hastily seized (Semitic), Mark 14:51; of the grave clothes of Jesus, probably *a piece of unused linen,* Mark 15:46, etc.

σινιάζω *I sift, winnow.*

σιρικός, ή, όν *silken;* neut. subs., *silk fabrics* or *garments* (an inexact spelling of σηρικός, an adj. formed from Σῆρες, *the Chinese,* from whose country silk was obtained).

σιρός (σιρά) see σειρός.

σιτευτός, ή, όν *fed up* (with grain), *fattened.*

σιτίον, ου, τό *food made of corn, bread.*

σιτιστός, ή, όν the same in meaning as the much commoner σιτευτός.

σιτομέτριον, ου, τό *measure of corn, portion of corn, allowance of corn.*

σῖτος, ου, ὁ *corn.*

Σιών, ἡ *Sion, Zion,* the mountain on which the Davidic citadel of Jerusalem was built, and thus the center of the life of the people Israel.

σιωπάω *I keep silence, I am silent.*

σκανδαλίζω *I put a stumbling block in the way of, I cause to stumble, I set a trap for* (in the moral sphere); a Hebraistic, biblical word.

σκάνδαλον, ου, τό (1) *stumbling, cause of stumbling* (in the moral sphere); πέτρα σκανδάλου (Isa 8:14), *the native rock* rising up through the earth, *which trips up* the traveler, hence, of Jesus the Messiah, to the Jews who refused him; (2) *some person* (Matt 13:41; 16:23) or *thing which leads one to sin;* a Hebraistic, biblical word.

σκάπτω *I dig.*

σκάφη, ης, ἡ *a small boat,* towed behind.

σκέλος, ους, τό *a leg.*

σκέπασμα, ατος, τό strictly *roofing, shelter,* but with special reference to *clothing.*

Σκευᾶς, ᾶ, ὁ *Sceva,* an inhabitant of Ephesus.

σκευή, ῆς, ἡ *tackle* (a collective noun).

σκεῦος, ους, τό (1) *a vessel,* generally of earthenware, e.g. John 19:29; τὰ σκεύη, *utensils, goods and chattels, effects, property;* (2) met. of persons, e.g. of Paul as chosen *repository* of the power of Jesus (Hebraistic), Acts 9:15; either of one's own body as the case enclosing the soul, or of one's wife, 1 Thess 4:4 (cf. 1 Pet 3:7); (3) *tackle, furniture* of a ship, Acts 27:17.

σκηνή, ῆς, ἡ *a tent; a hut;* usually with reference to the temporary abode of Yahweh, which preceded the Temple; ἡ σκηνὴ τοῦ μαρτυρίου, *the tent as a witness to the covenant between God and His people;* in Heb 9 the two parts of the one σκηνή, separated from one another by the curtain, are each called σκηνή.

σκηνοπηγία, ας, ἡ *the Feast of Tabernacles* (lit. *of booth building*), sometimes called ἑορτὴ [τῶν] σκηνῶν or ἑορτὴ [τῆς] σκηνοπηγίας, the great festival of the Jews, held in October, originally the Feast of Ingathering.

σκηνοποιός, οῦ, ὁ *a tentmaker.*

σκῆνος, ους, τό *a tent;* so met. (used in Pythagorean philosophy) of the body as the temporary dwelling place of the soul.

σκηνόω *I dwell as in a tent, I encamp.*

σκήνωμα, ατος, τό *a tent,* really a humble word for the permanent building aimed at, Acts 7:46; of the body as the temporary abode of the soul.

σκιά, ᾶς, ἡ *a shadow, darkness, shade;* contrasted with the body casting the shadow, and used met. somewhat like *a pale reflection,* Col 2:17; Heb 8:5; 10:1.

σκιρτάω *I leap, bound, jump.*

σκληροκαρδία, ας, ἡ *stiffness, stubbornness, unyieldingness, obduracy* Hebraistic, from σκληρός and καρδία, as the seat of the will).

σκληρός, ά, όν (properly *hard*), (1) *strong,* Jas 3:4; (2) met. *harsh, rough;* almost = *dangerous,* Acts 26:14.

σκληρότης, ητος, ἡ *obstinacy.*

σκληροτράχηλος, ον *stiff-necked, stubborn.*

σκληρύνω *I make unyielding.*
σκολιός, ά, όν *crooked;* hence met., *perverse,* of turning off from the truth, *crooked* in nature.
σκόλοψ, οπος, ὁ orig., *a stake;* but commonly in NT times *a thorn; a splinter;* met. referring to some physical trouble.
σκοπέω *I look upon, I gaze upon, watch.*
σκοπός, οῦ, ὁ *a mark* to be aimed at (e.g. by an archer).
σκορπίζω *I scatter.*
σκορπίος, ου, ὁ *a scorpion.*
σκοτεινός, ή, όν *dark.*
σκοτία, ας, ἡ *darkness;* hence met. of ignorance and sin.
σκοτίζω *I darken,* especially of an eclipse of the sun, cf. Luke 23:45 (var.); met. of blindness, Rom 11:10, ignorance, Rom 1:21.
σκότος, ους, τό *darkness;* frequent in the conceptions of Jewish eschatology, Matt 8:12; 22:13; 25:30; met. of *the darkness* of ignorance and sin, Luke 1:79; John 3:19, etc.
σκοτόω *I darken,* lit. or met.
σκύβαλον, ου, τό *sweepings, refuse,* especially *dirt, dung* (popularly used of the human skeleton).
Σκύθης, ου, ὁ *a Scythian,* an uncivilized inhabitant of northeast Europe.
σκυθρωπός, ή, όν *with downcast countenance; sad-faced; gloomy.*
σκύλλω (orig., *I flay, skin*), (1) *I tire out by hunting; I distress,* Matt 9:36; (2) (a slang usage in origin) *I worry, trouble.*
σκῦλον, ου, τό plur., *booty, spoils.*
σκωληκόβρωτος, ον *eaten by worms.*
σκώληξ, ηκος, ὁ *a worm.*
σμαράγδινος (ζμαράγδινος), η, ον *of an emerald.*
σμάραγδος (ζμάραγδος), ου, ὁ *an emerald.*
σμῆγμα, ατος, τό *ointment, salve.*
σμίγμα see μίγμα.
σμύρνα, ης, ἡ (= μύρρα), *myrrh,* a fragrant gum-resin from the Arabian Balsamodendron Myrrhae.
Σμύρνα (Ζμύρνα), ης, ἡ *Smyrna,* a great port of the Roman province Asia.
σμυρνίζω *I spice with myrrh.*
Σόδομα, ων, τό *Sodom,* a city submerged by the Dead Sea.
Σολομών, ῶνος (ῶντος), ὁ *Solomon,* son of David, King of Israel, and Bathsheba (oldest form Σαλωμών, next oldest Σαλομών).
σορός, οῦ, ἡ *a bier.*
σός, σή, σόν *your, thy, thine.*
σουδάριον, ου, τό *a handkerchief* [Lat., borrowed by Gk., and thence by Aram.].
Σουσάννα, ης, ἡ *Susannah,* a woman of the retinue of Jesus.
σοφία, ας, ἡ *wisdom,* the highest intellectual gift, of comprehensive insight into the ways and purposes of God; sometimes, e.g. Acts 6:3; 1 Cor 6:5; Jas 1:5, *practical wisdom,* that endowment of heart and mind which is needed for the right conduct of life.
σοφίζω *I make wise;* σεσοφισμένος, *fictitious,* 2 Pet 1:16.
σοφός, ή, όν *wise; skilled, an expert, a man of learning* (Hebraism), Matt 11:25; 1 Cor 3:10, etc.
Σπανία, ας, ἡ *Spain,* roughly coextensive with the mod. country of the name [Lat. *Hispania*].
σπάω mid. *I draw my* (sword).
σπαράσσω *I throw* on the ground.
σπαργανόω *I swathe.*
σπαρείς aor. pas. part. → σπείρω.
σπαταλάω *I live voluptuously* or *luxuriously.*
σπεῖρα, ης, ἡ *a cohort,* i.e., about 600 infantry, under the command of a tribune.
σπείρω *I sow,* lit. or met.

σπεκουλάτωρ, ορος, ὁ *a scout; a courier;* also *an executioner* [Lat.].

σπένδω *I pour out* an offering of wine to a god; hence pas. met., of the *outpouring* of one's life blood in service and suffering.

σπέρμα, ατος, τό (1) *seed,* commonly of cereals; (2) *offspring, descendants,* in the animal kingdom (frequent in Heb.).

σπερμολόγος, ου, ὁ (from σπέρμα and λέγω; a slang term in Acts), used properly of a bird *picking up seeds;* hence, *a parasite, hanger on;* also of one who *picks up scraps* of information and retails them at secondhand, *an ignorant plagiarist.*

σπεύδω *I hasten, hurry.*

σπήλαιον, ου, τό *a cave* (especially as inhabited).

σπιλάς, άδος, ἡ adjectivally used w. ἄνεμος understood, *a dirty, foul* (lit.), *miry wind,* perhaps of its effect on the water.

σπίλος, ου, ὁ *a spot* of disfigurement.

σπιλόω *I stain,* lit. or met.

σπλαγχνίζομαι *I am filled with pity, I have sympathy* (Hebraism).

σπλάγχνον, ου, τό (by form σπλάγχνα [fem.] in Phil 2:1, if text be genuine), usually plur. σπλάγχνα, *the nobler viscera,* heart, etc., and especially, Hebraistically, as the seat of certain feelings, or from the observed effect of emotion on them, *compassion* and *pity.*

σπόγγος, ου, ὁ *a sponge.*

σποδός, οῦ, ἡ *ashes.*

σπορά, ᾶς, ἡ quasicollective, *seed.*

σπόριμος, ου, τό *sown;* pl. subs., τὰ σπόριμα, *the crops.*

σπόρος, ου, ὁ *seed.*

σπουδάζω *I hasten; I am eager (zealous).*

σπουδαῖος, α, ον *eager, zealous; earnest.*

σπουδαίως adv., *eagerly, zealously; earnestly.*

σπουδή, ῆς, ἡ *haste; eagerness, zeal; carefulness, care, anxiety; diligence, earnestness* (characteristically in connection with religion).

σπυρίς (σφυρίς), ίδος, ἡ a flexible mat *basket* made of rushes and such like, and used to carry either fish or eatables generally, *a fish basket, a fisherman's basket.*

στάδιον, ου, ὁ *a stadium;* pl. *a stade* (a measurement of distance about 1/8 mile).

σταθείς aor. pas. part. → ἵστημι.

σταθῆναι aor. pas. infin. → ἵστημι.

σταθήσομαι fut. pas. → ἵστημι.

στάμνος, ου, ἡ *an earthenware pot (jar).*

στάς aor. act. part. → ἵστημι.

στασιαστής, οῦ, ὁ *a revolutionary.*

στάσις, εως, ἡ (1) *faction, sedition, discord; disturbance, upheaval, revolution, riot;* (2) in the more original but much rarer meaning, *standing, position, place,* Heb 9:8.

στατήρ, ῆρος, ὁ *a stater,* i.e., four drachmae (see δραχμή), the temple tax for two persons.

σταυρός, οῦ, ὁ *a cross,* strictly the transverse beam, which was placed at the top of the vertical part, thus forming a capital T. It was this transverse beam that was carried by the criminal; *the crucifixion* of Jesus.

σταυρόω *I crucify;* hence met., Gal 6:14.

σταφυλή, ῆς, ἡ *a grape.*

στάχυς, υος, ὁ *an ear (spike)* of corn.

Στάχυς, υος, ὁ a Christian man at Rome.

στέγη, ης, ἡ *a roof* (orig. poetical); in Mark 2:4 perhaps of thatch.

στέγω (1) *I roof over, cover;* hence, *I conceal, hide,* but not in NT; (2) *I*

keep out (weather); hence, *I keep close, put up with, endure patiently, bear up under.*
στεῖρα, ας, ἡ *a barren (childless) woman.*
στέλλω (orig., *I set, place;* hence, *I bring together. make compact;* then, *I restrain, check*), mid. *I draw (shrink) back* from anything.
στέμμα, ατος, τό (from στέφω, *I wreathe*), *a garland.*
στεναγμός, οῦ, ὁ *a groan.*
στενάζω *I groan.*
στενός, ή, όν *narrow.*
στενοχωρέω *I press upon, cramp, restrain* (στενός and χῶρος, cf. Eng. colloquial, *I keep some* one *in a tight place*).
στενοχωρία, ας, ἡ (lit. *confinement in a narrow space*), *restriction, restraint; anguish, great trouble.*
στερεός, ά, όν *solid; firm,* lit. or met.
στερεόω *I make firm,* or *solid;* met., Acts 16:5.
στερέωμα, ατος, τό *firm foundation, bulwark* (probably a military metaphor).
Στεφανᾶς, ᾶ, ὁ *Stephanas,* a Corinthian Christian (a pet form of Στεφανηφόρος).
Στέφανος, ου, ὁ *Stephen,* one of the seven original "deacons" at Jerusalem, and the first martyr.
στέφανος, ου, ὁ *a garland, wreath, chaplet, crown,* generally as the Greek victor's crown or chaplet, of perishable leaves (1 Cor 9:25), won in athletic and other contests, and familiar to the Jews for generations; ὁ στέφανος τῆς ζωῆς (Jas 1:12; Rev 2:10), *the crown (reward), which is life.*
στεφανόω *I wreathe, crown* as victor, 2 Tim 2:5, hence met.
στῆθος, ους, τό *the breast.*
στήκω *I stand; I remain standing, stand firm,* lit. or met. (form arising from the need for an act. form present in the intrans. sense, cf. ἵστημι).
στῆναι aor. act. infin. → ἵστημι.
στηριγμός, οῦ, ὁ *support.*
στηρίζω (1) *I fix firmly,* Luke 16:26; τὸ πρόσωπον (Hebraism) *I direct myself* towards, *I have my face turned steadfastly,* Luke 9:51; (2) generally met. *I buttress, prop, support; I strengthen, establish.*
στήσω fut. act. → ἵστημι.
στιβάς, άδος, ἡ *a wisp (bundle)* of brushwood, twigs or other light growth.
στίγμα, ατος, τό properly, *a brand* burned into, or *the mark* of a cut made in, the skin of a slave; in Gal 6:17 τὰ στίματα are the *marks* or *scars,* due to the lictor's rods at Pisidian Antioch and the stones at Lystra, *marking* Paul as the slave of Jesus.
στιγμή, ῆς, ἡ (lit. *a pricking*), *an instant, a moment.*
στίλβω *I gleam, flash.*
στοά, ᾶς, ἡ *a portico, colonnade, porch;* that "of Solomon" was on the east side of the Temple.
Στοϊκός, ή, όν *a Stoic,* a member of one of the two leading schools of philosophy (from στοιά, στοά, because of the original place of meeting).
στοιχεῖον, ου, τό (1) plur. *the heavenly bodies,* 2 Pet 3:10, 12; (2) *a rudiment, an element, a rudimentary principle, an elementary rule;* but in Gal 4:3 there is much to be said for taking the word in the sense of *spirit, demon* [possibly also in (1)]; pl., (physical) *elements, basic principles.*
στοιχέω *I walk* (properly, in a straight line, in rank).
στολή, ῆς, ἡ *a long robe,* worn by the upper classes in the east.

στόμα, ατος, τό *the mouth,* especially as an organ of speech in man and God; the sword has a mouth *(edge),* because it *drinks* blood, Luke 21:24; Heb 11:34; στόμα πρὸς στόμα (cf. πρόσωπον πρὸς πρόσωπον), *by word of mouth,* practically, *face to face.*

στόμαχος, ου, ὁ *the stomach.*

στρατεία, ας, ἡ *military service,* used met.

στράτευμα, ατος, τό *an army, a body of soldiers.*

στρατεύομαι *I serve in the army, I am in the army, I am a soldier* (whether on active service or not); hence met., *I make war, I take up war,* e.g. 1 Pet 2:11.

στρατηγός, οῦ, ὁ (1) in Jerusalem, ὁ στρατηγὸς τοῦ ἱεροῦ, *the commandant of the temple,* a priest, next in rank to the high priest, and commander of the priests and Levites who guarded the temple, Acts 4:1; 5:24, 26; under him were the στρατηγοί, *captains* of the temple guards, Luke 22:4 (var.), 52; (2) at Philippi, a Roman "colonia," *a praetor* or *a duumvir, a chief magistrate* of the "colonia" Acts 16 (there were probably two of them).

στρατιά, ᾶς, ἡ *an army.*

στρατιώτης, ου, ὁ *a soldier;* hence (perhaps under the influence of the language of the Mysteries and that of philosophy), the worshipper as *the soldier* of his God, cf. 2 Tim 2:3.

στρατολογέω trans., *I enroll in the army.*

στρατοπεδάρχης, ου, ὁ *the chief of the camp, the commander of the corps* connected with the commissariat, custody of prisoners, etc., which was on detached duty.

στρατόπεδον, ου, τό *a camp.*

στρεβλόω (lit. *I twist, warp, stretch on the rack*), hence met., *I twist, strain.*

στρέφω trans., *I turn;* hence, *I bring back(?),* Matt 27:3; *I change,* Rev 11:6; act. intrans., Acts 7:42; mid. and pas. intrans., *I turn,* also met. *I change.*

στρηνιάω *I am wanton, I wanton.*

στρῆνος, ους, τό *wantonness, luxury.*

στρουθίον, ου, τό *a sparrow,* the cheapest of all birds for food.

στρωννύω (στρώννυμι) *I spread out, strew;* in Mark 14:15; Luke 22:12 of the dining couches with the cushions ready for diners, cf. Acts 9:34 of *making* one's *bed.*

στυγητός, ή, όν *hated, hateful.*

στυγνάζω (1) *I am sad,* Mark 10:22; (2) *I am dull (overcast),* Matt 16:3.

στῦλος (στύλος), ου, ὁ *a pillar* for supporting an entablature or other structure; hence met.

Στωϊκός see Στοϊκός.

σύ, σοῦ (σου), σοί (σοι), σέ (σε) pl. ὑμεῖς, ὑμῶν, ὑμῖν, ὑμᾶς, *you;* τί ἡμῖν (ἐμοὶ) καὶ σοί; Matt 8:29, etc., *what have we (I) to do with you?* but in John 2:4 it is probable that we ought to translate, *what have you and I to do with it? what concern is it of ours? never mind!* note the order ἡμῖν καὶ ὑμῖν (Matt 25:9), as in Lat.; for καθ' ὑμᾶς, see κατά.

συγγένεια, ας, ἡ collective, *all the* συγγενεῖς, *kindred, kin, relations.*

συγγενής, οῦς, ὁ *a relation, relative, kinsman;* in Rom 9:3 the term is wide enough to include all Hebrews; in Rom 16:7, 11, 21 the reference may be narrower, to fellow members of the same (Jewish) tribe (φυλή) in the city of Tarsus.

συγγενίς, ίδος, ἡ *a kinswoman.*

συγγνώμη, ης, ἡ *indulgence, allowance* for circumstances.

συγκάθημαι *I am sitting (seated) with;* in Acts 26:30, perhaps to be compared w. Eng. *assessor.*

συγκαθίζω (1) trans., *I cause to sit along with;* (2) intrans., *I sit in company (together).*

συγκακοπαθέω *I am ill treated along with, I take my share of suffering* (in 2 Tim 1:8 the dat. is not governed by σύν, but = *for the benefit of*).

συγκακουχέομαι pas. *I suffer mistreatment with.*

συγκαλέω *I call together, invite, summon;* mid. *I call together to myself.*

συγκαλύπτω *I veil (cover) completely.*

συγκάμπτω *I bend low, I cause to stoop low.*

συγκαταβαίνω *I come down along with (together).*

συγκαταβάς aor. act. part. → συνκαταβαίνω.

συγκατάθεσις, εως, ἡ *agreement, union.*

συγκατανεύω *I agree, consent, join in agreeing.*

συγκατατίθεμαι *I agree with.*

συγκαταψηφίζω *I number (reckon) along with.*

συγκεκέραμαι perf. mid./pas. → συγκεράννυμι.

συγκεκέρασμαι perf. mid./pas. → συγκεράννυμι.

συγκεράννυμι (1) *I mix together, compound,* 1 Cor 12:24; (2) pas. w. dat. of instrument (πίστει), *I agree with,* Heb 4:2 (reading acc. plur.).

συγκέχυμαι perf. mid./pas. → συγχέω.

συγκινέω *I stir violently.*

συγκλείω *I shut together; I enclose, I shut in on all sides,* e.g. Rom 11:32.

συγκληρονόμος, ον *a joint heir, a fellow heir.*

συγκοινωνέω *I have partnership in, I share in* (with others).

συγκοινωνός, οῦ, ὁ *a fellow sharer* (in), *a joint partaker* (of).

συγκομίζω *I carry (convey) together,* i.e. to burial; or *I take up* for burial; hence, *I bury;* perhaps, however, *I get back, recover* (the συν- expressing the collecting of the mangled remains).

συγκρίνω *I compare.*

συγκύπτω *I am bent double, bent in two, bowed down.*

συγκυρία, ας, ἡ *coincidence, chance.*

συγχαίρω act. and pas. *I rejoice with;* perhaps *I congratulate.*

συγχέω *I confuse, confound, trouble.*

συγχράομαι *I associate with, have friendly dealings with.*

συγχύ(ν)νω see συγχέω.

σύγχυσις, εως, ἡ *confusion, disturbance.*

συζάω *I live along with (in company with).*

συζεύγνυμι *I yoke (harness) together, join.*

συζητέω (lit. *I seek in company*), *I discuss, debate, dispute.*

συζήτησις, εως, ἡ *discussion, debate.*

συζητητής, οῦ, ὁ *a discusser, debater.*

σύζυγος, ου, ὁ *yokefellow, companion, colleague* (perhaps a proper name).

συζωοποιέω *I make living along with.*

συκάμινος, ου, ἡ *the black mulberry tree* (a Semitic word).

συκῆ, ῆς, ἡ *a fig tree.*

συκομορέα (συκομωραία), ας, ἡ *a sycamore tree.*

σῦκον, ου, τό *a fig.*

συκοφαντέω *I accuse falsely.*

συλαγωγέω *I take away from as booty (plunder), I rob.*

συλάω *I rob.*

συλλαλέω *I speak together* (with).

συλλαμβάνω (1) act. and mid., *I arrest, catch, capture;* (2) *I conceive* (a child), cf. met. Jas 1:15; (3) mid. *I lend a hand to, I help,* Luke 5:7; Phil 4:3.

συλλυπέομαι *I am greatly pained (grieved) with;* pas. w. act. sense.

συλλέγω *I collect, gather together.*

συλλημφθῆναι aor. pas. infin. → συλλαμβάνω.

συλλογίζομαι *I reason together* with others.

συμβαίνω w. neut. subj. or impers., *I happen, occur; it happens.*

συμβαλεῖν aor. act. infin. → συμβάλλω.

συμβάλλω (1) w. λόγους expressed or understood, *I engage in discussion with,* Luke 11:53 (var.); Acts 4:15; 17:18; (2) *I reflect, ponder,* Luke 2:19; (3) *I meet with, I fall in with,* Acts 20:14; in hostile sense, *I enter into conflict with, attack,* Luke 14:31; (4) mid. *I contribute to, benefit.*

συμβασιλεύω *I reign along with (together with)* another, *I am a king with,* in met. sense.

συμβέβηκα perf. act. → συμβαίνω.

συμβιβάζω (1) *I bring together, join, unite,* Eph 4:16; Col 2:19; (2) *I put together, compare, examine closely,* hence, *I consider, conclude,* Acts 16:10; *I deduce, prove,* Acts 9:22; (3) *I teach, instruct* (a biblical sense, translation Gk.), Acts 19:33 (var.), 1 Cor 2:16; Col 2:2.

συμβουλεύω act. *I advise;* mid. συμβουλευόμεθα, *we counsel one another.*

συμβούλιον, ου, τό (1) *a body of advisers (assessors)* in a court, *a council,* Acts 25:12; (2) abstr., *consultation, counsel, advice; resolution, decree;* διδόναι (Aramaism) Mark 3:6.

σύμβουλος, ου, ὁ *an adviser.*

Συμεών, ὁ *Symeon,* (1) the patriarch, son of Jacob and founder of a tribe, Rev 7:7; (2) an ancestor of Jesus, Luke 3:30; (3) an inhabitant of Jerusalem, who blessed the babe Jesus, Luke 2:25, 34; (4) an Antiochian Christian, also called Niger, Acts 13:1; (5) a form of the Heb. name of Peter the Apostle, Acts 15:14; 2 Pet 1:1 (var.).

συμμαθητής, οῦ, ὁ *a fellow disciple, a fellow scholar.*

συμμαρτυρέω *I join in giving evidence (bearing witness)* with.

συμμερίζω *I cause to share with* (in the sacrifices); mid. *I share with* (w. dat.).

συμμέτοχος, ου, ὁ *a fellow sharer, a partner.*

συμμιμητής, οῦ, ὁ *a joint imitator, an imitator along (together) with* others.

συμμορφίζω lit. *I cause to share the form* (see μορφή) *of another,* hence in Phil 3:10, συμμορφιζόμενος = *being made to share the experience of.*

σύμμορφος, ον *sharing the form* of another.

συμπαθέω *I suffer along with.*

συμπαθής, ές *sharing the experiences* of others.

συμπαραγίνομαι *I arrive along with.*

συμπαρακαλέω *I cheer (encourage) along with;* pas., *receive encouragement together with.*

συμπαρακληθῆναι aor. act. infin. → συμπαρακαλέω.

συμπαραλαβεῖν aor. act. infin. → συμπαραλαμβάνω.

συμπαραλαμβάνω *I take along with me* (as helper).

συμπάρειμι *I am present (here) along with.*

συμπάσχω *I suffer together.*

συμπέμπω *I send along with.*

συμπεριλαμβάνω *I embrace closely.*

συμπίνω *I drink* (wine) *along with.*

συμπίπτω *I fall together, I fall in, I collapse.*

συμπληρόω (1) *I fill up,* hence

pas., by an idiom analogous to Eng., συνεπληροῦντο, Luke 8:23, *they were filling up* (where it was really the ship that was filling up); (2) *I complete* (Hebraistic), of the coming to an end of an interval of days before some event (in Acts 2:1 the day of the event may be partly included).

συμπνίγω met. *I choke utterly;* in Luke 8:42 by exaggeration (possibly slang), of *pressing very hard upon, hustling,* in a crowd (cf. the more correct συνθλίβω).

συμπολίτης, ου, ὁ *a fellow citizen.*

συμπορεύομαι *I journey with, I go with; I go together.*

συμπόσιον, ου, τό properly *a drinking bout,* following dinner; συμπόσια συμπόσια (colloquial), *in companies of diners.*

συμπρεσβύτερος, ου, ὁ *a fellow elder.*

συμφέρω (1) trans., *I collect, bring together,* Acts 19:19; (2) intrans. and generally impers., συμφέρει, *it is an advantage, it is expedient (beneficial);* συμφέρον (supply ἐστιν), 2 Cor 12:1 = συμφέρει; τὸ συμφέρον, as subs.

σύμφημι *I express agreement with, I agree with.*

σύμφορος, ου, τό *advantageous;* τὸ σύμφορον, as subs., *a benefit, advantage.*

συμφυλέτης, ου, ὁ *a fellow tribesman, one of the same tribe,* doubtless with reference to Jews in Thessalonica, all enrolled in one city-tribe.

σύμφυτος *grown along with, vitally one with, united with.*

συμφύω *I grow up together with* (another), 2 aor. pas. as act.

συμφωνέω (first of a harmony of voices, then) *I harmonize with, I agree with;* of more than one, *we agree together;* pas. impers. *it is agreed upon among* (possibly a Latinism, conuenit inter), Acts 5:9.

συμφώνησις, εως, ἡ *harmony, agreement.*

συμφωνία, ας, ἡ *bagpipes* (cf. Dan 3:5), but perhaps *music, symphony.*

σύμφωνος, ου, τό *agreeing;* neut. subs., *agreement;* ἐκ συμφώνου *by agreement.*

συμψηφίζω *I calculate together, I reckon up.*

σύμψυχος, ον *one in feeling with* others, *sharing the feelings of* others.

σύν prep. w. dat., *with* (Gk. allows either the sense *plus* or the sense *including*).

συναγαγεῖν aor. act. infin. → συνάγω.

συνάγω *I gather together, collect, assemble,* persons or things; συναγαγὼν πάντα implies the converting of the goods into money, *having sold all of,* Luke 15:13.

συναγωγή, ῆς, ἡ (in origin abstr., *a leading [bringing] together, convening* an assembly, then concr., *a [religious] meeting*), *a meeting (assembly), a place of meeting (assembly),* particularly of Jews for the reading of scripture and for worship, *a synagogue.* In certain passages it is doubtful whether the congregation (e.g. John 6:59; 18:20) or the place of meeting (e.g. Jas 2:2) is particularly intended, but the sense is not seriously affected by the doubt. In the OT συναγωγή and ἐκκλησία are practically synonymous, but in ordinary Christian writings the former is rarely used, and seemingly only of communities of Jews or Jewish Christians (e.g. Jas 2:2, where it is probably the building).

συναγωνίζομαι *I struggle (contend) in company with.*

συναθλέω *I compete together with*

others, originally of athletic contests, and then met.
συναθροίζω trans., *I gather together, assemble.*
συναίρω w. λόγον, *I compare (settle) accounts, make a reckoning.*
συναιχμάλωτος, ου, ὁ *a fellow captive, a fellow prisoner, a companion in chains.*
συνακολουθέω *I accompany.*
συναλίζομαι *I have table fellowship with, I share a common meal with, I meet with,* from time to time (from σύν, and ἅλς, "salt"; others take as from σύν and ἁλής, "crowded").
συναλλάσσω *I* attempt (seek) to *reconcile.*
συναναβαίνω *I go up with.*
συναναβάς aor. act. part. → συναναβαίνω.
συνανάκειμαι *I recline at* (dinner) *table with.*
συναναμίγνυμι mid. *I associate intimately with.*
συναναπαύομαι *I rest along with.*
συναντάω *I meet, encounter;* in Acts 20:22, w. inanimate subj.
συναντιλαμβάνομαι *I lend a hand along with, I take interest in* (a thing) *along with* (others), *I assist jointly* to perform some task, *I cooperate with, I take my share in.*
συναπάγω *I lead away with, I carry along with* (in good or bad sense according to context); mid. w. dat., *I condescend to,* Rom 12:16.
συναπέθανον aor. act. → συναποθνήσκω.
συναπέστειλα aor. act. → συναποστέλλω.
συναπήχθην aor. pas. → συναπάγομαι.
συναποθνήσκω *I die along with, I die together* (with others).
συναπόλλυμαι *I perish along with.*
συναποστέλλω *I send away in some one's company.*
συναπωλόμην aor. mid. → συναπόλλυμαι
συνᾶραι aor. act. infin. → συναίρω.
συναρμολογέω *I fit together* (by means of all the elaborate preparatory processes necessary); an architectural term, ἁρμός meaning "the side of a stone," and -λογεῖν added by analogy w. λιθολόγος without its proper force.
συναρπάζω *I keep a firm grip of.*
συναυξάνω *I make to increase (grow) together;* pas. *grow together.*
συναχθήσομαι fut. pas. → συνάγω.
συνβ. see συμβ.
συνγ. see συγγ.
σύνδεσμος, ου, ὁ *a binding together, a means of holding together, a bond,* lit. and met.; in Acts 8:23 the man is *in* (εἰς = ἐν) the grip of ἀδικία.
συνδέω *I bind along with another;* pas. συνδεδεμένοι, *fellow captives.*
συνδοξάζω *I glorify along with.*
σύνδουλος, ου, ὁ *a fellow slave,* either of an earthly master, or of the glorified Lord.
συνδρομή, ῆς, ἡ *a running together, a tumultuous concourse.*
συνέβην aor. act. → συμβαίνω.
συνεγείρω *I raise along with* the Messiah (from the dead, or from a dead spiritual state).
συνέδραμον aor. act. → συντρέχω.
συνέδριον, ου, τό *a council* of leading Jews, Mark 13:9; Matt 10:17, but elsewhere *the Jewish council at Jerusalem, the Sanhedrin* (Aram. form of συνέδριον), *the High Court, the Senate,* composed of seventy one members comprising members of high priestly families, Pharisees learned in the law, and a lay element of Elders.

συνέζευξα aor. act. → συζεύγνυμι.
συνέθεντο aor. mid. 3 plur. → συντίθημι.
συνείδησις, εως, ἡ (orig., *consciousness,* e.g. 1 Pet 2:19, where θεοῦ is obj. gen., but through the influence of the Stoic terminology) *conscience,* the innate power to discern what is good, an abiding consciousness bearing witness concerning a man's conduct.
συνεῖδον *I perceived, I was aware of, I saw distinctly, I realized;* see also the etymologically related σύνοιδα.
συνειδυῖα perf. act. part. fem. → σύνοιδα.
συνείληφα perf. act. → συλλαμβάνω.
σύνειμι *I am with, I am in company with, I join with* (from **εἰμί**).
σύνειμι *I come together,* Luke 8:4 (from **εἶμι**).
συνεισέρχομαι *I go in with, I enter with.*
συνεισῆλθον aor. act. → συνεισέρχομαι.
συνέκδημος, ου, ὁ *a traveling companion.*
συνεκέρασα aor. act. → συγκεράννυμι.
συνεκλεκτός, ή, όν *fellow-chosen, fellow-elect,* understand ἐκκλησία.
συνέλαβον aor. act. → συλλαμβάνω.
συνελήλυθα perf. act. → συνέρχομαι.
συνελθεῖν aor. act. infin. → συνέρχομαι.
συνενέγκας aor. act. part. → συμφέρω.
συνέπεσον aor. act. → συμπίπτω.
συνεπέστην aor. act. → συνεφίστημι.
συνεπιμαρτυρέω *I add my testimony to that already given.*
συνέπιον aor. act. → συμπίνω.
συνεπιτίθεμαι (lit. *I join in attacking*), *I join in the charge.*
συνέπομαι *I accompany.*
συνεργέω *I work along with, I cooperate with.*
συνεργός, οῦ, ὁ *a fellow worker.*
συνέρχομαι *I go along with, I accompany; I come (meet) together* with others, αὐτῷ in Mark 14:53 being = πρὸς αὐτόν; *have sexual intercourse,* Matt 1:18.
συνεσθίω *I eat in company with.*
σύνεσις, εως, ἡ *practical discernment, intelligence, understanding.*
συνεσπάραξα aor. act. → συσπαράσσω.
συνέσταλμαι perf. mid./pas. → συστέλλω.
συνέστειλα aor. act. → συστέλλω.
συνέστηκα perf. act. → συνίστημι.
συνέστησα aor. act. → συνίστημι.
συνεστώς perf. act. part. → συνίστημι.
συνέσχον aor. act. → συνέχω.
συνετάφην aor. pas. → συνθάπτω.
συνετός, ή, όν (lit. *one who can put things together,* from συνίημι), *intelligent;* in Matt 11:25; Luke 10:21 it doubtless refers to Pharisees learned in the law.
συνευδοκέω *I entirely approve of.*
συνευωχέομαι *I feast along with.*
συνέφαγον aor. act. → συνεσθίω.
συνεφίστημι (*the multitude) rose up together, set upon together,* 2 aor. intrans.
συνεχύθην aor. pas. → συγχέω.
συνέχυννον imperf. → συγχέω.
συνέχω (1) *I hold together,* hence, *I restrain; I close,* Acts 7:57; *I press from every side,* Luke 8:45; 19:43; (2) *I hold seized, I have in charge,* Luke 22:63, so pas. met. *I am pressed,* Acts 18:5; esp. in pas. w. datives, *I am seized (by), I am afflicted (by), I am suffering (from),* e.g. Matt 4:24; Luke 8:37; *I urge,*

impel, compel, Luke 12:50; 2 Cor 5:14; Phil 1:23.

συνζ. see συζ.

συνήγαγον aor. act. → συνάγω.

συνηγέρθην aor. pas. → συνεγείρω.

συνηγμένος perf. mid./pas. part. → συνάγω.

συνήδομαι *I delight in.*

συνήθεια, ας, ἡ *custom, habit;* w. gen. *habituation to, intercourse with, familiarity with,* 1 Cor 8:7.

συνῆκα aor. act. → συνίημι.

συνῆλθον aor. act. → συνέρχομαι.

συνηλικιώτης, ου, ὁ *a contemporary.*

συνηρπάκειν plup. act. → συναρπάζω.

συνήρπασα aor. act. → συναρπάζω.

συνήσω fut. act. → συνίημι.

συνήχθην aor. pas. → συνάγω.

συνθάπτω *I bury along with.*

συνθλάω *I break in pieces, break completely.*

συνθλίβω *I press closely upon, hustle.*

συνθρύπτω (lit. *I crush to pieces*), *I weaken thoroughly, unman.*

συνιδών aor. act. part. → συνοράω.

συνιέναι pres. act. infin. → συνίημι.

συνίημι *I understand; I have understanding.*

συνίστημι (συνιστάνω) (1) in trans. tenses, (a) *I recommend, commend, introduce,* Rom 16:1; 2 Cor 3:1; 4:2; 5:12; 6:4; 10:12, 18; 12:11, (b) *I show, prove,* Rom 3:5; 5:8; 2 Cor 7:11; Gal 2:18; (2) in intrans. tenses, (a) *I stand with (by),* Luke 9:32, (b) *I consist, I am held together,* Col 1:17; 2 Pet 3:5.

συνίων pres. act. part. → συνίημι.

συνιών pres. act. part. → σύνειμι.

συνκ. see συγκ.

συνλ. see συλλ.

συνμ. see συμμ.

συνοδεύω *I journey (travel) along with.*

συνοδία, ας, ἡ *a traveling company, caravan.*

σύνοιδα *I share knowledge with* another, *I am privy to* anything. In fact the word especially implies consciousness of *guilt,* e.g. 1 Cor 4:4.

συνοικέω *I cohabit with, live in wedlock with.*

συνοικοδομέω met. *I build together.*

συνομιλέω *I talk with.*

συνομορέω *I am contiguous with, I am next door to.*

συνοχή, ῆς, ἡ (lit. *compression;* then *narrowness*), met. *anxiety.*

συνπ. see συμπ.

συνσ. see συσ. and συσσ.

συντάσσω *I direct, instruct, command.*

συνταφείς aor. pas. part. → συνθάπτω.

συντέλεια, ας, ἡ w. αἰῶνος, a characteristic expression of Jewish apocalyptic, *conclusion, consummation, end* of the present period of time.

συντελέω *I bring to an end, complete, finish, exhaust; I accomplish, fulfill, bring to pass.*

συντέμνω *I cut down;* hence, *I contract, limit, restrict* the scope of.

συντετμημένος perf. mid./pas. part. → συντέμνω.

συντετρῖφθαι perf. mid./pas. infin. → συντρίβω.

συντηρέω *I keep safe.*

συντίθημι mid. and pas. *I make a compact (agreement) with (together), I covenant with, I agree.*

συντόμως adv., *briefly.*

συντρέχω *I run (rush) together,* lit. or met.

συντρίβω (1) *I break; I bruise;* (2) *I trample upon, crush,* Rom 16:20; *I maul,* Luke 9:39; (3) met.

pas. *I am stunned, crushed,* Luke 4:18 (var.).

σύντριμμα, ατος, τό *destruction, ruin.*

σύντροφος, ου, ὁ *foster brother;* such is the lit. rendering, but it would appear to be a court title, and might therefore be translated *a courtier.*

συντυγχάνω *I encounter, come up with, come close to.*

συντυχεῖν aor. act. infin. → συντυγχάνω.

Συντύχη, ης, ἡ *Syntyche,* a woman member of the church at Philippi.

συνυποκρίνομαι pas. *I dissemble along with.*

συνυπουργέω *I cooperate in a subordinate capacity.*

συνφ. see συμφ.

συνχ. see συγχ.

συνψ. see συμψ.

συνωδίνω *I unite in suffering travail (birth pangs, severe pain).*

συνωμοσία, ας, ἡ *a conspiracy, plot.*

Συράκουσαι, ῶν, ἡ *Syracuse,* in east Sicily (plur. because originally, as in many similar cases, both a citadel and a settlement in the valley).

Συρία, ας, ἡ *Syria,* a great Roman imperial province, united with Cilicia.

Σύρος, ου, ὁ *Syrian,* belonging to Syria.

Συροφοινίκισσα, ης, ἡ *Syrophoenician,* i.e. *Phoenician* (of Syria, in contrast to Carthage and its territory in N. Africa).

Σύρτις, εως, ἡ *Syrtis,* a quicksand off the coast of N. Africa.

σύρω *I drag, pull, draw.*

συσπαράσσω *I throw violently* on the ground.

σύσσημον, ου, ἡ *a signal agreed upon* between two parties.

σύσσωμος, ον *sharing in a body;* it has been taken as *fellow slave* (see σῶμα).

συστατικός, ἡ, όν *recommending, introducing.*

συσταυρόω *I crucify along with,* lit. or met.

συστέλλω (1) *I wrap round, swathe* in a sort of winding sheet, or possibly, *I lay out,* Acts 5:6; (2) *I contract, compress;* hence, *I shorten,* 1 Cor 7:29.

συστενάζω *I groan together.*

συστοιχέω (properly a military term, *I keep in line* or *file*), *I correspond exactly to.*

συστρατιώτης, ου, ὁ *a fellow soldier, comrade in arms.*

συστρέφω (1) trans., *I gather together, collect,* Acts 28:3; (2) mid. either, *I press together* (about one) or *I stroll.*

συστροφή, ῆς, ἡ *a crowding together;* hence, *a seditious meeting,* Acts 19:40; *a conspiracy,* Acts 23:12.

συσχηματίζω mid. *I fashion myself in agreement with, I conform myself outwardly to.*

Συχάρ, ἡ *Sychar,* a "city" of Samaria.

Συχέμ *Sychem, Shechem, Sicyma* (later *Neapolis,* from which mod. *Nablus*), a city of Samaria.

σφαγή, ῆς, ἡ *slaughter, sacrifice* (of an animal); πρόβατον σφαγῆς (Hebraism), *a sheep destined for sacrifice.*

σφάγιον, ου, τό *a sacrifice* (of an animal).

σφάζω *I slaughter; I sacrifice.*

σφόδρα adv., *greatly, exceedingly, very much.*

σφοδρῶς adv., *exceedingly.*

σφραγίζω (1) *I seal* and thus close, for guardianship or protection, Matt 27:66; Rev 20:3; (2) *I conceal,* Rev 10:4; 22:10; (3) *I mark* with the impress of the signet ring, lit. or met.; (4) *I confirm, make undoubted,* John 3:33; 6:27; mid. Rom 15:28 (cf. under [1]).

σφραγίς, ῖδος, ἡ *a seal,* a means not merely of attestation but also of closing, so that a cabinet, document, etc., could not be opened without breaking the seals.

σφυδρόν (σφυρόν), οῦ, τό *an ankle (bone).*

σφυρίς see σπυρίς.

σφυρόν see σφυδρόν.

σχεδόν adv., *almost, nearly.*

σχῆμα, ατος, τό *the* outward (changeable) *fashion* (*form*).

σχίζω *I cleave, split;* (of cloth) *I rend, tear;* of a crowd, *I divide* (sharply) *into two parties.*

σχίσμα, ατος, τό *a cleavage, cleft, split, rent;* so met, *a division* in a crowd, due to difference of opinion, *a party division.*

σχοινίον, ου, τό *a rope; a cable, hawser.*

σχολάζω (1) *I have leisure,* w. dat. for, 1 Cor 7:5; (2) *I stand empty,* of a house, Matt 12:44; Luke 11:25 (var.).

σχολή, ῆς, ἡ *a school,* or *lecture hall.*

σχῶ aor. act. subj. → ἔχω.

σῴζω (1) *I save, rescue* a life from death, e.g. Matt 8:25, a person from grave illness (and thus restore to health), e.g. Matt 9:21; (2) thus specially, of God and His Messiah, *I save, rescue, preserve,* from spiritual death (cf. Heb 5:7) or spiritual disease, i.e., from sin and its effects; the process is regarded as complete on God's part by the sacrifice of Jesus (e.g. Eph 2:5), but as progressive in our experience (1 Cor 1:18) or only to be realized in the future after acknowledgement of sin and expressed trust in Jesus.

σῶμα, ατος, τό (1) *the* human *body,* alive or dead (e.g. Matt 27:58); *the physical nature,* and thus in Gk. thought distinguished from πνεῦμα (e.g. 1 Cor 5:3) or ψυχή (e.g. 1 Thess 5:23); Hebraistic genitives (= adjs.) ἁμαρτίας, σαρκός, sometimes follow; (2) figuratively, the Church is *the Body* of the Messiah who is the Head (e.g. Eph 1:23); (3) *a slave,* as a mere body and nothing more, Rev 18:13.

σωματικός, ή, όν (1) *bodily,* hence, almost = *visible, tangible,* Luke 3:22; (2) *bodily, physical,* contrasted with "mental," "spiritual," 1 Tim 4:8.

σωματικῶς adv., *bodily, in a bodily way,* almost = visibly.

Σώπατρος, ου, ὁ *Sopater,* son of Pyrrhus, and a Christian of Beroea in Macedonia (a pet form of Σωσίπατρος).

σωρεύω *I heap;* w. acc. and dat., *I overwhelm* someone with something, 2 Tim 3:6.

Σωσθένης, ους, ὁ *Sosthenes,* the ruler of the synagogue at Corinth (Acts 18:17), probably to be identified with the Christian of 1 Cor 1:1.

Σωσίπατρος, ου, ὁ *Sosipater,* a Christian at Rome.

σωτήρ, ῆρος, ὁ *savior, rescuer, preserver,* a term applied to (the) God and to the Messiah with respect to the human race and sin and its consequences (a word familiar to the Graeco-Roman world as a constant epithet of kings like the Ptolemies and of the Roman emperors, especially in the phrase ὁ σωτὴρ τοῦ κόσμου [cf. John 4:42; 1 John 4:14], connoting probably *preserver* from the enemies of the nation or the empire, and thus *a maintainer* of life and prosperity).

σωτηρία, ας, ἡ *the salvation* to be wrought by the Messiah for the

Jews, the release from the foreign yoke in particular and the recovery of independence (cf. John 4:22); in purely Christian terminology, far fuller in content, including complete *recovery of health* from the disease of sin, *release* from captivity to it (in extrabiblical language has a reference generally to *bodily health, welfare* [so also Acts 27:34; Heb 11:7], especially as recovered after illness, but also to *deliverance* from every calamity, *victory* over enemies).

σωτήριον, ου, τό *the* Messianic *salvation* (cf. σωτηρία) in the wide sense (neut. of adj. σωτήριος used as subs., properly that which produces σωτηρία, a sacrifice or gift dedicated to bring salvation, or to give thanks for salvation).

σωτήριος, ον *bringing salvation, fraught with salvation.*

σωφρονέω (1) *I am in my senses,* Mark 5:15 (Luke 8:35); (2) *I am sober-minded, I am orderly* and *restrained* in all the relations of life.

σωφρονίζω (lit. *I make* σώφρων), hence, *I admonish, warn.*

σωφρονισμός, οῦ, ὁ *self-discipline.*

σωφρόνως adv., *sober-mindedly.*

σωφροσύνη, ης, ἡ *sound sense, sober-mindedness.*

σώφρων, ον *sober-minded, prudent* (from σῶς, *safe, sound,* and φρήν, *the mind*).

T

ταβέρναι, ῶν, αἱ *inns, taverns;* Τρεῖς Ταβέρναι, *Three Shops,* the name of a village or town on the Appian Way, about thirty-three miles from Rome [Lat. *Tres Tabernae*].

Ταβιθά (Ταβειθά), ἡ *Tabitha,* a Christian woman at Joppa.

τάγμα, ατος, τό *rank; division* (a military term).

τακτός, ή, όν *appointed, arranged.*

ταλαιπωρέω *I am wretched (afflicted, in distress).*

ταλαιπωρία, ας, ἡ *wretchedness, distress, misery.*

ταλαίπωρος, ον *wretched, miserable.*

ταλαντιαῖος, α, ον *a talent in weight* or *size.* (But ἀγῶνες ταλαντιαῖοι are games where the value of the prizes amounted to a talent.)

τάλαντον, ου, τό *a talent,* i.e., a talent weight (see ταλαντιαῖος) of silver, both the weight and the value being different in different countries and at different times. A common value was 6000 *denarii.*

ταλιθα (ταλειθά) *maiden* [Aram.].

ταμεῖον, ου, τό *an office, a private room;* also *a store,* Luke 12:24 (being derived from ταμίας, "a steward"); syncopated from ταμιεῖον, and first appearing in syncopated form in first cent. after Christ.

τάξις, εως, ἡ (1) *appointed order,* Luke 1:8; *regulation, rule,* perhaps *office,* Heb 5:6, etc.; (2) *right order,* 1 Cor 14:40, *orderly attitude,* Col 2:5.

ταπεινός, ή, όν *of low estate, poor* (and thus despised by the mass of mankind); also *poor in spirit, meek,* a notion often combined by the Jews with the previous.

ταπεινοφροσύνη, ης, ἡ *meekness; lowliness, humility.*

ταπεινόφρων, ον gen. **ονος** *meek minded; humble minded.*

ταπεινόω lit. *I make low, I lower,* Luke 3:5; generally met. *I humble.*

ταπείνωσις, εως, ἡ *a being brought low,* Acts 8:33; Jas 1:10; *meekness; humility.*

ταράσσω *I disturb, trouble.*

ταραχή, ῆς, ἡ *disturbing, ruffling.*

τάραχος, ου, ὁ *disturbance.*

Ταρσεύς, έως, ὁ *belonging to Tarsus, a Tarsian.*

Ταρσός, οῦ, ἡ *Tarsus,* the capital of the Roman province Cilicia.

ταρταρόω *I send to Tartarus* (Tartarus being in the Greek view a place of punishment under the earth, to which, for example, the Titans were sent).

τάσσω (1) *I put in its place, assign, fix,* Matt 8:9 (var.), Luke 7:8; Acts 13:48; 22:10; Rom 13:1; 1 Cor 16:15; (2) *I order,* w. acc. and inf. Acts 15:2; mid. *I order* by virtue of my power (authority), Matt 28:16; w. plur. subj., *we fix upon* among ourselves, Acts 28:23.

ταῦρος, ου, ὁ *a bull; an ox.*

ταφή, ῆς, ἡ *burial.*

τάφος, ου, ὁ *a tomb;* sepulchral *monument.*

τάχα adv., *perhaps.*

ταχέως adv., *quickly, swiftly, speedily;* compar. form τάχειον (w. superl. force in all places except John 20:4); superl. ὡς τάχιστα, *as quickly as possible.*

τάχιον (τάχειον) adv., see ταχέως.

ταχινός, ή, όν *speedy,* possibly *sudden.*

τάχιστα adv., see ταχέως.

τάχος, ους, τό *quickness;* ἐν τάχει, adverbially, *speedily, quickly.*

ταχύ adv., *quickly, speedily* (neut. of ταχύς, as adv.).

ταχύς, εῖα, ύ *quick.*

τέ *and,* an enclitic connective particle, weaker in force than καί, to which it is related as Lat. *-que* to *et (ac, atque);* τε . . . τε, τε . . . δέ, *both . . . and.*

τέθεικα perf. act. → τίθημι.

τεθῆναι aor. pas. infin. → τίθημι.

τέθλιμμαι perf. mid./pas. → θλίβω.

τεθλιμμένος perf. mid./pas. part. → θλίβω.

τέθνηκα perf. act. → θνήσκω.

τέθραμμαι perf. mid./pas. → τρέφω.

τεῖχος, ους, τό *a wall,* especially *the wall* of a city.

τεκεῖν aor. act. infin. → τίκτω.

τεκμήριον, ου, τό *an infallible proof,* a piece of certain (convincing) evidence.

τεκνογονέω *I bear a child (children), become a mother.*

τεκνίον, ου, τό *little child* (a diminutive form, suggesting affection, applied to grown up persons).

τεκνογονία, ας, ἡ *childbearing; motherhood.*

τέκνον, ου, τό (1) *a child,* used affectionately also of grown up persons; (2) met. (Hebraistic, cf. υἱός) w. gen., of those who show qualities like that expressed by the gen.; σοφίας, cf. Luke 7:35, those who draw from wisdom the impulses which mold their lives, and are as it were its representatives to others in speech and acts, *those who show* wisdom, φωτός Eph 5:8, ὑπακοῆς 1 Pet 1:14, τέκνα θεοῦ, *of godlike nature, of godly nature.*

τεκνοτροφέω *I bring up children.*

τέκτων, ονος, ὁ *a worker in wood, a carpenter.*

τέλειος, α, ον (1) *full grown, mature, complete,* having reached its utmost development, e.g. Eph 4:13; Heb 5:14; (2) *completely good* (simply), Jas 1:4; (3) *completely operative,* Jas 1:17; (4) *perfect,* as dealing with universal principles, Jas 1:25; (5) *perfect* in character, Matt 5:48; Jas 3:2, etc. (from τέλος, *final end*).

τελειότης, ητος, ἡ moral *completeness (perfection).*

τελειόω (1) *I bring to completion, I*

complete; of persons, *I bring to ethical* or *spiritual maturity (completeness); I fulfill,* John 19:28.

τελείως adv., *perfectly, absolutely,* w. νήφοντες, 1 Pet 1:13.

τελείωσις, εως, ἡ *a bringing to completion (perfection, fulfillment).*

τελειωτής, οῦ, ὁ *a completer, perfecter.*

τελεσφορέω *I bring* (fruit) *to maturity.*

τελευτάω *I die* (lit. *I end*).

τελευτή, ῆς, ἡ *death* (lit. *end*).

τελέω (1) *I end, complete, accomplish, finish;*(2) *I fulfill;* (3) in Gal 5:16, possibly *I perform;* (4) of taxes, dues, *I pay,* Matt 17:24; Rom 13:6.

τέλος, ους, τό (1) sing. *the end, the final end* of anything; εἰς τέλος, *continually,* Luke 18:5; (2) *the result, the culmination,* e.g. 1 Pet 1:9; (3) *fulfillment,* Luke 22:37; (4) especially plur. *revenues, dues,* Matt 17:25, also sing. Rom 13:7; of the spiritual *revenues* of the ages, 1 Cor 10:11.

τελώνης, ου, ὁ *collector (receiver) of customs, tax gatherer, revenue official,* of any rank, but especially of Jews of the lower rank, who collected revenue for the Roman overlord, detested by their fellow countrymen and practically identified w. ἁμαρτωλοί.

τελώνιον, ου, τό *a revenue office, a custom-house.*

τέξομαι fut. mid. → τίκτω.

τέρας, ατος, τό *a prodigy, an extraordinary occurrence (appearance, act), a startling portent.*

Τέρτιος, ου, ὁ *Tertius,* a Roman(?) Christian, who wrote the Epistle to the Romans at Paul's dictation [Lat.].

Τέρτυλλος, ου, ὁ *Tertullus,* a barrister acting as professional prosecutor of Paul at Caesarea [Lat.].

τεσσαράκοντα *forty.*

τεσσαρακονταετής, ές *of forty years, forty years long.*

τέσσαρες, τέσσαρα *four.*

τεσσαρεσκαιδέκατος, η, ον *fourteenth.*

τεσσερ- see τεσσαρ-.

τέταγμαι perf. mid./pas. → τάσσω.

τετάραγμαι perf. mid./pas. → ταράσσω.

τεταρταῖος, α, ον *of the fourth day* (Gk. idiom often personalizes such adjs.), *four days since* he died.

τέταρτος, η, ον *fourth.*

τεταχέναι perf. act. infin. → τάσσω.

τετρααρχέω (τετραρχέω) *I rule as tetrarch.*

τετραάρχης (τετράρχης), ου, ὁ *a tetrarch,* i.e., the ruler of a fourth part of a territory divided into four parts for efficient government, a division sometimes found in the Roman east.

τετράγωνος, ον *with four corners, square.*

τετράδιον, ου, τό *a quaternion,* a group of four soldiers.

τετρακισχίλιοι, αι, α *four thousand.*

τετρακόσιοι, αι, α *four hundred.*

τετράμηνος, ου, ἡ adj., *of four months* (understand χρόνος); hence, *four months.*

τετραπλοῦς, ῆ, οῦν *fourfold, four times as much.*

τετράπους, πουν, gen. **ποδος** *four footed; a quadruped.*

τετραρχ- see τετρααρχ-.

τέτυχα perf. act. → τυγχάνω.

τεφρόω *I cover with,* or *I convert into, ashes.*

τεχθείς aor. pas. part. → τίκτω.

τέχνη, ης, ἡ *art, handicraft, trade.*

τεχνίτης, ου, ὁ *a craftsman, an artisan;* w. gen. *a designer,* Heb 11:10.

τήκομαι pas. intrans., *I melt*

τηλαυγῶς adv., *clearly from afar, clearly* (so old MSS, but others of equal age read δηλαυγῶς, q.v.).

τηλικοῦτος, αύτη, οῦτο *so large, so great.*

τηρέω (1) lit. *I watch, observe;* (2) *I guard, preserve, keep, protect;* (3) of commandments and regulations, *I observe, keep, obey.*

τήρησις, εως, ἡ (1) *a keeping, an observance,* 1 Cor 7:19; (2) *a place of custody.*

Τιβεριάς, άδος, ἡ *Tiberias,* a town in Galilee on the western border of the sea called after it.

Τιβέριος, ου, ὁ *Tiberius,* the second Roman emperor (died A.D. 37).

τίθημι *I place, put, set forth;* sometimes w. two accusatives, the second in the pred., e.g. πατέρα πολλῶν ἐθνῶν τέθεικά σε, Rom 4:17, *I have made you a father,* etc.; τίθημι γόνατα, *I kneel;* τίθεμαι εἰς ὦτα, ἐν καρδίᾳ, *I put into my ears, into my mind,* i.e. *attend to,* e.g. Luke 1:66; 9:44; τίθημι ψυχήν, e.g. John 10:11 etc., for the synoptic and usual δίδωμι, *I give up my life, I offer up my life.*

τίκτω (of a woman), *I bear, give birth to, bring forth;* hence, met., of the earth, Heb 6:7, of evil desire, Jas 1:15.

τίλλω *I pluck, pull, pick.*

Τιμαῖος, ου, ὁ *Timaeus,* father of the blind beggar Bartimaeus.

τιμάω *I honor, give honor to.*

τιμή, ῆς, ἡ (1) *honor,* e.g. John 4:44; (2) *price,* e.g. Matt 27:6.

τίμιος, α, ον *precious, valuable,* in the lit. sense (of money value), e.g. Rev 17:4, and also, e.g. Acts 5:34, in an extended sense.

τιμιότης, ητος, ἡ *preciousness.*

Τιμόθεος, ου, ὁ *Timothy,* a Christian of Lystra, helper of Paul.

Τίμων, ωνος, ὁ *Timon,* one of the seven original "deacons" at Jerusalem.

τιμωρέω *I punish.*

τιμωρία, ας, ἡ (deserved) *punishment.*

τίνω *I pay.*

τίς masc. and fem., **τί** neut., gen. **τίνος,** dat. **τίνι,** acc. **τίνα, τί,** interrog. pron. and (sometimes) adj., *who? what? which?* (usually of more than two, but sometimes = πότερος, of two only, e.g. Matt 21:31); (1) τί = *what reward?* Matt 19:27; τί neut. as pred. to ταῦτα, e.g. Luke 15:26; Acts 17:20 (var.); John 6:9 (*what* use are they?); τί ἄρα ὁ Πέτρος ἐγένετο, *what then had happened to Peter,* Acts 12:18, τί ἄρα τὸ παιδίον τοῦτο ἔσται; Luke 1:66; Acts 5:24 (τί in pred.), abbreviated, οὗτος δὲ τί; *what will become of him?* John 21:21; (2) adverbially = *why?* Matt 6:28; Luke 2:48; Acts 14:15, like διὰ τί and ἵνα τί (supply γένηται), as well as τί ὅ, τι (ὅτι) = τί γέγονεν ὅτι (or δι' ὅ,τι) (cf. John 14:22); (3) (Hebraistic) *how,* Matt 7:14 (var.); Luke 12:49; 1 Cor 7:16; (4) τί πρὸς ἡμᾶς (supply ἐστιν); *what have we to do with it?* Matt 27:4, cf. John 21:22; 1 Cor 5:12 (see also under σύ); (5) τί γάρ; *what does it matter?* or *what difference does it make?* Rom 3:3; Phil 1:18; (6) τί οὖν (supply ἐροῦμεν?); Rom 6:15; (7) masc. ἐγὼ τίς ἤμην; Acts 11:17; (8) double interrog., τίς τί ἄρῃ, Mark 15:24, τίς τί *(what each)* διεπραγματεύσατο, Luke 19:15 (var.). Sometimes τίς is confused w. the rel. ὅστις, ὅς, which is rather a sign of illiteracy, Matt 10:19; Luke 17:8; Acts 13:25 (according to one punctuation); Jas 3:13 (if read as one sentence). In

Luke 11:5, 11, τίς (= εἴ τις, cf. Phil 2:1) is non-Gk. and Semitic.

τὶς, masc. and fem., **τὶ** neut., gen. **τινός,** dat. **τινί,** acc. **τινά, τὶ** (enclitic), indef. pron. and adj., (1) *some one, any one, something, anything;* (2) *a (an), a certain, any, some;* (3) special uses, (a) softening the metaphor, *so to speak, a sort of,* ἀπαρχήν τινα, Jas 1:18, (b) w. numbers, making indef., *about,* but τινας δύο, *a certain two,* Acts 23:23 (cf. Luke 22:50; John 11:49), (c) w. adjs., strengthening, Heb 10:27, cf. Acts 5:36; 8:9, (d) τι, *something special,* Gal 2:6; 6:3. Sometimes unexpressed, where it would be expected (Hebraism?), John 7:40; 16:17; Acts 19:33; 21:16, etc.

Τίτιος, ου, ὁ *Titius,* the second name (nomen) of a Christian Roman citizen at Corinth, his first name (praenomen) being unknown.

τίτλος, ου, ὁ *an inscription* [Lat., *titulus*].

Τίτος, ου, ὁ *Titus,* a Greek Christian, helper of Paul, perhaps also brother of Luke.

τοιγαροῦν *accordingly, wherefore.*

τοίνυν *so.*

τοιόσδε, άδε, όνδε, gen. **οῦδε, ᾶσδε, οῦδε** *of such character, to the following effect.*

τοιοῦτος, αύτη, οῦτον *of such a kind (character), such.*

τοῖχος, ου, ὁ *a wall.*

τόκος, ου, ὁ (from τίκτω), *interest* on money loaned.

τολμάω (1) *I have courage, I dare, I have the hardihood;* (2) *I take courage,* Mark 15:43; (3) *I submit to,* Rom 5:7.

τολμηρός, ά, όν *bold, courageous, audacious;* compar. adv. τολμηροτέρως or τολμηρότερον, *rather boldly.*

τολμητής, οῦ, ὁ *a shameless and headstrong man.*

τομός, ή, όν *cutting, with cutting power.*

τόξον, ου, τό *a bow* (and arrows).

τοπάζιον, ου, τό *a topaz.*

τόπος, ου, ὁ (1) *a place;* κατὰ τόπους, *in various places,* Mark 13:8, etc., διδόναι τόπον, *to make room for, give place to,* Luke 14:9, etc.; (2) met. *an opportunity,* Acts 25:16; Rom 15:23; Eph 4:27; Heb 12:17.

τοσοῦτος, αύτη, οῦτον (1) *so great, so large;* (2) of time, *so long,* plur. *so many;* (3) τοσούτου, *at such and such a price,* Acts 5:8.

τότε adv., *then, at that time;* ὁ τότε κόσμος, *the world of that day,* 2 Pet 3:6; ἀπὸ τότε, *from that time, thenceforward,* Matt 4:17, etc.; very often in Matt representing Heb. *waw* consecutive, and thus simply continuing the narrative.

τοὐναντίον as adv., *on the contrary* (syncopated from τὸ ἐναντίον, *the opposite*).

τοὔνομα as adv., *by name* (syncopated from τὸ ὄνομα).

τράγος, ου, ὁ *a goat.*

τράπεζα, ης, ἡ *a table.*

τραπεζίτης, ου, ὁ *a moneychanger, a banker* (from τράπεζα, moneychanger's *table*).

τραῦμα, ατος, τό *a wound.*

τραυματίζω *I wound.*

τραχηλίζω τετραχηλισμένα, *open, manifest* (from τράχηλος).

τράχηλος, ου, ὁ *the neck;* τὸν ἑαυτῶν τράχηλον ὑποθεῖναι, *to lay down their own necks,* i.e. *to risk their own lives.*

τραχύς, εῖα, ύ *rough.*

Τραχωνῖτις (Τραχωνιτίς), ιδος, ἡ *Trachonitic, belonging to Trachon,* adj. applied to a hilly region (inhabited by a nomad tribe), considerably to the south of Damascus, called also Ituraean.

τρεῖς, τρία gen. **τριῶν** dat. **τρισίν** *three;* μετὰ τρεῖς ἡμέρας = τῇ τρίτῃ ἡμέρᾳ.

τρέμω *I tremble.*

τρέφω (1) *I nourish, feed;* (2) *I bring up,* Luke 4:16; (2) met., Jas 5:5.

τρέχω (1) *I run;* sometimes w. acc. of the course, Heb 12:1; (2) met., e.g. Gal 2:2.

τρῆμα, ατος, τό (1) *opening, hole;* (2) *eye* of needle (perhaps a favorite term of medical writers).

τριάκοντα *thirty.*

τριακόσιοι, αι, α *three hundred.*

τρίβολος, ου, ὁ *a thistle.*

τρίβος, ου, ἡ *a path, track.*

τριετία, ας, ἡ *a period of three years, three years.*

τρίζω *I grind, crunch.*

τρίμηνος, η, ου *lasting three months;* acc. neut. as adv. *for three months.*

τρίς adv., *thrice, three times.*

τρίστεγος, η, ον (1) *having three roofs, with three floors (stories);* (2) hence, neut. as noun, *the third floor,* but it is uncertain whether the ground floor was counted or not in this enumeration; if so, we should have to translate, *the second floor.*

τρισχίλιοι, αι, α *three thousand.*

τρίτον acc. neut. of adj., generally w. def. article, as adv., (1) *the third time;* (2) *third, in the third place,* 1 Cor 12:28.

τρίτος, η, ον (see also τρίτον), *third;* ἐκ τρίτου, *a third time;* τῇ τρίτῃ ἡμέρᾳ (according to the ancient method of counting), *on the third day, two days after, on the next day but one, on the day after tomorrow.*

τρίχινος, η, ον *made of hair.*

τριχός gen. sing. → θρίξ.

τρόμος, ου, ὁ *trembling.*

τροπή, ῆς, ἡ (1) any *change* undergone by any object; (2) hence, referring to night and day, or the waxing and waning of the moon, the solstice, etc.

τρόπος, ου, ὁ (1) *manner, way;* (2) often acc. as adv. ὅν τρόπον, *in the way in which, as* (also w. κατά, etc.); (3) *manner of life,* Heb 13:5.

τροποφορέω *I bear (endure) the ways (disposition) of* (var.).

τροφή, ῆς, ἡ *nourishment, food, sustenance.*

Τρόφιμος, ου, ὁ *Trophimus,* a Christian of Ephesus in Asia.

τροφός, οῦ, ἡ *a nurse* (and thus of a mother who suckles her own children).

τροφοφορέω *I carry, dandle as a nurse* (var.).

τροχιά, ᾶς, ἡ *(a track);* hence, *a road.*

τροχός, οῦ, ὁ *(a wheel);* hence, *the chariot wheel* of man as he advances on the way of life, following his appointed course.

τρύβλιον, ου, τό *a dish.*

τρυγάω *I gather* (always of *grapes,* τρύξ).

τρυγών, όνος, ἡ *a turtledove.*

τρυμαλιά, ᾶς, ἡ (1) *an opening, hole;* (2) *an eye* of needle.

τρύπημα, ατος, τό (1) *a hole;* (2) *an eye.*

Τρύφαινα, ης, ἡ *Tryphaena,* a Christian woman in Rome.

τρυφάω *I live a luxurious life.*

τρυφή, ῆς, ἡ *luxury.*

Τρυφῶσα, ης, ἡ *Tryphosa,* a Christian woman in Rome, perhaps a sister of Tryphaena.

Τρῳάς, άδος, ἡ *Troas,* a harbor city of Mysia.

Τρωγύλλιον, ου, τό *Trogyllium,* a promontory somewhat to the south of Ephesus.

τρώγω (orig., *I munch, I eat*

audibly), *I eat.* (This word was displacing ἐσθίω in ordinary use.)

τυγχάνω (1) w. gen., *I obtain;* (2) absol., *I chance, happen;* (3) τυχών, *ordinary, everyday,* Acts 19:11; 28:2; (4) εἰ τύχοι (lit. *if it should happen*), *it may chance;* (5) old acc. absol., belonging to impers. verbs, τυχόν, *perhaps.*

τυμπανίζω *I break on the wheel* (from τύμπανον, "drum" used in worship, then "implement of torture").

τυπικῶς adv., either *by way of example,* or *typically, prefiguratively.*

τύπος, ου, ὁ (orig., *the mark* of a blow, cf. John 20:25; then *a stamp* struck by a die), (1) *a figure; a copy, image;* (2) *a pattern, model;* (3) *a type,* prefiguring something or somebody.

τύπτω *I strike.*

Τύραννος, ου, ὁ *Tyrannus* an inhabitant of Ephesus, probably a rhetorician.

τυρβάζομαι *be troubled, agitated.*

Τύριος, ου, ὁ *a Tyrian, an inhabitant of Tyre.*

Τύρος, ου, ἡ *Tyre,* an ancient city, the capital of Phoenicia.

τυφλός, ή, όν *blind,* either lit. or met.

τυφλόω *I blind, make blind,* lit. or met.

τύφομαι intrans., *I smoke.*

τυφόω pas. *I am puffed up, I am haughty.*

τυφωνικός, ή, όν (from τυφώς, *a vehement wind*); τυφωνικός ἄνεμος, *a heavy eddying squall.*

τυχεῖν aor. act. infin. → τυγχάνω.

Τυχικός, οῦ, ὁ (or Τύχικος), *Tychicus,* a Christian of the Roman province Asia.

τύχοι aor. opt. 3 sing. → τυγχάνω.

τυχόν aor. act. part. neut. → τυγχάνω.

Υ

ὑακίνθινος, η, ον *of the color of the martagon lily,* i.e., of a dusky red color.

ὑάκινθος, ου, ὁ *a sapphire* of dusky red color like the martagon lily.

ὑάλινος, η, ον *glassy, transparent as glass.*

ὕαλος, ου, ἡ *glass.*

ὑβρίζω *I treat insolently (outrageously), I insult.*

ὕβρις, εως, ἡ (1) *wanton insult, outrage,* 2 Cor 12:10; (2) *injury, loss,* due to the sea.

ὑβριστής, οῦ, ὁ noun as adj., *insolent, insulting, outrageous.*

ὑγιαίνω (1) *I am in* (good) *health, I am healthy (well);* (2) hence met. in connection with words and teaching, *I am right, reasonable.*

ὑγιής, ές, acc. **ὑγιῆ** (1) *whole, in health, sound;* (2) *restored to health;* (3) met. *reasonable.*

ὑγρός, ά, όν *moist, full of sap.*

ὑδρία, ας, ἡ a *water pot* (hence, of any pot).

ὑδροποτέω *I drink water* (alone, not mixed with wine).

ὑδρωπικός, ή, όν *afflicted with dropsy, edema.*

ὕδωρ, ὕδατος, τό *water;* ὕδωρ ζῶν, ζωῆς (Hebraistic gen.), *flowing water* (as opposed to stagnant), John 4:10, etc.

ὑετός, οῦ, ὁ (1) *a shower of rain;* (2) *rain.*

υἱοθεσία, ας, ἡ *adoption.*

υἱός, οῦ, ὁ (1) *a son* in the ordinary sense, with this difference, that one must keep in mind the greater solidarity of the family in ancient times and the greater ease in identifying father and son thence arising; also *a* male *descendant,* Matt 1:1, etc.; (2) in special senses: (a) w. a gen. of the Deity, θεοῦ, ὑψίστου, εὐλογητοῦ ("sons of God" in Job 1:6, etc., rendered by ἄγγελοι "angels," are members of the heavenly court gathered round Yahweh, and all men could be called "sons of God" as having been created by Him), rarely of a class of human beings, and in such cases only of those who perfectly perform God's will, those in and through whom His will is made known and who are thus like Him, e.g. Matt 5:9, (b) generally of Jesus, who as *God's Son* in an unique sense, as specially united with Him, is the Messiah, God's representative on earth, by whom His will is perfectly performed, and thus at times as it were identified with Him, Mark 1:11, etc., (c) ὁ υἱὸς τοῦ ἀνθρώπου (lit. *the Son of the Man*, an Aramaistic expression, originally equivalent to ὁ ἄνθρωπος, cf. Mark 3:28; Rev 1:13, *the man, the human being*, simply) at some stage become a Messianic title (cf. Dan 7:13 and *Parables of Enoch* for the growth in the use of the expression), used by Jesus Himself, representing the whole human race in the one Man, *the Son of Man*, who has to suffer but will be glorified, Mark 8:29, 31–32; Matt 16:13, 27–28, cf. Luke 9:18, 22–23, etc., (d) a similar Hebraism w. genitives indicating qualities, etc., ἀπειθείας, ἀπωλείας, γεέννης (cf. also διαβόλου), used of persons who so perfectly exemplify these qualities, etc., that they can be spoken of as having a family likeness to them (cf. τέκνον).

ὕλη, ης, ἡ *wood, timber, brushwood.*

Ὑμέναιος, ου, ὁ *Hymenaeus*, a backsliding Christian.

ὑμέτερος, α, ον *your.*

ὑμνέω (1) intrans., *I sing a hymn;* (2) trans., *I praise in a hymn.*

ὕμνος, ου, ὁ *a hymn*, especially of praise to God.

ὑπάγω (1) *I go away, withdraw, depart;* (2) *I depart this life*, Matt 26:24.

ὑπακοή, ῆς, ἡ *obedience.*

ὑπακούω *I obey;* w. infin., Heb 11:8.

ὕπανδρος, ον *under the authority of a husband.*

ὑπαντάω *I meet.*

ὑπάντησις, εως, ἡ *meeting, act of meeting.*

ὕπαρξις, εως, ἡ *a possession*, generally of *personal property.*

ὑπάρχω (1) *I am*, denoting originally a state or condition still subsisting in contrast to what is temporary or accidental; (2) τὰ ὑπάρχοντα, *one's belongings, possessions, personal property.*

ὑπέβαλον aor. act. → ὑποβάλλω.

ὑπέδειξα aor. act. → ὑποδείκνυμι.

ὑπέθηκα aor. act. → ὑποτίθημι.

ὑπείκω *I yield, submit.*

ὑπέλαβον aor. act. → ὑπολαμβάνω.

ὑπελείφθην aor. pas. → ὑπολείπω.

ὑπέμεινα aor. act. → ὑπομένω.

ὑπεμνήσθην aor. pas. → ὑπομιμνήσκω.

ὑπεναντίος, α, ον (1) *opposing, hostile;* (2) subs., *adversary*, Heb 10:27.

ὑπενεγκεῖν aor. act. infin. → ὑποφέρω.

ὑπέπλευσα aor. act. → ὑποπλέω.

ὑπέπνευσα aor. act. → ὑποπνέω.

ὑπέρ (1) prep. w. gen., (a) *for, on behalf of, for the sake of* (opp. to κατά, e.g. Mark 9:40), *as agent of*, Phlm 13; perhaps, *in memory of*, 1 Cor 15:29, (b) colorlessly, *concerning, about, as to*, John 1:30; 2 Cor 8:23; 12:8; Phil 1:7; 4:10; 2 Thess 2:1, (c) perhaps elsewhere of the goal one wants to reach, *with a view to*, 2 Cor 1:6; Phil 2:13; (2) prep. w. acc., (a) *over, beyond*, indicating excess, (b) w. the comp., *than,* Luke 16:8; John 12:43 (var.); Acts 20:35 (var.); Heb 4:12, and in compound expressions given below; (3) adv., *more* (than they), an ancient use.

ὑπεραίρω (1) lit. *I raise beyond;* (2) pas. met., *I am exceedingly uplifted.*

ὑπέρακμος, ον of doubtful meaning; probably *of excessive* sexual *vigor* (of the man), rather than *past the bloom of youth* (of the woman).

ὑπεράνω prep. w. gen., *far above.*

ὑπερασπίζω *I protect.*

ὑπεραυξάνω intrans., *I grow exceedingly.*

ὑπερβαίνω intrans., *I transgress.*

ὑπερβαλλόντως adv., *exceedingly.*

ὑπερβάλλω (1) intrans. w. gen., *I exceed, surpass;* (2) part. pres., absol., *excessive, extraordinary.*

ὑπερβολή, ῆς, ἡ (1) *excess, abundance;* (2) καθ᾽ ὑπερβολήν, *superlatively, exceedingly, beyond measure.*

ὑπερεῖδον aor. act. → ὑπεροράω.

ὑπερέκεινα adv. *beyond;* τὰ ὑπερέκεινα, *the places beyond.*

ὑπερεκπερισσοῦ adv., *most exceedingly, beyond all measure;* w. gen. of comparison, *exceedingly more than,* Eph 3:20.

ὑπερεκπερισσῶς adv., *most exceedingly, beyond all measure,* 1 Thess 5:13 (var.).

ὑπερεκτείνω trans., *I stretch beyond the measure assigned to me.*

ὑπερεκχύ(ν)νω *I pour out so that it overflows.*

ὑπερεντυγχάνω *I supplicate on behalf of.*

ὑπερέχω absol. or w. gen. or w. acc., (1) *I am superior, I am supreme;* (2) *I surpass.*

ὑπερηφανία, ας, ἡ *haughtiness, arrogance.*

ὑπερήφανος, ον *haughty, disdainful, arrogant.*

ὑπεριδών aor. act. part. → ὑπεροράω.

ὑπερλίαν adv. used as adj., (lit. *more than very much*); οἱ ὑπερλίαν ἀπόστολοι, in irony, *the super-apostles.*

ὑπερνικάω (1) *I score a heavy victory;* (2) *I am more than a conqueror.*

ὑπέρογκος, ον (lit. *of great* or *excessive bulk*), *arrogant.*

ὑπεροράω *I look past, overlook, pretend not to see.*

ὑπεροχή, ῆς, ἡ (1) *superiority,* 1 Cor 2:1; (2) *a position of superiority,* 1 Tim 2:2.

ὑπερπερισσεύω (1) intrans., *I abound exceedingly;* (2) mid. as act. *I overflow.*

ὑπερπερισσῶς adv., *most exceedingly.*

ὑπερπλεονάζω *I abound exceedingly, I am exceedingly abundant.*

ὑπερυψόω *I elevate greatly (exceedingly).*

ὑπερφρονέω *I have high notions.*

ὑπερῷον, ου, τό *an upper room, an upstairs room.*

ὑπεστειλάμην aor. mid. → ὑποστέλλω.

ὑπετάγην aor. pas. → ὑποτάσσω.

ὑπέταξα aor. act. → ὑποτάσσω.

ὑπέχω *I undergo.*

ὑπήκοος, ον *obedient.*

ὑπήνεγκα aor. act. → ὑποφέρω.

ὑπηρετέω *I serve, minister to.*

ὑπηρέτης, ου, ὁ *a servant, an attendant.*

ὕπνος, ου, ὁ *sleep.*

ὑπό prep. (1) w. gen., *by,* especially of a person as the original author (contrast διά), w. a verb pas. or quasi-pas. (cf. Rev 6:8); (2) w. acc., (a) both lit. and met., *under,* after a verb of motion, and so answering the question "to what place?"

(b) both lit. and met., after a verb of rest, and so answering the question "where?" (c) of time, *about*, Acts 5:21.

ὑποβάλλω *I suborn.*

ὑπογραμμός, οῦ, ὁ (properly a *piece of calligraphy, a copy,* for children to imitate); hence, *a model, a type,* which has to be followed.

ὑπόδειγμα, ατος, τό (1) *a sign, image* of something, Heb 8:5; 9:23; (2) *an example,* given for imitation.

ὑποδείκνυμι (1) *I point out, show;* (2) hence, *I advise, warn,* Matt 3:7; Luke 3:7.

ὑποδείξω fut. act. → ὑποδείκνυμι.

ὑποδέχομαι *I receive under my roof, I welcome to my house, I entertain hospitably.*

ὑποδέω (lit. *I bind under*), mid. *I put on* (my feet).

ὑπόδημα, ατος, τό *a shoe* (cf. ὑποδέω).

ὑπόδικος, ον (a forensic word), *liable to (brought under) the judgment of, answerable to.*

ὑποδραμών aor. act. part. → ὑποτρέχω.

ὑποζύγιον, ου, τό *a beast of burden,* either *an ass* or *a mule.*

ὑποζώννυμι *I undergird, frap,* i.e., I fasten cables vertically round the hull of the ship to prevent the timbers from straining or giving way.

ὑποκάτω prep. w. gen., *underneath.*

ὑποκρίνομαι *I act the part, pretend.*

ὑπόκρισις, εως, ἡ (*acting a part,* properly), *hypocrisy, pose.*

ὑποκριτής, οῦ, ὁ (properly *an actor*), *a hypocrite,* one who outwardly plays the part of a religious man to perfection, but is inwardly alien to the spirit of true religion.

ὑπολαμβάνω (1) *I receive from beneath, I take up,* Acts 1:9; (2) *I welcome, entertain,* 3 John 8; (3) *I catch up* in speech, by answering or contradicting or supplementing, Luke 10:30; (4) *I suppose, imagine.*

ὑπόλειμμα, ατος, τό *a remnant.*

ὑπολείπω *I leave behind.*

ὑπολήνιον, ου, τό *a winepress,* probably the *lower* (ὑπο-) trough, smaller but deeper than the ληνός proper, both being cut out of the solid rock.

ὑπολιμπάνω Ionic form of ὑπολείπω.

ὑπομεμενηκώς perf. act. part. → ὑπομένω.

ὑπομένω (1) *I remain behind,* Luke 2:43; Acts 17:14; (2) absol., *I stand my ground, I show endurance,* Matt 10:22, etc.; w. τῇ θλίψει, Rom 12:12, *in persecution, amid persecution,* w. εἰς = ἐν, Heb 12:7; (3) trans., *I endure, bear up against.*

ὑπομνῆσαι aor. act. infin. → ὑπομιμνήσκω.

ὑπομιμνήσκω (1) *I remind;* (2) pas. practically *I remember,* Luke 22:61.

ὑπόμνησις, εως, ἡ *remembrance, recollection.*

ὑπομνήσω fut. act. → ὑπομιμνήσκω.

ὑπομονή, ῆς, ἡ *steadfast endurance,* the virtue shown by martyrs.

ὑπονοέω *I suppose.*

ὑπόνοια, ας, ἡ *a supposition, suspicion.*

ὑποπλέω *I sail under the lee of (close to).*

ὑποπνέω *I blow moderately (gently).*

ὑποπόδιον, ου, τό *a footstool* (of the conquering king placing his foot on the neck of the conquered).

ὑπόστασις, εως, ἡ (lit. *an underlying*), (1) *confidence, assurance;* (2) *a giving substance* (or *reality*) *to,* or *a guaranteeing,* Heb 11:1 (where possibly *title deed* is the sense); (3) *substance, reality,* Heb 1:3.

ὑποστέλλω (1) act. trans., *I withdraw,* Gal 2:12; (2) mid. trans., *I keep back,* Acts 20:20; (3) intrans., *I withdraw,* Heb 10:38; (4) c. infin. and answering negative, *I shrink from, I shun,* Acts 20:27.

ὑποστολή, ῆς, ἡ (1) *withdrawal;* (2) *shrinking.*

ὑποστρέφω (1) intrans., *I return;* (2) met., *I withdraw,* 2 Pet 2:21.

ὑποστρωννύω (ὑποστρώννυμι) trans., *I spread underneath.*

ὑποταγή, ῆς, ἡ *subordination, subjection, submission.*

ὑποταγήσομαι fut. pas. → ὑποτάσσω.

ὑποτάσσω (1) *I subject, I put into subjection* (lit. *I put in a lower rank, I rank under,* a military term); (2) mid. and pas., *I subordinate myself, I put myself into subjection, I submit.*

ὑποτέταγμαι perf. mid./pas. → ὑποτάσσω.

ὑποτίθημι (1) *I place (put) under* some danger, *I expose;* (2) mid. *I suggest, advise.*

ὑποτρέχω *I run* before a wind *under* the lee of.

ὑποτύπωσις, εως, ἡ *a figurative representation,* serving as *an example.*

ὑποφέρω *I endure, suffer.*

ὑποχωρέω *I withdraw.*

ὑπωπιάζω (1) *I strike under the eye, bruise* (from ὑπώπιον, which is from ὑπό and ὤψ, "that part of the face under the eyes"); (2) hence, *I treat severely,* 1 Cor 9:27, *I molest, annoy, harass, worry, exhaust,* Luke 18:5.

ὗς, ὑός, ἡ *a sow.*

ὑσσός, οῦ, ὁ *a javelin.*

ὕσσωπος, ου, ὁ, ἡ, and **τό** *hyssop.* In John 19:29 ὑσσώπῳ is a graphic error for ὑσσῷ, *pike.*

ὑστερέω (1) act. intrans., (a) *I come late, I am late,* Heb 4:1, (b) *I am left behind in the race for, I have no part in,* w. ἀπό and the gen. of the end, Heb 12:15, (c) *I fall short, I am inferior,* Matt 19:20; 1 Cor 12:24 (var.); 2 Cor 11:5; 12:11, (d) *I am wanting (to),* Mark 10:21 (var.), John 2:3, (e) *I am without,* w. gen., Luke 22:35; (2) pas., (a) *I suffer from want,* absol., or w. gen., or w. ἐν and dat., (b) *I am worse off* (for honor), 1 Cor 8:8.

ὑστέρημα, ατος, τό (1) *that which is lacking,* of things or persons; (2) *want, poverty,* Luke 21:4; 2 Cor 8:14; 9:12; 11:9.

ὑστέρησις, εως, ἡ *poverty, want.*

ὕστερον adv., *later, afterwards.*

ὕστερος, α, ον (1) comp., *latter;* (2) superl., *last, latest.*

ὑφαίνω *I weave.*

ὑφαντός, ή, όν *woven.*

ὑψηλός, ή, όν (1) lit. *high, lofty;* (2) met. μετὰ βραχίονος ὑψηλοῦ (Hebraistic), of God; (3) w. φρονεῖν, of haughtiness, arrogance, boasting.

ὑψηλοφρονέω *I am haughty (arrogant).*

ὕψιστος, η, ον *highest,* always as epithet either of God, or of the region where He lives.

ὕψος, ους, τό (1) *height;* (2) *heaven,* Luke 1:78; 24:49; Eph 4:8; (3) met. spiritual *height.*

ὑψόω *I raise to a height, I lift up, I exalt,* usually met.

ὕψωμα, ατος, τό (1) *height,* Rom 8:39; (2) *loftiness, haughtiness, (self-) exaltation,* 2 Cor 10:5 (but including concr. as well as abstr., *whatever is lofty, etc.*).

Φ

φαγεῖν aor. act. infin. → ἐσθίω.

φάγομαι fut. mid. → ἐσθίω.

φάγος, ου, ὁ *a glutton, gourmand.*

φαιλόνης, ου, ὁ *a mantle, cloak;* a metathesis from φαινόλης.

φαίνω (1) act. *I shine, I shed light;* (2) pas., (a) *I shine,* (b) *I become visible, I appear,* cf. ἐφάνη, impers., Matt 9:33, (c) *I become clear, appear, show myself* as, Matt 6:5, 16, 18; 23:27; Rom 7:13; 2 Cor 13:7; 1 Pet 4:18, (d) of the mind and judgment (= δοκεῖ), Mark 14:64; Luke 24:11.

Φάλεκ, ὁ *Phalek,* son of Eber, and one of the ancestors of Jesus [Heb.].

φανερός, ά, όν (1) *clear, visible* (as opposed to "hidden," "secret"); (2) εἰς θανερὸν ἐλθεῖν, *to come into the open, to appear before the public,* Mark 4:22; Luke 8:17, ἐν τῷ φανερῷ, *in public.*

φανερόω *I make clear (visible, manifest).*

φανερῶς adv., *openly, overtly.*

φανέρωσις, εως, ἡ *a showing forth,* w. obj. gen.

φανός, οῦ, ὁ *(a light, a torch);* then, *a lantern.*

Φανουήλ, ὁ *Fanuhel, Phanuel,* father of Anna the prophetess.

φανοῦμαι fut. mid. → φαίνω.

φαντάζω *I make to appear;* τὸ φανταζόμενον, *the appearance.*

φαντασία, ας, ἡ *show, display.*

φάντασμα, ατος, τό (1) *an appearance;* (2) hence, *a ghost, a spirit.*

φάνω aor. pas. subj. → φαίνω.

φανῶ fut. act. → φαίνω.

φάραγξ, αγγος, ἡ *a hollow place, a hollow, a valley.*

Φαραώ, ὁ *Pharaoh,* a king of Egypt, properly a dynastic title (cf. Decebalus in Dacia, Candace in Ethiopia), but, though sometimes preceded by the def. article, probably everywhere understood as a proper name.

Φάρες (Φαρές), ὁ *Phares,* son of Judah and one of the ancestors of Jesus [Heb.].

Φαρισαῖος, ου, ὁ (lit. a Separatist, a Purist), *a Pharisee,* a member of the strict religious legalistic party in Judaism after the exile.

φαρμακία (φαρμακεία), ας, ἡ (1) *the practice of drugging, drugging;* (2) hence, especially, from the use of mysterious liquids, *sorcery, witchcraft,* inextricably combined with idolatry.

φάρμακον, ου, τό (1) *a drug;* (2) hence, plur., of those used in sorcery, and thus *sorcery,* Rev 9:21 (var.).

φάρμακος (φαρμακός), ου, ὁ *a sorcerer, magician* (see φαρμακία).

φασίν pres. act., 3 plur. → φημί.

φάσις, εως, ἡ *information* (from φαίνω).

φάσκω *I say,* either *I say frequently,* or *I allege.*

φάτνη, ης, ἡ *a manger, a feeding trough.*

φαῦλος, η, ον *worthless, low, paltry,* implying not so much what is evil as the limitations and paltrinesses belonging to a low order of things.

φέγγος, ους, τό *a light, ray, beam.*

φείδομαι *I spare,* I exempt from punishment or injury (death).

φειδομένως adv., *sparingly.*

φελόνης see φαιλόνης.

φέρω (1) *I carry, bear, bring;* (2) *I conduct, lead,* both trans. and intrans.; (3) perhaps, *I make publicly known,* Heb 9:16.

φεύγω (1) *I flee;* (2) *I escape.*

Φῆλιξ, ικος, ὁ *Felix,* third name of (Marcus) Antonius Felix, procurator of the Roman province Judaea from an uncertain date (before A.D. 52?) till A.D. 59 [Lat.].

φήμη, ης, ἡ *a report, a rumor.*

φημί *I say.*

φημίζω *I spread* a rumor, *(circulate)* a report.

φησίν pres. act. 3 sing. → φημί.

Φῆστος, ου, ὁ *Festus,* third name of(?) Porcius Festus, procurator of the Roman province Judaea from A.D. 59 [Lat.].

φθάνω (1) *I anticipate, I precede,* 1 Thess 4:15; (2) *I come, I arrive.*

φθαρήσομαι fut. pas. → φθείρω.

φθαρτός, ή, όν *perishable.*

φθέγγομαι *I utter* (a word), *I open the mouth in speech.*

φθείρω (1) lit., (a) *I destroy, I waste,* (b) *I damage, injure* (in being); (2) usually met., (a) *I corrupt morally, I deprave, injure* (in character), (b) *I seduce,* 2 Cor 11:3.

φθερῶ fut. act. → φθείρω.

φθινοπωρινός, ή, όν *autumnal, in autumn,* when fruit is expected (derived from τὸ φθινόπωρον, which itself = φθίνουσα ὀπώρα, "the concluding portion of the ὀπώρα").

φθόγγος, ου, ὁ (1) *a* measured harmonious *sound,* of voice or instrument; (2) *an utterance.*

φθονέω *I envy.*

φθόνος, ου, ὁ *envy, grudge;* plur. where related to various advantages.

φθορά, ᾶς, ἡ *rottenness, perishableness, corruption, decay, decomposition.*

φιάλη, ης, ἡ (1) strictly *a wine cup,* much like a modern champagne glass in shape; (2) hence, *a cup.*

φιλάγαθος, ον *loving what is good.*

φιλαδελφία, ας, ἡ (1) *love of brothers* for each other; (2) hence, *love of the brethren, love of fellow Christians,* all being sons of the same Father in a special sense.

Φιλαδέλφεια (Φιλαδελφία), ας, ἡ *Philadelphia,* a city of the Roman province Asia.

φιλάδελφος, ον *loving one's brothers (fellow Christians).*

φίλανδρος *loving one's husband.*

φιλανθρωπία, ας, ἡ (1) *love of (for) mankind;* (2) *humanity, kindness,* Acts 28:2.

φιλανθρώπως adv., *kindly.*

φιλαργυρία, ας, ἡ *love of money.*

φιλάργυρος, ον *loving money.*

φίλαυτος, ον *loving self.*

φιλέω (1) *I love,* of friendship (contrast ἔραμαι [of passion] and ἀγαπάω [of reverential love]); (2) *I kiss,* Mark 14:44; Matt 26:48; Luke 22:47.

φιλήδονος, ον *loving* (sensuous) *pleasure.*

φίλημα, ατος, τό *a kiss.*

Φιλήμων, ονος, ὁ *Philemon,* a Christian man of Colossae.

Φίλητος, ου, ὁ *Philetus,* a backsliding Christian at Rome.

φιλία, ας, ἡ *friendship.*

Φιλιππήσιος, ου, ὁ *a Philippian, an inhabitant of Philippi.*

Φίλιπποι, ων, ὁ *Philippi,* a great city of the Roman province Macedonia.

Φίλιππος, ου, ὁ *Philip* (a Gk. name); (1) one of the twelve disciples of Jesus; (2) tetrarch of the Ituraean and Trachonitic region, half brother of Herod Antipas, tetrarch of Galilee; perhaps another half brother is intended in Mark 6:17 and pars.; (3) one of the seven original "deacons" at Jerusalem and a missionary, Acts 6:5; 8:5–40; 21:8.

φιλόθεος, ον *loving God.*

Φιλόλογος, ου, ὁ *Philologus,* a Roman Christian.

φιλονεικία, ας, ἡ *emulation, rivalry* (see φιλόνεικος).

φιλόνεικος, ον *contentious* (φίλος and νείκη [νίκη] "victory").

φιλοξενία, ας, ἡ (1) *love to foreigners;* (2) *entertainment of strangers.*

φιλόξενος, ον (1) *friendly to foreigners;* (2) *hospitable.*

φιλοπρωτεύω *I love the first (chief) place.*

φίλος, η, ον (1) *friendly;* (2) subs. *a friend* (masc. or fem.).

φιλοσοφία, ας, ἡ *philosophy,* in a bad sense, and perhaps identified with ἀπάτη.

φιλόσοφος, ου, ὁ *a philosopher.*

φιλόστοργος, ον *loving warmly (strongly).*

φιλότεκνος, ον *loving one's children.*

φιλοτιμέομαι (earlier, *I am ambitious;* then, *I act with public spirit*); now, *I am zealous, I strive eagerly.*

φιλοφρόνως adv., *with friendly thoughtfulness.*

φιμόω (1) *I muzzle;* (2) hence, probably originally a slang use, *I silence,* φιμώθητι, *be quiet!* Mark 1:25, etc.

Φλέγων, οντος, ὁ *Phlegon,* a Roman Christian man.

φλογίζω *I set on fire.*

φλόξ, φλογός, ἡ (1) *a flame;* (2) πυρός (Hebraistic), *a fiery flame;* (3) spiritualized, 2 Thess 1:8.

φλυαρέω c. acc. *I chatter (gossip) against.*

φλύαρος, ον *chattering, gossiping.*

φοβέομαι *I fear, dread, reverence,* absol. or w. acc. or w. infin.; also w. cog. acc. φόβον, πτόησιν, *I fear greatly;* w. ἀπό and gen. (Hebraism), *I am afraid of,* Matt 10:28 (Luke 12:4); w. μή and conjunctive, *I fear lest, I fear that.*

φοβερός, ά, όν *fearful, terrible.*

φόβητρον (φόβηθρον), ου, τό *an instrument of terror, an object of fear, a bugbear.*

φόβος, ου, ὁ *fear, terror,* often fear on the reverential side, in reference to God, and such as inspires cautious dealing towards men, cf. 1 Pet 1:17.

Φοίβη, ης, ἡ *Phoebe,* a leading Christian woman in the church at Cenchreae.

Φοινίκη, ης, ἡ *Phoenice, Phoenicia,* a northern coast strip of the Roman province Syria.

Φοινίκισσα, ἡ *Phoenician;* see Συροφοινίκισσα (= Σύρο Φοινίκισσα).

φοῖνιξ, ικος, ὁ (1) *a palm tree,* John 12:13; (2) *a branch of a palm tree, a palm,* Rev 7:9.

Φοῖνιξ, ικος, ὁ *Phoenix* (perhaps modern Lutro), a bay on the south coast of Crete.

φονεύς, έως, ὁ *a murderer.*

φονεύω (1) c. acc. *I murder;* (2) absol. *I commit murder.*

φόνος, ου, ὁ *murder.*

φορέω (1) *I carry;* (2) hence, very often, *I wear.*

Φόρον, ου, τό *Forum, Market, Market Town* [Lat., *Forum*].

φόρος, ου, ὁ *tribute, war tax.*

φορτίζω *I load, burden.*

φορτίον, ου, τό (1) *a burden;* (2) *a cargo,* Acts 27:10.

Φορτουνᾶτος, ου, ὁ *Fortunatus,* a Christian of Corinth [Lat.].

φραγέλλιον, ου, τό *a lash* [by dissimilation from Lat., *flagellum*].

φραγελλόω *I lash, flog* [Lat., *flagello*].

φραγήσομαι fut. pas. → φράσσω.

φραγμός, οῦ, ὁ (1) *a hedge, a fence, a partition;* (2) hence, *a path* bounded by hedges or fences, Luke 14:23.

φράζω *I explain, I interpret.*

φράσσω *I stop, close.*

φρέαρ, ατος, τό (1) *a well;* (2) hence, transferred, Rev 9:1, 2.

φρεναπατάω (lit. *I deceive the mind*), *I deceive.*

φρεναπάτης, ου, ὁ (1) *a deceiver;* (2) *deceiving* (see φρεναπατάω).

φρήν, φρενός, ἡ *the mind.*

φρίσσω *I feel awe* (used properly of the standing of the hair on end with fear).

φρονέω (1) w. acc. *I have in my mind, I think of, I set my mind upon,* suggesting my moral interest, thought, and study, and not a mere unreflecting opinion; (2) intrans., *I think, I cherish a habit of thought.*

φρόνημα, ατος, τό *an object of thought* (or *endeavor*).
φρόνησις, εως, ἡ *understanding,* which leads to right action.
φρόνιμος, ον *sensible, prudent.*
φρονίμως adv., *wisely, sensibly, prudently.*
φροντίζω *I am careful, I take care.*
φρουρέω *I guard,* or rather *I garrison,* lit. and met.
φρυάσσω *I roar, rage* (properly, of the snorting and neighing of a high-spirited horse).
φρύγανον, ου, τό *brushwood, copse.*
Φρυγία, ας, ἡ *Phrygia,* an ethnic district in Asia Minor, the northwestern part of which was in the Roman province Asia, and the southeastern part in the Roman province Galatia; in Acts 16:6 φρυγίαν is adj.
φυγεῖν aor. act. infin. → φεύγω.
Φύγελος, ου, ὁ *Phygelus,* a Christian of the Roman province Asia who deserted Paul.
φυγή, ῆς, ἡ *flight.*
φυλακή, ῆς, ἡ (1) abstr., *guardianship, guard,* in cog. acc., Luke 2:8; Acts 12:6; (2) a *guard,* Acts 12:10; (3) much commoner, *a prison;* hence, *the place of confinement* of the spirits of the dead, 1 Pet 3:19; (4) as a division of the night, (a) perhaps according to the old Jewish system by which there were three divisions, Luke 12:38, (b) according to the Roman system, popularized in Judaea, by which there were four, Mark 6:48 (cf. 13:35), Matt 14:25; 24:43.
φυλακίζω *I put in prison, I imprison.*
φυλακτήριον, ου, τό *a phylactery, an amulet,* a parchment capsule containing little parchment rolls with the Heb. texts, Exod 13:1–10, 11–16; Deut 6:4–9; 11:13–21, affixed to the left upper arm or the forehead of men at morning prayer, and regarded as a protection (hence the name) against evil spirits.
φύλαξ, ακος, ὁ *a guard* (one person).
φυλάσσω (1) *I guard, protect,* w. pers. or other concr. obj., or (Luke 2:8) cog. acc.; mid. *I am on my guard,* Luke 12:15; (2) act. and mid., of customs or regulations, *I keep, I observe.*
φυλή, ῆς, ἡ *a tribe,* especially one of the twelve tribes of Israel, and perhaps (by analogy) of Christendom, Jas 1:1.
φύλλον, ου, τό *a leaf* of a tree.
φύραμα, ατος, τό (1) *a mixture;* (2) hence lit. or met., *a lump, a mass.*
φυσικός, ή, όν (1) *natural;* (2) φυσικά, 2 Pet 2:12, *creatures of instinct.*
φυσικῶς adv., *by instinct.*
φυσιόω (lit. *I inflate*), met. *I puff up,* with anger, conceit, etc.
φύσις, εως, ἡ *nature, inherent nature,* in NT nonmoral, neither good nor bad; φύσει, *by nature, in myself (itself,* etc.*).*
φυσίωσις, εως, ἡ *a puffing up* (due to conceit).
φυτεία, ας, ἡ (lit. *planting*), *a plant.*
φυτεύω *I plant.*
φύω *I grow, I grow up.*
φωλεός, οῦ, ὁ *a hole* in the earth.
φωνέω *I give forth a sound,* hence; (1) of a cock, *I crow;* (2) of men, *I shout;* (3) trans., (a) *I call* (to myself), *I summon, I invite,* Luke 14:12, (b) *I address,* John 13:13.
φωνή, ῆς, ἡ (1) *a sound;* (2) hence, *a voice.*
φῶς, φωτός, τό (1) *a light,* particularly *the light* of the sun, but also *the heavenly bodies* specially, Jas 1:17; (2) as indispensable to life, it comes to be associated with life (cf.

John 1:4), and as universal beneficence, with God and the Messiah (cf. John 1:8; 8:12), etc. (cf. John 12:36; Eph 5:8); (3) τὸ φῶς, *the (bright) fire,* Mark 14:54; Luke 22:56.

φωστήρ, ῆρος, ὁ (1) *a light,* perhaps *a sun,* Rev 21:11; (2) *a star,* Phil 2:15.

φωσφόρος, ου, ὁ (lit. *light-bringing,* lucifer), *the day star* (the planet Venus, probably).

φωτεινός, ή, όν *shining, brilliant.*

φωτίζω (1) *I shed light upon, I enlighten* (of the public disclosure of what has been kept secret); pas. w. acc. Eph 1:18; (2) *I bring to light,* Eph 3:9; (3) φωτισθέντες, *having received enlightenment,* having had experience of God's grace in conversion, Heb 6:4; 10:32.

φωτισμός, οῦ, ὁ (1) act. *enlightening,* 2 Cor 4:4; (2) pas. *enlightenment,* 2 Cor 4:6.

X

χαίρω (1) *I rejoice,* w. cog. acc. or w. dat., *I rejoice exceedingly;* (2) in the imper., χαῖρε, χαίρετε, a greeting, *farewell,* Christianized in Phil 3:1; 4:4 by the addition ἐν κυρίῳ (and generally mistranslated), cf. χαίρειν, imper. infin., e.g. Acts 15:23 (cf. 2 John 10); (3) *hail!* Mark 15:18; Matt 27:29.

χάλαζα, ης, ἡ *hail.*

χαλάω *I slacken.*

Χαλδαῖος, ου, ὁ *a Chaldaean,* one living in southern Armenia.

χαλεπός, ή, όν (1) *hard, difficult,* 2 Tim 3:1; (2) *difficult to restrain, dangerous,* Matt 8:28.

χαλιναγωγέω *I bridle,* met. *I keep in check, restrain.*

χαλινός, οῦ, ὁ *a bridle.*

χαλκεύς, έως, ὁ *a worker in bronze, a smith.*

χαλκηδών, όνος, ὁ *a chalcedony,* a small stone of various colors.

χαλκίον, ου, τό *a bronze vessel.*

χαλκολίβανος (ον), ου, ὁ or τό *brass, bronze;* a word of uncertain signification, translated *aeramentum turinum* (incense bronze) in certain Old Latin authorities, and *orichalcum* (= ὀρείχαλκος [mountain bronze]) in the Vulgate; the latter was understood to be a mixture of gold and copper.

χαλκός, οῦ, ὁ (1) *copper* or *bronze;* (2) hence, *a copper coin;* (3) *copper money,* Mark 6:8 (Matt 10:9). Mark 12:41.

χαλκοῦς, ῆ, οῦν made of bronze, bronze.

χαμαί adv., *on the ground.*

Χανάαν (Χαναάν), ἡ *Canaan,* the whole of Palestine (Acts 13:19) or Palestine west of the river Jordan (Acts 7:11).

Χαναναῖος, α, ον *Canaanitish, Canaanite,* a biblical and archaic name for *Phoenician.*

χαρά, ᾶς, ἡ (1) *joy;* (2) *delight.*

χάραγμα, ατος, τό (1) *an engraved work,* Acts 17:29; (2) *an inscription engraved, a stamp.*

χαρακτήρ, ῆρος, ὁ *a representation.*

χάραξ, ακος, ὁ *a mound, rampart.*

χαρῆναι aor. pas. infin. → χαίρω.

χαρήσομαι fut. mid. → χαίρω.

χαρίζομαι (1) *I graciously confer,* Luke 7:21, etc.; (2) *I pardon, forgive,* 2 Cor 2:7, 10; 12:13; Eph 4:32; Col 2:13; 3:13; (3) *I show kindness to,* Gal 3:18.

χάριν acc. sing. of χάρις, used as prep. w. gen., *for the sake of; by reason of, on account of.*

χάρις, ιτος, ἡ (1) *grace,* as a gift or blessing brought to man by Jesus Christ, John 1:14, 16, 17; (2) *favor,* as in LXX, i.e. Luke 1:30;

2:40, 52; Acts 2:47, etc.; (3) *gratitude,* Luke 6:32–34; 17:9; *thanks,* e.g. in χάρις τῷ θεῷ and ἔχειν χάριν *(to thank);* (4) *a favor,* Acts 24:27; 25:3, 9; (5) a new Christian sense, often w. a defining gen., of the divine *favor, grace,* the freeness and universality of which are shown in the inclusion of the Gentiles within the scope of the love and care of the God of the Jews. Paul, as the apostle to the Gentiles, and the proclaimer of the universal Gospel, naturally makes most use of this term (but cf. also Acts 13:43; 14:26, etc.), e.g. 1 Cor 3:10; 15:10; 1 Cor 1:4; 2 Cor 6:1; *grace* was given to him for his ministry to them, and to them through his ministry. (In early Gk. literature, *gracefulness, graciousness; favor; a favor; gratitude;* χάριν as above; in LXX especially of the *favor* which an inferior finds in the eyes of his superior).

χάρισμα, ατος, τό *a free (gracious) gift, a gift, an endowment,* especially from God.

χαριτόω *I endue with grace* (properly, *I endow with* χάρις, *the divine favor*); in Eph 1:6 followed by cog. acc. (gen.).

Χαρράν, ἡ *Haran,* identical with Carrae, in Mesopotamia.

χάρτης, ου, ὁ *papyrus, paper.*

χάσμα, ατος, τό (from χαίνω, *I yawn*), *an intervening space, a chasm.*

χεῖλος, ους, τό (1) *a lip;* (2) hence, *the edge,* Heb 11:12.

χειμάζομαι *I am in the grip of a storm.*

χείμαρρος, ου, ὁ *a winter torrent.*

χειμών, ῶνος, ὁ (1) *winter;* (2) *stormy weather,* Matt 16:3; Acts 27:20.

χείρ, χειρός, ἡ (1) *a hand;* (2) used also with reference to God, meaning, His power in action, Luke 1:66; 1 Pet 5:6, etc.; (3) διὰ χειρός (χειρῶν), *by the instrumentality of;* and so also ἐν χειρὶ (Hebraistic), Acts 7:35.

χειραγωγέω *I lead by the hand.*

χειραγωγός, οῦ, ὁ *one who leads* a helpless person *by the hand.*

χειρόγραφον, ου, τό properly, *a signature,* hence, as a term of a court of justice, (1) *a bill, bond, certificate of debt,* or (2) any *written obligation* or *agreement.*

χειροποίητος, ον *made by hand, handmade.*

χειροτονέω (lit. *I stretch out the hand,* thus expressing agreement with a motion, then, *I elect by show of hands* [of popular vote]), *I elect.*

χείρων, ον, gen. **ονος** comp., *worse;* ἐπὶ τὸ χεῖρον, *to the (a) worse result (degree).*

χερουβείν (-βίν, -βείμ, -βίμ), τό *cherubin, cherubim,* two golden figures of winged animals over the mercy seat (and the ark) in the Jewish tabernacle (χερουβείν is Aram., while -ειμ is Heb.).

χήρα, ας, ἡ *a widow.*

χιλίαρχος, ου, ὁ (lit. *a ruler of a thousand*), *a tribune,* a Roman officer commanding a cohort, i.e., about a thousand men), *a colonel.*

χιλιάς, άδος, ἡ *a thousand,* looked upon as a unit.

χίλιοι, αι, α *one thousand, a thousand.*

Χίος, ου, ἡ *Chios* (mod. Scio), an important island in the Aegean Sea, off the west central coast of Asia Minor.

χιτών, ῶνος, ὁ *a tunic, an undergarment* (a Semitic word).

χιών, όνος, ἡ *snow.*

χλαμύς, ύδος, ἡ *a cloak.*

χλευάζω *I scoff* by gesture and word.

χλιαρός, ά, όν *lukewarm, tepid.*

Χλόη, ης, ἡ *Chloe,* a woman, probably with business connections either in Corinth or in Ephesus or in both.

χλωρός, ά, όν *of the color of grass, green* or *yellow,* as the case may be (from χλόη).

χοϊκός, ή, όν *made of earth (dust)* and with the quality attaching to this origin (from χοῦς).

χοῖνιξ, ικος, ἡ a Greek dry *measure,* equivalent to 1.92 pints.

χοῖρος, ου, ὁ *a pig.*

χολάω *I am angry with.*

χολή, ῆς, ἡ (1) *gall, bile,* Matt 27:34; (2) met. *bitterness,* i.e., intense malignity. [In LXX represents three Heb. words meaning respectively, (1) *gall, bile,* (2) *wormwood,* (3) *poison.*]

χόος see χοῦς.

Χοραζίν (Χοραζείν), ἡ *Chorazin,* probably the present Kerâze, ruins northwest of Tell-hum (Capernaum?).

χορηγέω *I supply* (with lavish hand).

χορός, οῦ, ὁ *dancing.*

χορτάζω (from χόρτος, in earlier Gk. of feeding animals), *I feed to the full, I satisfy with food.*

χόρτασμα, ατος, τό *food, sustenance,* corn for man as well as beast.

χόρτος, ου, ὁ *grass, hay,* such grass or herbage as makes fodder.

Χουζᾶς, ᾶ, ὁ *Chuza,* a steward of Herod Antipas.

χοῦς, χοός, acc. **χοῦν, ὁ** *dust.*

χράομαι *I use, employ* (from χρή, "necessity," properly, "I make for myself what is necessary with something"); in 1 Cor 7:21 perhaps understand τῇ ἐλευθερίᾳ; w. persons, *I treat,* Acts 27:3.

χράω *I lend.*

χρεία, ας, ἡ (1) *need;* (2) any special *occasion* or *matter in hand,* Acts 6:3; Eph 4:29(?).

χρεοφειλέτης (χρεωφειλέτης), ου, ὁ *a debtor.*

χρή *it is fitting,* it is congruous to a law or rather standard; the word is somewhat vague.

χρῄζω *I need, have need.*

χρῆμα, ατος, τό (1) plur. *property, possessions, riches;* (2) sing. *the money got, the proceeds,* Acts 4:37.

χρηματίζω (orig., *I transact business*), (1) act., of God, *I warn,* Heb 12:25; pas. *I am warned by God* (properly in response to an inquiry as to one's duty), Matt 2:12, 22; Luke 2:26; Acts 10:22; Heb 8:5; 11:7; (2) *(I take a name from my public business),* hence, *I receive a name, I am publicly called . . .,* Acts 11:26; Rom 7:3.

χρηματισμός, οῦ, ὁ *a response of God* (to an inquiry as to one's duty), *an oracle.*

χρῆσαι aor. mid. imper. 2 sing. → χράομαι.

χρήσιμος, η, ον (1) *useful;* (2) neut. subs. *profit, value.*

χρῆσις, εως, ἡ *usage, use.*

χρῆσον aor. act. imper. → κίχρημι.

χρηστεύομαι *I play the part of a kind person* (full of service to others).

χρηστολογία, ας, ἡ *affectation of kind speech,* with insinuating tone.

χρηστός, ή, όν (1) *good;* (2) hence, *comfortable, kindly, not pressing,* Matt 11:30; (3) often has the idea of *kind.*

χρηστότης, ητος, ἡ *kindness, kindliness* (see χρηστός).

χρίσμα, ατος, τό *anointing,* referring to the gift of holy spirit.

Χριστιανός, οῦ, ὁ *Christian, a follower of Christ.* See χριστός. The formation is Lat., and indicates either *partisan of Christ* or more exactly *soldier of Christ,* cf. Fimbriani, Caesariani, Pompeiani.

Χριστός (χριστός), οῦ, ὁ (a rare verbal from χρίω, *"I anoint,"* and therefore *anointed,* ὁ χριστός being an epithet used at first practically in the sense of *the king*, anointing being the outward sign of his appointment to kingship, cf. 1 Sam 10:1; 12:3; 15:1 and often), (1) ὁ χριστός, *the anointed, the Messiah* (the Aram. equivalent of ὁ χριστός, John 1:41, *the* expected *king* of Israel, to be appointed by God as his vicegerent. In NT this epithet is, therefore, attached (either prefixed or affixed) to (ὁ) = Ἰησοῦς, *Jesus*, recognized by his followers as the expected Messiah. The epithet with or without article is also found alone referring to Jesus; (2) gradually it tends to lose the meaning it originally had and to become merely a proper name, *Christ*. (By many the curious word was confused with χρηστός, "good," which as a proper name was often a slave name, and thus Χριστιανοί became Χρηστιανοί, confusion being due to the fact that the two words were pronounced alike).

χρίω *I anoint*, to the kingly office, used generally with regard to dedication to Messiahship, etc.

χρονίζω *I delay*.

χρόνος, ου, ὁ (1) *time;* (2) *a time, period* (instrumental in Luke 8:27; Rom 16:25); (3) locative, πολλοῖς χρόνοις, *oftentimes*, Luke 8:29.

χρονοτριβέω *I waste time*.

χρυσίον, ου, τό (1) *gold;* (2) plur. *gold (golden) ornaments*, 1 Pet 3:3.

χρυσοδακτύλιος, ον *with (wearing) a* (one or more) *gold ring(s)* on the finger(s).

χρυσόλιθος, ου, ὁ a sparkling gem, of gold-yellow color, possibly our *topaz*, almost certainly not our *chrysolite*.

χρυσόπρασος, ου, ὁ a precious stone of leek-green color, which sparkled golden yellow, from India, perhaps *fluor-spar*, certainly not *chrysoprase*.

χρυσός, οῦ, ὁ *gold*.

χρυσοῦς (χρύσεος), ῆ, οῦν *made of gold, golden*.

χρυσόω *I adorn with gold, I overlay with gold*.

χρῶ pres. mid./pas. imper. 2 sing. → χράομαι.

χρώς, χρωτός, ὁ *skin*.

χωλός, ή, όν *lame;* generalizing neut., Heb 12:13.

χώρα, ας, ἡ (1) strictly used, *a region*, a great geographical (and sometimes administrative) division of a province, e.g. Acts 16:6; 18:23, but often more loosely, *country, district;* (2) hence met., e.g. Matt 4:16; (3) sometimes almost *a field*, John 4:35; Jas 5:4.

χωρέω (1) intrans., (a) *I go away, I withdraw, I come*, lit. and met., Matt 15:17; 2 Pet 3:9, (b) intrans., *I have room, find room*, John 8:37; (2) trans., (a) *I contain, am capable of receiving, hold, grasp*, Mark 2:2; Matt 19:11 etc., (b) *I make room for (I give a place to)* someone in my heart, *I take into* my heart, 2 Cor 7:2.

χωρίζω (1) act. trans., *I separate, I put apart;* (2) mid. or pas. *I separate myself, I depart*.

χωρίον, ου, τό (1) *a place;* (2) *a piece of land, a field*, enclosed (diminutive of χώρα or χῶρος).

χωρίς (1) prep. w. gen., *apart from, separate from, without;* (2) adv., *separately, apart, by itself*.

χῶρος, ου, ὁ *the northwest wind*, and so, the quarter of the sky from which it comes, *northwest* [Lat., *caurus, corus*].

Ψ

ψάλλω *I play on the harp* (or other stringed instrument).

ψαλῶ fut. act. → ψάλλω.

ψαλμός, οῦ, ὁ *a psalm,* i.e., a song of praise, etc., to God, with an accompaniment on the harp.
ψευδάδελφος, ου, ὁ *a false brother,* i.e. an unreal (insincere) Christian.
ψευδαπόστολος, ου, ὁ *a false apostle,* i.e. one who has received no commission from Jesus to preach the Gospel, though he pretends to have received it.
ψευδής, ές (1) *false;* (2) *untrue* in word, etc.
ψευδοδιδάσκαλος, ου, ὁ *a teacher of false things.*
ψευδολόγος, ου, ὁ (1) *speaking false things, lying;* (2) *a liar.*
ψεύδομαι (1) *I speak falsely;* (2) w. acc. *I deceive by words,* Acts 5:3.
ψευδομαρτυρέω *I give (bear) false witness.*
ψευδομαρτυρία, ας, ἡ (1) *giving of false evidence;* (2) *false witness.*
ψευδόμαρτυς (ψευδομάρτυς), υρος, ὁ *a false witness,* one who gives untrue evidence.
ψευδοπροφήτης, ου, ὁ *a false (untrue, unauthenticated) prophet.*
ψεῦδος, ους, τό (1) *that which is false, falsehood;* (2) *an untruth, a lie;* (2) *lying;* in Rom 1:25 abstr. for concr..
ψευδόχριστος, ου, ὁ *a false Messiah, a pretended Messiah.*
ψευδώνυμος, ον *falsely named.*
ψεῦσμα, ατος, τό *a lie.*
ψεύστης, ου, ὁ *a liar.*
ψηλαφάω *I touch;* in Heb 12:18 perhaps corrupt; πεφεψαλωμένῳ has been suggested, *burnt to ashes, calcined, volcanic.*
ψηφίζω *I count up* (lit. with pebbles).
ψῆφος, ου, ἡ (1) *a pebble,* Rev 2:17; (2) hence, from their use in voting, *a vote.*
ψιθυρισμός, οῦ, ὁ *whispering,* especially of secret attacks on a person's character.
ψιθυριστής, οῦ, ὁ *a whisperer* (cf. ψιθυρισμός).
ψίξ, ψιχός, ἡ *a crumb of bread.*
ψιχίον, ου, τό *a small crumb.*
ψυγήσομαι fut. pas. → ψύχομαι.
ψυχή, ῆς, ἡ (1) *life,* without any psychological content, Matt 2:20; John 10:11, 15, 17; Acts 15:26; Rom 11:3; 16:4; 1 Cor 15:45; 2 Cor 1:23; Phil 2:30; 1 Thess 2:8, etc.; (2) *an individual,* or as a strong pers. pron. (Hebraistic, cf. *nephesh*), cf. Mark 8:36 (contrast Luke 9:25); Acts 2:41, 43; 3:23; Rom 2:9; 13:1; 2 Cor 12:15; (3) psychical, *desire,* Eph 6:6; Phil 1:27; Col 3:23, cf. also 1 Thess 5:23, where the enumeration is not systematic. The general use of the word in the Bible is in the sense of whatever is felt to belong most essentially to man's life, when his bodily life has come to be regarded as a secondary thing. It comes near the modern conception, *self.* See also ψυχικός. In the LXX there is, in general, a lack of sharp distinction between ψυχή (lit. *breath, breath of life* in the individual), πνεῦμα and καρδία, though ψυχή generally refers to appetite and desire; it is there as a rule a translation of the Heb. *nefesh,* one of the words for the "breath-soul," the personal soul; in Paul, soul (ψυχή) and spirit (πνεῦμα) are hardly to be distinguished (yet cf. 1 Cor 15:45; cf. also πνεῦμα).
ψυχικός, ή, όν *emotional* or *sensuous* (from ψυχή, in the sense "the principle of life and the basis of its emotional aspect, animating the present body of flesh, in contrast to the higher life").
ψύχομαι *I become cold, I am extinguished* (of a flame), met.
ψῦχος, ους, τό *cold.*
ψυχρός, ά, όν (1) lit., *cold,* neut.

cold water, Matt 10:42; (2) met. *cold, frigid, indifferent, phlegmatic.*

ψωμίζω (1) *I confer a dole upon,* Rom 12:20; (2) *I dole out.*

ψωμίον, ου, τό *a little bit, morsel,* or *crumb* of food.

ψώχω *I rub.*

Ω

ὦ the last letter of the Gk. alphabet, *Omega* (at first the long and short o sounds were represented by one letter; when distinguished the short was called οὖ or ὂ μικρόν, the long ὦ or ὦ μέγα).

ὦ an interj. of address, *O.*

Ὠβήδ see Ἰωβήδ.

ὧδε adv., *here,* both of rest and of motion to *(hither);* τὰ ὧδε, *the things here, what is here, what is going on here, the state of affairs here.*

ᾠδή, ῆς, ἡ *a song.*

ὠδίν, ῖνος, ἡ (1) *pangs of childbirth, birth pangs,* 1 Thess 5:3; in Acts 2:24 Death is regarded as in *labor* and his pains as relieved by the birth of the child; (2) hence, of any *sharp sudden pain.*

ὠδίνω (1) *I suffer birth pangs,* w. acc. of the children that are being born; (2) met., Gal 4:19.

ὦμος, ου, ὁ *shoulder.*

ὤμοσα aor. act. → ὀμνύω.

ὠνέομαι *I buy.*

ᾠόν, οῦ, τό *an egg.*

ὥρα, ας, ἡ (1) *an hour,* i.e., a twelfth part of the period from sunrise to sunset, and thus of constantly changing length; (2) the shortest measurement of time among the ancients; (3) sometimes generally of *time;* ὥρα πολλή, *an advanced period of time, a considerable time,* Mark 6:35; πρὸς ὥραν, *for a* (little) *time.*

ὡραῖος, α, ον (lit. *in season*), *beautiful.*

ὤρυξα aor. act. → ὀρύσσω.

ὠρύομαι *I roar.*

ὡς adv. and conj., (1) w. superl., ὡς τάχιστα, *as quickly as possible,* Acts 17:15; w. comp., ambiguous, either *uncommonly . . .* or *very . . .,* Acts 17:22; (2) before numbers, etc., *about;* (3) exclamatory, *how,* e.g. Rom 10:15; (4) often in the pred. (nom. or acc.) *as,* e.g. Matt 14:5; 22:30; Luke 15:19; 2 Cor 10:2; (5) w. fut. part., *as such who have to . . .,* Heb 13:17; giving a reason, Luke 16:1; 23:4; Acts 3:12, etc.; part. sometimes has disappeared, e.g. Col 3:23; (6) w. absol. infin., ὡς ἔπος εἰπεῖν, *one might almost say,* Heb 7:9; (7) = ὥστε, *so as to,* Luke 9:52 (var.); Acts 20:24 (var.); (8) οὐχ ὡς, *not as if,* e.g. Acts 28:19; ὡς ὅτι = ὡς w. gen. absol., *as if;* 2 Cor 5:19; 11:21; 2 Thess 2:2; (9) ὡς correlative to οὕτως (with or without καί), *as . . . so;* (10) ὡς introducing a clause can also have something of a causal sense, Matt 6:12 (= Luke 11:4), etc., so, ὡς w. part., and w. preps. often in Hellenistic), cf. Acts 17:14 (var.); Rom 9:32; (11) (it is) *as* (when), without connection, either with what precedes or with what follows, Mark 13:34; (12) after verbs of saying, thinking, etc., *how;* (13) temp., *when, while, as long as,* Luke 1:23; Gal 6:10, etc.; ὡς ἄν, *when,* Rom 15:24; *as soon as,* 1 Cor 11:34; Phil 2:23 (but in 2 Cor 10:9, *as it were*).

ὡσαννά a cry of happiness, *hosanna!* [Aram. and Heb., originally a cry for help].

ὡσαύτως adv., *in the same way, likewise.*

ὡσεί (1) *as if, as it were, like;* (2) w. numbers, *about.*

Ὡσηέ (Ὡσηέ), ὁ *Hosea,* the OT prophet [Heb.].

ὠσί dat. plur. → οὖς.
ὥσπερ *even as, as.*
ὡσπερεί *even as if, as if* (= ὥσπερ εἰ).
ὥστε (1) w. an infin., expressing result, *so as to,* Luke 4:29 (var.), 9:52 (var.), 20:20 (var.), etc.; (2) (a) introducing an independent clause, in indic., imper., subjun. of exhortation, *so that,* John 3:16; Gal 2:13, (b) w. result stated merely as a new fact, *consequently, and so, therefore.*
ὦτα nom. and acc. plur. → οὖς.
ὠτάριον, ου, τό *an ear.*
ὠτίον, ου, τό *an ear* (see ὠτάριον).
ὠφέλεια, ας, ἡ *advantage.*
ὠφελέω *I help, benefit, do good, am useful (to);* (1) absol. Rom 2:25; (2) w. adv. acc. οὐδέν, *in no way,* τί, *in what way?;* (3) generally w. acc. of the person.
ὠφέλιμος, ον *beneficial, useful, serviceable.*
ὤφθην aor. pas. → ὁράω.